Breaching the C

EXPLORATIONS OF EDUCATIONAL PURPOSE

Volume 8

Founding Editor

Joe Kincheloe (1950-2008)

Series Editors

Shirley R. Steinberg, *McGill University, Montreal, Quebec, Canada*
Kenneth Tobin, *City University of New York, USA*

Editorial Board

Barrie Barrell, *Memorial University of Newfoundland, Canada*
Rochelle Brock, *University of Indiana, Gary, USA*
Stephen Petrina, *University of British Columbia, Canada*
Christine Quail, *State University of New York, Oneonta, USA*
Nelson Rodriguez, *College of New Jersey, USA*
Leila Villaverde, *University of North Carolina, Greensboro, USA*
John Willinsky, *Stanford University, USA*

Series Scope

In today's dominant modes of pedagogy, questions about issues of race, class, gender, sexuality, colonialism, religion, and other social dynamics are rarely asked. Questions about the social spaces where pedagogy takes place - in schools, media, and corporate think tanks - are not raised. And they need to be.

The *Explorations of Educational Purpose* book series can help establish a renewed interest in such questions and their centrality in the larger study of education and the preparation of teachers and other educational professionals. The editors of this series feel that education matters and that the world is in need of a rethinking of education and educational purpose.

Coming from a critical pedagogical orientation, *Explorations of Educational Purpose* aims to have the study of education transcend the trivialization that often degrades it. Rather than be content with the frivolous, scholarly lax forms of teacher education and weak teaching prevailing in the world today, we should work towards education that truly takes the unattained potential of human beings as its starting point. The series will present studies of all dimensions of education and offer alternatives. The ultimate aim of the series is to create new possibilities for people around the world who suffer under the current design of socio-political and educational institutions.

For other titles published in this series, go to
http://www.springer.com/series/7472

Arlo Kempf
Editor

Breaching the Colonial Contract

Anti-Colonialism in the US and Canada

 Springer

Editor
Arlo Kempf
Ontario Institute for Studies in Education
University of Toronto
Ontario, Canada

ISBN 978-90-481-3888-3   ISBN 978-1-4020-9944-1 (eBook)

Library of Congress Control Number: 2009920159

© Springer Science + Business Media B.V. 2010
No part of this work may be reproduced, stored in a retrieval system, or transmitted in any form or by any means, electronic, mechanical, photocopying, microfilming, recording or otherwise, without written permission from the Publisher, with the exception of any material supplied specifically for the purpose of being entered and executed on a computer system, for exclusive use by the purchaser of the work.

springer.com

For my mom, Patricia E. Smith (1948-1996), who left Tulsa running and never looked back.

Acknowledgements

I would first like to thank Joe L. Kincheloe (1950-2008) who made this book possible. Joe's tragic death in December of 2008 came as a tremendous shock to activists, scholars, students, family, friends and acquaintances around the world (I fit into the latter category). We are fortunate that his work lives on however, and that it surely will for some time. Over the better part of two years Joe supported this project, and of course countless others, as part of his and Shirley R. Steinberg's series *Explorations of Educational Purpose* with Springer. Joe's sustained enthusiasm and support for the work were both contagious and necessary for its completion. Let me get in line to thank you Joe.

Thanks are also due to the 18 contributors to this book. Clearly, without them there would be no book. In particular, I would like to thank Antonio Reyes Lopez, whose paper (now his chapter) at a conference in El Paso in the fall of 2006 provided the initial academic spark for the work. It's a lucky book. To begin with, I was able to include work from prominent senior scholars who I have been reading for a long time. This has been a most humbling honor and a wonderful privilege. An equally important part of this good fortune has been the inclusion of work from senior students and junior scholars whose works bring insightful analyses to issues of colonial relations in North America and around the world. I am profoundly grateful to have worked with this medley of voices. Thanks as well to Professor John Willinsky of Stanford University, for his guidance and for providing a pre-publication quote for the book (and more generally for his scholarship on colonialism and education).

At the Ontario Institute for Studies in Education of the University of Toronto (OISE/UT), I have to thank Professor and activist George Jerry Sefa Dei, whose work continues to guide my understandings of power and resistance, particularly with regard to anti-colonial studies. George Sefa Dei's work has been at the cutting edge of anti-colonial studies for some time and indeed it was his teaching and writing that brought me to the topic. A special thanks for writing the afterword. I also wish to thank Professor Peter Sawchuk whose continued support for the project and much needed guidance with the prospectus have been invaluable. To Professors Dei and Sawchuk, as well as to the Department of Sociology and Equity Studies in Education at OISE/UT, my sincere thanks for these and countless other supports over the past few years.

At Springer, I would like to acknowledge the tremendous work, patience and skill of Padmaja Sudhakher and Bernadette Ohmer who seemed to tolerate my learning curve and who have, I feel, turned out a very well-produced book. Thanks also to Harmen van Paradijs, Senior Publishing Editor for Education at Springer.

A special thanks to Melanie Tricker, of the Toronto District School Board, for reading and commenting on the manuscript.

Finally, I would like to thank my wonderful family: Randall Kempf for continuing to show me what lifelong learning and reflection look like; to Lola and Cy, for always being the brightest part of my day; to Darlene McKee, for providing me with the space and freedom to do this work; and finally to Meghan McKee, my partner with whom I stumble down this road – for all that you are and do. I love you madly.

Foreword

Every new colonial act re-imprints old forms of domination as well as reinstalls new ones and the emerging hybridity transcodes social relations of domination and exploitation such that it can appreciably be called a collective form of subjectification, more specifically, a perpetuated neocolonialism. What is interesting about many of these new forms of colonization is that they are now legitimized retroactively as kitsch art and media spectacles that colonize our subjectivities, and shape subalternity by giving impetus to the direction of our desiring. We are living in willing captivity to our worst nightmares, ensepulchred inside a pseudo-ethnographic pornscape of the exotico-folklorico, those savage documentaries of the 1960s that have their roots in such 1950s films as *Sex Madness, Savage Africa, Mau Mau, Cannibal Island, Continente Perduto, Magia Verde and L'Impero del Sole*—documentaries who go by such names as *Mondo Cane, Mondo Nudo, Mondo Freud, Hollywood's World of Flesh, Onna Onna Onna Monogatari, La Femme Spectacle*. If, decades ago, we sought out the bizarre and the lascivious in the thrill of *mondo* cinema, in films that exploited the abject other, sensationalizing and mythologizing the delights of the imperial unconscious, today we no longer need to seek out the repressed underside of the representational dreck that has garrisoned our white settler ideology, our empire of normative claims, since it is fully integrated into our daily lives.

Immersed in a popular culture unswervingly saturated by endless spectacles meant to divert attention from substantive political issues and debates and to proselytize for capital, we have become silent accomplices in the ravages of corporate expansionism and imperialism and the resultant dislocation and widespread misery. In the name of the most holy acts of consumption, the state media apparatuses, powered by turbines of moral turpitude, not only have failed to resist the complete takeover of the public sphere by the logic of capital, but actively promote capitalist logic. In other words, under the guise of de-fanging the alienation produced by the social labor of capital through forms of entertainment, or making us more critically informed citizens through its mission to educate and shape the character of the *vox populi*, the media actively promote such alienation.

We are living ablaze the spectatorial gaze of imperial desire in reality television shows, in porno sites that cater to every specialized sexual desire, in sci-fi channels where we can be destroyed or saved by alien life, in the "nature" channel where we can watch lions devour buffalo and fight hyenas and snakes injecting lethal poison into unsuspecting victims, in posted video streams where we can watch beatings of the homeless, teenage girls pummeling each other unconscious, Islamic militants beheading American contractors in Iraq or even suicides caught on videotape in sleepy suburban U.S. communities.

We know in advance that the outcomes we seek will never be realized, they will always the same, fixed in their present absence not by their own interior logic but by the rules of the capitalist game where a grotesque inequality possesses overwhelming preponderance. But it is the act of revelation that is important—that we will be victorious and will claim the planet for our own again—because then we can, if only briefly, suspend for a moment our knowledge that nothing will substantively change, and indulge ourselves in undermining our own fears with fantasies of hope—enjoying our symptoms as some Lacanians might put it. We have become imprisoned in basic Christian fantasies that a leader will magically appear at the gates of Jerusalem and turn the world upside down, putting it back on feet of righteousness. The promise of the American Dream has not lost its currency, but it is engaged as an empty promise, endlessly deferred, and recognized—resignedly—that it is now part of post-future America, not as an immoveable horizon but still something that might survive the current economic crisis, but in reverse-form, as a lurid parody of itself, as a kind of reversal of the Weberian notion that death has become more anguishing in modernity due to a perpetual postponement of happiness. The American Dream has become a promise from beyond, like the resurrection of the flesh at some unknown time in the future, when the oppressors and the oppressed join the lions and the lambs in the Elysian Fields watching Elvira Madigan and her lover gorge on an eternal supply of raspberries and cream.

Unable to impose limits to growth that sustains the current empire or operate outside the empire's own Manichean logic of "us-against-them", the current capitalist system has lashed us to the mast of the creditor class and its bubblemeisters, to the banking system of widespread negative equity (which included gangster capitalists who headed Citigroup as well as master manipulators who ran hedge funds attached to investment banks such as Lehman Bros. and Bear Stearns), to over-mortgaged real estate, and to over-indebted corporations.

Unbridled capitalism and the juggernaut of imperialism that follows in its wake has the potential to wreak havoc upon the world in terms of further imperialist wars for resources and strategic geo-political advantage, not to mention ecological destruction of the entire planet. And now the results are starting to reach into our neighborhoods.

Towns that rely on just a few major employers—or a single industry or company—are the most vulnerable during these tough economic times and it is not uncommon to see Depression-era scenes such as food lines. U.S. Senator Hilary Clinton's healthcare package was going to cost the government $110 billion a year, but the Federal Reserve just handed the American International Group Inc. $150 billion, and that was just the tip of the iceberg. We continue a policy of socialism for the rich and privatization of the trauma of the poor; with the latter carrying a debt burden conditioned by unbound capital and stoked by the market's hidden hand.

Foreword

Not far away from where I am writing this, in Echo Park, approximately five hundred people are gathering on the sidewalk, waiting for the weekly St. Paul Cathedral (Episcopalian) food handout consisting of beans, potatoes, onions, and cereal.

Those who suddenly become jobless often resort to suicide, murder, arson and robbery. Exurbs and suburbs are witnessing strange sights—people picking through green plastic garbage bags at home foreclosure sites as the former owners grab what they can and leave the rest.

The recent presidential election was perhaps little more than a rehearsal for a return of the same, a pretext for the restatement of business as usual in a different voice, whose message is more about timbre and pitch than policy. This is because the hope of which Obama speaks is impossible to achieve under capitalism. Even if Obama has the best intentions, and that look likely to be the case at this point in time, the rules of the game prevent the kind of difference that will make a real difference. Everything that could conceivably bring about the kind of social transformation that will dramatically change for the better the warp and woof of everyday life in America is unmasked as an impossible contradiction if we place it in the context of the persistence of capitalism as the only alternative way to organize the globe for overcoming necessity. The richest 400 Americans own more than the bottom 150 million Americans combined; their combined net worth is $1.6 trillion. During the Bush years, the nation's 15,000 richest families doubled their annual income, from $15 million to $30 million and corporate profits shot up by 68 percent while workers' wages have been steadily shrinking (and the workers are not the ones who are being bailed out by the government). That scenario isn't about to change radically with the election of Obama, whose administration is as likely to enhance the rule of capital as challenge it.

Arlo Kempf's important book, *Breaching the Colonial Contract*, is about hope, but it is specifically designed to counter the false revelations of hope and bring us directly into confrontation with the enduring crisis of colonialism through an astute archeology of the present. Kempf's book comes at a precipitous time in world history, when a new anti-colonial pedagogy is emerging to challenge the limitations of cultural critique and its postcolonial and poststructuralist advocates in a broad attempt to challenge race-based oppression, economic exploitation and cultural and economic imperialism.

Leaving aside the academic gallants of cultural critique, whose laborious expositions float down to the masses from the oxygen-starved summit of Mount Olympus like metaphysical flatulence and for whom decolonizing pedagogical practices have become a pathological transgression, it remains case that the educational establishment has impounded anti-colonial research as too polarizing or too extremist at a time when we must band together like brothers and sisters and fight the war against terrorism. And at a time when universities are turning out propagandists for imperialist wars that urge us to put an "Iraqi face" on the US occupation of Iraq, and an "Afghan face" on the war in Afghanistan, we can only wonder how well these nationalist masks are able to hide an imperial Michael Myers from *Halloween*. Probably very well. As Kempf notes in the introduction:

Secure in its place at the top of the evolutionary ladder, the US is now legitimized in its inward and outward projects of civilization. America is a feminist in Afghanistan, an anti-racist in Iran, a peacemaker in Israel, a champion of human rights in Cuba and an omniscient (and worthy) big brother at home. The US is now the world's foremost expert on tolerance, and those who say otherwise must, sadly, be themselves afflicted by intolerance. This mission, like all colonial missions, is a moral undertaking infused with a pedagogy of tolerance aimed to raise the most savage racist to a higher level – the highly Islamaphobic climate of the post 9–11 era is the most powerful marker of this phenomena.

We are living at a time that remains balefully oblivious to Marx's warning that the ruling ideas are the ideas of those who rule. Much of the poststructuralist attempts at rescuing difference from the process of capitalist commodification have only a contingently subversive capacity since in raising difference to a transcendental status they have too often scuttled the dialectic altogether. It is difficult to confront the notion that our pedagogies and research endeavors are worthy of the protagonistic praxis they are intended to generate when they surpass only superficially the necrophilic brand of liberal and left-liberal reformism that they try so hard to subvert. While critical and postcolonial educational critique has embraced mightily the possibility of decolonizing the conceptual, philosophical, epistemological and cultural dimensions of learning, many of these attempts have been expurgated by the flat-lined anti-politics of postmodernism.

Many post-structuralists unguardedly—and rightly—claim that we are semiotically situated in hermeneutic horizons, in gendered and racialized positionalities driven by power-sensitive and power-expansive relations of symmetrical privilege, and in social space aligned and vectored geopolitically and cross-hatched socioculturally, and this description is accurate as far as it goes. But too often it fails to take into account the totalizing power of capital and acknowledge that this power has created an overarching matrix of exploitation in which all of these antagonisms have been accorded value in relation to the sale of human labor power in the global marketplace. And during the current structural crisis of neoliberal capital that we are witnessing today, we are experiencing a particularly vicious time where, like force-fed swine made blind and crippled in preparation for mass consumption, men and women are led to the slaughterhouse of capital hoisted on hooks of poverty and debt. While it is important to explore and celebrate the ethnic heterogeneity and heterodox temporalities that power our subjectivity and building border identities that escape the lineaments of Eurocentric epistemes we need at the same time to recognize that the totalizing power of capital creates constitutive limitations in which subjectivities are formed. This, I have argued, can be seen as a form of controlled consent made possible by the production of social amnesia both generated and enforced by the corporate media, and the deep psychology that turns the engines of mass propaganda disguised as a free marketplace of ideas (where the only free cheese available is in the mousetrap). Democracy has become synonymous with profit-making, requiring a rollback of trade union power and a generalized hollowing out of social democracy, not by military dictatorship but by an endless stream of maledictions and execrations against leftist movements and Marxist analyses that deal with the totality of capitalist social relations and address questions of universality. Canadian theologian Gregory Baum (see Miller, 2005) has marshaled similar reservations with respect to contemporary postmodern thought:

> "I have ... quarrels with the 'linguistic turn' in postmodern thought. You cannot eat words! The linguistic turn corresponds to middle class preoccupations: it is of interest to people who have never suffered from hunger and thus makes the material basis of human existence invisible. Unemployment is not a purely linguistic issue either. I regret that so many philosophers are unwilling to ask themselves how their thought is related to their social location and what the social implications of their discourse are. Karl Manheim in Ideology and Utopia says that we cannot fully understand a sentence unless its social context has been clarified. A sentence by itself has no clear meaning. You must know on what occasion it is said, to whom, and under what conditions. When I teach this, I always give the example of the German anthem, 'Germany, Germany Above All.' In 1848, this was the song of the German revolution, and it meant: Germany above all the feudal structures. After Germany became an empire in 1871, the same song acquired an aggressive political message. 'We shall overcome' was the song of the powerless who hoped that justice would prevail: if the police department adopted this song, its meaning would be quite different. Thought is always related to a social base. Philosophers sometimes think that thought floats above history and above the economic order, but this is not true. In a context marked by grave inequalities and patterns of exclusion, thought either questions the existing order or contributes to its stability" (pp 28–29).

I wonder what members of the Abahlali base in Mjondolo would think of reading the arrests of their members as a poststructuralist text? Or the Movimento dos Trabalhadore Rurais Sem Terra, and other emerging antisystemic movements? This is not to say that linguistic analysis is not important, but any social critique needs to be at the same time conjugated with class and anti-racist struggle.

The paradigmatic innovation of anti-colonial analysis in North America has been significantly impacted by what has been taking place since capital began responding to the crisis of the 1970s of Fordist-Keynesian capitalism—which William Robinson has characterized as capital's ferocious quest to break free of nation state constraints to accumulation and 20th century regulated capital-labor relations based on some (at least a few) reciprocal commitments and rights—a move which has seen the development of a new transnational model of accumulation in which transnational fractions of capital have become dominant. New mechanisms of accumulation, as Robinson notes, include a cheapening of labor and the growth of flexible, deregulated and de-unionized labor where women always experience super-exploitation in relation to men, the dramatic expansion of capital itself; the creation of a global and regulatory structure to facilitate the emerging global circuits of accumulation; and, finally, neo-liberal structural adjustment programs which seek to create the conditions for unfettered operations of emerging transnational capital across borders and between countries. There still exists national capital, global capital, regional capitals, etc., but the hegemonic fraction of capital on a world scale is now transnational capital. So we are seeing the profound dismantling of national economies, the reorganization and reconstitution of national economies as component elements or segments of a larger global production and financial system which is organized in a globally fragmented way and a decentralized way but in manner in which power is concentrated and centralized. In other words, as Robinson notes, there is a decentralization and fragmentation of the actual national production process all over the globe while the control of these processes – these endless chains of accumulation—is concentrated and centralized at a global level by a transnationalist capitalist class.

The transnational capitalist class, that has inherited a nocuous rationality, understands that it costs less to keep workers alive in places like China or India or Mexico than it does in the United States because it is far easier to hire non-unionized workers with no medical benefits who are frantic at finding food and shelter and can be hired at a fraction of what U.S. workers would cost.

The most urgent issue for this time, living as we are at the razor-edge of a very dangerous historical juncture is to advance the struggle for a socialist alternative to capitalism, for a supersession of capitalism, for a breakthrough into a post-capitalist future.

Initially developed to repudiate the intemperate and highly reactionary attitudes—all too prevalent within the North American education establishment and redolent of the backlash against non-White immigrants—that affluence bestows intelligence, that working-class students are responsible for their own underachievement (achievement as measured against the standardized test scores of the children of the rich)—anti-colonial pedagogy has been astute in creating an archeology of the present that can develop (sociological, anthropological, philosophical, etc.) languages of analysis such that students and teachers ('educands') can begin to understand their experiences and subjectivities as 'constructed' through the intersection of a multiplicity of forces linked to the modes and social relations of production, to spaces and places of capitalist production, accumulation and circulation, to systems of mediation that involve their families, their religious upbringing, their class and racial formations, as well as organizations and institutions linked both to the state and civil society. Initiatives involving ideology critique, de-naturalizating what is assumed to be unchangeable, de-reifying human agency, and de-objectifying the commodity culture of contemporary capitalism have helped discourage progressive educators from a sole reliance on a politics of human rights antiseptically cleaved from the issue of economic rights and unburden cultural studies of its textuality of the negative, that presumably arrived on the wings of the Angel of History (thanks to the prayers of the postmodernists) to save us from the old bearded devil: Karl Marx.

Anti-colonial criticism has helped to deepen the purpose and challenge of critical/postcolonial pedagogy and free enterprise imperialism by asking questions and raising issues dealing with what Anibal Quijano (2000) has called "the coloniality of power": Are the transformations needed to eliminate oppression and exploitation achievable within the current value form of labor within existing capitalist economic arrangements? What are the limitations of liberal-democratic discourses of social, political, economic and educational equality when viewed in terms of the globalization of whiteness? How can we use anti-colonial work to de-commodify our subjectivities and help whom Kempf calls "people resisting erasure, amputation and genocide" fight the colonial matrix of power? How can education play a part (a necessary but, alas, not sufficient) in social revolution? These questions are far from

Foreword

mere academic exercises, not only because of the severity of the current crisis, but because the crisis has been acute for the past half millennium. Kempf notes:

> Almost a decade in, empire is the dominant mode of cultural production of the 21st Century. If we are unable excavate the archaeology of the present through a holistic and resistance based understanding of the workings of oppression, empire promises to be the definitive fact linking the dawn of this century with that of the next. Anti-colonial theory and practice bring such a reading to the workings of our world. Anti-colonialism responds to the system of imposition as well as to individual acts. An anti-colonial understanding is a holistic response to all, or to portions, of a given system or systems of power. While the implications if anti-colonial struggle vary in nature, and from context to context, two broad colonial trends are worth mentioning specifically when articulating an anti-colonialism of the 21st Century. First, Indigenous people are waging some form of anti-colonial struggle in every inhabited region of the world. This is the key form of anti-colonial resistance of our time. These are not abstract struggles against abstract phenomena; these are the struggles of people resisting erasure, amputation and genocide. Forced to battle the dominant narratives of historical memory, Indigenous people from throughout the world have no Israel to recover from their holocausts, and in many cases have seen no end to these holocausts. The bad guys are still winning. Although many of these struggles are old, they are phenomena of the present. In the North American, Australian and New Zealand contexts, Indigenous peoples are doing battle with the European colonialism of the 17th, 18th 19th and 20th centuries. In these contexts no new understanding of colonialism is needed to understand the perpetuated relevance of colonialism in the 21st Century. There is very little subtlety, nuance or sophistication needed to understand the injustice visited historically and currently upon indigenous peoples by colonial authorities. Subtlety, nuance and sophistication are needed instead when constructing the silence, ignorance and apathy characterizing public discourse around these injustices. It is to these processes of obfuscation, silencing and denial that we must bring a critical and self-interrogative anti-colonial approach to theory, practice, knowledge production and daily life.

Issues such as these, including related themes that draw attention to and frequently explode the limitations and complexities of the post-colonial approach, have been astutely raised in *Breaching the Colonial Contract*, a book that, through initiating an anti-colonial conversation, seeks a deeper means of challenging repressive and violent social structures brought into being by new incarnations of capitalist globalization. The book addresses numerous topics of major significance in the anti-colonial struggle which include the development of anti-colonial theory and practice; the discourse of critical whiteness through an anti-colonial framework; an anti-colonial approach to historiography; Fourth World liberation struggles; the organization of white settler ideologies and institutions through the lens of anti-colonial pedagogy; Paulo Freire and postcolonial criticism; the Chicana/o student walkouts and colonial schooling processes in the US/Mexico borderlands; the relationship between people of color and Aboriginal peoples in North America; the politics of African centered schools in Canada; anti-colonial trade unionism and community unionism; the politics of disability, the role of the "plantation approach" to the university and intellectual labor in Canada; and building anti-colonial spaces within classrooms. *Breaching the Colonial Contract* will help readers resist more fully the geopolitics of imperialism and to gain a deeper understanding of how such a politics gives birth to new colonial relationships. Only by re-centering ourselves with uncaptive minds in solidarity with the agency of the colonized, can we participate to our fullest capacity in breaching the colonial contract—what Ramon Grosfoguel and Ana Margarita Cervantes-Rodriguez (2002, xxviii) call a "second decolonization":

> In sum, developmentalism, Eurocentric universalist knowledges and the myth of decolonization have been crucial ideologies in concealing European/Euro-American responsibility in the fate of peripheral regions around the world. The world needs a second decolonization should address the global class, gender, racial, sexual, and regional asymmetries produced the hierarchical structures of he modern/colonial capitalist world-system.

Breaching the Colonial Contract not only assists us in undertaking a second decolonization, but provides innovative and important instantiations of anti-colonial pedagogy. Such a pedagogy stipulates that we must listen to our narratives of the self as carefully as we do our own heartbeats, from the context of the global totality, so that we can question as we walk, what the Zapatistas call *preguntando caminamos* (walking we question), a means of making the path critically by walking, facing our imperial custodians with an armed protagonistic agency. We don't march forward, berets tilted against the prevailing ideological winds, with crescendos of Rzewski' famous *36 Variations on Sergio Ortega's "El Pueblo Unido Jamas Sera Vencido"* animating our marching steps. We move forward without grandiose pronouncements, little by little, sometimes faltering, often invisible, but working tirelessly and consistently in every way we can—both large and small—to dismantle capital's law of value and the coloniality of power pumping through its veins that feeds the hammer fist of imperialism.

Peter McLaren

Notes

The author drew on several recent interviews for some of the material in this Preface.

References

Grosfoguel, Ramon, and Cervantes-Rodriguez, Ana Margarita. (2000). Unthinking Twentieth-Century Eurocentric Mythologies: Universalist Knowledges, Decolonialization, and Developmentalism. In *The Modern/Colonial Capitalist World-System in the Twentieth Century*. Edited by Ramon Grosfoguel and Ana Margarita Cervantes-Rodriguez (pp. xi–xxix). Westport, Connecticut and London: Praeger.

Miller, Adam. (2005). An Interview with Gregory Baum "Faith, Community, & Liberation" *Journal of Philosophy & Scripture*, Volume 2, Issue 2 | Spring. (pp. 23–30). Retrieved from: http://www.philosophyandscripture.org/Issue2-2/Baum/Baum.pdf

Quijano, Anibal. (2000) Coloniality of Power, Eurocentrism, and Latin America. *Nepantla: Views from South* 1.3, 533–580 [Translated by Michael Ennis]

Contents

Foreword ix
Peter McLaren

Introduction: The Politics of the North American Colonial in 2009 1

1 Contemporary Anticolonialism: A Transhistorical Perspective 13
  Arlo Kempf

2 Self-Determination and the Fourth World:
  An Introductory Survey 35
  Ward Churchill

3 Making Explicit the Jurisprudential Foundations
  of Multiculturalism: The Continuing Challenges
  of Colonial Education in US Schooling
  for Indigenous Education 53
  Dolores Calderón

4 Paulo Freire and the Politics of Postcolonialism 79
  Henry A. Giroux

5 Walking Out of Colonialism One Classroom
  at a Time: Student Walkouts and Colonial/Modern
  Disciplinarity in El Paso, Texas 91
  Antonio Reyes López

6 Indigenous Peoples and Black People
  in Canada: Settlers or Allies? 105
  Zainab Amadahy and Bonita Lawrence

7 Resistance from the Margin: Voices of African-Canadian
  Parents on Africentric Education 137
  Paul Adjei and Rosina Agyepong

8 Anticolonialism, Labor, and the Pedagogies
   of Community Unionism: The Case of Hotel
   Workers in Canada 159
   Peter H. Sawchuk

9 The Anguish of Power: Remapping Mental Diversity
   with an Anticolonial Compass 179
   Tanya Titchkosky and Katie Aubrecht

10 The Harvesting of Intellectuals
   and Intellectual Labor: The University System
   as a Reconstructed/Continued Colonial Space
   for the Acquisition of Knowledge 201
   Patrick S. De Walt

11 Building Anticolonial Spaces for Global Education:
   Challenges and Reflections 219
   Jonathan Langdon and Blane Harvey

12 The Eighteenth Brumaire of Gaius Baltar:
   Colonialism Reimagined in *Battlestar Galactica* 237
   Laura King and John Hutnyk

Afterword 251
George J. Sefa Dei

Index 259

Introduction: The Politics of the North American Colonial in 2009

Arlo Kempf

The common sense of empire is increasingly embedded in local, national, and international epistemologies. Counter-hegemonic discourse must increasingly confront and challenge dominant paradigms, research, policy, and practice. To do so requires a perspective that recognizes current discourses of "difference" and "resistance." Across much of the planet in disparate sites, ground-up resistance is in motion. As colonial relations are variegated, extended, and intensified, so must our resistance to these relations. In the fall of 2006, I attended a conference in El Paso, Texas, and had the opportunity to meet a number of local activists engaged in various radical (anti)border initiatives, who were articulating their struggles as a response to the ongoing colonial encounter: anticolonial struggle on North American soil. It seemed at the time that the anticolonial idea, or the anticolonial moment, was generally identified as happening elsewhere and in another time – basically in Africa from the 1950s through the 1970s and in Latin America up until the 1980s. While Canada and the United States in particular are frequently and accurately understood as colonial forces, the rise of anticolonialism within these two nations has been too often overlooked, despite the ongoing struggle of First Peoples for survival, autonomy, and justice which constitute the oldest social movements in both countries. There are, of course, anticolonial resistance, theorization, and even movements in the North American context, particularly if we read the notion of the "colonial" broadly. Anticolonial and antiracist education theorist Dei (2006) argues for a radical and important reconsideration of the notion of the "colonial." He writes: "[Colonial] refers to anything imposed and dominating rather than that which is simply foreign and alien" (p. 3). This is a departure from previous conceptions of colonialism constituted simply as various forms of territorial imperialism, or of state or cultural control through direct and/or indirect mechanisms. This radical reformulation allows for the recentering of objective assessments of power relations, of the myriad ways which colonialism has shed its skin only to reemerge in a new form – shape shifting to accommodate the needs of the colonizer (newly and broadly conceived). It is this reformulation that allows for a recentering of the agency of the colonized, alongside the accountability of the colonizer: the two pronged aim of this collection.

Although the degree to which the United States and Canada are transhistorically colonial powers is important, this work focuses on resistance and the degree to which anticolonial activism and theory are mobilizing in different sites (discursive and physical) across the United States and Canada. The works in this collection continue an anticolonial conversation already long underway, and add perhaps a small piece to a much larger discourse. We go to press as Barack Obama assumes the US presidency, as liberals prepare to declare the United States, and by extension the world, postracial. Juxtaposed with the new freedom of white commentators to speak race has been president Obama's color blind campaign, wherein everybody but the first black president was allowed to mention the man's color. As anti-Obama calls of "string him up" drifted through crowds at republican rallies (the party that received the other half of the vote), America prepared to declare an end to racism – an end to the past. The new North American racelessness is of course not content with the present – its reaches into both past and future possibilities, asserting a pedagogy of silence and denial around race-based oppression and struggle (as well as around the existence of race and racism). The consequence is a conference of illegitimacy on contemporary antiracist and anticolonial struggle. With Obama at the helm, America's long and uncomfortable march to civilization is complete. Indeed, in 2009 the notion of a black president and the notion of America are mutually civilizing ideas – each conferring legitimacy on the other.

From all sides of the political middle, Barack Obama's body – his color – is seen to heal a sick America. If any pop culture figure can be said to speak for (and to) the mainstream left, it is Jon Stewart, and his highly popular *The Daily Show*. Speaking on Obama's victory, Stewart declared:

> [T]here are very few countries in the world that live up to their creed, that live up to the documents of their founding that all men are created equal, and tonight, America has proven itself on a world stage as a show country, not a tell country. They have shown that we have lived up to our creed. We are what we say we are. ... America tonight lives up to its promise. (Comedy Network 2008)

Mission accomplished then – cheers to a job well done – this from a leading "critical" voice. As the bombs continue to rain down in Iraq and Afghanistan; as American policy, money, and weapons kill Palestinians, Somalis, and Columbians; as millions of Americans fall further down the economic rabbit hole of late capitalism; as people of color continue to face criminalization and impoverishment at disproportionately high rates; as people socialized as disabled struggle against social and economic marginalization; as American women continue to face gendered violence at alarming rates across the country; as the word "queer" remains a loaded weapon for most who use it – America is redeemed.

Canada is of course above this pedestrian struggle with race and inequality. Canadians have watched, both smug and surprised, as the United States elected an African-American man as president. Underlying such presumptions about US voters lay the implication that Americans were caught in a struggle to correct historical wrongs, get over a racial hump, and catch up. For many Canadians, Canada is above and beyond such a struggle, both currently and historically. The Canadian narrative insists that Canada is tolerant, inclusive, and intrinsically multicultural. Canadians watch contentedly with their feet up – resting on these assumptions – as the United States finally comes around. Slavery, segregation, lynching, and other red flag markers of racism are for many Canadians phenomena associated only with the United States, despite the historical presence of each of these in Canada. Martin Luther King Jr. and Malcolm X are embraced by Canadians as heroes and healers of a sick nation whose disease, however, was never contagious and certainly never made its way north. Canadians are raised on an ontological diet of "mosaic" (not melting pot) and "multiculturalism" which serve to disguise colonial privilege and punishment. This dovetails with the myth of Canada as an international force for peace and tolerance (particularly in contrast to the United States), and defines the very notion of what it means to be Canadian as a conceptual paradigm which simultaneously takes credit for some degree of inclusion and good will, while working to exclude many (by virtue of race, class, gender, disability and sexuality) through an "us" (white middle-class) and "them" (everybody else) framework.

The Canadian narrative tends to see the absence of popular and powerful black leaders in Canada as an indication that such leaders, as well as a public discussion of race and inequity, are somehow unnecessary. While Canadians have their eyes trained keenly on race relations in the United States, their 20/20 vision fades when it comes to their own backyard. The ongoing assault on First Nations and First Nations People by the Canadian settler/occupier state remains the elephant in the room of Canadian left-wing politics. As Churchill (1996) and others have argued, the struggle for equity and equality among all of North America's immigrants proceeds on Indigenous land. In the United States, Barack Obama's historic fulfillment of America's promise is indeed unprecedented: no person of color has ever been handed the keys to the stolen castle.

As is the case in the United States, the election captured the Canadian racial imagination (and imaginary) as well. Almost overnight Canadians were talking about race, representation, and politics. As the Canadian federal election proceeded simultaneously, race and inequality, however, were kept neatly in the closet. A look at the racial breakdown of the candidates in each of Canada's four federal parties reveals that the racial laurels on which the Canadian narrative rests are perhaps less inclusive than commonly thought – particularly by racially privileged Canadians. Of the approximately 1,232 candidates who ran for Canada's 308 federal parliamentary seats, only 132 were people of color (10.7%). Highly underrepresented were Latino and black Canadians, with almost no candidates in most regions of the country. As for Canada's great black hope to the south, and whether or not Canadians would elect him, they probably would not get the chance. Obama would have a near impossible time finding his way to the leadership of any federal Canadian party. The paucity of black candidates at all levels was striking: 16 of 1,232 (1.2%) in total. In Canada, Mr. Obama would have a hard time finding a seat, to say nothing of the country's highest office. While Canadians may love the notion of black leadership as well as racial progress, they seem to do so only at a comfortable distance. The same holds true in the United States in its historical mission of exporting values and discourse in its various internal and external civilizing missions.

Secure in its place at the top of the evolutionary ladder, the United States is now legitimized in its inward and outward projects of civilization. America is a feminist in Afghanistan, an antiracist in Iran, a peacemaker in Israel, a champion of human rights in Cuba, and an omniscient (and worthy) big brother at home. The United States is now the world's foremost expert on tolerance, and those who say otherwise must, sadly, be themselves afflicted by intolerance. This mission, like all colonial missions, is a moral undertaking infused with a pedagogy of tolerance aimed to raise the most savage racist to a higher level – the highly Islamaphobic climate of the post 9/11 era is the most powerful marker of this phenomenon. While overseeing a campaign of domestic and international targeting of Muslim groups and individuals, former President Bush reassured us in 2004 that "[t]here's a lot of people in the world who don't believe that people whose skin color may not be the same as ours can be free and self-governing. I reject that. I reject that strongly. I believe that people who practice the Muslim faith can self-govern. I believe that people whose skins [sic] aren't necessarily ah, are a different color than White, can self-govern" (White House Web site 2004). Although these ideas are rarely expressed so blatantly, they clearly underpin the current US and Canadian recolonization of parts of the Middle East. They also speak to the shock and hope that surrounds Obama's success in a game heretofore belonging entirely to whites. Bush's quote implies that Muslim self-governance – or a non-white self-governance – is a wild idea that, well, just might work. The former president locates the West and (himself) as visionary on the subject, all the while engaging in the destabilizing of Muslim governments, communities, and individuals in various parts of the world (Dei and Kempf 2007).

For this experiment to work, however, the worthy must be separated from the heretical. In the finest colonial tradition, the battle of good and other operates with the United States at the helm, burdened with the Manichean task of separating barbarian from hero, good Muslim from bad Muslim, moderate from militant, tolerant from intolerant. Publicly cleansed and separated from his Church, his activism as a community organizer, and from any discussion of the saliency of race, Obama is pronounced by the electorate (and his party) as ready to lead. The good (his good) separated from the other (his other). This did not, however, stop me or thousands of others from crying when we watched his acceptance speech. Despite the power of colonial hegemony expressed through racial, capitalist, gendered, embodied, and sexualized logic, another form of commonsense persists: that of resistance on the one hand, and to borrow a phrase, hope, on the other. Our bodies, our spirit, and indeed the rich history of anticolonial struggle tell us that another story is possible. The rise of the new left in South America tells us that it is possible. The activism of our marginalized communities tells us it is possible. Emerging scholarship reflecting a rich tradition of anticolonial thought tells us it is possible. The fact that no oppression goes unresisted tells us it is possible.

Almost a decade in, empire is the dominant mode of cultural production of the twenty-first century. If we are unable to excavate the archaeology of the present through a holistic and resistance-based understanding of the workings of oppression, empire promises to be the definitive fact linking the dawn of this century with that of the next. Anticolonial theory and practice bring just such a reading to the workings of our world. Anticolonialism responds to the system of imposition as well as to individual acts. An anticolonial understanding is a holistic response to all, or to portions, of a given system or systems of power. While the implications of anticolonial struggle vary in nature, and from context to context, two broad colonial trends are worth mentioning specifically when articulating anticolonialism of the twenty-first century.

First, Indigenous people are waging some form of anticolonial struggle in every inhabited region of the world. This is the key form of anticolonial resistance of our time. These are not abstract struggles against abstract phenomena; these are the struggles of people resisting erasure, amputation, and genocide. Forced to battle the dominant narratives of historical memory, Indigenous people from throughout the world have no Israel to recover from their holocausts, and in many cases have seen no end to these holocausts. The bad guys are still winning. Although many of these struggles have a significant and long history, they are phenomena of the present. In the North American, Australian, and New Zealand contexts, Indigenous peoples are battling with the European colonialism of the seventeenth to twentieth centuries. In these contexts, no new understanding of colonialism is needed to understand the perpetuated relevance of colonialism in the twenty-first century. There is very little subtlety, nuance, or sophistication needed to understand the injustice visited historically or currently upon Indigenous peoples by colonial authorities. Subtlety, nuance, and sophistication are needed instead when constructing the silence, ignorance, and apathy characterizing public discourse around these injustices. It is to these processes of obfuscation, silencing, and denial that we must bring a critical and self-interrogative anticolonial approach to theory, practice, knowledge production, and daily life.

Second, alongside economic imperialism, cultural Americanization and even tourism or cultural performance dynamics of global imperialism, we can also identify the globalization of whiteness. This is a process whereby, as a constituent part and function of the exportation and spread of mainstream Euro/American cultural values, a colored epistemology is produced and reproduced in varied contexts around the globe. Production occurs when local sociocultural practices are displaced either partially through a devaluation of those practices, or completely by way of an entirely new set of practices. Reproduction occurs when global cultural capital formation works with and reifies existing systems of whiteness. By existing, I refer to the historical and/or transhistorical presence of, and context for, a currency of whiteness. The widespread pursuit of straight hair and lighter skin cannot be separated from the cultural aspects of globalization. It is related as well, however, to the historical context of the European (British, Dutch, Swedish, and Spanish) whites, having committed mass murder, mass exploitation, and mass colonization of Ghanaians. The globalization of whiteness is linked to other social locations (e.g., class and gender) and should be understood as an interlocked and intersecting element of the continuing colonial project. The resultant cultural hierarchy comes with gender and sexuality strictures that are equally as problematic. In many colonial contexts the culture of the dominant, or whiteness, takes on a commodity form, with economic and cultural implications. The motivation to retain and pass down local languages and cultural practices is diminished in many colonial settings. The language of the dominant or colonizer takes on the form of a currency to which value is assigned. In *Black Skin, White Masks*, Fanon writes:

> The Negro of the Antilles will be proportionately whiter – that is, he will come closer to being a real human being – in direct ratio to his mastery of the French language. ... A man who has a language consequently possesses the world expressed and implied by the language. ... What we are getting at becomes plain. Mastery of language affords remarkable power. (1967, p. 18)

With telemarketers in India trained to mimic the accents of people in certain US and Canadian regions (so that incoming calls sound "local" to First World ears), we can see that with the intensification of the global market comes an intensification of cultural and economic imperialism. Much of the current colonial impulse – the current colonial project – is ultimately generated in the European–American homelands of the dominant. Alongside an analysis of anticolonial struggles around the world, we have to look at oppression and resistance here and now. If we cannot bring home "our" troops, at least we can bring home our analysis, our struggle, our hearts, and our minds.

With contributors from a variety of academic and professional fields from across the United States and Canada, this work offers an anticolonial analysis of a broad spectrum of topics and contexts. Although postcolonialism as an area of research and writing is widely taken up, anticolonialism offers a relevant critique of the limitations and complexities of the postcolonial approach, and serves to challenge both the persistence of colonial imposition and the ways in which that persistence is understood and misunderstood.

Chapter 1, *Contemporary Anti-colonialism: A Transhistorical Perspective* by Arlo Kempf, sets out the theoretical landscape of contemporary anticolonialism, arguing for the relevance of anticolonialism for twenty-first-century North America. By looking at the transhistorical nature of anticolonial struggle, this chapter also situates current anticolonial moments within a broader chronological context, one that we may both learn from and upon which we may improve. Beginning with an introduction to anticolonialism and its contemporary implications, this chapter provides an explication and investigation of both colonialism and anticolonialism, including an examination of some of the key concepts and mechanisms at work in each. The chapter then fleshes out the implications of articulating a discourse of critical whiteness through the anticolonial framework, and stresses the need to investigate the implications of anticolonialism for dominant accountability. The final section of the chapter looks briefly at anticolonialism in history, and as well examines the anticolonial approach to historiography. A very brief conclusion follows.

In Chapter 2, *Self-determination and the Fourth World: An Introductory Survey*, Ward Churchill counterposes the idea of Third World liberation to that of the Fourth, tracing the development and implications of both Third and Fourth World struggles. Churchill's highly annotated piece maps the terrain of the struggle of Indigenous peoples around the globe against myriad aspects and elements of the ongoing colonial encounter with attention to the North American, African, Asian, the Middle Eastern, Latin American, and Oceanic contexts. Churchill sets out the current and historical trajectory of the discourse surrounding the Third World and

Fourth World struggles, with attention to the degree to which Third World liberation has come largely at the expense of the peoples of the Fourth World. Churchill also challenges the postcolonial (mis)understanding of Indigenous peoples. In addition to providing a comparative analysis of global Indigenous resistance to colonialism, this exhaustively referenced chapter is a source guide for anyone interested in the contemporary Fourth World struggle.

In Chapter 3, *Making Explicit the Jurisprudential Foundations of Multiculturalism: The Continuing Challenges of Colonial Education in US Schooling for Indigenous Education*, Dolores Calderón argues that a major issue facing educational research in the United States in general and multicultural education in particular is the lack of interrogation of the Western metaphysics, or worldviews, that shape and define the parameters of how we conceive and talk about education. Indigenous educational issues are thus placed in the same context as the challenges faced by black, Asian-American, and Latino/Latina communities. This collapsing of "minority" educational issues into a standardized, "colonial blind" discourse of multiculturalism ignores native self-determination, its accompanying nation-building projects, and does not take into account the importance of native culture and knowledge in maintaining native sovereignty. She traces this collapsing of "minority" treatment to jurisprudence, examining central legal sources of Civil Rights and Federal Indian Law to explore how colonization has organized white-settler ideologies and institutions in the United States. Calderón investigates how multicultural frameworks in education reproduce these ideas through promotion of concepts such as citizenship, equality, and diversity, which preclude engagement with Native-informed frameworks. Therefore, to encourage anticolonial practices in education, she concludes that serious reassessment of the common racial remedies offered by Civil Rights law, embodied in multicultural education, is required.

Chapter 4, *Paulo Freire and the Politics of Postcolonialism* by Henry A. Giroux, argues that, increasingly, Freire's work has become the standard reference for engaging in what is often referred to as teaching for critical thinking, dialogical pedagogy, or critical literacy. His scholarship has passed from the origins of its production in Brazil, through Latin America and Africa, to the hybrid borderlands of North America – frequently appropriated by academics, adult educators, and others who inhabit the ideology of the West in ways that often reduce it to a pedagogical technique or method. What has been increasingly lost in the North American and Western appropriation of Freire's work is the profound and radical nature of its theory and practice as an anticolonial and postcolonial discourse. Giroux argues that Paulo Freire's work must be read as a postcolonial text and that North Americans, in particular, must engage in a radical form of intellectual and pedagogical border-crossing in order to reconstruct Freire's work in the specificity of its historical and political construction. Specifically, this means making problematic a politics of location situated in the privilege and power of the West and how engaging the question of the ideological weight of such a position constructs one's specific reading of Freire's work. At the same time, becoming a border crosser engaged in a productive dialogue with others means producing a space in which those dominant social relations, ideologies, and practices that erase the specificity of the voice of the other must be challenged and overcome.

Chapter 5, *Disrupting the Colonial Present: Chicana/Chicano Student Walkouts, United States Colonialism, and Disciplinarity in El Paso, Texas* by Antonio Reyes López, provides the initial spark for the idea of this book. Within the spatial confines of missions, boarding schools, and public school classrooms, colonized youth in the US–Mexican borderlands were targeted by colonial regimes for cultural transformation. Seeking to create ideal citizens that consented to colonial relations of power, state-sanctioned educational facilities functioned as an effective space of disciplinarity. Through a theoretical discussion of the central location of colonized youth in colonial regimes of power, the silencing of US colonialism in scholarly and popular discourses, and the disciplinary function of the colonialist classroom in the region, López examines the student walkouts that took place in El Paso, Texas, in March 2006 as acts of anticolonial resistance that disrupt colonial disciplinarity in the city. The author evaluates historical sources, oral histories, participant accounts of the student walkouts, and public reactions in the city to evaluate the persistence of colonial relations of domination and how a discursive regime of truth serves to silence US colonialism and manage anticolonial resistance in El Paso, Texas. In examining US colonialism in the borderlands through the lens of disciplinarity, this chapter argues that power relations, public discourse, and student activism have to be analyzed within the context of ongoing colonialism.

López's look at colonial schooling processes in the US–Mexico borderland communities illustrates the parallels in colonial processes from one region as well as time to another. While the US and Spanish authorities were snatching Mexican and Indigenous children from their homes, Canadian and British authorities were busy with the same processes of kidnapping 3,000 miles to the north. The complex material and discursive web involved in colonial education in Canada was also at work in the borderlands López describes so eloquently with the notion of colonial disciplinarity. López also looks at the gender reformation necessary for the colonial imperative to proceed. His analysis powerfully demonstrates the ways in which the mobilization of different sites of oppression were constituent elements of US and Spanish colonialism. His parallels to contemporary education in the border region remind us that many of these same processes are at work in the twenty-first century and govern contemporary colonial relations in that region and elsewhere.

Chapter 6, *Indigenous Peoples and Black People in Canada: Settlers or Allies?* by Zainab Amadahy and Bonita Lawrence, addresses the current and historical implications of the relationship between people of color and aboriginal peoples in North America. In Canada, recent attempts to delineate the relationship of people of color to aboriginal people have concluded that despite sharing experiences of racism, people of color maintain a settler relationship with aboriginal peoples. However, the ambiguities of this relationship are nowhere more complex than between African-descended and aboriginal people. The relationship is complicated by the fact that generations of African descendants are here not as settlers but as descendants of enslaved people brought here by force, and that more recent African-descended peoples come as migrant workers and refugees who have been massively displaced by colonialism and racism on an international scale, by the uniqueness of the semi-colonized marginal position that most African nations still occupy globally, and by the fact that black people are the only racialized people who have extensively intermarried with aboriginal people, and indeed, for years, in many parts of the Americas, were given refuge in Indigenous communities. In the interests of alliance-building, the authors explore the tensions and points of connection between black and aboriginal communities, in Canada, with reference to the United States and other settler nations in the Americas. They also begin to explore the struggles of people who are both black and aboriginal to express their identities as black Indians.

Chapter 7, *Resistance from the Margin: Voices of African-Canadian Parents on Black-Focused Education* by Paul Adjei and Rosina Agyepong, investigates the colonial and anticolonial underpinnings of the struggle for Afrocentric public schooling in Toronto, Canada. For many, the recent call for Afrocentric schools as an alternative form of education for African-Canadian youth in Toronto has amounted to a call for racial (re)segregation of schools in Toronto. This objection rests on the illusive assumption that the present arrangement is devoid of segregation and exclusionary practices. Unfortunately, the coded messages engraved within curricula and classrooms are administered to criminalize black students. While much of the African-Canadian community believes that schools have the best of intentions for every student, available research findings clearly show that many black youths do not feel welcome in schools in Toronto due to racism, classism, and other inequitable practices. The authors bring an anticolonial reading to the philosophy and politics of Afrocentric schools. Adjei and Agyepong use original research findings alongside historical documents to argue that the African-Canadian community cannot afford to rely on the current school system to address problems facing black youths. The chapter concludes with an analysis of the pedagogic relevance of having such alternative education in Toronto. Grounded in the voices of African-Canadian parents, those who are living this controversy, the authors place an emphasis on resistance and agency in the epistemological formulations of the community involved.

Chapter 8, *Through the Lobby and into the Streets: Toward a Pedagogy of Anticolonial Trade Unionism in Canada* by Peter Sawchuk, brings an anticolonial lens to the context of union movements in Canada. In Toronto today, where hotel workers have turned a new page in their own lives, they have also begun to turn a new page in the collective life of the trade union movement – they are organizing. In Canada, these efforts represent a movement of distinction: at the center of a coalition of largely female and largely immigrant workers of color, an increasingly coherent, increasingly militant form of organizing has moved north and taken root. In this chapter Sawchuk explores one of a growing number of examples in which the logics of race, gender, and class – systematically and at great material and ideological effort kept isolated from each other – converge. It is an example of a moment of undeniable possibility in which what Raymond Williams has referred to as "commitment" is overcome by raw "alignment" of subaltern forces. In order to assess these events and possibilities, here the author draws on a potentially unifying marxist, anticolonialist social analysis. The colonization process, in this sense, describes the simultaneity of race, gender, and class reproduction across individual mental life, groups and community practice, and economic institutions. Colonized experience, then, is understood as a potential unifying analytic method with the potential to detail the confluence of alienation, exploitation, and oppression across a range of lived forms. In so doing, and in keeping with the tenor of this collection, it challenges conceptions of postcolonial thought as a form of nostalgia, traced through lives lived well within the walls of advanced capitalist development of a country open and proud in its claim of multiculturalism. Outlining first the state of the hospitality sector in conjunction with the state of the urbanized, demographic landscape of twenty-first-century Canada, Sawchuk offers a critical review of social movement theory with special attention to the emerging scholarship on Community Unionism. What we see is a picture of an accelerated economic apartheid, an emboldened colonizing project of the First World as well as its challenger: a pedagogy of social movement building; a pedagogy through which one of the most potent forces for transformation beyond capitalism, the union movement, must necessarily learn a new identity; a pedagogy that necessarily must march past the classroom, through the lobby and into the streets.

Chapter 9, *The Anguish of Power: Remapping Mental Diversity with an Anticolonial Compass* by Katie Aubrecht and Tanya Titchkosky, argues that an analysis informed by anticolonial principles "challenges the normalizing gaze of the dominant in the construction of what constitutes valid knowledge and experience" (Kempf, chapter One). This chapter aims to participate in that challenge by exposing how, at the level of embodiment, colonization has worked to oppress diversity and to make the possibility of valued bodily, sensorial, and mental differences all but disappear. Moreover, the ordinary ways that embodied responses develop in relation to the violence of prevailing discourses of power are often assimilated under colonial knowledge regimes. The authors explore mental illness as both a form of devalued embodiment and as an assimilated response. As a way to pursue this examination, this chapter conducts a textual analysis of the way disability is defined and studied by the World Health Organization and the World Bank. Specific attention is cast on how mental differences and anguish are framed by the normalizing gaze of dominant health agencies. This normalizing gaze makes ways of experiencing embodied differences appear invalid while distancing people from the need to reflect on power. By exposing how colonial power is at work organizing how disability can and cannot be known, this chapter aims to demonstrate the generative potential of conceptualizing embodiment otherwise. Aubrecht and Titchkosky demonstrate how embodiment is a space of knowledge and experience where power relations can be revealed and rethought.

Chapter 10, *The Harvesting of Intellectuals and Intellectual Labor: The University System as a Reconstructed/Continued Colonial Space for the Acquisition of Knowledge* by Patrick S. De Walt, provides a critical analysis highlighting the multiple roles university intellectuals enact as both colonized and colonizer, using a fusion of Du Boisian, Fanonian, Gramscian, Marxian, and anticolonial thought. The author argues that this phenomenon occurs within the colonial university's capitalistic mission to plant and harvest knowledge through the exploitation of faculty and student labor. This exploitation begins in K–12 school models, creating a transition from an emphasis on physical labor, that is, the workforce, to what is sought by universities, intellectual labor. The author identifies and maps a "plantational approach," with which the university works to sustain and reproduce itself by developing a "university brand" for marketing and recruiting future intellectual laborers. Once within colonial universities, hierarchical institutional power dynamics (HIPDs) emulate the psychosocial mechanisms occurring on US antebellum plantations. Tracing the historical development of education for African descendants in the United States, De Walt draws a powerful connection between plantation labor formations and the current "colonial" university system, raising multiple key questions on the nature of duality and involuntary hybridity, as created by colonial labor formations both currently and historically.

Chapter 11, *Building Anticolonial Spaces of Education: Challenges and Reflections* by Jonathon Langdon and Blane Harvey, takes as its starting point the challenging process of building anticolonial spaces within classrooms, without reapplying new forms of dominance and imposition. More specifically, the chapter focuses on a particular example of an undergraduate course in "Global Education," where the authors sought to both introduce and model anticolonial pedagogy. This classroom was constituted in a democratic way, where team teaching and collaborative activity attempted to open up space for different truths, and for debate around these truths – opening up alternative narratives to dominant colonial legacies around knowledge construction. Together with a group of student teachers from this class, the authors reflect on the successes and challenges that arose in using an anticolonial pedagogy. The chapter concludes by underscoring the need for critical reflection to be linked with concrete action, and argues that anticolonial education must conceptualize the classroom as only the starting point to action.

References

Churchill, W. (1996). *From A Native Son: Selected Essays on Indigenism, 1985–1995*. Cambridge: South End Press.
Comedy Network. (2008). *The Colbert Report: Indecision 2008: America's Choice*. Originally aired November 4. Accessed November 18, 2008 at: http://watch.thecomedynetwork.ca/#clip109409
Dei, G.J.S. (2006). *Mapping the Terrain: Towards a New Politics of Resistance*. In Dei, G.S. and Kempf, A. (eds.), Anti-Colonialism and Education: The Politics of Resistance (pp. 1–23). Rotterdam: Sense Publishers.
Dei, G.J.S. and Kempf, A. (2007). Katrina and Other Colonial Levees Breaking: Empire in 2006. A Dialogue with George Sefa Dei and Arlo Kempf. *Journal of Contemporary Issues in Education*. 1(2). pp. 4–25.
Fanon, F. (1967). *Black Skin, White Masks*. New York: Grove Press.
Whitehouse Web site. (2004). April 30, Joint press conference. Retrieved from http://www.whitehouse.gov/news/releases/2004/04/20040430-2.html on December 19, 2005.

Chapter 1
Contemporary Anticolonialism: A Transhistorical Perspective

Arlo Kempf

1.1 Introduction

Ours is a time of sophisticated empire on high. We need look no further than the US and Canadian military occupations in Iraq and Afghanistan to see the blunt end of the colonial encounter. This is but a fraction of the colonial tale. The US invasions of Iraq have produced an extreme, although not unfamiliar, insider–outsider paradigm, one expressed physically in Iraq (by the division between the Green Zone in central Baghdad and the rest of the country) and discursively in the United States (by the division between those "for us" and those "against us"). Naomi Klein has described a "global green zone," an idea which sees the world and its people divided into binary spaces, thus: those inside the green zone have adequate infrastructure, food, security, water, and other resources; those outside this zone do not (The Possibility of Hope 2007). When extended by the anticolonial approach, this analysis can be applied to discursive as well as physical spaces. All green zones are, of course, contested spaces – spaces constituted as much by that within their borders as by that which is absent therein. Contestation, conflict, resistance, and domination create such spaces be they physical or discursive. While residents of Klein's green zone enjoy food, water, and at least some ability to control their surroundings, residents/members of a discursive green zone enjoy epistemic entitlement and legitimacy as well as the ability to confer normative truths on their mental surroundings. As the child of conflict, the green zone is conflicted; it understands itself by virtue of what it is not, and exists in perpetual opposition to this absence. Further, the green zone and its surroundings are mutually constitutive, thus blurring the binary. The dynamic relations between center and periphery on the one hand, and the overlap of the two spaces on the other makes one impossible without the other and makes the two zones indistinguishable at times (e.g., certain residents of Baghdad's Green Zone face gender and ethnic oppression despite their insider status, while many living outside of the Green Zone enjoy greater material and immaterial comforts than those on the inside). Foundational anticolonial theorist Memmi (1965) as well as contemporary scholar Minh-ha (2000) point out that within each colonizer there is a colonized, and vice versa – the same overlap found in the green zones. Green zones are empty without notions of identity and history, yet they also create both identity and history. The struggles (both military and discursive) of the twenty-first century are colonial in nature. Today's wars are the well-endowed grandchildren of European colonialism – the continuation of the family business. Colonialism has not been alone in its journey through the ages, however; with it has come resistance, refusal, and the agency of the oppressed. With it has come anticolonialism.

This chapter seeks to flesh out the contemporary meanings and workings of anticolonialism, within a transhistorical epoch. The term anticolonialism brings to mind different things for different people. For some it is the African struggles for independence against European colonialism in the 1950s, 1960s, and 1970s. Others conflate it with terms such as neocolonialism and postcolonialism. While the African liberation movements of the twentieth century are key sites of anticolonial resistance that produced and inspired key literature on the topic, anticolonialism has a much broader history in regions and spaces around the globe. Further, although anticolonialism draws on certain postcolonial and neocolonial works, it is by no means synonymous with these approaches – a departure discussed below. First and foremost, anticolonialism brings a newly holistic reading to domination and resistance, raising important questions around the intersections of class, gender, ethnicity, disability, sexuality, racial, linguistic, and religion-based oppressions. This approach challenges the normalizing gaze of the dominant in the construction of what constitutes valid and invalid knowledge and experience (see Dei 2006). While anticolonialism is in many ways a language of resistance for and from the oppressed (see Dei and Asgharzadeh 2001), the dominant must also participate in the anticolonial struggle, as the colonizer is no less colonized than any of his victims. Where anticolonialism is a tool used to invoke resistance for the colonized, it is a tool used to invoke accountability for the colonizer. In both cases, it serves to reveal and challenge the assumptions, silences, and common sense of dominant relations. Working with, and extending the theoretical implications of, early anticolonial works by Memmi (1965), Fanon (1967a and 1967b), and Césaire (1972), this chapter foregrounds dominant accountability alongside resistance as a key tenet of anticolonial thought.

By focusing on relations of resistance and domination in both the physical and discursive spheres, anticolonialism challenges all relations of domination. As Dei (2006) has argued, all domination and imposition constitute a form of colonization. Although this approach begs certain questions concerning the operations of these relations, Dei's redefinition allows for an expansion of our ideas of colonization, from nation-on-nation Euro-American-style colonization to more subtle, intricate, sophisticated, and nuanced forms of colonial oppression. While the example of the most recent US invasion and occupation of Iraq is clearly indicative of colonial relations at work, so too are the myriad epistemological battles and contestations taking place in Iraq and the United States. The anticolonial approach brings a complex reading of history, possibility, and resistance. The anticolonial approach invokes a literacy of resistance – this is to say a reading against domination and imposition. This chapter provides an introduction to anticolonialism and its contemporary implications. Section 1.2 attempts an explication and investigation of both colonialism and anticolonialism, including an examination of some of the key concepts and mechanisms at work in each. Section 1.3 briefly fleshes out the implications of articulating a discourse of critical whiteness through the anticolonial framework, and stresses the need to investigate the implications of anticolonialism for the notion of accountability. In this section, I also address what brings me personally to the topic at hand, and how I understand my own position in relation to anticolonial theory and practice. Section 1.4 looks briefly at anticolonialism in history, and examines the anticolonial approach to historiography. A very brief conclusion follows.

1.2 Colonialism and Anticolonialism

> In your excitement you have forgotten what we have been considering. We brought the English, and we keep them. Why do you forget that our adoption of their civilization makes their presence in India at all possible? Mahatma Gandhi (1997, p. 74)

The anticolonial framework casts a critical gaze wherever imposition occurs. Epistemologically, anticolonialism is guided by the knowledge of the oppressed and is informed as well by the drive for the accountability of the oppressor. Axiologically, it works with the contextual, temporal, and historical determinants of a given situation in order to establish a course of resistance and social transformation. Ontologically, it works from the premises that change is possible; that oppression can be overcome; and that the tools for such liberation lie in the mental, physical, and emotional/spiritual abilities of oppressed people. Anticolonialism is a strategic approach to decolonization. In order to understand oppression in a concrete sense, the anticolonial approach looks at the day-to-day material and immaterial operations and manifestations of oppression. Having said all this, however, anticolonialism can really be understood only by first coming literally to terms with colonialism.

1.2.1 Mechanics

Modern colonialism is not simply something Europe did to the rest of the world between the sixteenth and twentieth centuries. Nor is it reducible to the ongoing global expansion and penetration of Euro-American culture and priorities. Although these instances provide important examples of the act of colonization, these acts in and of themselves do not provide quite enough information. Dei (2006) has defined colonization as anything dominating or imposing. This begs the question, however, of how colonialism functions. Anticolonialism is a resistance-oriented lens for understanding history, politics, education, and power relations more generally. To confront oppressive power relations we must understand them. This means looking at various sites of oppression including race, class, gender, ethnicity, ability, sexuality, religion, geographic/immigration status, etc., as well as their interconnectivity. All of these are, of course, abstract concepts. They become concrete when they are operationalized to confer power and/or punishment. This operationalization is the colonial moment.

Colonization is the process whereby abstract social locations become sites for concrete oppression. The concrete includes material and nonmaterial elements of existence. What Fanon (1967a) calls amputation, what Dei and Asgharzadeh (2001) describe as spirit injury, and what Marx famously identifies as alienation fall into the category of the concrete nonmaterial. Anticolonialism is the de-operationalization of social locations as sites of concrete (material and nonmaterial) oppression. The colonial moment occurs when behavior, based on social location, has concrete negative consequences for one actor or group, and concrete positive consequences for another. See Fig. 1.1 below.

To flesh out this idea, the case of Ghana's liberation from Britain provides a useful example. Ghana's independence in 1957 marked the first successful anticolonial struggle in West Africa. Ghana's was a liberation won from the blood, sweat, and ingenuity of the Ghanaian people. We can ask, however, what changed as a result of the transformation from foreign to local rule? The rise to power of Dr. Kwame Nkrumah, although important as an act of representation, insured little but hope. What made the struggle of the Ghanaian people, as well as their new government, anticolonial? In other words, how were sites of oppression de-operationalized as

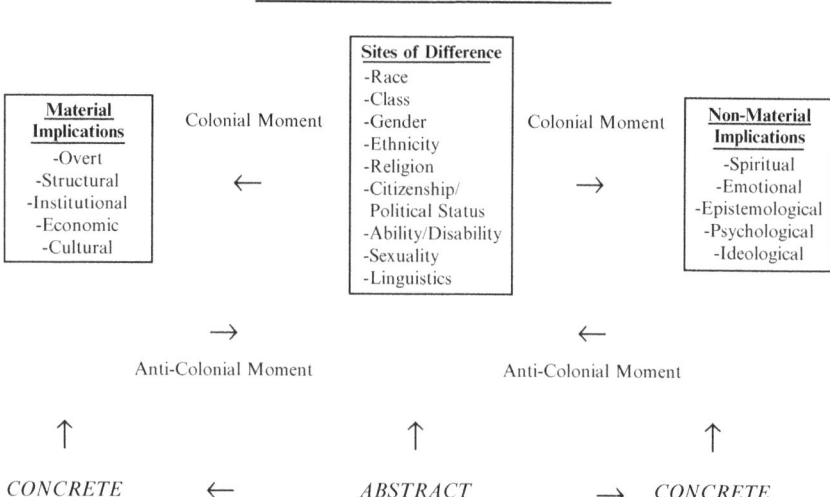

Fig. 1.1 Concrete implications of oppression

such? How was concrete oppression ended along material and nonmaterial lines? Two major areas stand out among the many sweeping changes brought forth by the Nkrumah government: one, formal racial barriers were largely dismantled (de-operationalizing many sites of racial oppression); and two, state resources were enriched and redistributed to the people (de-operationalizing many areas of class oppression). This is to say that not just any revolution (or revolutionary) will do. A simple change of hands – or a simple change in the color, class, or gender of those hands – is inadequate in and of itself. I suggest that President Obama, for example, must be understood in these terms. While representation, color, and bodies matter, these are insufficient in and of themselves. The salient markers are the content and character of the change as well as the way the dynamics of privilege and punishment are recreated by a given transformation. This applies to international revolutions as well as the smallest interpersonal encounters. The deconstruction of oppression reveals the links and the locks between different sites of oppression. While the anticolonial prism is focused on multiple sites and locations, it is also crucial to note and challenge the tendency of race to disappear when different sites of oppression assemble for the purpose of disassembly. As antiracist scholarship has long cautioned, class and gender are too often addressed to the exclusion of race (Brandt 1986; Miles 1993; Omi and Winant 1994; Crenshaw et al. 1995; Delgado and Stefancic 2001; Dei 1996). This should not, however, prevent an embrace of the multicentric approach. In the US and Canadian contexts, black feminists have argued that mainstream (white) feminism currently and historically excludes the struggles and concerns of black women (see Hill-Collins 1990; Wane et al. 2001). Subsequent to the organization of a black feminist discourse, queer theory scholars argued that black feminism excluded and delegitimized the struggles of lesbians of color (hooks 2000; Lorde 1984; Silvera 1992). So the reproduction of colonial relations (of inclusion and exclusion) takes place even in progressive discursive activist contexts – necessitating a holistic multicentric approach from the onset.

1.2.2 Saliency and Entry Points

The notion of privilege is crucial to anticolonialism because it provides us with an avenue for assessing accountability. Interrogating privilege provides a guide for anti-oppression – to undo the colonial relations around us as well as those in which we play a role. We can thus outline an anticolonial categorical imperative whereby, in addition to resisting the ways we are oppressed, we should first enjoy only those privileges that do not punish others; and second, at the individual and societal levels, we should actively seek to undo any privileges, which punish others. Another way of putting it is to say that we must use the means at our disposal to effect the elimination of colonialism and colonization.

The vast majority of the world's population enjoys some form of colonial privilege at the expense of somebody else. So, although white men like me are most in need of a critical analysis of their privilege, anticolonialism is an approach which applies to any privileged body, to anyone positioned to oppress another person or group. Further, by looking at the links between different components of the colonial structure, we can better theorize resistance to them. Oppression is assembled. It thus needs to be disassembled. This is only possible if we understand each of the parts that make up the sum, as well as the way they work together. For instance, how do the politics of the home and of the personal impact the politics of a national revolution, consciousness, and transformation? Like integrative antiracism theories (Dei 1996), this approach recognizes the interlocking and intersecting nature of different sites of oppressions. Unlike antiracism, however, which argues for the saliency of race within the integrative approach (Dei 1996), anticolonialism argues that the saliency of one issue over another must be temporally and contextually determined, working with the material and immaterial effects of oppression and domination as dictated by what is most pressing and most strategically viable. It is crucial here to stress that an integrative approach is necessary when conceiving of oppression and resistance to oppression. The notion of saliency is best understood as an entry point. Every context demands a contextual analysis to determine the entry point that best responds to the lived reality (meaning the material and nonmaterial consequences) of oppression and privilege. For the oppressor, this means looking at the ways we most oppress, as well as any connections to other relations of oppression. It also means determining where we can be most useful in effecting change. No one form of oppression will be the most pressing in every context around the globe – further, the title of "most pressing" site of resistance is often contested. From region to region, country to country, city to city, and home to home different types of oppression are salient.

Colonialism, of course, is not confined to individual actions or reactions – it works on various interactive levels: nation to nation, person to person, region to region, etc. Colonialism is also at play in intra-sectional contexts: intra-national, intra-regional, and intrapersonal. These different levels are often mutually supportive – and mutually constitutive. The US invasion of Iraq, for example, involves an international imposition of material and nonmaterial objectives. This is nation-to-nation colonialism. The project is supported by corollary intra-national battles for hearts and minds in both the US and Iraqi contexts. A certain amount of US domestic support (be it passive ignorance or flag-waving enthusiasm) for the occupation of Iraq is key to the maintenance and reproduction of the mission. What passage or phrase in a textbook is required in Minneapolis for American soldiers to bomb a school in Teqrit? What must power relations look like in Tulsa for Americans to rape and photograph prisoners at the Abu Gharib prison facility? What truths and common sense are necessary for a nation to stand by a colonial war with benefits invisible to the average American? The colonial project is no greater than the sum of its parts. There is no magical synergy, economy of scale, or organic colonial inertia propelling the project forward on its own steam. Rather, domination occurs through individual, systemic, and institutional acts, and at times, differing levels of consent to those acts. Individually, we may oppress at one level and fight oppression at another. How we understand ourselves in connection to the relations of domination in which we participate is key.

1.3 Anticolonialism and Whiteness: On Location, Privilege, and Accountability

> [The colonizer who refuses] discovers that if the colonized have justice on their side, if he can go so far as to give them his approval and even his assistance, his solidarity stops there; he is not one of them and has no desire to be one. He vaguely foresees the day of their liberation and the reconquest of their rights, but does not seriously plan to share their existence, even if they are freed. Memmi (1965, p. 22)

I come to anticolonialism, an approach that seeks to counter racial, gender, class, sexuality, ethnicity, and ability-based oppressions, as a straight white guy, with no visible disability. I come with Memmi's above critique as a permanent check against my intentions as far as discussing oppression, oppressors, and oppressed people. As argued in Section 1.2, anticolonialism necessarily works with the knowledge of the oppressed. So what do I bring to anticolonialism? I bring various layers of latent racism and sexism. I bring what I assume is a full-scale misunderstanding of the struggles faced by people socialized/medicalized as disabled. I bring an overly dismissive attitude toward the oppression of queer bodies – especially those that are rich, white, and male. I am by no means proud of the preceding basket of political goodies and I bring them up for a reason. These blind spots help to confer, at times invisibly so, various elements of my dominant privilege. As Sawchuk (2007) has asked with regard to race and gender privilege in the Canadian academy: Who is most often made to feel like a fish in water? Who is made to forget the water is there to begin with? In the North American context, I have all the tools not only to feel like a fish in most North American waters, but also to cash in my unearned markers at will.

Among a few other things, I am a teacher. When students are reading a text, I often ask them to imagine the author – to piece her or him together based on the writing. Allow me to save you the trouble. Picture a big white guy in front of a computer and you've got me. I grew up in a working-class family in Toronto, with two American expatriate hippies who raised me as a good lefty and I quickly took up what I thought was an antiestablishment, anti-imperialist position. I went to alternative schools, I did social justice work in Latin America, and I became involved with a few small somewhat radical organizations in Canada. My politics reflected a working-class and pro-working-class consciousness. This is my political heritage. While we did talk politics around the table, we did not talk about race or racial privilege. We talked about the forms of oppression affecting us, but not about the forms of oppression that we ourselves effected and enjoyed. The blinders of racial, gender, ethnic, and ability-based privilege limited my early critical understandings – this is still the case, although I hope to a lesser degree. I was raised with the privilege of ignorance and the ignorance of privilege to think that class struggle was the only crucial part of the emancipatory puzzle.

To begin to address the tensions in doing anti-oppression work as a dominant body, I continually ask myself three questions: (1) What power do I have? (2) How did I get it? (3) What am I doing with it? The processes of decolonization and questioning do not end with the completion of one paper, book, or conversation. This is something with which and through which I must work, for as long as inequity and power are configured in their current state (Kempf 2006). This process is guided, for me, by the anticolonial conversation.

As a formal discourse, anticolonialism emerged in the early to mid-twentieth century as an expression of the voices of the colonized, and as an interrogation of the nature of colonial/anticolonial relations. Writers like Frantz Fanon, Aimé Césaire (1972), Amilcar Cabral (1970), Albert Memmi (1965), Mahatma Gandhi (1967 and 1997), Ernesto "Che" Guevara (1997), Maurice Bishop (1983), and others arrived organically at their understanding of oppression. Their entry points, although characterized to a certain degree by a colonizer–colonized duality, stemmed from their experience of oppression – from their resistance to the victimization of colonialism. For a dominant body/person (like me), the entry point is resistance to the perpetration of colonialism. While anticolonialism works with the knowledge of the oppressed, it also works with a holistic understanding of oppression and of resistance. The oppressor must resist, a fact often expressed but denied by dominant bodies. For privilege to function, it must create the conditions for its own invisibility. Resisting privilege means countering that invisibility, as well as the resulting privilege. For dominant bodies and for analyses of dominance more generally, the issue of accountability is paramount. Dominant bodies must work primarily against the oppression by which they are privileged and in which they thus participate. This is the essence of an entry point because, by its very nature, it involves a simultaneity of the theoretical and the practical, the saying and the doing. Anticolonial resistance at the personal level has to come about whenever possible, however, through engagement in a wider community. For a white male like me, an engagement with race cannot be a purely personal thing. It must involve becoming a transformative member of one's community.

My entry point into anticolonialism is through a critical analysis of white privilege – a privilege that interlocks and intersects with a number of other markers of social location and position including gender, ethnicity, sexuality, ability, and geographic/immigration status. Although critical whiteness as an area of study has emerged as a field of its own over the past 20 years (with such works as López 2005; Jensen 2005; Frankenberg 2004; Wise 2002; Wildman and Davis 2002; Hayes 2001; Twine 2004; Gaine 2000; Gallagher 2000; Kincheloe et al. 1998; Hill 1997; Delgado and Stefanic 1997; Lawrence 1997; Maher and Tetreault 1997; Scheurich 1997; Roediger, 1991; Macintosh 1988), many of the salient ideas at the core of critical whiteness, such as focusing on accountability, confronting Eurocentricity, assessing the cost of domination to the dominant, holding systems as well as individuals to account for racial privilege and punishment, and analyzing the epistemic underpinnings of racial punishment and privilege, can trace their roots to some of the key anticolonial thinkers (see also Dei 2004).

In *Toward the African Revolution*, Fanon argues: "Racism is not the whole but the most visible, the most day-to-day and, not to mince matters, the crudest element of a given structure" (1967b, p. 32). Commenting on the failure of phenotypical explanations of race differentiation and racism, Fanon continues: "[T]hese old fashioned positions tend in any case to disappear. This racism that aspires to be rational, individual, genotypically and phenotypically determined becomes transformed into cultural racism. The object of racism is no longer the individual man but a certain form of existing" (1967b, p. 32). We can extend this to notions of performing whiteness, whereby what Fanon calls "certain forms of existing" are preferred over others. Existence in this sense includes the physical, spiritual, and mental elements of day-to-day life. We see this locally in the histories of *shadism, passing,* and the voluntary/involuntary performance of whiteness in Canada and the United States, and internationally as Africans throughout the diaspora are now asked to perform the dominant trope in the public (and sometimes private) sphere of their existence.[1] In many countries around the world, finding skin whitener[2] is easier than finding a pack of cigarettes, while Euro-American cultural norms continue to permeate via media, colonial education, and colonial civil structures. In another work Fanon discusses the oppression of Africans in the Antilles and the colonial notion of ascending to the dominant culture: "Every people in whose soul an inferiority complex has been created by the death and burial of its cultural originality – finds itself face to face ... with the culture of the [dominant] mother country. The colonized is elevated above his jungle status in proportion to his adoption of the mother country's cultural standards" (1967a, p. 18). With a focus on language specifically, he continues: "[T]he Negro of the Antilles will be proportionately whiter – that is, he will come closer to being a real human being – in direct ratio to his mastery of the French language" (1967a, p. 18). In colonial contexts around the world, language continues to be an important barrier, keeping some people in and others out. Think of American television English (the "neutral" white accent) used to perform and define cultural norms for the nation. What does the voice of power sound like? What does the voice of the margin sound like? The ability of the colonial to adapt (and adapt to) any available space (be it physical or discursive) is reflective of the transhistorical imperative of the present contained in the colonial moment. In *Wretched of the Earth*, Fanon writes:

> [C]olonialism is not content to impose its rule upon the present and the future of a dominated country. Colonialism is not satisfied with holding a people in its grip and emptying the native's brain of all form and content. By a kind of perverted logic, it turns to the past of the oppressed people, and distorts, disfigures and destroys it. This work of devaluing colonial history takes on a dialectical significance today. (1963, p. 210)

Indeed all societies are characterized by official and unofficial discourses of memory, with holy memories dialectically dueling and defining (and being defined by) their heretical counterparts. This comes with both demonic and angelic bodies, with saviors and saved. Colonial imposition is not simply a closed door on the histories of the oppressed, but a ravaging of the legitimacy of all that exists behind that door – a condemnation in abstentia of all that existed *before*, alongside banishment to the past of "precolonial" cultures which have the audacity to survive Europe's genocidal march toward totality. Thus, struggles against what Dei (2007) has called "cultural closure," as well as against what Fanon has termed "amputation," are indeed anticolonial in nature.

Césaire's famous polemic *A Discourse on Colonialism* was one of the first published works to center critically on the colonial question. Césaire brings questions of systemic accountability to bear. His indictment of the journalists, the academics, intellectuals, pundits, and all others engaged in the colonial moment either actively or passively, and who sometimes appear to be the good liberals of the occasion, instructs us to train the gaze of accountability on all levels and to think critically around the entire spectrum of our epistemological building blocks. He argues:

> Therefore, comrade, you will hold as enemies ... not only sadistic governors and greedy bankers ... but likewise and for the same reason, venomous journalists, goitrous academics ... and in general, all those who performing their functions in the sordid division of labour for the defense of Western Bourgeois society ... split up the forces of [revolutionary] progress. (1972, p. 54)

The problem for Césaire is not simply the individual colonialists or their intentions – be they right or wrong – but the structure within which they perform their duties. He continues:

> And do not seek to know whether these gentlemen personally are in good or bad faith. ... Whether personally – that is, in the private conscious of Peter or Paul – they are or are not colonialists, because the essential thing is that their highly problematical subjective good faith is entirely irrelevant to the objective and social implications of the evil work they perform as watchdogs of colonialism. (1972, p. 55)

For Césaire, then, one's position dictates the impact of his or her existence on others. Until subverted, one's position trumps one's intentions. The same can be said about the way whites are structurally positioned as dominant bodies – racist, until that position is subverted. As I have argued elsewhere, any white person who does not actively subvert his or her racial privilege and the racism around him or her is racist. The key is to reveal race's hiding places. For example, many whites I know often make the distinction between making a racist remark, and actually being a racist. The idea is that saying racist things, or saying *a* racist thing, does not necessarily make the speaker a racist. I have used this evasion myself when, after having called a friend on racist remarks, I have wanted to patch up the hole I just created in our invisible script. The distinction between someone making a racist remark and someone being a racist serves three dangerous purposes: First, it hides the source and existence of racism; second, it separates the speaker from his or her thoughts and ideas, and from taking the necessary responsibility for them; and third, it places the blame on the remark, rather than on what motivates the remark. In this sense, the problem with the remark is not that it was thought, felt, or considered, but that it was voiced. When the time comes to hold someone or something accountable for the comment, the speaker answers only for breaching the script – not for why he or she said it, and not even necessarily for the content of the comment (Kempf 2008). The remark is rendered meaningless beyond the fact that it is a breach. The workings of oppression hide in the same places over and over again. In the above case, language provides the cover necessary to reimpose silence and invisibility on race in the face of blatant expressions of racism. Anticolonialism must answer these mechanisms of obfuscation, with counter mechanisms of resistance and accountability.

Bringing the mutually constituting relationship between colonizer and colonized into focus, Césaire further inverts the creative–destructive paradox whereby, in Césaire's time, Europe was in effect created by the third world which it was busy destroying. In 2008, the global South creates the Euro-American North. In *A Poetics of Anticolonialism*, Kelley notes: "[T]he colonial encounter … requires a reinvention of the colonizer" (2000, p. 9). There is nothing subjective, benign, or obfuscating about this binding together of colonizer and colonized, however, and Césaire is quick to demonstrate the myriad forms of domination emerging from these relations. In *Discourse*, he looks at the degree to which European colonizers, Belgians in particular, integrated themselves (in their own minds) into the spiritual and political hierarchies of the Bantus and as a way to justify European presence and involvement in African Bantu homelands. The Europeans, explains Césaire, were received by the Bantus and assumed a place at the height of the local hierarchy. Thus the European was loved and honored by the Bantu, while the Bantus were left accountable for European domination. This presumes a simultaneous and related domination and holiness in the colonial–colonized relationship. Following this, inadequacies of the colonizer (like "they ruined our society") are really a matter of the locals placing divine expectations on the European saviors (Cesaire 1972). Césaire also critiques the psychological and theological aspects and approaches of colonialism, arguing that they are false ontological spaces wherein notions of dependence and freedom are manipulated and constructed. This is evidenced in the twenty-first century as the practice of colonialism continues to be a process that pulls the colonizer and the colonized ever deeper into barbarism. This is by no means an abstract concept but one evident in the world's richest nations and their activities in their colonial in-posts and outposts. So with the United States in Iraq (outpost), we get the heinous abuses at the Abu Gharib prison, while with the United States in New Orleans (in-post) during the Katrina disaster, we get roving bands of white vigilantes hunting African-American "looters."

Finally, Césaire provides one of the first *classed* antiracist articulations and one of the first *raced* anticapitalist formulations. He works with notions of intersectionality and racist colonialism, as trumping simple class analyses. Simultaneously, his antiracism is deeply rooted in an anticapitalist critique. He stayed true to his communist roots while formulating an inclusive race-based analysis of colonial relations. While he is vehemently anticapitalist, his entry point via colonialism is largely but not exclusively centered around race. He demonstrates the way race can be used as an entry point without working to the detriment or exclusion of other sites of resistance/oppression. Negritude, as theorized by Césaire, was a liberation philosophy (and movement) that centered around race but worked powerfully against other forms of oppression. Manthia Diawara, quoted in Kelly (2000, p. 26), describes this phenomenon:

> The awareness of our new historical mission [enabled by Negritude] freed us … it freed us from race and banished our fear of the whiteness of French identity. To be labeled the saviors of humanity when only recently we had been colonized and despised by the world, gave us a feeling of righteousness, which bred contempt for capitalism, racialism of all origins, and tribalism.

Indeed such a race-based analysis may have been necessary to get to the anticapitalist position described therein. Similarly, for the racially dominant, a class-based analysis may be the gateway to a better understanding of antiracism. A 1932 letter by the Surrealist Group of France, of which Césaire was a member, charts the progression from a class-based analysis to a race-based analysis. It states:

> In a France hideously inflated from having dismembered Europe, made mincemeat of Africa, polluted Oceania and ravaged whole tracts of Asia, we surrealists pronounced ourselves in favor of changing the imperialist war, in its chronic and colonial form, into a civil war. Thus we placed our energies in the service of the revolution – of the proletariat and its struggles – and defined our attitude toward the colonial problem, and hence toward the color question. (Surrealist Group of France 1932)

The final phrase "and hence toward the color question" speaks to the nature of intersecting and interlocking oppression and resistance. The anticolonial framework engages the materiality of these intersections between class and race, as well as between and among other sites of resistance/oppression.

The Tunisian theorist and writer Albert Memmi provides a crucial analysis of the epistemic workings of colonialism in his seminal anticolonial work, *The Colonizer and the Colonized* (1965). Extending Césaire's analysis of the mutually constituting relationship between the colonizer and the colony, Memmi investigates the psychology of the colonizing mind, arguing: "[T]he colonialist realizes that without the colonized, the colony would no longer have any meaning. This intolerable contradiction fills him with a rage, a loathing, always ready to be loosed on the colonized" (1965, p. 66). Memmi's look at the colonized, the colonizer, and the ambiguities of such strict dualism make *The Colonizer and the Colonized* one of the key texts in anticolonial literature. Further, Memmi provides some of the clearest links between anticolonialism and accountability. The book's first section, "Portrait of the Colonizer," fleshes out some of the key epistemological functions of the colonial paradigm, many of which directly parallel the workings of (among other things) white privilege in the European and North American contexts. He writes: "[T]he most favored colonized will never be anything but colonized people, in other words … certain rights will forever be refused them and certain advantages are reserved for [the colonizer]" (1965, p. 9). In a foreshadowing of Peggy Macintosh's famous 1988 work, he continues: "[F]rom the time of his birth [the colonizer] possesses a qualification independent of his personal merits or his actual class. He is part of a group of colonizers whose values are sovereign. The colony follows the cadence of his traditional holidays, even religious holidays" (1965, pp. 12–13). The idea of unearned racial privilege is at the heart of critical whiteness. Like Césaire and Fanon before him, Memmi points to the deterministic role played by the system of colonial relations, arguing: "Whether he expressly wishes it or not [the colonizer] is received as a privileged person by the institutions, customs and people. From the time he lands or is born, he finds himself in a factual position which is common to all Europeans living in a colony, a position which turns him into a colonizer" (1965, p. 17). Applied to an analysis of racial oppression, we see the conferred inescapability of race. At birth, race inexorably confers privilege, punishment, or sometimes forms of both simultaneously. Memmi also points to a moral imperative for the dominant. He writes: "If every colonial immediately assumes the role of colonizer, every colonizer does not necessarily become a colonialist. However the facts of colonial life are not simply ideas, but the general effect of actual conditions. To refuse means either withdrawing physically from those conditions or remaining to fight and change them" (1965, p. 19). Applied to race and racism, the colonizer is of course the racial dominant. According to Memmi, the colonizer has two options for refusal: leave or fight to change the system. Only those choosing to leave truly exercise refusal. For those who remain, even reluctantly, their decision to participate (passively or otherwise) in the colonial project is clear. Memmi elucidates the mechanisms used to obtain, maintain, and reproduce myriad forms of power by those who choose to stay. The colonizer, he argues, "endeavors to falsify history, he rewrites laws, he would extinguish memories. Anything to succeed in transforming his usurpation into legitimacy" (p. 52).[3] The colonizer, for Memmi, is thus aware of his own illegitimacy. Race is thus powerfully invoked by the colonizer to delegitimize the humanity of the colonized, and to confer an inverse worth on the colonizer (himself) for which he is so desperate. Memmi writes: "All efforts of the colonialist are directed towards maintaining the social immobility [of the colonized], and racism is the surest weapon for this aim" (1965, p. 74). The implications of Memmi's work for an intersectional analysis are slightly different from those emerging from Dei, Fanon, and Memmi. For Memmi, race is a weapon used to protect a larger power – colonial power. This power has many elements but is largely made up of economic privilege and oppression. Memmi perhaps misses that race takes on a life of its own; that the weapon inevitably comes to guard itself and its own legitimacy, as much it protects that for which it was originally unsheathed to look after. Once this has been achieved, race and racism can thus no longer be distinguished from each other or from the general schema of oppressive relations. People are understood in a way that justifies the assumptions of racialized discourses – people are made in the image of a monster and indeed cannot be understood any longer without a nod to the beast. Once perhaps only a symptom, race becomes a disease – one requiring a remedy befitting its unique discursive and material pathology.

The work of Fanon, Césairé, and Memmi, as understood in the preceding paragraphs, demonstrates some of the key initial connections between anticolonialism and both critical whiteness and antiracism.

1.3.1 From Postcolonialism to Anticolonialism

Often conflated with anticolonialism, postcolonial scholarship has brought an important analysis of colonial relations, particularly as far as the eighteenth, nineteenth, and twentieth centuries. Scholars such as López (2005), Achebe (1994, 2002), Bhabha (1990, 1995), Spivak (1988), Spivak and Guha (1988), Said (1985, 1993), Appiah (2005), Guha (1997, 2002), JanMohamed (1992, 1995), Loomba (1998), Mohanty (1991), Mohanty and Alexander (1997), Mukherjee (1998), Wa Thiong'o (1965, 1972), Sangari (1999), and Sara Suleri (1992) have offered important analyses of various colonial encounters. Foregrounding issues of hybridity and identity, postcolonial theorists have flushed and fleshed out many of the complexities of colonial relations. The implications of postcolonialism for an anticolonial approach are broad and varied. Indeed, many postcolonial theorists can also be called anticolonial thinkers (e.g., Wa Thiong'o).[4] The connections between the two are therefore as important as the disconnections. Having said this, an anticolonial approach challenges the implication of the "post" in postcolonialism and asserts that the colonial encounter is transhistorical rather than historical – arguing that it persists in colonized and colonizing nations.[5] Education, politics, and culture are key contemporary sites of social construction where difference is ignored, suppressed, or taken up. Colonialism is alive and well in our classrooms, curricula, popular press, and popular culture. It is not only under the instruction of invading colonizing regimes that people find themselves excluded from the format and content of dominant culture and norms. Anticolonialism posits that people are made foreigners in their own lands by way of the colonial encounter, and that numerous markers of difference (class, ethnicity, race, gender, sexuality, ability, and others) serve as the basis for exclusion from/by dominant pedagogical, political, and cultural practices (Kempf 2006). With a focus on resistance and accountability, anticolonialism is interested in the complexities of identity only as far as they serve these ends – be it through offering a better understanding of power relations or through specific strategic offerings. Further, a politics of identity – or a politics of essentialism – often offers what Dei (2006) has called a "slippery slope" toward recolonization with certain issues dominating at the expense of others.

Another term commonly associated with anticolonialism is neocolonialism. Although the two are related, a distinction is worth making: Neocolonialism refers to new forms and instances of colonialism, while anticolonialism refers to a resistance-based approach to understanding and countering colonialism. Further, it is useful to ask whether or not there is such a thing as new colonialism. At its essence, colonialism describes relations of domination and resistance. Although colonialism may adapt or demonstrate new levels of sophistication and nuance, we should not confuse evolution for a new species altogether. The colonial workings of European empire through the ages demonstrate this point.

Classical Athens, still regarded by many as the jewel of Europe's ancient past, provides a model by which colonial powers still operate today. With one third of its population enslaved, and women of all classes severely oppressed, Athens was ripe with internal colonial relations. Externally, it was the leading European imperial power of its time, rivaled only by Sparta. Despite popular misconceptions, Athens was a highly repressive society with a largely illiterate and disenfranchised population (Freeman 1996, pp. 206–207). It was not without its apologists however, in whose charge lay the task of winning hearts and minds. To reconcile the lofty rhetoric of Athenian democracy with the unsightly but ubiquitous institution of slavery, we find the work of ruling-class philosopher Aristotle and his famous defense of slavery. A slave owner himself, Aristotle argues that certain people are slaves by nature (Aristotle 1976, Books III–V). For the requisite adulation on the international front, Athens had ruling-class historian and sycophant Thucydides (1982), and his epic *the Peloponnesian War*, which lent glory to Athens' possessive imperial exploits by detailing Athens' triumph over Persia and fellow Greeks, Sparta. Despite the near-official musings of the apologist literati, Athens was a society rotting from within – with wealth, education, and rights reserved for the few; and poverty, illiteracy, and marginalization reserved for the rest. One key notion for an anticolonial approach to this history is that such inequity was by no means an aberration of an otherwise good system – the point of the system was just such inequity as far as it served the interests of the tiny ruling class. The pattern continued into Roman times. A centralized system of oppression spanning three continents needed its very own epistemic justificatory pillars. Among its apologists were the poet Virgil who canonized the divine origins of Rome and its emperor Augustus in his *Aeneid*, as well as the famous senator and orator (and racist slumlord) Cicero, who worked incessantly to discredit and villainize Rome's popular reformers like Cataline. Bequeathed to its continental brothers to the north via the Holy Roman Empire and subsequent Ottoman expansionism and middle feudalism, the ancient European colonial found a home in the modern world. Indeed, this colonial hegemony has been at the core of Europe's development over the past 500 years. Working to manufacture subjects at home and abroad, with insider–outsider paradigms between and within the metropolis and the periphery, little has changed as far as the colonial model. In fact, the current US war of/on terror, has employed a 2,500-year-old Athenian tactic. In 477 BC, an international military and economic organization was established called the Delian League. Its formal purpose was to provide a unified military defense against invasion from neighboring Persia. Athens was the most powerful member of the new alliance, providing the vast majority of its military and economic force. Athens also appointed all treasurers and enjoyed an unofficial status as head of the organization (Freeman 1996, pp. 197–199). Under the guise of a multinational initiative, Athens expanded its power and influence, as well as enriched its treasury. The US-led "coalition of the willing" is a fitting parallel of this ancient colonial phenomenon.

If we understand colonialism in a transhistorical context, neocolonialism is somewhat bereft of meaning. If we understand ancient Greek and Roman colonial exercises as fruit from the same tree which bore later European colonialism, to be thus called by the same name, then colonial relations of the twenty-first century need no new name. The evolution of our response is more important than that of the nomenclature.

1.4 Anticolonial Historiography

> [F]rom the west's vantage point, the discovery myth is true. The history of the other side is also mythic. But while Western myths are triumphalist, those of the "losers" have to explain and overcome catastrophe. If the vanquished culture is to survive at all, its myths must provide it with a rugged terrain in which to resist the invader and do battle with his myths. (Wright 1993, p. 5)

Domination produces the circumstances of its own rejection. Colonialism thus has as its corollary anticolonialism. The history of colonialism brings with it the history of resistance to colonialism. Parenti (2001) has pointed out that Aristotle's defense of slavery (found in his famous work *The Politics*) by its very existence provides evidence of resistance to slavery. Why else, Parenti asks, would a defense be necessary? Oppression should never be taken for granted as a product of its time, or a product of necessity. Although little written evidence of antislavery sentiment in Ancient Greece remains, Aristotle alludes to those in his time who were opposed to the institution. He writes: "Against this right many of those versed in law protest that [slavery] is in fact contrary to law, which should exercise restraint upon violence. They hold it to be indefensible that a man who has been overpowered by the violence and superior might of another should become his property" (1976, p. 35). Another group consistently oppressed by slavery voiced its objection with its feet – through constant attempts at escape and revolt. It is safe to say that very few enslaved people (from any epoch) would argue for the necessity of slavery, or that any enslaved person would be content by arguments for historical relativism (Parenti 2001). The immorality of oppression is transhistorical. Slavery, for example, is neither more sensible nor more excusable in some situations or times than others. The enslaved boys and girls tortured by Alexander the Great faced the same evil as their enslaved sisters would 2,000 years later at the hands of famous statesman and accused rapist Thomas Jefferson (see Leyton-Brown and Cleveland [1992] for Alexander, and Stevenson [1996] for Jefferson). When Spartacus assembled 60,000 enslaved men and women to overthrow the Roman government, they were battling the same iniquity as Toussaint L'Ouverture and others in the late 1700s, who fought and won the first third world revolution in San Domingo (present-day Haiti) (see Freeman 1996 for Spartacus, and James 1963 for L'Ouverture). While Spartacus may be the most famous unsuccessful revolutionary in western history, the Thracian hero is perhaps the only anti-imperialist celebrated by dominant history. As Zinn (1999) points out, historical interpretation and distortion are ideological rather than technical phenomena. Anticolonial struggles and ideas have been, through processes of omission, denial, and marginalization largely written out of dominant history. The anticolonial response must counter and resist not only these processes (of denial, omission, and marginalization) but also the fruits of these processes – which is to say the dominant narratives of mainstream history. Marginalized perspectives (those of the minoritized and those which subvert privilege) must be brought to the center. History need not be the spoil of the "victor." The human impulse to resist oppression must be rescued from the margins of the dominant narrative. Anticolonial history speaks not only of the margins but also from them.

Fanon (1967a), Memmi (1969), and Dei (1996) all discuss the amputation resulting from colonial educational and cultural processes, which sever the colonized from her past (and thus present and future). Memmi writes:

> [T]he colonized observes all [of the colonizer's] religious holidays. These holidays are located at the beginning of history, rather than in history. From the time they were instituted, nothing else has happened in the life of that people. That is nothing particular to their own existence which deserves to be retained by the collective consciousness and celebrated. Nothing except a great void. ... The history which is assigned [the colonized] is not his own. ... Far from preparing the adolescent to find himself completely, school creates a permanent duality in him. (1969, pp. 104–106)

1 Contemporary Anticolonialism

As scholars and activists like Said (1985), Wright (1993), Asante (2000), Parenti (2003), and Zinn (1999) have done in the cases of the Middle East, the Americas, Egypt, ancient Rome, and the United States, respectively, we must tell new truths about the past, alongside critical interrogations of the old ones. We must contest both the content and the telling of dominant history.

Reading against the grain gets easier the closer we are to the event in question. Picking up the pieces of an anticolonial history for ancient Greece and Rome, for example, is a difficult undertaking given the lack of written record representing the experiences, struggles, and ideas of the oppressed. Although an exhaustive attempt is beyond the scope of this work, such an enterprise would begin with a look at the ways in which oppressed people exercised agency and resistance in these societies, as well as a corollary examination of the way celebrated individuals and systems contributed directly and indirectly to the oppression of minoritized groups and individuals.

Colonialism and anticolonialism, of course, are by no means exclusively European phenomena – there are perhaps no populated parts of the planet untouched by colonial oppression. Although there is no race, religion, or ethnicity that has not oppressed others along one or more lines of difference, this discussion has focused primarily on European colonialism historically and transhistorically because we are living in an era defined by white supremacist US–European colonialism. While other cultures and peoples have dominated and have been dominated, it is the historical construction of the present that guides the critical lens of this chapter. If I were a privileged Akan, living at the height of Ashanti dominion in western Africa, my critique would have very little to do with Europe and whiteness. We are living in an age bequeathed to us by Europe's earliest colonizers. So while history may teach that nobody is above domination or racism, the hegemonic domination and racism of our time are not Ashanti, Aztec, Mohawk, or Maori phenomena. Although race and racism seem to be mobilized for oppression by segments of numerous nondominant groups, the scale of impact is delimited internally, and is thus incomparable to Euro–American colonial relations. Further, as far as accountability is concerned, it is not Hutu discrimination against Tutsis, for example, that directly affords me a global racial privilege.[6] Interrogating my privilege, my participation in colonialism, and my potential for anticolonialism involves making the connections between my day-to-day race, gender, ethnicity, and ability-related advantages and the historical circumstances which produce them. For example how does European epistemological universalism, alongside contemporary US exceptionalism, provide a foundation for various types of privilege, as well as the conditions for the invisibility thereof? My colonial power, for example, is defined in part by all the things I am not: gay, a woman, black, from the global South, etc. How do I understand myself in relation to these variables and the people who inhabit them? And vice versa? I cannot be white unless I know who's/what's not. I cannot be a man, unless I know who's/what's not. It was the Macedonians that conceptually allowed the Athenians to construct the idea of the superiority of their civilization (a civilization with beautiful philosophical prose for even the ugliest social institutions). It was the serfs who allowed the lords to define their place at the helm of the feudal economies. It was the savaged "savages" of Asia, Africa, and the Americas who gifted civilization to European colonists. What is America without Afghanistan and Iraq? The anticolonial gaze brings a critical reading to these mutually constitutive binaries, revealing just how important it is that they be subverted when understanding human history and its implications for the present and the future.

One discursive mechanism necessary for a colonial understanding of history is the conflation of ubiquitous human activity with human nature. A common argument for domination is a pronouncement on human nature claiming that people are intrinsically inclined to dominate and be dominated. This idea generally posits that once freed from their oppression, the dominated will themselves dominate once given the chance. While humans enjoy a history often characterized by oppressive relations, this same history reveals a constant opposition to these relations. Following the logic that domination is natural because it is found throughout human history, so too is resistance to that domination. In just the last 500 years (a tiny fraction of human history) the people of Africa, North America, South America, Australia, New Zealand, Asia, Europe, Central America, the Caribbean, Polynesia, and the Indian Subcontinent have all engaged in anticolonial struggle. A complete history of anticolonialism is well beyond the scope and reach of this chapter, and perhaps beyond the capabilities of the written word. Delimiting a portion of this history is similarly difficult – the twentieth century for example, saw nationalist anticolonial struggles throughout Latin America, Africa, and Asia.[7] Alongside these we find social, local, regional, and intra-national struggles throughout the world. Thus, in place of a complete history of any epoch, I propose the following as a sort of closing heuristic: human history heretofore as the history of anticolonialism. This is a normative statement, the validity of which can be established not just by the events of the past but also by the way we choose to read and understand those events.

1.5 Conclusion

Anticolonialism offers a lens for understanding oppression in and around multiple sites. It also offers a strategic approach to action-oriented social change. This chapter is only a beginning. Alongside my white-guy enthusiasm for a multicentric approach, a quick caution is worth repeating: Race is too often the first casualty of a multicentric analysis. Vigilance is thus required to ensure that race is neither subsumed nor negated within an integrative approach. We must fight the rise of whiteness as power (which inherently denies the nature of racial oppression) within multicentric anticolonial thinking. Having said this, the possibilities for thinking and working with and across difference are numerous. When we work strategically with an anticolonial multicentric lens, we can draw revolutionary and transformative tactics from a wide spectrum of disciplines and situations. For example, what might an antiracist socialist framework look like? What are the possibilities for Afrocentric socialism in the twenty-first century? A number of essentially class-oriented authors have developed models of localism and are challenging capitalist notions of "progress for the sake of progress" (see LaTouche 2003, 2005, Magnaghi 2003). How can such approaches be guided by principles of difference and anti-colonialism? How might we theorize and operationalize a theory of anticolonial development, authored by those for whom the development is occurring? This chapter addresses only a fraction of the questions raised by an expanded notion of the colonial. Although beyond the scope of this chapter, relations of gender, sex, family, the body, and the home are of particular relevance for a more nuanced understanding of colonialism and anticolonialism. How might dinner at someone's house tell the story of their engagement with colonial or anticolonial relations? I have talked about my political heritage and my white privilege but I have not talked about the politics of my sex life, the labor breakdown in my home, or the ways I (intentionally or not) impose gender on my two children. The personal gets a free pass in far too many activist and academic endeavors, yet it is the personal in which our lives are primarily embedded.

Resistance is necessary and possible. If anticolonialism is going to challenge what Smith (1990) has called the relations of ruling, we need to continue thinking strategically both within and beyond our own sites of oppression. We must keep a keen eye on the ways we participate in the oppression of others: locally and internationally. Change is inevitable, so the question is not how it will affect us, but how we will effect change – in our world, our communities, our families, and our homes.

Notes

1. Notions of passing, as well as issues of shadism, persist in contexts around the globe.
2. Skin whitening in service to imperial ideals and control is an old colonial idea, well documented by McClintock (1995) and others.
3. This speaks to Fanon's notion of amputation.
4. See Giroux, Chapter 4, this volume. Although not necessarily a postcolonial scholar, he powerfully and critically invokes the postcolonial in his piece on the use of Freire's work.
5. Postcolonial studies have themselves been highly self-reflective, and numerous postcolonial scholars have problematized the notion of the postcolonial (see McClintock, 1992 and Bahri, 1995).
6. The European role (Belgium's in particular) in the creation of this and other "intertribal" conflicts should not be overlooked. Part of the colonial project has always been divisive practices often resulting in local violence between the colonized.
7. Although many of the anticolonial struggles in these regions focused on issues of class inequality, the anticolonial revolutions of the twentieth century were not, on the whole, exclusively socialist. Nkrumah (1999/2000) points out that many aspects of various anticolonial struggles were explicitly unaligned with socialist economic philosophy (e.g., the Negritude movement). In many cases, cultural transformation was made salient, with economic policy as a secondary concern.

References

Achebe, C. (1994). *Things Fall Apart*. New York: Anchor Books.
Achebe, C. (2002). The Epic Imagination: A Conversation with Chinua Achebe at Annandale-on-Hudson, October 31, 1998. *Callaloo*, 2(25), Spring. pp. 505–526.
Appiah, K. (2005). *The Ethics of Identity*. New York: Princeton University Press.
Aristotle. (1976). *The Politics*. Translated by Thomas Alan Sinclair. Middlesex: Penguin.
Asante, M. K. (2000). *The Egyptian Philosophers: Ancient Voices from Imhotep to Akhenaten*. Philadelphia, PA: Temple Press.
Bahri, D. (1995). Once More with Feeling: What is Postcolonialism? *Ariel*, 1(26), 51–82.
Bhabha, H. (1990). *Nation and Narration*. New York: Routledge and Kegan Paul.
Bhabha, H. (1995). Signs Taken for Wonders. In Ashcroft, B., Griffiths, G., and Thiophene, H. (eds.), *The Post-Colonial Studies Reader* (pp. 29–35). New York: Routledge.
Bishop, M. (1983). *Maurice Bishop Speaks: The Grenada Revolution and its Overthrow 1979–83*. New York: Pathfinder.
Brandt G.L. (1986). *The Realization of Anti-Racist Teaching*. London: Falmer Press.
Cabral, A. (1970). *National liberation and culture*. New York: Syracuse University Press.
Césaire, A. (1972). *Discourse on Colonialism*. New York: Monthly Review Press.
Crenshaw, K., Gotanda, N., and Thomas, K. (eds.). (1995). *Critical Race Theory: The Key Writings that Formed the Movement*. New York: The New Press.
Dei, G. J. S. (1996). *Anti-Racism Education in Theory and Practice*. Halifax: Fernwood Publishing.
Dei, G. J. S. (2004). Unpublished draft. Lecture Notes: SES 3914H: Anti-Colonial Thought: Pedagogical Challenges. Toronto: OISE, University of Toronto.
Dei, G. J. S. (2006). Mapping the Terrain: Towards a New Politics of Resistance. In Dei, G. S. and Kempf, A. (eds.), *Anti-Colonialism and Education: The Politics of Resistance* (pp. 1–23). Rotterdam: Sense Publishers.
Dei, G. S. and Asgharzadeh, A. (2001). The Power of Social Theory: Towards an Anti-Colonial Discursive Framework. *Journal of Educational Thought*, 35(3), 297–323.
Delgado, R. and Stefancic, J. (eds.). (1997). *Critical White Studies: Looking Behind the Mirror*. Philadelphia, PA: Temple Press.
Delgado, R. and Stefancic, J. (2001). *Critical Race Theory: An Introduction*. New York: NYU Press.
Fanon, F. (1963). *The Wretched of the Earth*. New York: Grove Weidenfeld.
Fanon, F. (1967a). *Black Skin, White Masks*. New York: Grove Press.
Fanon, F. (1967b). *Toward the African Revolution*. New York: Grove Press.
Frankenberg, R. (2004). On Unsteady Ground: Crafting and Engaging in the Critical Study of Whiteness. In Bulmer, M. and Solomos, J. (eds.), *Researching Race and Racism* (pp. 104–118). London: Routledge.
Freeman, C. (1996). *Egypt, Greece and Rome: Civilizations of the Ancient Mediterranean*. Oxford: Oxford University Press.
Gaine, C. 2000. Anti-Racist Education in 'White' Areas: The Limits and Possibilities of Change. *Race, Ethnicity and Education*, 3(1), 65–79.
Gallagher, C. 2000. White Like Me? Methods, Meaning, and Manipulation in the Field of White Studies. In Twine, F. W. and Warren, J. (eds.), *Racing Research, Researching Race: Methodological Dilemmas in Critical Race Studies* (pp. 67–92). New York: New York University Press.
Gandhi, M. (1967). *Political and National Life and Affairs*. Ahmedabad: Navijivan Press.
Gandhi, M. (1997). How Can India Become Free? In Parel, A. J. (ed.), *M.K. Gandhi: Hind Swaraj and Other Writings* (pp. 72–74). New York: Cambridge University Press.
Guevara, E. C. (1997). The Essence of Guerrilla Struggle. In Deutchmann, D. (ed.), *Che Guevara Reader* (pp. 66–72). New York: Ocean Press.
Guha, R. (ed.). (1997). *Subaltern Studies Reader: 1986–1995*. Minneapolis, MN: University of Minnesota Press.

Guha, R. (2002). *History at the Limit of World-History. (Italian Academy Lectures)*. New York: Columbia University Press.
Hayes, M. T. (2001). A Journey Through Dangerous Places: Reflections on a Theory of White Racial Identity as Political Alliance. *Contemporary Issues in Early Childhood*, 1(2), 15–30.
Hill, M. (ed.). (1997). *Whiteness: A Critical Reader*. New York: New York University Press.
Hill-Collins, P. (1990). *Black Feminist Thought: Knowledge, Consciousness, and the Politics of Empowerment*. Boston, MA: Unwin Hyman.
hooks, b. (2000). Homophobia in Black Communities. In Simms, D. S. (ed.), *The Greatest Taboo: Homosexuality in Black Communities* (pp. 67–73). New York: Alyson Books.
James, C. L. R. (1963). *The Black Jacobins: Toussaint L'Ourverture and the San Domingo Revolution*. New York: Vintage.
JanMohamed, A. (1992). Worldliness-Without-World, Homelessness-as-Home: Toward a Definition of the Specular Border Intellectual. In Sprinker, M. (ed.), *Edward Said: A Critical Reader* (pp. 96–120). Oxford: Basil Blackwell.
JanMohamed, A. (1995). Refiguring Values, Power, Knowledge or Foucault's Disavowal of Marx. In Magnus, B. and Cullenberg, S. (eds.), *Whither Marxism?: Global Crises in International Perspective* (pp. 31–64). New York/London: Routledge.
Jensen, R. (2005). *The Heart of Whiteness: Confronting Race, Racism and White Privilege*. Columbus, OH: City Lights Books.
Kempf, A. 2006. Anti-Colonial Historiography: Interrogating Colonial Education. In G. Dei and A Kempf (eds.) Anti-Colonialism and Education: The Politics of Resistance. Rotterdam: Sense. (pp. 129–158)
Kempf, A. 2008. *On The Souls of White Folks: Notes on the White Crash Conversation*. In P. Howard and G Dei (eds.) Crash Politics and Anti-Racism: Interrogations of Liberal Race Discourses. New York: Peter Lang. (pp. 91–108)
Kelley, R.D.G. *A Poetics of Anti-Colonialism*. Introduction to Cesaire, A. (1972) Discourse on Colonialism. New York: Monthly Review Press. (pp. 7–28)
Kincheloe, J. L., Steinberg, S. R., Rodriguez, N. M., et al. (eds.). (1998). *White Reign: Deploying Whiteness in America*. New York: St Martin's Press.
LaTouche, S. (2003). Would the World Be Happy with Less? *Le Monde Diplomatique*. December 16.
LaTouche, S. (2005). The Globe Downshifted. *Le Monde Diplomatique*. January. http://mondediplo.com/2006/01/13degrowth
Lawrence, S. (1997). Beyond Race Awareness: White Racial Identity and Multicultural Teaching. *Journal of Teacher Education*, 48(2), 108–117.
Leyton-Brown, K. and Cleveland, R. (1992). *Alexander the Great: An Exercise in History*. New York: High Butte Books.
Loomba, A. (1998). *Colonialism/Postcolonialism*. London: Routledge.
López, A. (ed). (2005). *Post Colonial Whiteness: A Critical Reader on Race and Empire*. New York: State University of New York Press.
Lorde, A. (1984). *Sister Outsider*. New York: The Crossing Press.
Macintosh, P. (1988). White Privilege: Unpacking the Invisible Knapsack. Available at: http://www.racismagainstindians.org/whitePrivilege/InvisibleKnapsack.htm. Retrieved April 2, 2007.
McClintock, A. (1992). The Angel of Progress: Pitfalls of the Term 'Post-Colonialism'. *Social Text*, 31–32(Spring), 1–15.
McClintock, A. (1995). *Imperial Leather: Race, Gender and Sexuality in the Colonial Encounter*. New York: Routledge.
Magnaghi, A. (2003). *Le Projet Local*. Brussels: Mardaga.
Maher, F. and Tetreault, T. (1997). Learning in the Dark: How Assumptions of Whiteness Shape Classroom Knowledge. *Harvard Educational Review*, 67(2 Summer), 321–349.
Memmi, A. (1969). *The Colonizer and the Colonized*. Boston, MA: Beacon Press.
Miles, R. (1993). *Racism After 'Race Relations'*. London: Routledge.
Minh-ha, T. (2000). Not You/Like You: Postcolonial Women and the Interlocking Questions of Identity and Difference. In Brydon, D. (ed.), *Postcolonialism: Critical Concepts in Literary and Cultural Studies, Volume III* (pp. 1210–1215). London/New York: Routledge.

Mohanty, C. (1991). *Third World Women and the Politics of Feminism*, co-edited with Lourdes Torres and Ann Russo. Bloomington, IA: Indiana University Press.
Mohanty, C. and Alexander, J. M. (eds.). (1997). *Feminist Genealogies, Colonial Legacies, Democratic Futures*. New York: Routledge.
Mukherjee, A. (1998). *Towards an Aesthetic of Opposition: Essays on Literature, Criticism and Cultural Imperialism*. New York: Williams-Wallace.
Nkrumah, G. (1999/2000). Past Over Present. *Al Ahram*, No. 462, 30 Dec–5 Jan 2000.
Omi, M. and Winant, H. (1994). *Racial Formation in the United States, 2nd Edition*. New York: Routledge.
Parenti, M. (1992). *Racism and the Ideology of Slavery*. Speech given in Berkeley California, September 25.
Parenti, M. (2003) *The Assassination of Julius Caesar: A People's History of the Roman Republic*. New York: Knopff.
Roediger, D. (1991). *The Wages of Whiteness: Race and the Making of the American Working Class*. New York: Verso.
Said, E. (1985). *Orientalism: Western Representations of the Orient*. New York: Penguin.
Said, E. (1993). *Culture and Imperialism*. New York: Vintage Books.
Sangari, K. (1999). *Politics of the Possible: Essays on Gender, History, Narrative, Colonial English*. New Delhi: Vedams.
Sawchuk, P. (2007). Personal Electronic Correspondence. Ontario Institute for Studies in Education, May 19.
Scheurich, J. (1997). Toward a White Discourse on White Racism: An Early Attempt at an Archaeological Approach. In *Research Method in the Postmodern* (pp. 119–131). London: The Falmer Press.
Silvera, M. (ed). (1992). *Piece of My Heart: A Lesbian of Color Anthology*. Toronto: Sister Vision Press.
Smith, D. (1990). *Texts, Facts, and Femininity: Exploring the Relations of Ruling*. London: Routledge.
Spivak, G. (1988). Can the Subaltern Speak? In Nelson, C. and Grossberg, L. (eds.), *Marxism and the Interpretation of Culture* (pp. 271–313). Chicago, IL: University of Illinois Press.
Spivak, G. and Guha, R. (eds.). (1988). *Selected Subaltern Studies*. Oxford: Oxford University Press.
Stevenson, B. (1996). *Life in Black and White: Family and Community in the Slave South*. New York: Oxford University Press.
Suleri, S. (1992). Woman Skin Deep: Feminism and the Postcolonial Condition. *Critical Inquiry*, 18(Summer), 756–769.
Surrealist Group of France (Breton, A., Caillois, R., Char, R., Crevel, R., Eluard, P., Monnerot, J.M., Péret, B., Tanguy, Y., Thirion, A., Unik, P., and Yoyotte, P.) 1934. *Murderous Humanitarianism*. In Nancy Cunard (ed.), Negro Anthology. Translated by Samuel Beckett. New York: Harper Collins.
Thucydides. (1982). *The Peloponnesian War*. New York: The Modern Library.
Twine, F. W. (2004). A White Side of Black Britain: The Concept of Racial Literacy. *Ethnic and Racial Studies*, 27(6), 878–907.
Wane, N., Deliovsky, K., and Lawson, E. (eds.). (2001). *Back to the Drawing Board: African-Canadian Feminisms*. Toronto: Sumach Press.
Wa Thiong'o, N. (1965). *The River Between*. London: Heinemann.
Wa Thiong'o, N. (1986). *Decolonizing the Mind: The Politics of Language in African Literature*. Oxford: James Currey Publishers.
Wildman, S. M. and Davis, A. D. (2002). Making Systems of Privilege Visible. In Rothenberg, P. (ed.), *White Privilege: Essential Readings on the Other Side of Racism* (pp. 89–95). New York: Worth Publishers.
Wise, T. (2002). White Like Me: Race and Identity Through Majority Eyes. In Singley, B. (ed.), *When Race Becomes Real* (pp. 225–239). New York: Lawrence Hill Books.
Wright, R. (1993). *Stolen Continents: The 'New World' Through Indian Eyes*. Toronto: Penguin.
Zinn, H. (1999). *A People's History of the United States: 1492–Present*. New York: Perennial Classics.

Chapter 2
Self-Determination and the Fourth World: An Introductory Survey*

Ward Churchill

> *The Fourth World has always been here...*
>
> (George Manuel 1974)

At the 1955 Bandung Conference, Mao Zedong's famous vision of a planet divided into three "worlds" was set forth by Chou En-lai.[1] The 1955 conference conducted in the city of Bandung, on the island of Java, has been described as "the most significant congress of the Third World" to occur before the huge Non-Aligned Conference held in Algeria a quarter century later (Horne 2002, p. 559). In Mao's view, the "First World" consisted of industrialized capitalist states in the northern hemisphere, overwhelmingly white in racial composition, and pitted – economically, philosophically, and militarily – against a "Second World" of their industrially developed socialist counterparts. There was as well a "Third World,"[2] he said, composed of countries or "territories," mostly to the south of the other two and populated almost exclusively by peoples of color, which were either maintained as colonies within the ambit of several First World imperial powers, or had recently freed themselves from colonial domination. Perhaps the best explication remains Peter Worsely's (1967) *The Third World*.[3]

The Third World, in Mao's view, was inherently aligned with neither side in the First or Second World conflict.[4] Rather, its agenda was situationally defined within each colony or former colony in accordance with the requirements of attaining political self-determination and economic development. In other words, the overarching goal of what soon came to be known as the "Third World Revolution" was "national liberation" on whatever terms and by any/every means through which it could be attained. In many instances, this involved the waging of "popular war[s] of liberation, appealing to the peasant masses and mobilizing them for help and shelter and flight, as Mao had recommended and Guevara had practiced" (Smith 1983, p. 107). The underlying premises were set forth most clearly in Lin Piao's "Mao Tse-Tung's

---

*An earlier and unannotated version of this chapter appeared in *Left Turn*, No. 25 (July/August 2007).

Theory of People's War," quoted extensively by Richard J. Barnet (1972, pp. 87–89) in his *Intervention and Revolution: The United States in the Third World*.[5] It was a potent recipe, all in all, giving both shape and voice to sustained struggles which led, between 1945 and 1990, to an across-the-board decolonization of Africa and Asia and a corresponding repeal of European imperialism in its classic form.[6]

For all its undeniable triumphs, however, the Third Worldist formulation was afflicted from the outset by many conceptual deficiencies. Certain of these contradictions seem to have been inherent even within Mao's own ostensible paradigm, a matter presented quite succinctly by Arif Dirlik (1994, pp. 46–47) in his *After the Revolution: Waking to Global Capitalism*.[7] Insufficient weight was placed upon the prospect that the extent of colonialism's often protracted underdevelopment of the Third World might have created structural conditions within the newly independent countries that would leave them virtually defenseless against "neocolonialist" exploitation by their former colonizers.[8] Nor, despite the warnings implicit to pioneering studies undertaken by Mannoni, Fanon, Memmi, and others, was the virulence and intractability of the psychological maiming inflicted upon those subjugated under colonialism's genocidal yoke ever truly taken into account.[9]

Scant attention was paid as well to the implications of the reality that those who typically instigated and led the Third World liberation struggles, thereby assuming control of the state apparatus in the wake of formal decolonization, had themselves been "educated" in imperial institutions. As a result, their perspectives and priorities – even their most personal sensibilities – often displayed a far greater commonality with those of their former colonizers than with those of the grassroots populations whose destinies they now presumed to decide and direct. Although undoubtedly unintended as such, a good survey of these tendencies will be found in A. B. Assensoh (1998), *African Political Leadership: Jomo Kenyatta, Kwame Nkrumah, and Joseph Nyerere*. For an especially emphatic – and no doubt even more unintended – assertion of the virtues supposedly inhering in the "transcendence" of African tradition, see Elenga M'buyinga (1982), *Pan Africanism of Neo-Colonialism: The Bankruptcy of the O.A.U.*

In short order, the ostensible constituents of many such "revolutionary leaders" had come to complain that they were "more European than the Europeans" and were often "worse than the Europeans themselves."[10] Perhaps most significant in this regard, little or no consideration was given in the canons of Third Worldism to the fact that the territorial boundaries of what were now proclaiming "sovereign states" had been drawn by the colonizers, *not* the colonized. In Africa, the boundaries by and large had been established during an 1885 conference of Europe's colonial powers convened for that purpose in Berlin; J. M. McKenzie (1983), *The Partition of Africa, 1880–1900*; Thomas Packenham (1991, pp. 239–255), *The Scramble for Africa: The White Man's Conquest of the Dark Continent, 1876–1912*. As concerns the territorial delineation of India and other South Asian states, see K. M. Panikar (1953), *Asia and Western Dominance*.[11] The geographical demarcations defining the "possessions" of each imperial power were established in a manner amalgamating or partitioning the homelands of various peoples indigenous to the areas cast as "colonial compartments," their right to govern themselves in accordance with their own traditions usurped by the centralized authority embodied in colonial administrations, their very identities *as peoples* subsumed under the homogenizing nomenclature of "colonial subjects."

Such circumstances have been not only extended but in many respects intensified under the rubric of Western-style "citizenship" during the "postcolonial" period. Throughout sub-Saharan Africa, for example, there

> is no "nation" ... in any way co-extensive with [a] state's [colonially defined] boundaries, or congruent with [any] state's culture. Such a congruent and coextensive nation is a mere project today, a "nation of intent" to be forged out of the territorial state. As in Western Europe ["postcolonial"], African rulers and intelligentsia aim to create such nations, and merge the political culture of the state with the several ethnic cultures of the peoples that compose it. (Smith 1983, pp. 125–126)

As in Western Europe during its formative phases, the means employed to this end have typically been coercive in the extreme; see, for example, John Smith Ikpuk (1995), *Militarization of Politics and Neo-Colonialism: The Nigerian Experience, 1966–90*.[12]

Thus, while "liberation" has been seen by Third Worldists as the transformation of Europe's overseas colonies into states independently governed by their former subjects, the subjects themselves often envisioned it in dramatically different terms, that is, the restoration of control over their traditional territory to each of the peoples encompassed within colonial boundaries and, on that basis, resumption of their self-determining modes of governance, social organization, and economy. The principle is by no means obscure. It was in fact articulated officially – and quite clearly – by Belgium during the early 1950s (Belgian Government Information Center 1953). Instructively, the right of self-determination recognized in the United Nations Charter as inhering in *all* peoples was deeply circumscribed a decade later by an overseas requirement advocated by the ostensibly anticolonialist Organization of African Unity – and endorsed by virtually every UN member-state – which defined colonies as consisting exclusively of territorial entities separated from their colonizers by at least 30 miles of ocean. Plainly, the OAU's "Blue" or "Salt Water" requirement was designed to legally preclude peoples whose territories were/are encapsulated *within* the borders of various states to assert their rights to decolonize (Nirmal 1999, pp. 103–108).[13]

In substance, these indigenous peoples – nations, actually[14] – comprised a "*Fourth* World," unmentioned by Mao and his adherents, upon the expropriation of whose lands and resources *all* states depend for their very existence.[15] Contrary to popular (mis)perception, the term "state" is by no means synonymous with "nation," albeit the conflation has been institutionalized via the United *Nations*, membership in which is strictly restricted to *states*. While nations exhibit a vast diversity of governmental forms, the statist form of government is by definition highly centralized and coercive. While the world is currently divided among roughly 200 recognized states more than 4,000 distinct nations are identifiable. For discussion, see Hugh Seton-Watson (1977), *Nations and States: An Inquiry into the Origins of Nations and the Politics of Nationalism*.[16]

It follows that for Fourth World peoples the success of Third World revolutions added up not to a repeal of the system of subjugation imposed under European imperialism but instead to something more nearly resembling a consummation of such oppression. The conceptual bases for this are again brought out quite clearly in Partha Chatterjee (1986, esp. pp. 36–53), *Nationalist Thought in the Colonial World: A Derivative Discourse*.[17] Certainly, any difference between the forcible subordination of indigenous nations by a colonial regime imported from overseas and relegation to the same status by a "domestically constituted" central government was/is negligible at best. In effect, colonialism in its classic form was merely supplanted by a still more insidious "internal" form resembling that which had facilitated consolidation of Europe's imperial states themselves a few centuries earlier.[18]

The results, while often misinterpreted, were both predictable and soon apparent. In "India," an entity which did not exist until it was forcibly synthesized by British colonizers from the territories of nearly 300 indigenous nationalities, the Nagas – to offer but one example – were waging what turns out to be an ongoing armed struggle to recover self-governing control over their traditional homeland even before the "broader" society's independence was announced in 1947.[19] Across the European-drawn border separating India from "Burma," the Karins had commenced a similar struggle in the south, as had the Kachins in the north (Mirante 1987).[20] So, too, in what was known until 1954 as "French Indochina," especially as regards the Hmongs in Laos and the various "Montagnard" peoples of Vietnam's highland regions (Connor 1984, as well as Churchill and Morris 2005).[21]

By the 1970s, such resistance had emerged in Indonesia, notably among the Papuans of "New Guinea" and the peoples of East Timor (Chomsky and Herman 1979, pp. 129–204; Taylor 1991; Nevins 2005). In the Philippines as well, native peoples of Luzon and the more southerly islands like Mindanao had begun to actively pursue agendas of their own, distinct in many ways from that of the maoist guerrillas operating in such locales (Swenson 1987, pp. 199–209, on the maoist insurgency, see pp. 316–317).[22] Across the vast reaches of Micronesia, from Samoa, Palau, and the Solomons in the south; northward through the Marianas; westward to Okinawa and other islands along the Ryukyu chain; and eastward through the so-called Marianas Marshall Islands to the Hawaiian Archipelago, comparably "indigenist" phenomena could be discerned (Halliday and McCormack 1973; Robie 1989; Roberts 1995, esp. pp. 271–279; Trask 1999, esp. pp. 51–74).

Much the same process began to unfold in Africa almost from the outset, probably the most notable example being the bloody and protracted effort mounted by Katangese "secessionists" during the early 1960s to free themselves from the Congo, created as a personal holding by Belgium's King Leopold toward the end on the nineteenth century.[23] Scores of similar struggles materialized throughout the sub-Saharan regions of the "Dark Continent" over the next decade – the Ibos' attempt to separate their Biafran homeland from Nigeria, for instance[24] – a matter that so eroded claims of cohesion both within and between the various components of Africa's emergent statist system that Kwame Nkrumah, a leading advocate of a Pan-African Union, was led to observe that "tribalism" rather than the ravages of neocolonialism stood as the primary barrier to actualization of the Third Worldist vision. Predictably enough, those seeking to deny the devastation imposed upon "postcolonial" Africa have seized upon precisely this argument to obfuscate the unpleasant realities, thereby shifting the onus of responsibility onto the victims themselves (see, e.g., Coquery-Vidrovitch 1988, p. 133).[25]

Nor have North Africa or the Middle East been immune. Since 1948, by far the most visible has of course been the sustained resistance of indigenous Palestinians to the impositions of the Israeli state. In contrast to most of the struggles mentioned herein, analysis of the conflict between the Israelis and Palestinians is voluminous. Among the works I've found most useful are Said, *The Question of Palestine* (1980) and *The Politics of Dispossession: The Struggle for Palestinian Self-Determination, 1969–1994* (1994); Morris, *1948 and After: Israel and the Palestinians* (1990); Sternhell, *The Founding Myths of Israel: Nationalism, Socialism, and the Making of the Jewish State* (1998); Shlaim, *The Iron Wall: Israel and the Arab World* (2000); Rogan and Shlaim, *The War for Palestine: Rewriting the History of 1948* (2001); and Pappe, *The Ethnic Cleansing of Palestine* (2006).

Less noticed, but sustained over an even longer period, has been the struggle of the Kurds to free their traditional territory, spanning the borders of Turkey, Iraq, Iran, and Armenia.[26] By the 1970s, Bedouin resistance to statist rule in the western Sahara had also congealed into the Polisario Liberation Front, a movement aimed mainly at securing the self-determining rights of tribal peoples against the self-anointed authority of Morocco's central government.[27]

Throughout Latin America, what might otherwise be viewed as typical Third World national liberation struggles and/or their precursors have all along exhibited a pronouncedly indigenist dynamic.[28] This became apparent at least as early as 1900, with the attempt by the Yaquis to (re)establish their own "free state," separate from that born of the Mexican revolution. Actually, the effort – which lasted until the Indians were finally defeated in 1917 – began in 1899, when Yaqui leaders announced that "we want … all whites and troops [to] get out" of Yaqui territory. "If they go for good … there will be peace; if not, we declare war" (Hu-DeHart 1984, esp. pp. 155–200).

Comparable objectives were apparent in the "Land or Death" program for reorganizing property relations in the Andes advanced by Quechan revolutionary Hugo Blanco during the 1960s,[29] and in the armed resistance of the Miskitos and other natives for the consolidation of the Nicaraguan state by the Sandinista government 20 years later (Blanco 1972). Blanco was a marxist – hence, his characterization of Indians as "peasants" – and at least nominally a trotskyite. During the 1980s, efforts by Marxian organizations like the Sendero Luminoso (Shining Path) guerrillas to facilitate a revolution among the Quechans of Peru's Andean highlands assumed a self-consciously maoist cant.[30] More recent struggles undertaken in the same vein include those of the Mayan population of Chiapas to assert their autonomy from Mexico's central government, an initiative presently being replicated in the provinces of Guerrero, Oaxaca, and Sonora. Among the better discussions are a pair of books by John Ross: *Rebellion from the Roots: Indian Uprising in Chiapas* (1995) and *The War Against Oblivion: The Zapatista Chronicles* (2000).[31]

In Venezuela, President Hugo Chávez, having apparently reconsidered certain tenets of Third Worldism, has become the first self-consciously revolutionary head of state to restore lands and rights to indigenous peoples (whether this initiative was gestural or programmatic remains to be seen).[32] Meanwhile, in Bolivia – demographically, the most overwhelmingly indigenous of all the Andean states – Evo Morales, a Guaraní, has been elected president, largely on a promise to usher in a "new day" for the country's native peoples (what this means, and where it might lead, also remain to be seen).[33]

The issue of demographics brings up yet another major mode of colonialism left unaddressed in the maoist "Three Worlds" paradigm. This is that of "settler states," wherein a colonizing European population, having sufficiently established itself in its new overseas domain, declares itself, or is otherwise declared, to constitute a country in its own right, independent of the colonizing power from whence it sprang. For the seminal formulation of the settler state concept – at least as it is employed herein – see A. Grenfell Price, *White Settlers and Native Peoples: An Historical Study of Racial Contacts between English-speaking Whites and Aboriginal peoples in the United States, Canada, Australia, and New Zealand* (1950).

Structurally, settler states – prominent examples include United States and Canada,[34] Australia,[35] New Zealand,[36] Israel,[37] Northern Ireland, and, until lately, the ugly duo of Rhodesia (now Zimbabwe)[38] and South Africa[39] – resemble the above-discussed internal colonial model embodied in most "liberated" Third World states, their primary distinction being that the dominant population is of immigrant rather than native descent. True, the latter circumstances have served to foster conditions radically different from those prevailing in Third World settings. Since the society "freed" by the attainment of settler state independence was that of the colonizers themselves, for those actually colonized colonial domination has not only been sustained but in most cases intensified in the "postcolonial" context. This intractable reality – discerned and cogently addressed by a number of theorists – cuts to the very heart of the recently voguish notion of "post-coloniality."[40]

There has been sufficient developmental continuity to place virtually every such entity on a First World footing. Nonetheless, Fourth World liberation struggles have been every bit as apparent in the most advanced of the First World settler states as they have in the least developed states in the Third World, oftentimes more so. An especially insidious dimension of this circumstance is that the original colonizing population – i.e., settlers – are thereby positioned to substitute themselves for the genuinely colonized in the context of "decolonization," thus rendering both the still-subjugated and the ongoing fact of colonialism itself effectively invisible. A classic illustration is that of Eurocanadian scholar Diana Brydon, who argued in all seriousness that if "contemporary 'mainstream' critics are truly interested in postcolonial literatures and perspectives, they will come to us." By "us," of course, Brydon meant Eurocanadians like herself (Moore-Gilbert, p. 207, n. 16, quoting Diana Brydon 1989, p. 95). Moore-Gilbert points out that Eurocanadian theorists have "blithely" sought to place the work of their literary counterparts on the same "postcolonial" footing as that of West Indian writers like C. L. R. James.

While the efforts of Australia's aboriginal peoples have been quite fruitful,[41] as have those of the Maoris in Aotearoa (New Zealand),[42] the sharpest confrontations have been in North America, a reality highlighted by the American Indian Movement's (AIM's) 1972 seizure of the U.S. Bureau of Indian Affairs building in Washington, DC[43]; AIM's 71-day armed defense of Wounded Knee in 1973[44]; the ongoing and sometimes armed resistance of the Big Mountain Dine (Navajos) to forced removal from their land, beginning in 1974[45]; the armed occupation of Montreal's Mercier Bridge by the Mohawk Warrior Society in 1990[46]; the armed occupation of traditional lands at Gustafsen Lake, British Columbia, during the mid-1990s[47]; and, currently, the struggle being waged by the Mohawks and others of the six-nation Haudenosaunee confederation to regain control over their traditional territory around Caledonia, in the Canadian province of Québec.[48]

Other examples abound: the long struggle of the Newes (Western Shoshone), spearheaded by the sisters Mary and Carrie Dann, to assert their right under the Ruby Valley Treaty to most of present-day Nevada[49]; the protracted struggle of the Lubicon Cree to preserve and protect the traditional territory in northern Alberta[50]; the hard-fought campaign by the Kanaka Maoli (Native Hawaiians) to assert their rights under international law to land and self-governance[51]; the Makahs' assertion of their right to maintain their traditional whaling economy[52]; the successful drive by the James Bay Cree to block hydroelectric projects that would have submerged their entire homeland under 200 feet of water.[53] The list goes on and on, from the Dene campaign to enforce their treaty rights in Canada's Northwest Territories, to the Mi'kmaq insistence upon their treaty-guaranteed right to fish and take lobsters off the coast of Nova Scotia,[54] to the ongoing Lakota effort to recover the Black Hills, guaranteed them in perpetuity under the 1868 Fort Laramie Treaty.[55] For background, see Mel Watkins, *Dene Nation: The Colony Within* (1977) and Ila Bussidor and Üstün Milgen-Reinhart, *Night Spirits: The Story of the Relocation of the Sayisi Dene* (1997). For insight on why Canada's usurpation of Dene rights has become increasingly pronounced over the past 20 years, see Ellen Bielawski, *Rogue Diamonds: Northern Riches on Dene Land* (2003).

Even in the European "mother countries" themselves, the Fourth World has increasingly made its presence known over the past 50 years,[56] most spectacularly by a 30-year intensification, beginning in 1970, of the 800-year-long Irish struggle to evict the last vestiges of British colonialism from their homeland.[57] Less conspicuous have been similar processes at work in Celtic Cymru (Wales) and Alba (Scotland). Also at issue are Breizh (Brittany), Kernow (Cornwall), and Mannin (the Isle of Mann).[58] Elsewhere, the Basques have also engaged in an armed struggle to free their homeland, Euskadi, from its status of forcible incorporation into the Spanish state, while the Catalans have recently begun to openly pursue a similar agenda.[59] So, too, the native Corsicans, whose island homeland in the Mediterranean has long been held as a settler possession by France. In "Discussing Autonomy and Independence for Corsica," Gunter Lauwers writes:

> The emergence of the Corsican demand for independence dates back to the mid-1970s. Until that time, nationalist Corsicans did not seek independent statehood but merely political autonomy within France. However, ... the fact that this demand for autonomy was not given due consideration led to a radicalization of the movement. [At this point,] Corsica has been the scene of separatist violence for decades. Assassination and bomb attacks seem to be an ingredient of everyday politics. ... A comparison with Northern Ireland or the Basque country is never far away. (Lauwers 2003, p. 49)[60]

Far to the north, in the Arctic region of Scandinavia, the Samis (Lapps) are also seeking to resume their traditional autonomy vis-à-vis Norway, Sweden, and Finland.[61]

Where does all this lead? One possibility is perpetual low-intensity warfare. Indeed, of 122 armed conflicts catalogued by cultural geographer Bernard Neitschmann in 1993, 97 – roughly 85% of the total – devolved upon efforts by indigenous nations to free themselves from forced incorporation into one or more states, or against military operations designed to compel (re)incorporation (Neitschmann 1987, p. 237).[62] Moreover, 23 additional conflicts were classified simply as state "counterinsurgency" operations, a rather ambiguous and perhaps misleading designation in view of the fact that the bulk of the "insurgents" involved were often native people. At the same time, Neitschmann could identify only a single instance in which an armed conflict was occurring *between* states (ibid.). For a useful survey, see Lisa Gross, *Handbook of Leftist Guerrilla Groups in Latin America and the Caribbean* (1995). A close reading reveals that many of these organizations appear to be motivated by agendas markedly different from those prescribed by traditional left-wing ideologies.

In the alternative, the steadily increasing proliferation of Fourth World liberation struggles may ultimately produce genuine and complete rather than partial or figurative decolonization on a planetary basis. This would inherently entail a redefinition of the relations between peoples in terms of the mutual acknowledgement of fundamental rights – hence, mutual respect – a matter establishing self-determination and free association as the cardinal principles upon which the affairs of nations are conducted. These principles conform very well with those traditionally embraced throughout the Fourth World. See, for example, Franke Wilmer, *The Indigenous Voice in World Politics* (1993). Also see Sharon Helen Venne, *Our Elders Understand Our Rights: Evolving International Law Regarding Indigenous Rights* (1998).

Perhaps self-evidently, such principles preclude the exercise of the kind of centralized, arbitrary, and inherently coercive authority which constitutes the very essence of statist organization. This, in turn, would serve to delegitimate in its entirety the seventeenth-century Westphalian system of international relations, wherein states are the *only* entities deemed to be legitimate for purposes of deciding questions of world order. For a succinct account of the origins of the decisively Eurocentric Westphalian system, see Hedley Bull, "The Importance of Grotius in the Study of International relations," in *Hugo Grotius and International Relations* (1992, pp. 75–91). It is worth mentioning, however, that non-statist or even antistatist alternatives have long been posed from within the European tradition itself. For a brief historical survey, see Richard Falk, "Anarchism and World Order," in his *The End of World Order: Essays on Normative International Relations* (1983, pp. 277–298). Also see the essays collected in Demko and Wood, *Reordering the World* (1994).

The upshot of a Fourth World approach would be a multiplicity of sociopolitical environments, wherein decision-making processes are inherently geared to what Kirkpatrick Sale once and aptly described in *Human Scale* (1980). All but inevitably, this would lead to the contours of the resulting societies conforming closely to bioregional realities, a circumstance that would go far toward shaping the nature of their economies and facilitating a high degree of interactivity among/between societies through the medium of satisfying reciprocal needs.[63] Much more could and no doubt needs to be said, but constraints on length prevent it being said herein.

To cut a long story short, what has just been sketched goes a long way toward describing the restoration of the Fourth World, the indigenous or "host" world upon which all three of those identified by Mao were built, and without the perpetual subjugation/nullification of which none of the three could/can exist. Such an outcome would be entirely consistent with that advocated by the groundbreaking anarchist theorist Leopold Kohr; see, as examples, his *The Breakdown of Nations* (1957) as well as his *The Overdeveloped Nations: The Diseconomies of Scale* (1978). My personal preference of a term by which to refer to pursuit of Fourth World restoration is "indigenism," although it shares much in common with certain variants of anarchism, a promise which seems worthy of further exploration. That too, however, is a discussion consigned by the limits of space to be had another day.

Notes

1. For Western overviews, see George McT. Kahin (1956), Carlos P. Romulo (1956), and James Mackie (2005). On Chou's role, see Harold C. Hinton (1972, p. 77).
2. The term "Third World" itself apparently originated with Alfred Sauvy, a French economist, in 1952 (Malley 1996, p. 78). The association of the term with the maoist conception of global revolution is nonetheless clear; see Eqbal Ahmed (1971, pp. 137–213), Gérard Chaliand (1977, esp. pp. 17–24), and Robert J. Alexander (1999).
3. Also see David C. Gordon (1971) as well as Heydar Reghaby (1974).
4. See generally, Lawrence W. Martin (1973) as well as Robert Mortimer (1984).
5. Also see Mao Tse-Tung (1961), Che Guevara (1962), Vo Nguyen Giap (1962), Amilcar Cabral (1969, esp. pp. 112–126). For a broader survey of such material, see William J. Pomeroy (1968).
6. See generally, Stewart C. Easton (1964), Tony Heath (1975), V.G. Kiernan (1982), and Franz Ansprenger (1989).
7. Also see Smith (1983, pp. 1–17, 122–135) and Walker Connor (1984, pp. 67–100). For elaboration of a different route to essentially the same end, see Emmanuel Terray (1972).
8. For early recognition of this reality, see Kwame Nkrumah (1965). For subsequent analyses, drawn from several perspectives, see Arghiri Emmanuel (1972), Samir Amin (1976), Stephen Krasner (1985), and Nigel Harris (1986).
9. See esp., O. Mannoni (1990 translation of 1950 original), Frantz Fanon (1966), and Albert Memmi (1965, 1968).
10. For explication, see Arif Dirlik (1997). Also see Ngugi Wa Thiong'o (1986).
11. Further, the implications are in some respects usefully explored in Basil Davidson (1992, esp. pp. 101–117).
12. On South Asia, see, e.g., David Ludden (1992, pp. 247–287).
13. Also see Lee Buchheit (1978).
14. This is literally true by definition. According to the current edition of the *Encarta World English Dictionary*, a **nation** is "1. a community of people or peoples who live in a defined territory and are organized under a single government 2. a community of people who share a common ethnic origin, culture, historical tradition, and, frequently, language, whether or not they live together in one territory or have their own government, 3. a Native American people or federation of peoples 4. A territory occupied by a Native American nation."
15. See, e.g., Bernard Neitschmann (1994, pp. 225–242). For what may be the seminal framing(s) of the term, see Ben Whitaker (1972) and George Manuel and Michael Posluns (1974).

16. Also see Connor (1984, esp. pp. 5–27) Joseph Stalin (1975, esp. pp. 18–58).
17. Also see Ronaldo Munck (1986, esp. pp. 162–178).
18. See, e.g., Michael Hector (1975). More broadly, see Robert Bartlett and Angus Mackay (1989) and Robert Bartlett (1993).
19. See Neville Maxwell (1980), M.K. Akbar (1985), and Isak Chisi Swu and Th. Muivah (1993).
20. Also see Sadruddin Aga Khan and Hassan bin Tala (1987, pp. 131–134).
21. For further context, see Fred Branfman (1970, esp. pp. 244–255) and John Prados (1986, pp. 255–256).
22. Also see Alexander (1999).
23. See Jules Gerard-Libois (1966). On the formation of the Congo as Leopold's private domain, see Packenham (1991, pp. 239–255) and Adam Hothschild (1998, esp. pp. 61–74).
24. See Arthur A. Nwanko (1969); Peter Schwab (1971).
25. Kwame Nkrumah (1961, pp. 167–168).
26. See Susan Meiselas (1997) and Denise Natali (2005). For additional perspectives, see Gerald Chaliand (1993).
27. John Gretton (1976), Tony Hodges (1980), Suresh Chandra Saxena (1995), and Toby Shelley (2004).
28. The meanings of the terms "indigenism" and "indigenist," used herein, may be self-evident. Those in need of explanation, or desiring a fuller understanding, will find it useful to refer to Roxanne Dunbar Ortiz (1984, pp. 83–85), Alcida Rita Ramos (1998, esp. pp. 3–5, 121–144), and Ronald Niezen (2003).
29. See Gustavo Gorriti (1999 trans. of 1990 Spanish language original).
30. For the best overview, see Bernard Neitschmann (1989). Also see Klaudine Ohland and Robin Schneider (1983) and Americas Watch, *The Miskitos in Nicaragua* (1986). New York: Human Rights Watch.
31. Also see Elaine Katzenberger (1995).
32. See, e.g., Maurice Lemoine (2007). For context, see Steve Ellner (2008).
33. See Nancy Postero (2005, pp. 73–87). For background, see Silvia María Hirsch (2003, esp. pp. 84–93).
34. See Manuel and Posluns (1974). More comprehensively see Anthony J. Hall (2003).
35. See Henry Reynolds (1989) and Bruce Elder (1998).
36. See Claudia Orange (1987) and (1999).
37. Two of the better analyses are Maxime Rodinson's (1973), and Lorenzo Veracini's more recent (2006). Also see the various works regarding Israel cited above.
38. See generally, Ronald Weitzer (1990). For further background, see Brendan O'Brien (1993), David Martin and Phyllis Johnson (1981), and Gerald Horne (2001).
39. For background, see Noel Mostert (1992), Jeff Guy (1979), Merle Lipton (1986). On the liberation struggle, see Francis Meli (1988) and Maria van Diepen (1988).
40. See, as critical examples, Anne McClintock (1992, pp. 1–15), Deepra Bahri (1995, pp. 51–82), and Stuart Hall (1996, pp. 242–260). Also see Dirlik (1997).
41. See generally, Peter H. Russell (2005).
42. See generally, Jane Kelsey (1993).
43. See generally, Vine Deloria, Jr. (1985) and Rex Weyler (1992, pp. 35–57).
44. See generally, Robert Burnette and John Koster (1974) and Paul Chaat Smith and Robert Warrior (1996).
45. See generally, Jerry Kammer (1980), Anita Parlow (1988), and Emily Benedek (1992).
46. See generally, Geoffrey York and Loreen Pindera (1991), Donna Goodleaf (1995), and Linda Pertusati (1997).
47. See generally, Janice G.A.E. Switlo (1997).
48. For the fullest available information on the struggle at Caledonia, see Tehaliwaskenhas (Bob Kennedy, 2008) Also see the Wikipedia (2008a) entry for "Caledonia land dispute."
49. See generally, Ward Churchill (2002, pp. 173–189).
50. See generally, John Goddard (1991).
51. See generally, Huanani-Kay Trask (1999) and Ward Churchill (2003, pp. 73–123).

52. Although it is in some respects badly flawed, the best readily accessible source is probably by Robert Sullivan (2000).
53. See generally, Grand Council of the Crees (Eeyo Astchee, 1998).
54. On the "Burnt Church Crisis" see the Wikipedia (2008b) entry bearing that title. For background, see L.F.S. Upton (1979) and Geoffrey York (1989, pp. 54–79).
55. See Edward Lazarus (1991) and Mario Gonzalez and Elizabeth Cook-Lynne (1999).
56. For background, see generally, Mikulás Teich and Roy Porter (1993).
57. See O'Brien (1993) and Ed Moloney (2002). For an especially good case study, see Ciaran De Baroid (2000).
58. See Peter Berresford Ellis (1985) and Gwynfor Evans (1991).
59. See Cyrus Zirakzadeh (1977), Joseba Zulaika (1988), Robert P. Clark (1990), and Paddy Woodworth (2001).
60. For a description of the Army of the Corsican People see the entry under that name in the US Department of Homeland Security-sponsored MIPT Terrorism Knowledge Base (available at http://www.ikb.org/Group.jsp?groupID=4413).
61. See Hannum (1990, pp. 247–262).
62. Also see R. Brian Ferguson and Neil Lancelot Whitehead (1992) and Ted Robert Gurr (1993).
63. See his *Dwellers in the Land: The Bioregional Vision* (San Francisco: Sierra Club Books, 1985). Also see my own "I Am Indigenist: Notes on the Ideology of the Fourth World," in Churchill, W. (2003). *Acts of rebellion: The Ward Churchill reader* (pp. 275-99). New York: Routledge

References

Aga Khan, S. and Tala, H.B. (1987). *Indigenous peoples: A global quest for justice*. London: Zed Books.
Ahmed, E. (1971). Revolutionary warfare and counterinsurgency. In Miller, N. and Aya, R. (eds.), *National liberation: Revolution in the Third World*. New York: Free Press.
Akbar, M.K. (1985). *India: The siege within*. London: Penguin.
Alexander, R.J. (1999). *International Maoism in the developing world*. New York: Praeger.
Amin, S. (1976). *Unequal development: An essay on the social formations of peripheral capitalism*. New York: Monthly Review Press.
Ansprenger, F. (1989). *The dissolution of colonial empires*. New York: Routledge.
Assensoh, A.B. (1998). *African political leadership: Jomo Kenyatta, Kwame Nkrumah, and Joseph Nyerere*. Malabar, FL: Kreiger.
Bahri, D. (1995). Once more with feeling: What is postcolonialism? *Ariel*, 26, 1(Jan), 51–82.
Barnet, R.J. (1972). *Intervention and revolution: The United States in the third world*. New York: Mentor Books.
Bartlett, R. (1993). *The making of Europe: Conquest, colonization and cultural change, 950–1350*. Princeton, NJ: Princeton University Press.
Bartlett, R. and Mackay, A. (1989). *Medieval frontier societies*. Oxford: Clarendon Press.
Bell, J.B. (1993). *The Irish troubles: A generation of violence, 1967–1992*. New York: St. Martin's Press.
Benedek, E. (1992). *The wind won't know me: A history of the Navajo-Hopi land dispute*. New York: Alfred A. Knopf.
Bielawski, E. (2003). *Rogue diamonds: Northern riches on Dene land*. Vancouver: Douglas & McIntyre.
Blanco, H. (1972). *Land or death: The peasant struggle in Peru*. New York: Pathfinder Press.
Branfman, F. (1970). Presidential war in Laos, 1964–70. In Adams, N.S. and McCoy, A.W. (eds.), *Laos: War and revolution*. New York: Harper's, pp. 213–280.
Brydon, D. (1989). New approaches to the new literatures in English. In Maes-Jelinek, H., Peterson, K.H., and Rutherford, A. (eds.), *A shaping of connections: Commonwealth literature studies – essays in honor of A.N. Jeffries*. Mundlestrup: Dangaroo.

Buchheit, L. (1978). *Secession: The legitimacy of self-determination.* New Haven, CT: Yale University Press.

Bull, H. (1992). The importance of Grotius in the study of international relations. In Bull, H., Kingsbury, B., and Roberts, A. (eds.), *Hugo Grotius and international relations* (pp. 75–91). Oxford: Clarendon Press.

Burnette, R. and Koster, J. (1974). *The road to Wounded Knee.* New York: Bantam Books.

Bussidor, I. and Milgen-Reinhart, U. (1997). *Night spirits: The story of the relocation of the Sayisi Dene.* Winnipeg: University of Manitoba Press.

Cabral, A. (1969). *Revolution in Guinea.* New York: Monthly Review Press.

Chaliand, G. (1977). *Revolution in the third world: Myths and prospects.* New York: Viking.

Chaliand, G. (1993). *People without a country: The Kurds and Kurdistan.* New York: Olive Branch Press.

Chatterjee, P. (1986). *Nationalist thought in the colonial world: A derivative discourse.* London: Zed Books.

Chomsky, N. and Herman, E.S. (1979). *The political economy of human rights, Vol. 1: The Washington connection and third world fascism.* Boston, MA: South End Press.

Churchill, W. (2002). The struggle for New Segobia: The Western Shoshone battle for their homeland. In Churchill, W. (ed.), *Struggle for the land: Native North American resistance to genocide, ecocide and colonization* (pp. 173–189). San Francisco, CA: City Lights.

Churchill, W. (2003). Stolen kingdom: The right of Hawai'i to decolonization. In Churchill, W., *Perversions of justice: Indigenous peoples and Angloamerican law* (pp. 73–123). San Francisco, CA: City Lights.

Churchill W. and Morris, G.T. (2005). Between a rock and a hard place: Left-wing revolution, right-wing reaction, and the destruction of Indigenous peoples. In Churchill, W. (ed.), *Since predator came: Notes on the struggle for American Indian liberation* (pp. 329–348). Oakland, CA: AK Press.

Clark, R.P. (1990). *Negotiating with ETA: Obstacles to peace in the Basque country, 1975–1988.* Reno, NV: University of Nevada Press.

Connor, W. (1984). *The national question in Marxist-Leninist theory and strategy.* Princeton, NJ: Princeton University Press.

Coppieters, B. and Sakwa, R. (2003). *Contextualizing secession: Normative studies in comparative perspective.* Oxford: Oxford University Press.

Coquery-Vidrovitch, C. (1988). *Africa: Endurance and change south of the Sahara.* Berkeley, CA: University of California Press.

Davidson, B. (1992). *The black man's burden: Africa and the curse of the nation-state.* New York: Times Books.

De Baroid, C. (2000). *Ballymurphy and the Irish war.* London: Pluto Press.

Deloria, V., Jr. (1985). *Behind the trail of broken treaties: An Indian declaration of independence.* Austin, TX: University of Texas Press.

Dirlik, A. (1994). *After the revolution: Waking to global capitalism.* Hanover, NH: Wesleyan University Press.

Dirlik, A. (1997). *The postcolonial aura: Third world criticism in the age of global capitalism.* Boulder, CO: Westview Press.

Easton, S.E. (1964). *The rise and fall of western colonialism: An historical survey from the early nineteenth century to the present.* New York: Praeger.

Elder, B. (1998). *Blood on the wattle: Massacres and maltreatment of Aboriginal Australians since 1788.* Sydney: New Holland.

Ellis, P.B. (1985). *The Celtic revolution: A study in anti-imperialism.* Talybont, Dyfed: Y Lolfa Cyf.

Ellner, S. (2008). *Rethinking Venezuelan politics: Class, conflict, and the Chavez phenomenon.* Boulder, CO: Lynne Rienner.

Emmanuel, A. (1972). *Unequal exchange: A study in the imperialism of trade.* New York: Monthly Review Press.

Evans, G. (1991). *Fighting for Wales.* Talybont, Dyfed: Y Lolfa Cyf.

Falk, R. (1983). Anarchism and world order. In Falk, R. (ed.), *The end of world order: Essays on normative international relations* (pp. 277–298). New York: Holmes & Meier.
Fanon, F. (1966). *The wretched of the earth*. New York: Grove Press.
Ferguson R.B. and Whitehead, N.L. (1992). *War in the tribal zone: Expanding states and indigenous warfare*. Seattle, WA: School of American Research/University of Washington Press.
Gerard-Libois, J. (1966). *Katanga secession*. Madison, WI: University of Wisconsin Press.
Giap, V.N. (1962). *People's war, people's army*. New York: Praeger.
Goddard, J. (1991). *Last Stand of the Lubicon Cree*. Vancouver: Douglas & McIntyre.
Gonzalez M. and Cook-Lynne, E. (1999). *The politics of hallowed ground: Wounded Knee and the struggle for Indian sovereignty*. Urbana, IL: University of Illinois Press.
Goodleaf, D. (1995). *Entering the war zone: A Mohawk perspective on resisting invasions*. Penticton: Theytus Books.
Gordon, D.C. (1971). *Self-determination and history in the third world*. Princeton, NJ: Princeton University Press.
Gorriti, G. (1999). *The Shining Path: A history of the millenarian war in Peru*. Chapel Hill, NC: University of North Carolina Press.
Government of Belgium. (1953). *The Belgian thesis; The sacred mission of civilization: To which peoples should the benefit be extended?* New York: Belgian Government Information Center.
Grand Council of the Crees (Eeyo Astchee). (1998). *Never without consent: James Bay Crees' stand against forcible inclusion in an independent Québec*. Toronto: ECW Press.
Gretton, J. (1976). *Western Sahara: The fight for self-determination*. London: Anti-Slavery Society.
Gross, L. (1995). *Handbook of leftist guerrilla groups in Latin America and the Caribbean*. Boulder, CO: Westview Press.
Guevara, E.C. (1962). *Guerrilla warfare*. New York: Praeger.
Gurr, T.R. (1993). *Minorities at risk: A global survey of ethnopolitical conflict*. Washington, DC: State Institute of Peace Press.
Guy, J. (1979). *The destruction of the Zulu kingdom*. London: Longman.
Hall, A.J. (2003). *The American empire and the fourth world: The bowl with one spoon*. Montreal: McGill-Queen's University Press.
Hall, S. (1996). When was 'the post-colonial'? Thinking at the limit. In Chambers, I. & Curti, L. (eds.), *The post-colonial question: Common skies, divided horizons* (pp. 242–260). New York: Routledge.
Halliday, J. and McCormack, G. (1973). *Japanese imperialism today*. New York: Monthly Review Press.
Hannum, H. (1990). *Autonomy, sovereignty, and self-determination: The accommodation of conflicting rights*. Philadelphia, PA: University of Pennsylvania Press.
Harris, N. (1986). *The end of the third world: Newly industrializing countries and the decline of an ideology*. New York: Meredith Press.
Heath, T. (1975). *The end of European empire: Decolonization after World War II*. Lexington, MA: D.C. Heath.
Hector, M. (1975). *Internal colonialism: The Celtic fringe in British national development, 1536–1966*. Berkeley, CA: University of California Press.
Hinton, H.C. (1972). *China's turbulent quest: An analysis of China's foreign relations since 1949*. Bloomington, IA: Indian University Press.
Hirsch, S.M. (2003). The emergence of political organizations among the Guaraní Indians of Bolivia and Argentina: A comparative perspective. In Langer E.D. and Muñoz, E. (eds.), *Contemporary Indigenous movements in Latin America* (pp. 84–93). Wilmington, DE: Scholarly Resource Books.
Hodges, T. (1980). *Western Sahara: The roots of a desert war*. Westport, CT: Lawrence Hill.
Horne, A. (2002). *Savage war of peace: Algeria, 1954–1962*. New York: History Book Club.
Horne, G. (2001). *From the barrel of a gun: The United States and the war against Zimbabwe 1965–1980*. Chapel Hill, NC: University of North Carolina Press.
Hothschild, A. (1998). *King Leopold's ghost: A story of greed, terror and heroism in colonial Africa*. New York: Houghton-Mifflin.

Hu-DeHart, E. (1984). *Yaqui resistance and survival: The struggle for land and autonomy, 1821–1910*. Madison, WI: University of Wisconsin Press.

Ikpuk, J.S. (1995). *Militarization of politics and neo-colonialism: The Nigerian experience, 1966–90*. London: Janus.

Kahin, G. (1956). *The Asian-African conference: Bandung, Indonesia, April 1955*. Ithaca, NY: Cornell University Press.

Kammer, J. (1980). *The second long walk: The Navajo-Hopi Land Dispute*. Albuquerque, NM: University of New Mexico Press.

Katzenberger, E. (ed.) (1995). *First world, ha-ha-ha! The Zapatista challenge*. San Francisco, CA: City Lights.

Kelsey, J. (1993). *Rolling back the state: Privatisation of power in Aotearoa/New Zealand*. Wellington: Bridget Williams Books.

Kiernan, V.G. (1982). *European empires from conquest to collapse, 1815–1960*. Leicester: Leicester University Press.

Kohr, L. (1957). *The breakdown of nations*. London: Routledge and Kegan Paul.

Kohr, L. (1978). *The overdeveloped nations: The diseconomies of scale*. New York: Schocken Books.

Krasner, S. (1985). *Structural conflict: The third world against global liberalism*. Berkeley, CA: University of California Press.

Lauwers, G. (2003). Discussing independence for Corsica. In Coppieters, B., and Sakwa, R. (eds.), *Contextualizing secession: Normative studies in comparative perspective*. Oxford, UK: Oxford University Press.

Lazarus, E. (1991). *Black Hills, white justice: The Sioux Nation versus the United States, 1775 to the present*. New York: HarperCollins.

Lipton, M. (1986). *Capitalism and apartheid: South Africa, 1910–1986*. Aldershot: Wildwood House.

Ludden, D. (1992). India's Development Regime. In Dirks, N.B. (ed.), *Colonialism and culture* (pp. 247–287). Ann Arbor, MI: University of Michigan Press.

M'buyinga, E. (1982). *Pan Africanism of neo-colonialism: The bankruptcy of the O.A.U.* London: Zed Books.

Mackie, J. (2005). *Bandung 1955: Non-alignment and Afro-Asian solidarity*. Paris: Editions Duduer Millet.

Malley, R. (1996). *The call from Algeria: Third worldism, revolution, and the turn to Islam*. Berkeley, CA: University of California Press.

Mannoni, O. (1990). *Prospero and Caliban: The psychology of colonization*. Ann Arbor, MI: University of Michigan Press.

Manuel G. and Posluns, M. (1974). *The fourth world: An Indian reality*. New York: Free Press.

Mao, T. (1961). *On guerrilla warfare*. New York: Praeger.

Martin, D. and Johnson, P. (1981). *The struggle for Zimbabwe: The Chimurenga war*. New York: Monthly Review Press.

Martin, L.W. (1973). *Neutralism and non-alignment: The new states in world affairs*. Westport, CT: Greenwood Press.

Maxwell, N. (1980). *India, the Nagas and the northeast*. London: Minority Rights Group.

McClintock, A. (1992). The angel of progress: Pitfalls of the term 'post-colonialism'. *Social Text*, 31–32 (Spring), 1–15.

McKenzie, J.M. (1983). *The partition of Africa, 1880–1900*. London: Metheun.

Meiselas, S. (1997). *Kurdistan: In the shadow of history*. New York: Random House.

Meli, F. (1988). *South Africa belongs to us! A brief history of the ANC*. Harare: Zimbabwe Publishing House.

Memmi, A. (1965). *The colonizer and the colonized*. New York: Orion Press.

Memmi, A. (1968). *Dominated man: Notes towards a portrait*. New York: Orion Press.

MIPT Terrorism Knowledge Base (available at http://www.ikb.org/Group.jsp?groupID = 4413).

Mirante, E.T. (1987). Ethnic minorities of the Burma borders and their resistance organizations. In *Southeast Asian tribal groups and ethnic minorities*. Cambridge, MA: *Cultural Survival Report* (22), 59–71. Moloney, E. (2002). *A secret history of the IRA*. New York: W.W. Norton.

Moore-Gilbert, B. (1997). *Postcolonial theory: Contexts, practices, politics*. London: Verso.
Morris, B. (1990). *1948 and after: Israel and the Palestinians*. New York: Oxford University Press.
Mortimer, R. (1984). *The third world coalition in international politics*. Boulder, CO: Westview Press.
Mostert, N. (1992). *Frontiers: The epic of South Africa's creation and the destruction of the Xhosa people*. London: Jonathan Cape.
Munck, R. (1986). *The difficult dialogue: Marxism and nationalism*. London: Zed Books.
Natali, D. (2005). *The Kurds and the state: Evolving national identity in Iraq, Turkey, and Iran*. Syracuse, NY: Syracuse University Press.
Neitschmann, B. (1987). Militarization and indigenous peoples: The third world war. *Cultural Survival Quarterly*, 3(11).
Neitschmann, B. (1989). *The unknown war: The Miskito Nation, Nicaragua, and the United States*. Lanham, MD: Freedom House.
Neitschmann, B. (1994). The Fourth World: Nations versus states. In Demko G.J. and Wood, W.B. (eds.), *Reordering the world: Geopolitical perspectives on the 21st Century* (pp. 225–242). Boulder, CO: Westview Press.
Nevins, J. (2005). *A Not-so-distant horror: Mass violence in East Timor*. Ithaca, NY: Cornell University Press.
Niezen, R. (2003). *The origins of indigenism: Human rights and the politics of identity*. Berkeley, CA: University of California Press.
Nirmal, R.M. (1999). *The right to self-determination in international law*. New Delhi: Deep & Deep.
Nkrumah, K. (1961). *I speak of freedom: A statement of African ideology*. New York: Praeger.
Nkrumah, K. (1965). *Neo-colonialism: The last stage of imperialism*. New York: International.
Nwanko, A.A. (1969). *Biafra: The making of a nation*. New York: Praeger.
O'Brien, B. (1993). *The long war: The IRA and Sinn Fein*. Syracuse, NY: Syracuse University Press.
Ohland, K. and Schneider, R. (1983). *National revolution and Indigenous identity*. Copenhagen: IWGIA Doc. 47.
Orange, C. (1987). *The Treaty of Waitangi*. Wellington: Allen & Unwin.
Ortiz, R.D. (1984). *Indians of the Americas: Human rights and self-determination*. London: Zed Books.
Packenham, T. (1991). *The scramble for Africa: The white man's conquest of the dark continent, 1876–1912*. New York: Random House.
Panikar, K.M. (1953). *Asia and western dominance*. London: Allen & Unwin.
Pappe, I. (2006). *The ethnic cleansing of Palestine*. Oxford: Oneworld.
Parlow, A. (1988). *Cry, sacred ground: Big Mountain, U.S.A.* Washington, DC: Christic Institute.
Pertusati, L. (1997). *In defense of Mohawk land: Ethnopolitical conflict in native North America*. Albany, NY: State University of New York Press.
Pomeroy, W.J. (1968). *Guerrilla warfare and Marxism*. New York: International.
Postero, N. (2005). Indigenous responses to neoliberalism: A look at the Bolivian uprising of 2003. *Political and Legal Anthropology Review*, 73 (May), 73–87.
Prados, J. (1986). *Presidents' secret wars: Pentagon and CIA secret operations since World War II*. New York: William Morrow.
Price, A.G. (1950). *White settlers and Native peoples: An historical study of racial contacts between English-speaking Whites and Aboriginal peoples in the United States, Canada, Australia, and New Zealand*. Melbourne/Cambridge: Georgian House/Cambridge University Press.
Ramos, A.R. (1998). *Indigenism: Ethnic politics in Brazil*. Madison, WI: University of Wisconsin Press.
Reghaby, H. (1974). *Philosophy of the third world*. Berkeley, CA: Lewis.
Reynolds, H. (1989). *Dispossession: Black Australians and white invaders*. St. Leonards, NSW: Allen & Unwin.
Roberts, R.F. (1995). *Destiny's landfall: A history of Guam*. Honolulu: University of Hawai'i Press.
Robie, D. (1989). *Blood on their banner: Nationalist struggles in the South Pacific*. Leichardt, NSW: Pluto Press Australia.

Rodinson, M. (1973). *Israel: A colonial settler state?* New York: Pathfinder Press.
Rogan, E.L. and Shlaim, A. (2001). *The war for Palestine: Rewriting the history of 1948.* Cambridge: Cambridge University Press.
Romulo, C.P. (1956). *The meaning of Bandung.* Chapel Hill, NC: University of North Carolina Press.
Ross, J. (1995). *Rebellion at the roots: Indian uprising in Chiapas.* Monroe, ME: Common Courage Press.
Ross, J. (2000). *The war against oblivion: The Zapatista chronicles.* Monroe, ME: Common Courage Press.
Russell, P.H. (2005). *Recognizing Aboriginal title: The Mabo case and Indigenous resistance to English-settler colonialism.* Toronto: University of Toronto Press.
Said, E.W. (1980). *The question of Palestine.* New York: Times Books.
Said, E.W. (1994). *The politics of dispossession: The struggle for Palestinian self-determination, 1969–1994.* New York: Pantheon.
Sale, K. (1980). *Human scale.* New York: Coward, McCann & Geoghegan.
Saxena, S. C. (1995). *Western Sahara: No alternative to armed struggle.* Delhi: Kalinga.
Schwab, P. (1971). *Biafra.* New York: Facts on File.
Seton-Watson, H. (1977). *Nations and states: An enquiry into the origins of nations and the politics of nationalism.* Boulder, CO: Westview Press.
Shelley, T. (2004). *Endgame in the Western Sahara: What future for Africa's last colony?* London: Zed Books.
Shlaim, A. (2000). *The iron wall: Israel and the Arab world.* New York: W.W. Norton.
Smith, A.D. (1983). *State and Nation in the Third World: The Western State and African Nationalism.* New York: St. Martin's Press.
Smith, P.C. and Warrior, R.A. (1996). *Like a hurricane: The American Indian Movement from Alcatraz to Wounded Knee.* New York: New Press.
Stalin, J. (1975). Marxism and the national question. In Stalin, J. (ed.), *Marxism and the national-colonial question.* San Francisco, CA: Proletarian, pp. 7–68.
Sternhell, Z. (1998). *The founding myths of Israel: Nationalism, socialism, and the making of the Jewish state.* Princeton, NJ: Princeton University Press.
Sullivan R. (2000). *A whale hunt.* New York: Scribner.
Swenson, S. (1987). National minorities. In Schirmer, D.B. and Shalom S.R. (eds.), *The Philippines reader: A history of colonialism, neocolonialism, dictatorship and resistance* (pp. 199–209). Boston, MA: South End Press.
Switlo, J.G.A.E. (1997). *Gustafsen Lake under siege: Exposing the truth behind the Gustafsen Lake stand-off.* Peachland: TIAC Communications.
Swu, I.C. and Muivah, T.H. (1993). *Free Nagaland manifesto.* Oking: National Socialist Council of Nagaland.
Taylor, J.G. (1991). *Indonesia's forgotten war: The hidden history of East Timor.* London: Zed Books.
Tehaliwaskenhas (Kennedy, B.). (2008). Kanenhstaton: The protected place. In *Turtle Island Network News*, Feb. 28. Available at http://www.turtleisland.org/news/news-sixnations.html.
Teich, M. and Porter, R. (1993). *The national question in Europe in historical context.* Cambridge: Cambridge University Press.
Terray, E. (1972). *Marxism and "primitive" societies: Two studies.* New York: Monthly Review Press.
Trask, H.K. (1999). Kupa'a "Aina: Native nationalism in Hawai'i." In Trask, H.K. (ed), *From a Native daughter: Colonialism and sovereignty in Hawai'i* (pp. 87–110). Honolulu: University of Hawai'i Press.
Upton, L.F.S. (1979). *Micmacs and colonists: Indian-white relations in the Maritimes, 1713–1867.* Vancouver: University of British Columbia Press.
van Diepen, M. (1988). *The national question in South Africa.* London: Zed Books.
Venne, S.H. (1998). *Our elders understand our rights: Evolving international law regarding Indigenous rights.* Penticton: Theytus Books.

Veracini, L. (2006). *Israel and settler society*. London: Pluto Press.
Wa Thiong'o, N. (1986). *Decolonizing the mind: The politics of language in African literature*. Oxford/Portsmouth, NH: James Curry/Heineman.
Ward, A. (1999). *An unsettled history: Treaty claims in New Zealand today*. Wellington: Bridget Williams Books.
Watkins, M. (1977). *Dene Nation: The colony within*. Toronto: University of Toronto Press.
Weitzer, R. (1990). *Transforming settler states: Communal conflict and internal security in Northern Ireland and Zimbabwe*. Berkeley, CA: University of California Press.
Weyler, R. (1992). *Blood of the land: The government and corporate war against First Nations*. Philadelphia, PA: New Society.
Whitaker, B. (1972). *The Fourth World: Victims of group oppression*. London: Sidgwick & Jackson.
Wikipedia (2008a). Caledonia land dispute. Available at http://en.wikipedia.org/wiki/Caledonia_land_dispute).
Wikipedia (2008b). Burnt Church crisis. Available at http://en.wikipedia.org/wiki/Burnt_Church_Crisis).
Wilmer, F. (1993). *The Indigenous voice in world politics*. Newbury Park, CA: Sage.
Woodworth, P. (2001). *Dirty war, clean hands: ETA, the GAL and Spanish democracy*. Cork, Ireland: Cork University Press.
Worsely, P. (1967). *The third world*. Chicago, IL: University of Chicago Press.
York, G. (1989). *The dispossessed: Life and death in native Canada*. Toronto: Lester & Orpen Dennys.
York G. and Pindera, L. (1991). *People of the pines: The warriors and the legacy of Oka*. Toronto: Little, Brown Canada.
Zirakzadeh, C. (1977). *A rebellious people: Basques, protests, and politics*. Reno, NV: University of Nevada Press.
Zulaika, J. (1988). *Basque violence: Metaphor and sacrament*. Reno, NV: University of Nevada Press.

Chapter 3
Making Explicit the Jurisprudential Foundations of Multiculturalism: The Continuing Challenges of Colonial Education in US Schooling for Indigenous Education

Dolores Calderón

Education in the United States today is not merely a legacy of the colonial project – it is a functionary arm of colonialism that acts to absorb even progressive educational movements. Willinsky (1998) contends that education continues to be shaped by the legacy of imperialism, and this legacy has mapped and named the world, "bringing it within a single system of thought" (pp. 9–10). Willinsky (1998) continues: "[T]he lessons that were drawn from centuries of European expansion continue to influence the way we see this world" (p. 25). In this chapter, I extend Willinsky's important insights to examine how education is framed by what I assert is the often invisible foundation of the colonial project in the West – Western metaphysics[1] focusing on prominent discourses in multicultural education. I build upon the work of indigenous scholars such as Vine Deloria and others who have developed the critique of Western metaphysics in education (Cajete 1994; Calderón 2008; Champagne 2005; Deloria and Wildcat 2001).

I focus on what I define as Normative Multicultural Education which is characterized by the following features: It folds native Americans into minority discourses with African-Americans, Asian-Americans, and Latinos/Latinas; defines multiculturalism within settler-state discourses and institutions; emphasizes multicultural goals in relation to equality and citizenship rights; perpetuates colonial models of education; and operates within traditional western metaphysical frameworks. In addition, Normative Multicultural Education (NMCE) contains a major blind spot. This blind spot, or *colonial blind* pattern, is a recurrent phenomenon in both educational practices and research. I define *colonial blind*[2] as practices that normalize Western knowledge organization and assumptions, promote Western notions of being (metaphysics), and promote Westernization of knowledge and its institutionalization through means perceived as neutral. NMCE fails to engage how Western metaphysical or worldviews, including anthropocentrism, individualism, and linear narratives inform the parameters of discourse and practice in education. Specifically, many of the key themes tackled by NMCE including citizenship, equality, and diversity embody Western assumptions that are not congruent with indigenous needs[3] and are *colonial blind*. Therefore, it is important to engage both the colonial practices that operate both explicitly and implicitly in education in order to better achieve anticolonial practices.

As stated, indigenous[4] educational issues are usually placed in the same context as the challenges faced by black, Asian-American, and Latino/Latina communities. This collapsing of "minority" educational issues, into a standardized approach, or a discourse of NMCE, is blind to native self-determination, its accompanying nation-building projects, and it does not take into account the importance of native cultures and knowledge in maintaining native sovereignty. In this way, NMCE discourses perpetuate the Colonial Models of Education (Calderón 2008) forced upon indigenous peoples in the United States, a white settler nation.[5]

In order to achieve truly anticolonial education, we must first make Western metaphysics or worldviews explicit, by shattering *colonial blind* ideologies. The history of Western metaphysics precedes the Enlightenment project. Indeed many of the core foundational elements of Western metaphysics are products of Judeo-Christian worldviews (Deloria 1992). While the Enlightenment project claimed to replace church doctrine with scientific rationality and objectivity, both belief systems nevertheless rely on the same epistemological assumptions of universalism, historicity, linearity, dualism, and humanism. Rubenstein (2003) explains: "Today we tend to think of science and orthodox religion as inherently and perpetually in conflict," but this is not the case (p. 7). Rubenstein (2003) continues: "[B]y marrying Christian theology to Aristotelian science, they [church leaders] committed the West to an ethic of rational inquiry that would generate a succession of 'scientific revolutions' as well as unforeseen upheavals in social and religious thought" (p. 9). A product of these "scientific revolutions" are the systems of law developed in the West – particularly the United States – that created rationales for empire and colonialism, and institutionalize *colonial blind* ideologies and practices.

Therefore, in this chapter, I turn to legal jurisprudence for concrete evidence of the behaviors of Western metaphysics and construction of colonial blind ideologies. I examine two bodies of law – Civil Rights (CR) and Federal Indian Law (FIL) – in order to outline how these legal narratives have created and framed the parameters around key concepts, such as citizenship, equality, and diversity used in NMCE. While FIL has produced concepts concerning the Doctrine of Discovery, the Trust Relationship, and Self-Determination to name a few, these concepts have not made their way to educational discourses. While the concept of self-determination is referred to at times in curriculums incorporating multicultural perspectives, Native American educational issues are nevertheless integrated with minority group issues in education (Calderón 2008). I am not advocating that NMCE look toward the concepts developed in FIL to "pluralize" their conceptual hermeneutics; rather what I demonstrate is that reliance on CR ideology in NMCE reifies the notion of a *colonial ontology*.[6] This reification results in the alienation of Indian educational issues (reproducing the goals of colonial education toward Indians), and reasserts the primary position of Western metaphysics (as embodied in law). Finally, I turn to Derrick Bell and Robert Williams to show how both bodies of law are so entrenched in the Western project that they ultimately fail both Indians and communities of color.

3.1 How Colonization Has Organized Identity Within the United States: An Examination of Central Legal Sources

The role of law in framing parameters around identity remains central in how we "talk" about rights today, in particular how we talk about educational rights, and how we talk in sightless ways. Law and society scholar Dudas (2005) explains: "Sociolegal scholars, for example, have established that rights talk is a primary method by which we at once perceive our interests, communicate them to each other, and negotiate disputes that are based upon those interests" (p. 731). Legal scholar Mertz (1995) expands on Dudas' (2005) insights, pointing out that the language of law imposes social ideologies on social life, and "legal language is at once a conceptual framework and powerful social praxis" (pp. 361, 380). For this reason, I focus on US Supreme Court case law, as the development of law is one of the clearest evidentiary guides we have today to analyze the implementation and continuance of colonialism and its underlying Western metaphysics. Specifically, I analyze how the US Supreme Court has framed key concepts in Civil Rights law and Federal Indian Law. Two appendices are included at the end of this chapter. The first is a full list of the cases discussed in this chapter, as well as the years they were decided. The second provides a graphic organizer and outline of United States Supreme Court Settler Nation Law Jurisprudence discussed in this chapter for clarification, as well as for easy use in the classroom.

The Supreme Court does two important things to both these bodies of law: first, it demarcates the relationships (political, economic, and social) national minorities and Indians have with the United States as a settler nation; and second, it produces important concepts and ideologies that subsequently shape movements within the United States (such as affirmative action, multicultural education, bilingual education, etc.). These two functions, institutionalized by the Supreme Court, I argue, have created an entire ontological project that I characterize as *colonial ontology*.[7] I find that many of the most visible national minority rights movements firmly locate their conceptual and policy frameworks within this ontological project.

As Kempf argues: "Colonization is the process whereby abstract social locations become sites for concrete oppression" and the "colonial moment occurs when behaviour, based on social location, has concrete negative consequences for one actor and concrete positive consequences for another" (Arlo Kempf, Chapter 1, this volume). Therefore, from an anticolonial perspective, it is important to make clear that these national minority rights movements are vital and necessary, as they indeed embody social transformation. However, I am interested in taking this anticolonial analysis further, by arguing that we must also turn a critical gaze toward the types of assumptions maintained and produced by national minority rights discourses. Additionally, while the Supreme Court's

Federal Indian Law differentiates Indian rights from racial or minority rights, this body of law nevertheless frames Indian rights solely within the colonial context, never recognizing indigenous origins of sovereignty. As we shall see below, the ontological project of Civil Rights frames national minority rights in relation to the settler nation.

3.1.1 National Minority Rights

In this section, I analyze how the Supreme Court has defined key concepts in relation to national minority rights. I focus on national minority rights contained within the Civil Rights body of law, particularly the concepts of citizenship, equality, and diversity. These three concepts represent key themes and principles also contained in Normative Multicultural Education (NMCE) discourses and practices today. I use the term national minority rights to refer generally to the history and development of racialized rights, typically associated with African-American, Latinos, Asian Americans, and other marginalized groups within the context of the United States. I couple the terms "national" and "minority rights" in order to indicate that these rights have developed within the context of a white settler nation, the United States.

3.1.1.1 Citizenship and the Nation–State–Race and Minority Rights

An important legal framework relating to minority rights within the settler state has to do with citizenship. In particular, minority rights movements have been concerned with access to the full rights of citizenship in the United States. Secondary or subsidiary categories to citizenship are related to issues of access, integration, and equality. While minorities are considered citizens, there are both historic and contemporary ideologies and structures that function to impede full enjoyment of citizenship for minorities that are indeed afforded to whites in the United States.[8] The framing of minority rights within the context of citizenship necessarily ties these movements and their ideological, theoretical, and policy projects to the colonial settler project.

Specifically, minority rights are framed in relation to the nation-state, and in the United States, minority rights are framed around the construction of race. Koopmans and Statham (1999) provide a useful definition of citizenship, as "the set of rights, duties, roles, and identities linking citizens to the nation-state" (p. 654). While I analyze cases that focus mostly on African-Americans, the Civil Rights movement is a legacy that shapes the rights of communities of color in the United States in general.

To begin, I explore the legacy of slavery in shaping Civil Rights law. Prior to the civil war, African-American slaves and former slaves were not considered citizens. For example, in the Supreme Court Case *Dred Scott v. Sandford* (1856) the court had the following question before it:

> Can a negro, whose ancestors were imported into this country, and sold as slaves, become a member of the political community formed and brought into existence by the Constitution

of the United States, and as such become entitled to all the rights, and privileges, and immunities, guaranteed by that instrument to the "citizen?" (60 U.S. 393, 403).

The Court held:

> We think they [slaves/former slaves] are not [citizens], and that they are not included, and were not intended to be included, under the word "citizens" in the Constitution, and can therefore claim none of the rights and privileges which that instrument provides for and secures to citizens of the United States. (60 U.S. 393, 404–405)

The Thirteenth Amendment, ratified in 1865, abolished slavery, but states responded by keeping in place a system designed to keep former slaves in conditions of virtual servitude (Ides and May 2001, p. 5). The Bill of Rights at this point was only applicable to national and not state action; therefore, states did not have to legally abide by the Thirteenth Amendment.

Ides and May (2001) explain that post civil war, a series of laws, the Black Codes, were enacted in southern states, which restricted the rights of former slaves, "including the rights to enter into contracts, to purchase property, and to sit on juries," all rights of citizenship enjoyed by whites (p. 5). In 1868, the Fourteenth Amendment was adopted. It provides: "All persons born or naturalized in the United States and subject to the jurisdiction thereof, are citizens of the United States and of the State wherein they reside" (Ides and May 2001). The intent of the Fourteenth Amendment, along with the Thirteenth Amendment's abolishment of slavery, was "designed to repeal" the *Dred Scott* (1856) decision, although it took decades of Supreme Court cases to establish the foundations of modern Fourteenth Amendment interpretation (Ides and May 2001). One important aspect of the history of Civil Rights that I emphasize here is how the Fourteenth Amendment essentially established "federal supremacy within this realm of rights" over states' rights (Ides and May 2001). This latter role of federal supremacy, as I will show, becomes primary in later Civil Rights cases as well as in Federal Indian Law.

3.1.1.2 The Separate but Equal Doctrine

The question before the US Supreme Court in *Plessy v. Ferguson* (1896) was whether the act of the general assembly of the state of Louisiana, passed in 1890, "providing for separate railway carriages for the white and colored races" violated the Thirteenth and Fourteenth Amendments (163 U.S. 537, 540). The petitioner argued, for example, that the act violated the Fourteenth Amendment on the basis that

> all person born or naturalized in the United States, and subject to the jurisdiction thereof, are made citizens of the United States and of the states where in they reside; and the states are forbidden from making or enforcing any law which abridge the privileges or immunities of citizens of the United States, or shall deprive any person of life, liberty, or property without due process of law, or deny to any person within their jurisdiction the equal protection of the law. (163 U.S. 537, 543)

The Court held that the Louisiana Act "does not conflict with the thirteenth amendment" (ibid.). The Court reasoned: "A statute which implies merely a legal distinction between the white and colored races – a distinction which is founded in the color of the two races, and which must always exist so long as white men are distinguished from the other race by color – has no tendency to destroy the legal equality of the two races, or re-establish a state of involuntary servitude" (ibid.). With regard to the Fourteenth Amendment, the Court held that the act is a reasonable regulation, reasoning that the state of Louisiana "is at liberty to act with reference to the established usages, customs, and traditions of the people, and with a view to the promotion of their comfort, and the preservation of the public peace and good order" (163 U.S. 537, 550). Woll's (2006) *American Government: Readings and Cases*, a text approved for use in many school districts across the United States, explains that the Court held that the separate but equal practices "did not violate the Equal Protection of the Laws Clause of the Fourteenth Amendment" (p. 136).

Citizenship rights, however, have not been guaranteed for minority groups viewed as perpetual foreigners such as Asian-Americans. Although not within the typical trajectory of Civil Rights cases, the case of *Korematsu v. United States* (1944) serves as the most egregious example of the precariousness of citizenship for minority groups. With regard to this case, Johnson (2002) explains that the Court "rejected constitutional challenges to the US government's internment of people of Japanese ancestry" (p. 190). Johnson (2002) also notes that "the government did not distinguish between non-citizens who had immigrated from Japan and US citizens of Japanese ancestry" (p. 190). While *Korematsu* (1944) reminds us of the precariousness of national minority rights, the Civil Rights cases maintain a central and paradigmatic role within minority rights discourses today.

3.1.1.3 The Battle for Equality: *Brown v. Board of Education* and the Dream of Integration

In education, like all institutions of public life in the United States, the separate but equal doctrine remained the law of the land. African-Americans, however, continued to fight the separate but equal doctrine, with the NAACP leading this battle. Derrick Bell (1995) describes this history:

> By the early thirties, the NAACP, with the support of a foundation grant, had organized a concerted program of legal attacks on racial segregation. … These strategies were intended to eliminate racial segregation, not merely in the public schools but throughout society. The public schools were chosen because they presented a far more compelling symbol of the evils of segregation and a far more vulnerable target than segregated railroad cars, restaurants or restrooms (p. 6).

In *Brown v. Board of Education of Topeka (I)(II)* (1954)(1955), the question before the Court was: "Does segregation of children in public schools solely on the basis of race, even though the physical facilities and other 'tangible' factors may be equal, deprive the children of the minority group of equal educational opportunities?" (347 U.S. 483, 493). The Court held:

> We conclude that in the field of public education the doctrine of "separate but equal" has no place. Separate educational facilities are inherently unequal. Therefore, we hold that the

plaintiffs and others similarly situated for whom the actions have been brought are, by reason of the segregation complained of, deprived of the equal protection of the laws guaranteed by the Fourteenth Amendment. (347 U.S. 483, 495)

Brown (1954, 1955) represents the most enduring legacy of the Civil Rights cases, and it is generally viewed as the central source for validating minority rights with regards to equal opportunity. Similarly, the diversity raitonale, developed by the Court in latter cases, has been used to promote racialized minority groups integration through education.

3.1.1.4 The Diversity Rationale in Education: The Perceived Value for Whites

The diversity rationale was developed by a series of cases that examined race in relation to admissions programs. Moses and Chang (2006) trace the origins of this legal concept to the cases *Sweatt v. Painter* (1950) and *McLaurin v. Oklahoma State Regents* (1950). In *Sweatt*, the question before the Court was whether a Texas law school could deny admission to blacks, but the Court held that the "law school must admit Blacks because there were gross disparities between that school and the separate law school for Blacks" (Moses and Chang 2006; p. 7). Moses and Chang (2006) point out that in the *Sweatt* decision, a type of diversity rationale was indeed at work. The authors describe that in *Sweatt*, Chief Justice Fred M. Vinson, who wrote for a unanimous Court, held that a law school cannot be effective when it is isolated from the "individuals and institutions with which the law interacts," and students should not study in "an academic vacuum" (p. 7). In *McLaurin*, according to Moses and Chang (2007) the Court invalidated the University of Oklahoma's

> policy of restricting Black graduate students' use of the library, classrooms, and school cafeteria, arguing that it contributed to educational inequality by prohibiting "the intellectual commingling of students" and limited Black students' ability "to engage in discussions and exchange views with other students," thereby handicapping their "pursuit of effective graduate education." (p. 7)

Furthermore, Moses and Chang (2006), point out that this reasoning presents a type of diversity rational, relying on the perceived value that blacks receive from interacting with whites without mentioning "what White students could gain through interaction with their Black peers" (p. 7). Moses and Change (2006) conclude that the diversity rationale's perceived value for whites is more "obvious in Justice Powell's opinion in the well-known case of *Bakke*" (p. 7).

The most famous use of the diversity rationale is found in *Regents of the University of California v. Bakke* (1978), in which the Court held that the Davis admissions "quota" program violated the Equal Protection Clause of the Fourteenth Amendment. In addition, the Court held that "when a State's distribution of benefits or imposition of burdens hinges on ancestry or the color of a person's skin, that individual is entitled to a demonstration that the challenged classification is necessary to promote a substantial state interest"; in other words, use of race is subject to strict scrutiny, no matter what the race of the impacted individual is (438 U.S.

265, 320). The Court goes on to clarify, stating: "In enjoining petitioner from ever considering the race of any applicant, however, the courts below failed to recognize that the State has a substantial interest that legitimately may be served by a properly devised admissions program involving the competitive consideration of race and ethnic origin," thus allowing the use of race as a criterion in admissions processes constitutional (ibid).

Moses and Chang (2006) explain the importance of Powell's decision in maintaining race as a factor that can be considered in university admissions:

> [A] diverse student body broadens the range of viewpoints collectively held by students and subsequently allows a university to provide an atmosphere that improves the quality of higher education through greater speculation and experimentation. This type of atmosphere, he believed, enhances the training of the student body and better equips the institution's graduates. (p. 7)

Powell reasoned that this type of diversity is essential for the future of the United States, and when the use of race is narrowly tailored, it meets this compelling state interest. More recent cases such as *Grutter v. Bollinger* (2003) and *Gratz v. Bollinger* (2003) have further defined the use of race and the diversity rational in admissions processes.

Specifically in *Grutter*, the question before the Court was whether the use of race in the University of Michigan Law School's admission's program violated the Equal Protection Clause of the Fourteenth Amendment. In *Grutter*, the Court found that "the Law School's narrowly tailored use of race in admissions decisions to further a compelling interest in obtaining the educational benefits that flow from a diverse student body is not prohibited by the Equal Protection Clause" (539 U.S. 306, 307). The Court reasoned:

> To be narrowly tailored, a race-conscious admissions program cannot "insulat[e] each category of applicants with certain desired qualifications from competition with all other applicants" (Opinion of J. Powell). Instead, it may consider race or ethnicity only as a "'plus' in a particular applicant's file"; i.e., it must be "flexible enough to consider all pertinent elements of diversity in light of the particular qualifications of each applicant, and to place them on the same footing for consideration, although not necessarily according them the same weight." It follows that universities cannot establish quotas for members of certain racial or ethnic groups or put them on separate admissions tracks. The Law School's admissions program, like the Harvard plan approved by Justice Powell, satisfies these requirements. (539 U.S. 306, 309)

In *Gratz*, on the other hand, the Court found that unlike the University of Michigan Law School's admissions program, its undergraduate admissions program violated the Equal Protection Clause of the Fourteenth Amendment because it was not narrowly tailored.

3.1.1.5 Colorblindness and the Diminishing Legacy of Brown

The US Supreme Court's most recent decision, *Parents Involved in Community Schools v. Seattle School District No. 1* (2007), represents the most recent Supreme Court entrance on the use of race to promote the legacy of *Brown*. The Court in

Parents v. Seattle held that the school district's policies of using "racial classifications as a 'tiebreaker' to allocate slots in particular high schools" is in violation of the Equal Protection Clause of the Fourteenth Amendment (p. 1). The Court reasoned that Seattle's program was not narrowly tailored to meet the compelling government interest of diversity and therefore did not meet the standards of *Grutter*:

> The school districts have not carried their heavy burden of showing that the interest they seek to achieve justifies the extreme means they have chosen – discriminating among individual students based on race by relying upon racial classifications in making school assignments. ... Although remedying the effects of past intentional discrimination is a compelling interest under the strict scrutiny test, *that interest is not involved here because the Seattle schools were never segregated by law nor subject to court ordered desegregation, and the desegregation decree to which the Jefferson County schools were previously subject has been dissolved.* [Emphasis mine] (pp. 2–3).

Furthermore, Chief Justice Roberts, writing the majority opinion differentiates the recent *Grutter v. Bollinger* (2003) decision "in which the Court held that, for strict scrutiny purposes, a government interest in student body diversity 'in the context of higher education' is compelling" (p. 3). In *Parents* (2007), Roberts counters: "[R]ace is not considered as part of a broader effort to achieve 'exposure to widely diverse people, cultures, ideas, and viewpoints,' for some students, is determinative standing alone" (ibid.).

In addition, Chief Justice Roberts differentiates *Parents v. Seattle* (2007) from the diversity rationale outlined in *Bakke* (1978):

> Quoting Justice Powell's articulation of diversity in *Regents of the University of California v. Bakke*, the *Grutter* Court noted that "'it is not an interest in simple ethnic diversity, in which a specified percentage of the student body is in effect guaranteed to be members of selected ethnic groups,' that can justify the use of race," ... but "'a far broader array of qualifications and characteristics of which racial or ethnic origin is but a single though important element.'" In the present cases, by contrast, race is not considered as part of a broader effort to achieve "exposure to widely diverse people, cultures, ideas, and viewpoints"; race, for some students, is determinative standing alone. The districts argue that other factors, such as student preferences, affect assignment decisions under their plans, but under each plan when race comes into play, it is decisive by itself. It is not simply one factor weighed with others in reaching a decision, as in *Grutter*; it is the factor. See *Gratz v. Bollinger*, 539 U.S. 244, 275. Even as to race, the plans here employ only a limited notion of diversity, viewing race exclusively in white/nonwhite terms in Seattle and black/"other" terms in Jefferson County. (p. 3)

This lengthy quote demonstrates that for schools to continue to use race as a factor in desegregation, integration, and admissions, it must be so narrowly tailored, to meet the stringent diversity rational outlined in *Grutter* (2003) and *Gratz* (2003).

These series of Supreme Court cases shape the fundamental legal jurisprudence concerning citizenship, equality, and diversity characterized in education. The cases demonstrate that national minority rights are not set in stone and are subject to the changing nature of political, economic, and social ideology. For this reason, it is important to critically examine how and why normative multicultural frameworks continue to rely on the concepts of citizenship, equality, and diversity to promote the educational needs of communities of color. However, before delving into an analysis of how normative multicultural concepts of citizenship, equality, and diversity are in essence the same concepts constructed by the Court, I examine and contrast how indigenous rights have been constructed by US legal jurisprudence to flesh out the colonial ontology that dominates US law.

3.1.2 Indigenous Rights

In this section I analyze how the United States has framed indigenous rights, by looking at key Supreme Court cases within the area of Federal Indian Law, focusing on the development of the concepts domestic dependent nation, trust responsibility, and self-determination. While the body of Federal Indian Law follows a considerably different legal trajectory than Civil Rights law, proponents of sovereignty in Federal Indian Law have drawn inspiration from the Civil Rights cases to promote their goals.[9] Wilkins (1994), however, cautions us to consider "the political/legal 'cloaking' tools generated by the US Supreme Court and practiced by Congress which placed tribes in the particularly enigmatic position of being recognized sovereigns with rights that can be systematically quashed" (p. 2). Like the ever-changing nature of Civil Rights law, Federal Indian Law and policy likewise vacillates (Lomawaima and McCarty 2006).

3.1.2.1 Federal Supremacy – Domestic Dependent Nation Rationale and the Trust Relationship

In the nineteenth-century Supreme Court Chief Justice John Marshall played a central role in Federal Indian law through a series of cases known as the Marshall trilogy, which established the foundations for the continued colonial domination of Indian peoples in the United States. In *Johnson v. McIntosh* (1823), Chief Justice John Marshall's majority opinion laid out the Doctrine of Discovery and denial of Indian territorial sovereignty. In it, Marshall denied Indians' natural law rights to land by incorporating the Doctrine of Discovery which granted "the discovering European Nation 'an exclusive right to extinguish the Indian title of occupancy, either by purchase or by conquest,'" which in turn, was transferred to, and adopted by, the United States following the American Revolution (Williams 1990, p. 313). The plaintiffs in this case had purchased lands directly from Western Indian tribes while the defendant had obtained title to the same lands from a patent issued from the federal government. According to the Marshall opinion in *McIntosh*, the "purchases of lands from the Western Indian tribes without the approval or sanction of either the discovering European nation or its successor in interest, the United States, could not be recognized as valid in a United States court" (Williams 1990, p. 313). Underlying Marshall's legal reasoning was the idea that

> once a European nation firmly established its occupancy of territories discovered in the New World, relations with the Indigenous inhabitants of that region became matters of

exclusively domestic concern between the tribes and the particular invading European sovereign. Any independent rights of the tribes to their aboriginal lands or to sovereignty had been subsumed within the hierarchical, universalized conceptions centering European political and legal theory toward alien peoples. (Williams in Goldberg 2002, p. 60)

In the second case of the Marshall Trilogy, *Cherokee Nation v. Georgia* (1831), the issue before the Supreme Court was whether the Cherokee nation is a foreign state and could therefore sue the state of Georgia in federal court under diversity jurisdiction. Marshall wrote in the majority opinion that as "domestic dependent nations" the Cherokee are not "foreign nations" and therefore the Court has no jurisdiction. Chief Justice John Marshall continued:

> [Y]et it may well be doubted, whether those tribes which reside within the acknowledged boundaries of the United States can, with strict accuracy, be denominated foreign nations. They may, more correctly, perhaps, be denominated domestic dependent nations. They occupy a territory to which we assert a title independent of their will, which must take effect in point of possession, when their right of possession ceases. Meanwhile, they are in a state of pupilage. Their relation to the United States resembles that of a ward to his guardian. (30 U.S. 1, 17)

Undoubtedly, this case establishes the controversial domestic dependent nation status and federal trusteeship over Indian tribes in the United States.

In the third case of the Marshall Trilogy, *Worcester v. Georgia* (1832), Chief Justice Marshall again wrote the majority opinion:

> [T]he Cherokee nation, then, is a distinct community, occupying its own territory, with boundaries accurately described, in which the laws of Georgia can have no force, and which the citizens of Georgia have no right to enter, but with assent of the Cherokees themselves, or in conformity with treaties, and with the acts of Congress. (31 U.S. 515, 529)

In other words, the federal government, and not the states, possesses "the exclusive right to exercise control over Indian affairs" (Williams 1990, p. 63). The holding of *Georgia* reaffirms tribal sovereignty, by affirming a model of federal supremacy in which the federal government, and not the states, has the authority to convey trust status and thus regulate tribes, protecting tribes from state encroachment (Williams 1990).

Indeed the Marshall trilogy is the foundation of Federal Indian Law in the United States. In the twentieth century, another justice greatly influenced this body of law.

3.1.2.2 Twentieth-Century Federal Indian Law: Thurgood Marshall's Opinions and Indian Self-Determination

Similarly, in the twentieth century, Justice Thurgood Marshall's opinions in areas of federal Indian law upheld a "vision of sovereignty based on federal supremacy." Although Justice Thurgood Marshall's decisions enumerate different aspects of tribal sovereignty, they also maintain federal supremacy with relation to tribal activities. For example, in *Merrion v. Jicarilla Apache Tribe* (1982), Justice Marshall held that the Jicarilla tribe has the inherent power to "impose a severance tax on 'any oil and natural gas severed, saved and removed from Tribal lands' ... as part of its power to govern and to pay for the costs of self-government" (455 U.S. 130, 133). Although Justice Marshall also "qualified the tribe's authority to tax nonmembers by acknowledging that the federal government has the power to limit or completely divest the tribe of this power" (Tsosie 1994, p. 510). In *McClanahan v. Arizona State Tax Commission* (1973), the Court reaffirmed its position on limiting states' rights with regards to tribes. The Court held that "by imposing the tax in question on this appellant, the State has interfered with matters which the relevant treaty and statutes leave to the exclusive province of the Federal Government and the Indians themselves. The tax is therefore unlawful as applied to reservation Indians with income derived wholly from reservation sources" (411 U.S. 164, 165). As is evident from his rulings, Marshall upholds federal supremacy in relation to tribes over states' authority.

In *Santa Clara Pueblo v. Martinez* (1978), a female member of the Santa Clara Pueblo claimed that an "ordinance of the tribe denying tribal membership to the children of female tribe members who married outside the tribe, while extending membership to the children of male members who married outside the tribe, violated the provision of Title 1" of the Indian Civil Rights Act (436 U.S. 49). Justice Thurgood Marshall held that litigants using the Indian Civil Rights Act "were limited to tribal forum for relief, except for the express federal remedy of habeas corpus" (Tsosie 1994, p. 515). Justice Marshall's reasoning followed Federal Indian Law precedent not treating the case as a federal Civil Rights case, concluding tribal membership is a political right and not a constitutional right; thus the "Indian nation, rather than the federal government" has the "ultimate authority to make this decision" (ibid., pp. 515–518). *Santa Clara* (1978) is not the only case where minority rights are differentiated from Indian Law.

3.1.2.3 Court Differentiation of Indian and Race/Minority Rights

A series of cases differentiate national minority rights from indigenous rights. The *Dred Scott* (1857) case, for instance, centered on the question of whether a former slave could be considered a citizen, the court nevertheless made an interesting point relating to Indians:

> The situation of this population [slaves/former slaves] was altogether unlike that of the Indian race. The latter, it is true, formed no part of the colonial communities, and never amalgamated with them in social connections or in government. But although they were uncivilized, they were yet a free and independent people, associated together in nations or tribes, and governed by their own laws. ... It is true that the course of events has brought the Indian tribes within the limits of the United States under subjection to the white race; and it has been found necessary, for their sake as well as our own, to regard them as in a state of pupilage, and to legislate to a certain extent over them and the territory they occupy. (60 U.S. 393, 403–404)

Interestingly, this excerpt represents an extension of the ideology of white supremacy over Indians, slaves, and former slaves.

In *Morton v. Mancari* (1974) non-Indian employees of the Bureau of Indian Affairs (BIA) claimed that the "employment preference for qualified Indians in the BIA provided by the Indian Reorganization Act of 1934 contravened the antidiscrimination provisions of the Equal Employment Opportunities Act of 1972" (417 U.S. 535). The Court held that the employment did not violate the Equal Employment Opportunities Act because "preference, as applied, is granted to Indians not as a discrete racial group, but, rather, as members of quasi-sovereign tribal entities whose lives and activities are governed by the BIA in a unique fashion" (417 U.S. 535, 554). The Court reasoned that "the legal status of the BIA is truly sui generis," and the employment "applies only to employment in the Indian service" (ibid.). The Court found that the employment preference in place was reasonable and "directly related to a legitimate, nonracially based goal" (ibid.).

In *Regents of the University of California v. Bakke* (1978), the petitioner in *Bakke* attempted to use *Mancari* "for the proposition that the State may prefer members of traditionally disadvantaged groups" (438 U.S. 265, 304). The Court differentiated the facts of *Mancari* from *Bakke*, stating the preference challenged in *Mancari* "was not racial at all, but 'an employment criterion reasonably designed to further the cause of Indian self-government and to make the BIA more responsive to ... groups ... whose lives and activities are governed by the BIA in a unique fashion'" (438 U.S. 265, 304). Indian preferences are not measured by the same preferences granted to national minorities. In *Rice v. Cayetano* (2000), the Court held that Native Hawaiians do not share the same legal status as Indians organized in tribes: "Congress may not authorize a State to establish a voting scheme that limits the electorate for its public officials to a class of tribal Indians to the exclusion of all non-Indian citizens" (528 U.S. 495, 511). The Court argued that the voting scheme in question was solely based on race. Therefore, the *Mancari* exception does not apply. The Court stated: "The National Government and the States may not violate a fundamental principle: They may not deny or abridge the right to vote on account of race. Color and previous condition of servitude, too, are forbidden criteria or classifications, though it is unnecessary to consider them in the present case" (528 U.S. 495, 511–512).

It is worth noting that the rights of Indian tribes do not originate in Federal Indian Law; rather they are inherent. However, Federal Indian Law informs the political parameters of these rights vis-à-vis the United States, and like Civil Rights, the sovereign rights of tribes face a contracting jurisprudence.

3.1.2.4 The Diminishment of Tribal Sovereignty: Equal Protection and Individual Rights

Like the narrowing of the diversity rational posed by the cases of *Bakke*, *Grutter*, and *Gratz*, tribal sovereignty established by Federal Indian Law has been similarly restricted. Legal scholar Carole Goldberg (2002) explains: "Non-Indians seeking immediate access to Indians' natural resources have often attacked these special benefits through equal rights rhetoric. Over time, the rhetoric has shifted from concern for equal treatment of Indians to fear of unequal treatment of whites" (p. 2). In a six to two opinion authored by Justice Rehnquist, the Court in *Oliphant v. Suquamish Indian Tribe* (1978) concluded that tribal courts do not have criminal jurisdiction over non-Indians. Justice Thurgood Marshall's dissent in *Oliphant*, joined by Chief Justice Warren Burger, agreed, in part, with the majority that "the power to preserve order on the reservation ... is a *sine qua non* of the sovereignty that the Suquamish originally possessed" (435 U.S. 191, 224). Conversely, Justice Marshal argued, contrary to the majority opinion, "in the absence of affirmative withdrawal by treaty or status ... Indian tribes enjoy as a necessary aspect of their retained sovereignty the right to try and punish all persons who commit offenses against tribal law within the reservation" (ibid.). Another major limitation of tribal sovereignty came about with *Montana v. United States* (1981) in which the Supreme Court, relying on *Oliphant*, held that the sovereign powers of a tribe only extend to members of the tribe and do not extend to non-members, unless otherwise enacted by Congress.

Relying on *Montana* (1981), the courts further limited tribal sovereignty in *Nevada v. Hicks* (2001) and *Atkinson v. Shirley* (2001). In *Atkinson Trading v. Shirley* the question before the Court was whether the hotel occupancy tax applied to non-Indian owned hotels within the exterior boundaries of the reservation by the Navajo Nation was invalidated by *Montana*. The Court held the Navajo Nation's imposition of a hotel occupancy tax upon nonmembers on non-Indian fee land[10] within its reservation was invalid because tribes lack civil authority over the conduct of nonmembers on non-Indian fee land within the reservation, limiting the sovereign power of tribes to tax. Similarly, in *Nevada v. Hicks* the Court held that since

> [t]ribes lacked legislative authority to restrict, condition, or otherwise regulate the ability of state officials to investigate off-reservation violations of state law, they also lacked adjudicative authority to hear respondent's claim that those officials violated tribal law in the performance of their duties. ... State officials operating on a reservation to investigate off reservation violations of state law are properly held accountable for tortious conduct and civil rights violations in either state or federal court, but not in tribal court. (533 U.S. 353, 374)

Hicks (2001) is an especially important case in this analysis because it represents a dangerous reversal of previous precedent.

Legal scholar Gould (2003) contends that *Nevada v. Hicks* (2001) "ignored a principle laid down almost half a century ago – that states cannot regulate the affairs of Indians on reservations without authority from Congress" as established in *Worcester* (p. 671). Gould (2003) raises the alarm that "in deciding that a tribal court did not have jurisdiction over a civil proceeding brought against state game wardens for conduct occurring on tribal land, the Court embraced a converse principle" (p. 671). And not surprisingly, going against established precedent, Justice Scalia, wrote that "states possess 'inherent jurisdiction' over reservations, except where their authority is limited by Congress" reasoning that " 'it was long ago' that 'the Court departed from Chief Justice Marshall's view' that 'the laws of [a State] can have no force' within reservation boundaries. 'Ordinarily,' it is now clear, 'an Indian reservation is considered part of the territory of the State' " (p. 671).

Gould (2003), like Goldberg (2002), argues that the court has taken this stance, not because they intend to strengthen states' rights or due to a conservative shift in the court, but rather that

3 Making Explicit the Jurisprudential Foundations of Multiculturalism

> [t]he root cause of the Court's unwillingness to vest tribes with regulatory or adjudicatory jurisdiction over non-Indians and nonmembers is its inability to reconcile the constitutional protection of individual rights with the tribal conception of group rights. There is virtually no textual basis in the Constitution to support tribal authority over nonmembers, while the rights of individuals to due process and equal protection are hallmarks of the Constitution and the Court's modern jurisprudence. Hence, when contests have pitted a tribe against an individual, unless the individual was a member of the tribe, the tribe has almost always failed. (p. 674)

The diminishment of tribal sovereignty is due to a combination of issues, including those described by Gould (2003) and Goldberg (2002). Similarly, the diminishment of equal protections for minority groups in the United States is due to the Court's reliance on individual rights – leaving open the claims of reverse discrimination that have constituted cases such as *Bakke*, *Grutter*, *Gratz*, and *Seattle*.

Wilkins' (1994) reminder to examine what he calls the political and legal cloaking devices used by the Supreme Court to quash tribal sovereignty may also be applied to the Civil Rights cases. For this reason, it is important to examine how it is that Normative Multicultural Education (NMCE) discourses and practices perpetuate citizenship, equality, and diversity rationales incorporated from Civil Rights legal jurisprudence. Rather than challenging the ontological processes embodied in Civil Rights jurisprudence, NMCE incorporates these processes. To be sure, I do not argue that multicultural education look toward Federal Indian Law as this simply replaces one colonial ontology with another.

3.2 From Supreme Court Precedent to Normative Multicultural Education: The Central Role of Citizenship, Equality, and Diversity in Multiculturalism

Citizenship, equality, and diversity narratives have become the mainstays of normative multiculturalism in education or Normative Multicultural Education (NMCE; Calderón 2008). NMCE promotes education in relation to the nation-state and explicitly or implicitly perpetuates the ideological foundations at the expense of peoples that do not define themselves in relation to the nation-state. In this chapter, I examine how Civil Rights jurisprudence constructs citizenship, equality, and diversity rationales. In this section, I investigate how NMCE incorporates framings of citizenship, equality, and diversity that reproduce the jurisprudential view of these concepts. Furthermore, I turn a critical gaze toward the propensity of NMCE to fold native education issues into a standardized discourse of minority education. Duane Champagne (2007) argues this standardizing of minority education discourses occurs because "the American public understands even less of Indian legal, political and cultural views, and still generally expects us to enter general society as a race or ethnic group" (p. 1). He elaborates that "[t]here are many disadvantages to American Indian interests when the public, and institutions, do not understand or recognize Indian viewpoints" (p. 1). In this same way NMCE maintain a *colonial blind* perspective.

Supreme Court jurisprudence develops interpretative mechanisms in order to protect full enjoyment of citizenship rights, equality, and safeguard from discrimination of diversity. These interpretive mechanisms maintain a central discursive and conceptual role in NMCE. Multicultural education is not a singular discourse; rather it ranges from conservative multiculturalism, liberal multiculturalism, left–liberal multiculturalism, to critical multiculturalism (McLaren 1994). Despite these diverse forms of multiculturalism, they subscribe to similar foundational assumptions, and are subsequently a part of the larger NMCE. Multiculturalism in education is characterized, according to McCarthy (1994), as "a product of a particular conjuncture of relations among the state, contending racial minority and majority groups, educators, and policy intellectuals in the United States, in which the discourse over schools has become increasingly racialized" (pp. 81–82). The focus of multicultural education, James Banks (2004) writes, is "on ethnic, racial, cultural, language, and gender groups within the boundaries of a nations-state, such as the United States" (p. xii). Both views maintain NMCE discourses and practices that center on rights defined in relation to racial minorities.

For the sake of brevity, I focus on the report *Diversity Within Unity: Essential Principles for Teaching and Learning Within a Multicultural Society* and the work of James Banks. The report presents the findings of "consensus panel of interdisciplinary scholars" that "worked over a four-year period to determine what we know from research and experience about education and diversity," and as such represents a valuable insight into assumptions of NMCE (Banks et al. 2001). It states:

> An important goal of the schools should be to forge a *common nation* and destiny from the tremendous ethnic, cultural, and language *diversity*. To forge a common destiny, educators must respect and build upon the cultural strengths and characteristics that students from *diverse* groups bring to school. At the same time, educators must help all students acquire the knowledge, skills, and values needed to become participating *citizens* of the commonwealth. Cultural, ethnic, and language *diversity* provide the *nation* and the schools with rich opportunities to incorporate *diverse* perspectives, issues, and characteristics into the nation and the schools in order to strengthen both [emphasis mine]." (p. 5)

Citizenship, in this instance, is solely regarded in relationship to the United States, and likewise, diversity is presented as an interpretive mechanism to provide a plurality of ideas for the benefit of the nation.

As stated, NMCE discourses can be understood to represent progressive ends, yet even these types of discourses promote and reify constructions of citizenship that reaffirm its jurisprudential origins. For example, James Banks (1998) writes:

> To educate *citizens* for the next century, it is also important to revise the school curriculum in substantial ways so that it reflects the *nation's* new, emerging *national identity* and describes the process of becoming *American*. Students from *diverse* groups will be able to identity with a curriculum that fosters an overarching *American identity* only to the extent that it mirrors their perspectives, struggles, hopes, and possibilities. A curriculum that incorporates only the knowledge, values, experiences, and perspectives of mainstream powerful groups marginalizes the experiences of students of color and low-income students. Such a curriculum will not foster an overarching American identity because students will view it as one that has been created and constructed by outsiders, people who do not know or understand their experiences. Educators should try to create a curriculum that will be perceived by all students as being in the *broad public interest* [emphasis mine]. (p. 15)

Banks' intent is to promote a vision of citizenship that embraces the increasing diversity of the United States. Explicit in his argument, is the belief that curriculum, like citizenship, must be open to embrace the experiences of all citizens, and by doing so achieving a "broad public interest" for the benefit of the Nation. The "public interest," however, does not include sovereignty (Champagne 2005; Lomawaima and McCarty 2006; Wilkins 1994). It is not my intent to diminish the importance of Banks' work – it is my point here simply to offer how well-meaning scholars can inadvertently smuggle in concepts that not only alienate indigenous peoples but can also fail communities of color (Bell 1995b, c; Peller 1995; Wilkins 2002).

Likewise, equality is a constant theme in NMCE. Continuing in my examination of Banks (2004) work, he states that a major goal of multicultural education "is to reform the schools and other educational institutions so that students from diverse racial, ethnic, and social-class groups will experience educational *equality*" (p. 3). However, this educational equality does not translate to indigenous educational desires for self-determination (Calderón 2008; Champagne 2005). Interestingly, in order to achieve equality in education, a key tool used to achieve it is diversity, paralleling the legal use of the diversity rationale in cases promoting minority access to higher education. For instance, Banks (2004) argues for a type of multicultural framework that promotes five dimensions, one of which he defines as the equity pedagogy dimension, which "exists when teachers use techniques and methods that facilitate the academic achievement of students from *diverse* racial, ethnic, and social-class groups" (p. 5). This approach, while laudable, does not go far enough to challenge the colonial origins of the techniques and methods developed in education.

Diversity themes in NMCE, also consistently affirm their jurisprudential origins – as a means to promote equity and citizenship. The report *Diversity Within Unity: Essential Principles for Teaching and Learning Within a Multicultural Society* states the following concerning diversity:

> *Diversity* in the nation's schools is both an opportunity and a challenge. The *nation* is enriched by the ethnic, cultural, and language *diversity* among its *citizens* and within its schools. However, whenever diverse groups interact, inter-group tension, stereotypes, and institutionalized discrimination develop. Schools must find ways to respect the *diversity* of their students as well as help to create a *unified nation* state to which all of the *nation's citizens* have allegiance. Structural inclusion into the nation-state and power sharing will engender feelings of allegiance among diverse groups. E pluribus unum – diversity within unity – is the delicate goal toward which our nation and its schools should strive [emphasis mine]. (p. 13)

Diversity and citizenship concepts used in this report reproduce the diversity rationale employed by the Supreme Court. This perspective of diversity affirms the jurisprudential construction of diversity as a compelling interest of the nation-state. However, this diversity is aimed at facilitating assimilation to a singular idea of citizenship, leaving little to no room for discussions of tribes' desires for measured separatism (Williams 2005).

As Gay (2004) points out: "Multicultural education is essentially an affective, humanistic, and transformative enterprise situated within the sociocultural, political, and historical contexts of the United States" (p. 39). This point of contention is emblematic of the problems I see in attempting to incorporate and or utilize NMCE with indigenous peoples. Gay (2004) provides an important insight concerning multicultural education that is applicable to NMCE. She offers the explanation that "because multiculturalism originates in the liberal pluralist paradigm it is limited in its ability to create long-lasting substantive social change" (p. 54). Likewise, NMCE models originate from Western metaphysical paradigms, and are therefore limited in their ability to speak to organic native educational needs.[11]

To be sure, NMCE is the prominent method used to incorporate and speak to nonwhite communities. Nevertheless, it is firmly situated within the colonial ontology of the United States as I demonstrate above. This colonial ontology has led to the development of a particular type of educative model, which favors settler narratives, actively delinks present settler dominance from historical genocide of Indians, and actively erases engagement with tribal nations and sovereignty. I name this educative model the Colonial Model of Education, which I "define as the education practices, discourses and policies prominent in settler states that promote assimilatory curriculums and educational practices" (Calderón 2008, p. 1).

3.3 The Maintenance of the Colonial Project in Law and Normative Multicultural Education: The Challenge for Both Native Peoples and Communities of Color

The Colonial Model of Education (CME) promotes assimilation through language policy designed to eradicate or diminish fluency in native languages (Calderón 2008). It adopts and disseminates curriculum that serves to invalidate and contradict native cultures, while promoting the institutions and values of settler culture and promotes policies and practices that advance integration of native children in settler society (ibid.). It validates the legal authority of the white settler nation's governing institutions, practices, and beliefs, and promotes Judeo-Christian values and worldviews with the intent to Christianize and/or de-Indianize students (ibid.). Normative Multicultural Education (NMCE) ideologies and practices, as shown in the previous section, perpetuate the CME by insisting upon concepts guided by colonial ideologies of the nation-state not limited to citizenship, equality, and diversity.

While NMCE ideologies seek integration to the nation-state and promotion of minority rights, through a variety of legal mechanisms, American Indians demand and articulate an entirely different set of educational needs.[12] Native peoples, for example, center tribal citizenship and seek measured economic, cultural, and political separation from the United States. Wilkins (1994) clarifies that "although tribal nations share minority characteristics … with other minority groups, the differences distinguishing tribes from the other groups grossly exceed the similarities" (p. 1). Wilkins (1994) explains that "tribes are indigenous or original to the United States while all other individuals and groups [such as minorities] are immigrants" (p. 2). With regards to tribal sovereignty Wilkins (1994) illustrates, that in conjunction with tribes' indigenous status "is the fact that many tribes still have and exercise a number of elements of inherent sovereignty" and in essence, are also governments in and of themselves (p. 2). Both Duane Champagne (2007) and Wilkins (2004) agree that this status does not originate with the United States, nor is it granted to tribes by the federal government (Champagne 2007; Wilkins 1994). Unlike minority groups, the "tribal relationship to the United States is a political one, not a racial one, per se" as is the relationship of minorities such as African-Americans, Asian-Americas, and Latinos to the United States (Wilkins 1994, p. 2).

In addition, Champagne (2007) clarifies that the "roots of American Indian self-government ... precede the treaties and the formation of the U.S. Constitution. American Indian nations are not parties to the U.S. Constitution, and therefore not part of the original consensus that is American government" (p. 1). Unlike racialized minorities, who are party to the US Constitution, Wilkins (1994) continues, "Indians' legal status, then, derives from their recognized citizenship in a tribal nation, a status no other minority group can claim" (p. 2). However, as the outline of Indian Law in previous sections demonstrates, the Supreme Court historically and currently continues to impose legal narratives upon indigenous peoples. Federal Indian Law contradicts Indian views of sovereignty, yet Indians also face the contradiction that they engage this legal jurisprudence in order to protect their interests against a colonial system that perpetually attempts to eradicate them. In addition, many tribes look toward education to promote their values and worldviews through the creation and implementation of community-controlled schools (Manuelito 2005; Szasz 1974; Tippeconnic 2001). Like Indian law though, schooling is tied to the colonial system, and is therefore subject to its conceptual parameters (Senese 1991; Snyder-Joy 1994). Indian peoples, thus, are experts at navigating these contradictions and provide important models of anticolonialism.

As argued, citizenship, equality, and diversity narratives have become the mainstays of normative multiculturalism in education. In the previous section, I investigated how NMCE incorporates notions of citizenship, equality, and diversity that reproduce the jurisprudential view of these concepts. Furthermore, I offered a critical gaze toward the propensity of NMCE to fold native education issues into a standardized discourse of minority education. Then again, Supreme Court case history demonstrates that the concepts examined above, developed originally for the benefit of minorities, are constricted by that same Court. Like the critiques posed by Indian Law scholars concerning the volatility of tribal sovereignty in relation to "special rights" challenges, Civil Rights law has experienced the same challenges, particularly under the guise of reverse discrimination.

It is thus incumbent upon proponents of NMCE to join in anticolonial movements. NMCE advocates can begin with the work of Derrick Bell and other critical race theorists who, like Robert Williams and David Wilkins for indigenous peoples, articulate useful critiques of Civil Rights discourses (Bell 2004; Crenshaw et al. 1995; Williams 2005).

3.4 Conclusion: Interest Convergence and the Singularity Thesis: Rely on US Law at Your Own Peril

In this chapter I begin to unravel the embedded ideologies of colonialism, indeed the colonial blind ideologies and practices from Civil Rights law and Federal Indian Law prevalent in Normative Multicultural Education. To conclude, I turn to the work of two critical race theorists, who draw from their lived experiences as a black legal scholar and an indigenous legal scholar, to begin to shatter these colonial blind ideologies. Derrick Bell and Robert Williams have each turned critical perspectives to Civil Rights and Federal Indian Law, arriving at insights that provide powerful anti-colonial perspectives.

Derrick Bell's (1995a) interest convergence theory functions similarly to the critiques mentioned earlier by Goldberg (2002), Gould (2003), and Wilkins (1994) concerning the threat posed to tribal sovereignty by the populace. With regard to *Brown* and the Civil Rights cases, Bell (1995a) argues that on "a normative level … the notion of racial equality appears to be the proper basis on which *Brown* rests … yet the reality," according to Bell (1995a), is that "racial equality is not deemed legitimate by large segments of the American people, at least to the extent it threatens to impair the societal status of whites" (p. 22). In this way, dominant groups can challenge what they perceive to be threats to the colonial order, in the case of the United States, perceived white settler privilege (Calderón 2008). Bell (1995a) names this the "interest convergence dilemma," in which the "interest of blacks in achieving racial equality will be accommodated only when it converges with the interests of whites" (p. 22). The most recent Supreme Court decision of *Seattle* further limits the legacy of *Brown*, reminding us that racial minorities cannot depend on the courts to protect their interests.

For this reason, Derrick Bell (2004) urges civil rights leaders to reconsider their racial goals: "We need to examine what it was about our reliance on racial remedies that may have prevented us from recognizing that these legal rights could do little more than bring about the cessation of one form of discriminatory conduct that soon appeared in a more subtle though no less discriminatory form" (p. 187). Bell (2004) affirms that minority rights movements for equal justice that took place within the courts, simply served to legitimate the system. The law, Bell (2004) explains, functions as a tool to "induce both the dominant [settler society] and dominated classes [racial minorities and Indians] to accept the hierarchy" (p. 188). The law accomplishes this, Bell (2004) maintains, "by appearing to be universal and operating with a degree of independence by making it 'possible for other classes to use the system against itself … and force it to make good on its utopian promises'" (p. 188). For this reason, Bell (2004) makes the case that it is important not to confuse principles with tactics. While the principle of gaining equality of education is, according to Bell (2004), appropriate, the tactics employed can serve to reify the status quo and fail at a later date when the rights granted do not converge with the needs of the dominant classes (Bell 2004).

NMCE proponents endorse discourses and practices that affirm the status quo or the colonial project evidenced in Civil Rights law. Similarly, Federal Indian Law functions to maintain the hierarchy named by Bell (2004). While the principles of maintaining and protecting sovereignty are appropriate, the tactic of relying solely on federal courts to protect sovereignty threaten to diminish sovereignty when these rights do not converge with those of the dominant classes. In particular, the rights Indians are seeking from the courts are, according to Williams (2005) "much different from the types of minority rights that were and remain at the center for the continuing struggle for racial equality represented by cases like *Brown*"; and the rights Indians seek to protect, are much more prone to fail because the "unique types of autochthonous rights that tribal Indians want protected under US law … are inherently problematic for the dominant non-Indian society and its judges in a way that the more general types of minority individual rights" are not (p. xxxv). Rather than an interest convergence dilemma, Williams (2005) declares that Indians have a "singular" dilemma, or "singularity thesis" – based on the Indian desires to maintain a "measured separatism" (p. xxxv). It is difficult to convince Americans "that it is in their material interests" to recognize Indian self-rule, and support egalitarian configurations of racial equality (Williams 2005, p. 36).

It is difficult to translate this "singular dilemma" into educational practice because dominant education ideas and practices are produced within the Colonial Model of Education. This model of education, in turn, embodies the colonial ontologies I identify in Supreme Court jurisprudence. By subscribing to NMCE, borrowing from Bell (2004), educators reproduce ideologies that serve to protect white settler societies, appearing to advocate for communities of color by promoting equality and diversity as a means for inclusion, yet remain blind to endemic colonialism. Like the law, NMCE induces people to accept these colonial ontologies as proper and meritorious ideologies and values. Anticolonial practices in education force us to examine and make explicit the dominance of white settler ideologies, institutions, and practices.

Without a doubt, it is much harder to work toward true pluralism, which demands an anticolonial reconfiguration of current educational models. This demands a rejection of Western metaphysics, a move toward epistemological and ontological diversification, and the shattering of colonial blind ideologies and practices. In other words a diversity that truly embraces different ways of *seeing*, *being*, and *embodying* the world around us.

Notes

1. I define Western metaphysics as the set of assumptions and systems of knowledge derived from European traditions, their historical origins, and colonialism that form the foundations of education in the United States. Western metaphysics include universalism, linearity, historicism, humanism, dualism, and compartmentalization.
2. "Colonial blind" is a play on the term color-blind.
3. NMCE also cannot shed light on the complex realities of transnational communities.
4. I use the terms American Indians, Indians, indigenous, and native interchangeably.
5. For instance, early educational practices encouraged and institutionalized by the US government toward tribes were founded upon the assumptions that American Indians needed to be

civilized, which could be accomplished through conversion to Christianity (Lomawaima, 2001, p. 7). Initially, the US government paid religious groups to operate mission schools, and in 1879 began its own boarding schools (Hamme, 1995). The primary goals of boarding schools were to: "keep students apart from their parents for years at a time, teach the students Christianity, and punish them for speaking their Native languages" (Trujillo & Alston, 2005, p. 6) in order to assimilate to white society.
6. I define *colonial ontology* as a project that promotes a hierarchy of being in which white settler state citizenship is defined as the dominant form, and the racialized "minority" other is defined as the subordinate. This hierarchy of being is mediated by a number of corollary rights defining the parameters of access to this ontology (such as integration, diversity, and equity), and promoting settler dominance over indigenous groups (doctrine of discovery, federal supremacy, and limited sovereignty).
7. See note 6.
8. Indeed, African-Americans set the legal stage for battles that would influence other racialized groups. However, it is also important to point out that citizenship has been denied to Asian and Latino communities through different mechanisms under the guise of immigration. Immigration laws, policies, and the generally promoted state of xenophobia keep these groups from accessing the full rights of citizenship. For a more thorough treatment of this debate, see Johnson (2002) and Torres (1998).
9. The Civil Rights movement inspired a generation of native activists that utilized the courts in a similar manner to accomplish goals specific to native nations. Dumas (2005) describes: "In the early 1960s … a generation of Native American activists who were inspired by the civil rights movement began to mobilize their long-neglected treaty fishing rights, both in and out of court. Their direct action tactics culminated in the mid-1960s in a series of 'fish-ins' in which activists flouted state regulations, fishing at traditional off-reservation grounds in accord with their treaty rights. Meanwhile, the activists' tribal governments pursued fishing rights in court, filing a series of suits against Washington State's Departments of Game and Fisheries (the agencies that oversaw the state's wildlife resources). Judge Boldt's opinion in *United States v. Washington* (1974) which, in addition to the 50% allocation, invalidated Game's and Fisheries' regulations of off-reservation tribal fishing was thus a successful culmination of more than a decade of fishing-rights activism" (p. 739).
10. Fee land is a concept of modern law where an individual has absolute ownership of property.
11. Marxist orientations for example promote humanist and universal critiques of current relations, and do not provide promise for native views that are animist in nature, and maintain geographic–cosmological worldviews. For Native peoples, marxism leaves little room for tribal self-determination and the right to maintain separate and unique native cultural arrangements from the nation-state. I limit my arguments in this chapter to normative multicultural forms of educational discourse, but similar analysis can be made for critical theory perspectives.
12. There are exceptions to this, but for the sake of this chapter, I will focus on the majority trends in Indian country.

References

Atkinson Trading v. Shirley, 532 U.S. 645 (2001).
Banks, J. A. (1998). The lives and values of researchers: Implications for educating citizens in a multicultural society. *Educational Researcher, 27*(2), 4–17.
Banks, J. A. (2004). Multicultural education: Historical development, dimensions, and practice. In J. A. Banks and C. A. M. Banks (Eds.), *Handbook of research on multicultural education* (second ed.). San Francisco, CA: Wiley.
Banks, J. A., Cookson, P., Gay, G., Hawley, W. D., Irvine, J. J., Nieto, S., et al. (2001). *Diversity within unity: Essential principles for teaching and learning within a multicultural society*. Seattle, WA: Center for Multicultural Education, University of Washington.

Bell, D. A. (1995a). *Brown v. Board of education* and the interest convergence dilemma. In K. Crenshaw, N. Gotanda, G. Peller, and K. Thomas (Eds.), *Critical race theory: The key writings that formed the movement.* New York: The New Press.
Bell, D. A. (1995b). Racial realism. In N. G. Kimberly Crenshaw (Ed.), *Critical race theory: The key writings that formed the movement.* New York: The New Press.
Bell, D. A. (1995c). Serving two masters: Integration ideals and client interests in school desegregation litigation. In K. Crenshaw, N. Gotanda, G. Peller, and K. Thomas (Eds.), *Critical race theory: The key writings that formed the movement.* New York: The New Press.
Bell, D. A. (2004). *Silent covenants: Brown v. Board of education and the unfulfilled hopes for racial reform.* Oxford: Oxford University Press.
Brown v. Board of Education (I), 347 U.S. 483 (1954).
Brown v. Board of Education (II), 349 U.S. 294 (1955).
Cajete, G. (1994). *Look to the mountain: An ecology of indigenous education.* Skyland: Kivaki Press.
Calderón, D. (2008). Indigenous metaphysics: Challenging western knowledge organization in social studies curriculum. University of California, Los Angeles.
Champagne, D. (2005). Education, culture and nation building: Development of the tribal learning community and educational exchange. In D. Champagne and I. Abu-Saad (Eds.), *Indigenous and minority education: International perspectives on empowerment.* Beer-Shiva, Israel: Negev Center for Regional Development.
Champagne, D. (2007). Self-government's roots: Communities. *Indian Country Today, 2007,* January 19, 2007.
Crenshaw, K., Gotanda, N., Peller, G., and Thomas, K. (Eds.). (1995). *Critical race theory: The key writings that formed the movement.* New York: The New Press.
Cherokee Nation v. Georgia, 30 U.S. 1 (1831).
Deloria, V. (1992). *God is red: A native view of religion.* Golden, CO: Fulcrum.
Deloria, V. and Wildcat, D. (2001). *Power and place: Indian education in America.* Golden, CO: Fulcrum.
Dred Scott v. Sandford, 60 U.S. 393 (1857).
Dudas, J. R. (2005). In the name of equal rights: "Special" rights and the politics of resentment in post-civil rights America. *Law & Society Review, 39*(4), 723–758.
Gay, G. (2004). Curriculum theory and multicultural education. In J. A. Banks and C. A. M. Banks (Eds.), *Handbook of research on multicultural education.* San Francisco, CA: Wiley.
Goldberg, C. (2002). American Indians and "preferential" treatment. *UCLA Law Review, 49*(4), 1–47.
Gould, L. S. (2003). Tough love for tribes: Sovereignty after *Atkinson* and *Hicks. New England Law Review, 37*(3), 669–693.
Gratz v. Bollinger, 539 U.S. 244 (2003).
Grutter v. Bollinger, 539 U.S. 306 (2003).
Hamme, L. V. (1995). American Indian cultures and the classroom. *Journal of American Indian Education, 35*(2).
Ides, A., and May, C. N. (2001). *Constitutional law, individual rights: Examples and explanations* (second ed.). New York: Aspen Law and Business.
Johnson, K. R. (2002). Race and the immigration laws: The need for critical inquiry. In F. Vales, J. M. Culp, and A. P. Harris (Eds.), *Crossroads, directions, and a new critical race theory* (pp. 187–198). Philadelphia, PA: Temple University Press.
Johnson v. McIntosh, 21 U.S. 543 (1823).
Korematsu v. United States, 323 U.S. 214 (1944).
Lomawaima, K. T. (2001). The unnatural history of American Indian education. In K. G. Swisher and J. W. Tippeconnic (Eds.), *Next steps: Research and practice to advance Indian education* (second ed.). Charleston, WV: Clearinghouse on Rural Education and Small Schools.
Lomawaima, K. T. and McCarty, T. L. (2006). *To remain and Indian: Lessons in democracy from a century of Native American education* New York: Teachers College Press.
Manuelito, K. (2005). The role of education in American Indian self-determination: Lessons from the Ramah Navajo community schools. *Anthropology and Education Quarterly, 36*(1), 73–87.

McCarthy, C. (1994). Multicultural discourses and curriculum reform: A critical perspective. *Educational Theory, 44*(1), 81–98.
McClanahan v. Arizona State Tax Commission, 411 U.S. 164 (1973).
McLaren, P. (1994). White terror and oppositional agency: Towards a critical multiculturalism. In D. T. Goldberg (Ed.), *Multiculturalism: A critical reader*. Cambridge, MA: Blackwell.
McLaurin v. Oklahoma State Regents, 339 U.S. 637 (1950).
Merrion v. Jicarilla Apache Tribe, 455 U.S. 130 (1982).
Mertz, E. (1995). The uses of history: Language, ideology, and law in the United States and South Africa. In R. L. Abel (Ed.), *The law and society reader*. New York: New York University Press.
Montana v. United States, 450 U.S. 544 (1981).
Morton v. Mancari, 417 U.S. 535 (1974).
Moses, M. S., and Chang, M. J. (2006). Toward a deeper understanding of the diversity rationale. *Educational Researcher, 35*(1), 6–11.
Nevada v. Hicks, 533 U.S. 353 (2001).
Oliphant v. Suquamish Indian Tribe, 435 U.S. 191 (1978).
Parents Involved in Community Schools v. Seattle School District No. 1, 551 U.S. (2007).
Peller, G. (1995). Race-consciousness. In K. Crenshaw, N. Gotanda, G. Peller, and K. Thomas (Eds.), *Critical race theory: The key writings that formed the movement*. New York: The New Press.
Plessy v. Ferguson, 163 U.S. 537 (1896).
Regents of the University of California v. Bakke, 438 U.S. 265 (1978).
Rice v. Cayetano, 528 U.S. 495 (2000).
Santa Clara Pueblo v. Martinez, 436 U.S. 49 (1978).
Senese, G. (1991). *Self-determination and the social education of Native Americans*. New York: Praeger.
Snyder-Joy, Z. K. (1994). Self-determination in American Indian education: Educators' perspectives on grant, contract, and BIA-administered schools. *Journal of American Indian Education, 34*(1), 1–11.
Sweatt v. Painter, 339 U.S. 629 (1950).
Szasz, M. C. (1974). *Education and the American Indian: The road to self-determination since 1928*. Albuquerque: University of New Mexico Press.
Tippeconnic, J. W. (2001). Tribal control of American Indian education: Observations since the 1960s with implications for the future. In K. G. Swisher and J. W. Tippeconnic (Eds.), *Next steps: Research and practice to advance Indian education* (second ed.). Charleston, WV: Clearinghouse on Rural Education and Small Schools.
Torres, M. D. L. A. (1998). Transnational political and cultural identities: Crossing theoretical borders. In F. Bonilla, E. Melendez, R. Morales and M. d. l. A. Torres (Eds.), *Borderless borders: U.S. Latinos, Latin Americans, and the paradox of independence*. Philadelphia, PA: Temple University Press.
Trujillo, O. V. and Alston, D. A. (2005). *Report on the status of American Indians and Alaska Natives in education: Historical legacy to cultural empowerment*. Washington, DC: National Education Association of the United States.
Tsosie, R. (1994). Separate sovereigns, civil rights, and the sacred text: The legacy of justice Thurgood Marshall's Indian law jurisprudence. *Arizona State Law Journal, 26*, 495–584.
Willkins, D. E. (1994). The cloaking of justice: The Supreme Court's role in the application of western law to America' indigenous peoples. *Wicazo Sa Review: A Journal of Native American Studies, 10*(1), 1–13.
Willinsky, John. (1998). *Learning to Divide the world: Education at Empire's End*. Minneapolis: University of Minnesota press.
Willkins, D. E. (2002). Indian peoples are nations, not minorities. In *American Indian politics and the American political system* (pp. 41–62). Oxford: Rowman & Littlefield.
Williams, R. A. (1990). *The American Indian in western legal thought: The discourses of conquest*. New York: Oxford University Press.

Williams, R. A. (2005). *Like a loaded weapon: The Rehnquist court, Indian rights, and the legal history of racism in America*. Minneapolis, MN: University of Minnesota Press.

Woll, P. (2006). *American government: Readings and cases* (sixteenth ed.). New York: Pearson-Longman.

Worcester v. Georgia, 31 U.S. 515 (1832).

Appendix

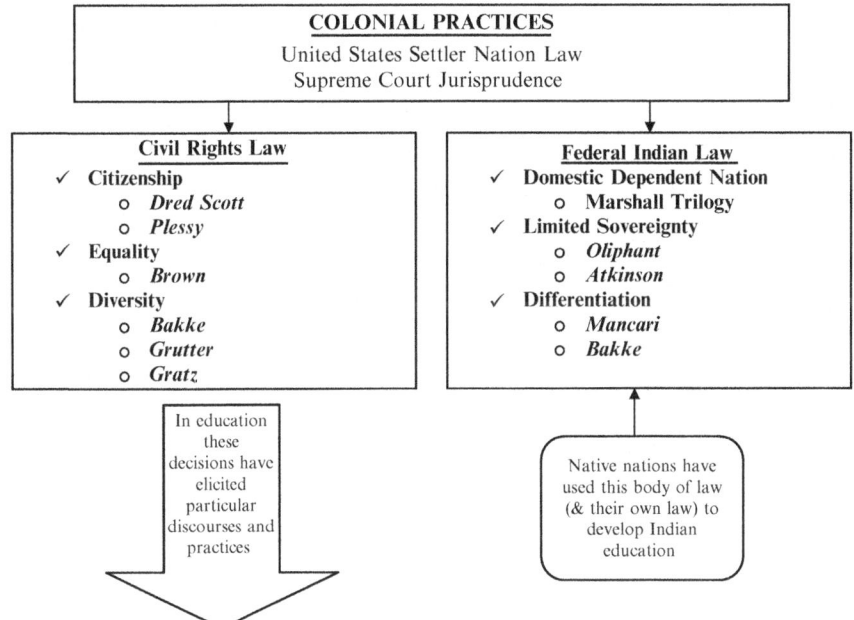

Case/Law	Year Decided	Page Number
Johnson v. McIntosh	1823	p. 15
Cherokee Nation v. Georgia	1831	p. 16
Worcester v. Georgia	1832	p. 16
Dred Scott v. Sanford	1857	p. 7
Fourteenth Amendment adopted	1868	p. 7
Louisiana Act	1890	p. 8
Plessy v. Ferguson	1896	p. 8
Korematsu v. United States	1944	p. 9
Sweatt v. Painter	1950	p. 10
McLaurin v. Oklahoma State Regents for Higher Education	1950	p. 10
Brown v. Board of Education of Topeka (I)(II)	1954, 1955	p. 9
Morton v Mancari	1974	p. 18
Regents of the University of California v. Bakke,	1978	p. 11
Santa Clara Pueblo v. Martinez	1978	p. 17
Oliphant v. Suquamish Indian Tribe	1978	p. 19
Montana v. United States	1981	p. 20
Merrion v. Jicarilla Apache Tribe	1982	p. 17
McClanahn v. Arizona State Tax Commission	1982	p. 17
Rice v. Cayetano	1999	p. 20
Nevada v. Hicks	2001	p. 20
Atkinson v. Shirley	2001	p. 20
Grutter v. Bollinger	2003	p. 12
Gratz v. Bollinger	2003	p. 12
Parents Involved in Community Schools v. Seattle School District No. 1	(2007)	p. 13

Chapter 4
Paulo Freire and the Politics of Postcolonialism

Henry A. Giroux

> Yet we have different privileges and different compensations for our positions in the field of power relations. My caution is against a form of theoretical tourism on the part of the first world critic, where the margin becomes a linguistic or critical vacation, a new poetics of the exotic. (Caren Kaplan 1987)

The work of Paulo Freire continues to exercise a strong influence on a variety of liberal and radical educators. In some quarters his name has become synonymous with the very concept and practice of critical pedagogy. Increasingly, Freire's work has become the standard reference for engaging in what is often referred to as teaching for critical thinking, dialogical pedagogy, or critical literacy. As Freire's work has passed from the origins of its production in Brazil, through Latin America and Africa to the hybrid borderlands of North America, it has been frequently appropriated by academics, adult educators, and others who inhabit the ideology of the West in ways that often reduce it to a pedagogical technique or method. Of course, the requisite descriptions generally invoke terms like "politically charged," "problem-posing," or the mandatory "education for critical consciousness" and often contradict the use of Freire's work as a revolutionary pedagogical practice.[1] But in such a context, these are terms that speak less to a political project constructed amidst concrete struggles than they do to the insipid and dreary demands for pedagogical recipes dressed up in the jargon of abstracted progressive labels. What has been increasingly lost in the North American and Western appropriation of Freire's work is the profound and radical nature of its theory and practice as an anticolonial and postcolonial discourse. More specifically, Freire's work is often appropriated and taught "without any consideration of imperialism and its cultural representation. This lacuna itself suggests the continuing ideological dissimulation of imperialism today" (Young 1990, p. 158). This suggests that Freire's work has been appropriated in ways that denude it of some of its most important political insights. Similarly, it testifies to how a politics of location works in the interest of privilege and power to cross-cultural, political, and textual borders so as to deny the specificity of the other and to reimpose the discourse and practice of colonial hegemony.

I want to argue that Paulo Freire's work must be read as a postcolonial text and that North Americans, in particular, must engage in a radical form of border crossing in order to reconstruct Freire's work in the specificity of its historical and political construction. At the same time, becoming a border crosser engaged in a productive dialogue with others means producing a space in which those dominant social relations, ideologies, and practices that erase the specificity of the voice of the other must be challenged and overcome.

4.1 Homelessness and the Border Intellectual

In order to understand Freire's work in terms of its historical and political importance, cultural workers have to become border crossers. This means that teachers and other intellectuals have to take leave of the cultural, theoretical, and ideological borders that enclose them within the safety of "those places and spaces we inherit and occupy, which frame our lives in very specific and concrete ways" (Borsa 1990, p. 36). Being a border crosser suggests that one has to reinvent traditions not within the discourse of submission, reverence, and repetition, but "as transformation and critique." That is, "[o]ne must construct one's discourse as difference in relation to that tradition and this implies at the same time continuities and discontinuities" (Laclau 1988, p. 12). At the same time, border crossing engages intellectual work not only in its specificity and partiality, but also in terms of the intellectual function itself as part of the discourse of invention and construction, rather than a discourse of recognition whose aim is reduced to revealing and transmitting universal truths. In this case, it is important to highlight intellectual work as being forged in the intersection of contingency and history arising not from the "exclusive hunting grounds of an elite [but] from all points of the social fabric" (Laclau 1988, p. 27).

This task becomes all the more difficult with Freire because the borders that define his work have shifted over time in ways that parallel his own exile and movement from Brazil to Chile, Mexico, the United States, Geneva, and back to Brazil. Freire's work not only draws heavily upon European discourses, but also upon the thought and language of theorists in Latin America, Africa, and North America. Freire's ongoing political project raises enormous difficulties for educators who situate Freire's work in the reified language of methodologies and in empty calls that enshrine the practical at the expense of the theoretical and political.

Freire is an exile for whom being home is often tantamount to being "homeless," and for whom his own identity and the identities of others are viewed as sites of struggle over the politics of representation, the exercise of power, and the function of social memory.[2] It is important to note that the concept of "home" being used here does not refer exclusively to those places in which one sleeps, eats, raises children, and sustains a certain level of comfort. For some, this particular notion of "home" is too mythic, especially for those who literally have no home in this sense; it also becomes a reification when it signifies a place of safety which excludes the lives, identities, and experiences of the other, that is, when it becomes synonymous with the cultural capital of white, middle-class subjects.

"Home," in the sense I am using it, refers to the cultural, social, and political boundaries that demarcate varying spaces of comfort, suffering, abuse, and security that define an individual's or group's location and positionality. To move away from "home" is to question in historical, semiotic, and structural terms how the boundaries and meanings of "home" are constructed in self-evident ways often outside of criticism. "Home" is about those cultural spaces and social formations which work hegemonically and as sites of resistance. In the first instance, "home" is safe by virtue of its repressive exclusions and hegemonic location of individuals and groups outside of history. In the second case, home becomes a form of "homelessness," a shifting site of identity, resistance, and opposition that enables conditions of self and social formation. JanMohammed captures this distinction quite lucidly:

> "Home" comes to be associated with "culture" as an environment, process, and hegemony that determine individuals through complicated mechanisms. Culture is productive of the necessary sense of belonging, of "home;" it attempts to suture ... collective and individual subjectivity. But culture is also divisive, producing boundaries that distinguish the collectivity and what lies outside it and that define hierarchic organizations within the collectivity. "Homelessness," on the other hand, is ... an enabling concept ... associated with ... the civil and political space that hegemony cannot suture, a space in which alternative acts and alternative intentions which are not yet articulated as a social institution or even project can survive. "Homelessness," then, is a situation wherein utopian potentiality can endure. (*Worldliness*, p. 27)

For Freire, the task of being an intellectual has always been forged within the trope of homelessness: between different zones of theoretical and cultural difference, and between the borders of non-European and European cultures. In effect, Freire is a border intellectual,[3] whose allegiance has not been to a specific class and culture as in Gramsci's notion of the organic intellectual; instead, Freire's writings embody a mode of discursive struggle and opposition that not only challenges the oppressive machinery of the state but is also sympathetic to the formation of new cultural subjects and movements engaged in the struggle over the modernist values of freedom, equality, and justice. In part, this explains Freire's interest for educators, feminists, and revolutionaries in Africa and Latin America.

As a border intellectual, Freire ruptures the relationship between individual identity and collective subjectivity. He makes visible a politics that links human suffering with a project of possibility, not as a static plunge into a textuality disembodied from human struggles, but as a politics of literacy forged in the political and material dislocations of regimes that exploit, oppress, expel, maim, and ruin human life. As a border intellectual, Freire occupies a terrain of "homelessness" in the postmodern sense that suggests there is little possibility of ideological and hegemonic closure, no relief from the incessant tensions and contradictions that inform one's own identity, ideological struggles, and project of possibility. It is this sense of "homelessness," this constant crossing over into terrains of otherness, that characterizes both Freire's life and work. It is as an exile; a border being, an intellectual posed between different cultural, epistemological, and spatial borders that Freire has undertaken to situate his own politics of location as a border crosser.

4.2 Freire as Border Crosser

It is to Freire's credit as a critical educator and cultural worker that he has always been extremely conscious about the intentions, goals, and effects of crossing borders, and how such movements offer the opportunity for new subject positions, identities, and social relations that can produce resistance to, and relief from, the structures of domination and oppression. While such an insight has continuously invested his work with a healthy "restlessness," it has not meant that Freire's work has developed unproblematically. For example, in his earlier work, Freire attempted to reconcile an emancipatory politics of literacy and a struggle over identity and difference with certain problematic elements of modernism. Freire's incessant attempts to construct a new language, produce new spaces of resistance, imagine new ends and opportunities to reach them were sometimes constrained in totalizing narratives and binarisms that de-emphasized the mutually contradictory and multiple characters of domination and struggle. In this sense, Freire's earlier reliance on emancipation as one and the same with class struggle sometimes erased how women were subjected differently to patriarchal structures; similarly, his call for members of the dominating groups to commit class suicide downplayed the complex, multiple, and contradictory nature of human subjectivity. Finally, Freire's reference to the "masses" or oppressed as being inscribed in a culture of silence appeared to be at odds with both the varied forms of domination these groups labored under and Freire's own belief in the diverse ways in which the oppressed struggle and manifest elements of practical and political agency. While it is crucial to acknowledge the theoretical and political brilliance that informed much of this work, it is also necessary to recognize that it bore slight traces of vanguardism. This is evident not only in the binarisms that inform *Pedagogy of the Oppressed* but also in *Pedagogy in Process: The Letters to Guinea-Bissau*, particularly in those sections in which Freire argues that the culture of the masses must develop on the basis of science and that emancipatory pedagogy must be aligned with the struggle for national reconstruction.

Without adequately addressing the contradictions these issues raise between the objectives of the state, the discourse of everyday life, and the potential for pedagogical violence being done in the name of political correctness, Freire's work is open to the charge made by some leftist theorists of being overly totalizing. But this can be read less as a reductive critique of Freire's work than as an indication of the need to subject it and all forms of social criticism to analyses that engage its strengths and limitations as part of a wider dialogue in the service of an emancipatory politics. The contradictions raised in Freire's work offer a number of questions that need to be addressed by critical educators about not only Freire's earlier work but also about their own. For instance, what happens when the language of the educator is not the same as that of the oppressed? How is it possible to be vigilant against taking up a notion of language, politics, and rationality that undermines recognizing one's own partiality and the voices and experiences of others? How does one explore the contradiction between validating certain forms of "correct" thinking and the pedagogical task of helping

4 Paulo Freire and the Politics of Postcolonialism

students assume rather than simply follow the dictates of authority, regardless of how radical the project informed by such authority. Of course, it cannot be forgotten that the strength of Freire's early discourse rests, in part, with its making visible not merely the ideological struggle against domination and colonialism but also the material substance of human suffering, pain, and imperialism. Forged in the heat of life-and-death struggles, Freire's recourse to binarisms such as the oppressed versus the oppressor, problem-solving versus problem-posing, science versus magic, raged bravely against dominant languages and configurations of power that refused to address their own politics by appealing to the imperatives of politeness, objectivity, and neutrality. Here Freire strides the boundary between modernist and anti-colonialist discourse; he struggles against colonialism, but in doing so he often reverses rather than ruptures its basic problematic. Benita Parry locates a similar problem in the work of Frantz Fanon: "What happens is that heterogeneity is repressed in the monolithic figures and stereotypes of colonialist representations. ... [But] the founding concepts of the problematic must be refused (Parry 1987, p. 28).

In his later work, particularly in his work with Donaldo Macedo (Freire 1985), in his numerous interviews, and in his talking books with authors such as Ira Shor (Shor and Freire 1987), Antonio Faundez (Freire and Faundez 1989), and Myles Horton (Horton and Freire 1990), Freire undertakes a form of social criticism and cultural politics that pushes against those boundaries that invoke the discourse of the unified, humanist subject, universal historical agents, and Enlightenment rationality. Refusing the privilege of home as a border intellectual situated in the shifting and ever-changing universe of struggle, Freire invokes and constructs elements of a social criticism that shares an affinity with emancipatory strands of postmodern discourse. That is, in his refusal of a transcendent ethics, epistemological foundationalism, and political teleology, he further develops a provisional ethical and political discourse subject to the play of history, culture, and power. As a border intellectual, he constantly reexamines and raises questions about what kind of borders are being crossed and revisited; what kind of identities are being remade and refigured within new historical, social, and political borderlands; and what effects such crossings have for redefining pedagogical practice. For Freire, pedagogy is seen as a cultural practice and politics that takes place not only in schools but in all cultural spheres. In this instance, all cultural work is pedagogical, and cultural workers inhabit a number of sites that include but are not limited to schools. Most recently in a dialogue with Antonio Faundez, Freire talks about his own self-formation as an exile and border crosser. He writes:

> It was by travelling all over the world, it was by travelling through Africa, it was by travelling through Asia, through Australia and New Zealand, and through the islands of the South Pacific, it was by travelling through the whole of Latin America, the Caribbean, North America and Europe – it was by passing through all these different parts of the world as an exile that I came to understand my own country better. It was by seeing it from a distance, it was by standing back from it, that I came to understand myself better. It was by being confronted with another self that I discovered more easily my own identity. And thus I overcame the risk which exiles sometimes run of being too remote in their work as intellectuals from the most real, most concrete experiences, and of being somewhat lost, and

even somewhat contented, because they are lost in a game of words, what I usually rather humorously call "specializing in the ballet of concepts." (1989, p. 13)

It is here that we get further indications of some of the principles that inform Freire as a revolutionary. It is in this work and his work with Donaldo Macedo, Ira Shor, and others that we see traces, images, and representations of a political project inextricably linked to Freire's own self-formation. It is here that Freire is at his most prescient in unraveling and dismantling ideologies and structures of domination as they emerge in his confrontation with the ongoing exigencies of daily life as manifested differently in the tensions, suffering, and hope between the diverse margins and centers of power that have come to characterize a postmodern/postcolonial world.

Reading Freire's work for the last 15 years has drawn me closer to Adorno's insight that "[i]t is part of morality not to be at home in one's home" (quoted in *Reflections* by Said 1990, p. 365). Adorno was also an exile, raging against the horror and evil of another era, but he was also insistent that it was the role of intellectuals, in part, to challenge those places bounded by terror, exploitation, and human suffering. He also called for intellectuals to refuse and transgress those systems of standardization, commodification, and administration pressed into the service of an ideology and language of "home" that occupied or were complicitous with oppressive centers of power. Freire differs from Adorno in that there is a more profound sense of rupture, transgression, and hope, intellectually and politically, in his work. This is evident in his call for educators, social critics, and cultural workers to fashion a notion of politics and pedagogy outside of established disciplinary borders; outside of the division between high and popular culture; outside of "stable notions of self and identity ... based on exclusion and secured by terror" (Martin and Mohanty 1986, p. 197); outside of homogeneous public spheres; and outside of boundaries that separate desire from rationality, body from mind.

Of course, this is not to suggest that intellectuals have to go into exile to take up Freire's work, but it does suggest that in becoming border crossers it is not uncommon for many of them to engage his work as an act of bad faith. Refusing to negotiate or deconstruct the borders that define their own politics of location, they have little sense of moving into an "imagined space," a positionality from which they can unsettle, disrupt, and "illuminate that which is no longer home-like, heimlich, about one's home" (Becker 1991, p. 1). From the comforting perspective of the colonizing gaze, such theorists often appropriate Freire's work without engaging its historical specificity and ongoing political project. The gaze in this case becomes self-serving and self-referential, its principles shaped by technical and methodological considerations. Its perspective, in spite of itself, is largely "panoptic and thus dominating" (JanMohamed, *Worldliness*, p. 10). To be sure, such intellectuals cross borders less as exiles than as colonialists. Hence, they often refuse to hold up to critical scrutiny their own complicity in producing and maintaining specific injustices, practices, and forms of oppression that deeply inscribe the legacy and heritage of colonialism. Edward Said captures the tension between exile and critic, home and "homelessness" in his comment on Adorno, though it is just as applicable to Paulo Freire:

To follow Adorno is to stand away from "home" in order to look at it with the exile's detachment. For there is considerable merit in the practice of noting the discrepancies between various concepts and ideas and what they actually produce. We take home and language for granted; they become nature and their underlying assumptions recede into dogma and orthodoxy. The exile knows that in a secular and contingent world, homes are always provisional. Borders and barriers, which enclose us within the safety of familiar territory can also become prisons, and are often defended beyond reason or necessity. Exiles cross borders, break barriers of thought and experience. (1990, p. 365)

Of course, intellectuals from the First World, especially white academics, run the risk of acting in bad faith when they appropriate the work of a Third World intellectual such as Freire without "mapping the politics of their forays into other cultures," theoretical discourses, and historical experiences (JanMohamed, *Worldliness*, p. 3). It is truly disconcerting that First World educators rarely articulate the politics and privileges of their own location, in this case, so at the very least to be self-conscious about not repeating the type of appropriations that inform the legacy of what Said (1979) calls "orientialist" scholarship (orientalism).

4.3 Freire and Postcolonial Discourse

I want to conclude by raising some issues regarding what it might mean for cultural workers to resist the recuperation of Freire's work as an academic commodity, a recipe for all times and places. Similarly, I want to offer some broad considerations for reinventing the radicality of Freire's work within the emergence of a postcolonial discourse informed by what Cornel West terms the "decolonization of the Third World," and characterized by "the exercise of ... agency and the [production of] new ... subjectivities and identities put forward by those persons who had been degraded, devalued, hunted, and harassed, exploited and oppressed by the European maritime empires (West 1991, p. 4). The challenge presented by Freire and other postcolonial critics offers new theoretical possibilities to address the authority and discourses of those practices wedded to the legacy of a colonialism that either directly construct, or are implicated in, social relations that keep privilege and oppression alive as active constituting forces of daily life within the centers and margins of power.

Postcolonial discourses have made clear that the old legacies of the political left, center, and right can no longer be so easily defined. Indeed, postcolonial critics have gone further and provided important theoretical insights into how such discourses either actively construct colonial relations or are implicated in their construction. From this perspective, Robert Young argues that postcolonialism is a dislocating discourse that raises theoretical questions regarding how dominant and radical theories "have themselves been implicated in the long history of European colonialism – and, above all, the extent to which [they] continue to determine both the institutional conditions of knowledge as well as the terms of contemporary institutional practices – practices which extend beyond the limits of the academic institution" (Young 1990, p. viii). This is especially true for many of the theorists in a variety of social movements who have taken up the language of difference and a concern for the politics of the other. In many instances, theorists within these new social movements have addressed political and pedagogical issues through the construction of binary oppositions that not only contain traces of racism and theoretical vanguardism but also fall into the trap of simply reversing the old colonial legacy and problematic of oppressed versus oppressor. In doing so, they have often unwittingly imitated the colonial model of erasing the complexity, complicity, diverse agents, and multiple situations that constitute the enclaves of colonial/hegemonic discourse and practice.[4]

Postcolonial discourses have both extended and moved beyond the parameters of this debate in a number of ways. First, postcolonial critics have argued that the history and politics of difference are often informed by a legacy of colonialism that warrants analyzing the exclusions and repressions that allow specific forms of privilege to remain unacknowledged in the language of Western educators and cultural workers. At stake here is the task of demystifying and deconstructing forms of privilege that benefit maleness, whiteness, and property as well as those conditions that have disabled others to speak in places where those who are privileged by virtue of the legacy of colonial power assume authority and the conditions for human agency. This suggests, as Gayatri Spivak has pointed out, that more is at stake than problematizing discourse. More importantly, educators and cultural workers must be engaged in "the unlearning of one's own privilege. So that, not only does one become able to listen to that other constituency, but one learns to speak in such a way that one will be taken seriously by that other constituency" (Spivak 1990, p. 42). In this instance, postcolonial discourse extends the radical implications of difference and location by making such concepts attentive to providing the grounds for forms of self-representation and collective knowledge in which the subject and object of European culture are problematized.[5]

Second, postcolonial discourse rewrites the relationship between the margin and the center by deconstructing the colonialist and imperialist ideologies that structure Western knowledge, texts, and social practices. In this case, there is an attempt to demonstrate how European culture and colonialism "are deeply implicated in each other" (Young 1990, p. 119). This suggests more than rewriting or recovering the repressed stories and social memories of the other; it means understanding and rendering visible how Western knowledge is encased in historical and institutional structures that both privilege and exclude particular readings, particular voices, certain aesthetics, forms of authority, specific representations, and modes of sociality. The West and otherness relate not as polarities or binarisms in postcolonial discourse but in ways in which both are complicitous and resistant, victim and accomplice. In this instance, criticism of the dominating other returns as a form of self-criticism. Linda Hutcheon captures the importance of this issue with her question: "How do we construct a discourse which displaces the effects of the colonizing gaze while we are still under its influence?" (Hutcheon 1990, p. 176).

While it cannot be forgotten that the legacy of colonialism has meant large-scale death and destruction as well as cultural imperialism for the other, the other is not merely the opposite of Western colonialism, nor is the West a homogeneous trope of imperialism. This suggests a third rupture provided by postcolonial discourses. The current concern with the "death of the subject" cannot be confused with the necessity of affirming the complex and contradictory character of human agency. Postcolonial discourse reminds us that it is ideologically convenient and politically suspect for Western intellectuals to talk about the disappearance of the speaking subject from within institutions of privilege and power. This is not to suggest that postcolonial theorists accept the humanist notion of the subject as a unified and static identity. On the contrary, postcolonial discourse agrees that the speaking subject must be decentered, but this does not mean that all notions of human agency and social change must be dismissed. Understood in these terms, the postmodernist notion of the subject must be accepted and modified in order to extend rather than erase the possibility for creating the enabling conditions for human agency. At the very least, this would mean coming to understand the strengths and limits of practical reason, the importance of affective investments, the discourse of ethics as a resource for social vision, and the availability of multiple discourses and cultural resources that provide the very grounds and necessity for agency.[6]

Of course, while the burden of engaging these postcolonial concerns must be taken up by those who appropriate Freire's work, it is also necessary for Freire to be more specific about the politics of his own location and what the emerging discourses of postmodernism and postcolonialism mean for self-reflectively engaging both his own work and his current location as an intellectual aligned with the state (Brazil). If Freire has the right to draw upon his own experiences, how do these get reinvented so as to prevent their incorporation by First World theorists within colonialist rather than decolonizing terms and practices? But in raising that question, I want to emphasize that what makes Freire's work important is that it does not stand still. It is not a text for but against cultural monumentalism, one that offers itself up to different readings, audiences, and contexts. Moreover, Freire's work has to be read in its totality to gain a sense of how it has engaged the postcolonial age. Freire's work cannot be separated from either its history or its author, but it also cannot be reduced to the specificity of intentions or historical location.

Maybe the power and forcefulness of Freire's works are to be found in the tension, poetry, and politics that make it a project for border crossers, those who read history as a way of reclaiming power and identity by rewriting the space and practice of cultural and political resistance. Freire's work represents a textual borderland where poetry slips into politics, and solidarity becomes a song for the present begun in the past while waiting to be heard in the future.

Notes

1. See Stygall (1989) for an excellent analysis of this problem among Freire's followers.
2. My use of the terms "exile" and "homelessness" have been deeply influenced by essays by Becker, JanMohamed ("Worldliness"), Said, Martin and Mohanty, and Kaplan. See also selected essays in bell hooks (1989, 1990).

3. I have taken this term from JanMohamed, "Worldliness."
4. For an excellent discussion of these issues as they specifically relate to postcolonial theory, see Parry (1987), JanMohamed (1983), Spivak (1990), Young (1990), and Bhabha (1990). The ways in which binary oppositions can trap a particular author into the most essentialist arguments can be seen in a recent work by Patti Lather (1991). What is so unusual about this text is that its call for openness, partiality, and multiple perspectives is badly undermined by the binarisms which structure around a simple gendered relation of truth to illusion.
5. This position is explored in Tiffin (1987, 1988).
6. I explore this issue in *Border Crossings* (Giroux 2005).

Reference

Becker, C. (1991). Imaginative Geography. *School of the Art Institute of Chicago*. Unpublished paper.
Bhabha, H.K. (ed.). (1990). *Nation and Narration*. New York: Routledge.
Borsa, J. (1990). Towards a Politics of Location: Rethinking Marginality. *Canadian Women Studies*, 11, 36–39.
Freire, P. (1985). *The Politics of Education: Culture, Power, and Liberation*. Translated by Donaldo Macedo. South Hadley, MA: Bergin.
Freire, P. and Faundez, A. (1989). *Learning to Question: A Pedagogy of Liberation*. New York: Continuum.
Giroux, H.A. (2005). *Border Crossings: Cultural Workers and the Politics of Education*, 2nd edition. New York: Routledge.
hooks, b. (1989). *Talking Back: Thinking Feminist, Thinking Black*. Boston, MA: South End.
hooks, b. (1990). *Yearning: Race and Gender in the Cultural Marketplace*. Boston, MA: South End.
Horton, M. and Freire, P. (1990). *We Make the Road by Walking: Conversations on Education and Social Change*. Edited by Bell, B., Gaventa, J., and Peters. J. Philadelphia, PA: Temple UP.
Hutcheon, L. (1990). Circling the Downspout of Empire. In Adam, I. and Tiffin, H. (eds.), *Past the Last Post*. Calgary, Canada: University of Calgary Press.
JanMohamed, A.R. (Unpublished). *Worldliness-Without-World, Homelessness-as-Home: Toward a Definition of Border Intellectual*. University of California, Berkeley, CA. Unpublished paper.
Kaplan, C. (1987). Deterritorializations: The Rewriting of Home and Exile in Western Feminist Discourse. *Cultural Critique*, 6, 187–198.
Laclau, E. (1988). Building a New Left: An Interview with Ernesto Laclau. *Strategies* 1, 10–28.
Lather, P. (1991). *Getting Smart: Feminist Research and Pedagogy Within the Postmodern*. New York: Routledge.
Martin, B. and Mohanty, C.T. (1986). Feminist Politics: What's Home Got to Do with It? In de Lauretis, T. (ed.), *Feminist Studies/Critical Studies*. Bloomington, IA: Indiana University Press.
Parry, B. (1987). Problems in Current Theories of Colonial Discourse. *The Oxford Literary Review*, 9, 27–58.
Said, E.W. (1979). *Orientalism*. New York: Vantage.
Said, E.W. (1990). Reflections on Exile. In Ferguson, R., Gever, M., Minh-ha, T.T., and West, C. (eds.), *Out There: Marginalization and Contemporary Cultures*. New York: New Museum of Contemporary Art and MIT Press.
Shor, I. and Freire, P. (1987). *A Pedagogy for Liberation: Dialogues on Transforming Education*. South Hadley, MA: Bergen.
Spivak, G.C. (1990). *The Post-Colonial Critic: Interviews, Strategies, Dialogues*. Edited by Sarah Harasym. New York: Routledge.

Stygall, G. (1989). Teaching Freire in North America. *Journal of Teaching Writing*, 8, 113–125.
Tiffin, H. (1987). Post-Colonial Literatures and Counter-Discourse. *Kunapipi*, 9(3), 17–34.
Tiffin, H. (1988). Post-Colonialism, Post-Modernism, and the Rehabilitation of Post-Colonial History. *Journal of Commonwealth Literature*, 23(1), pp. 169–181.
Young, R. (1990). *White Mythologies: Writing History and the West*. New York: Routledge.
West, C. (1991). Decentering Europe: A Memorial Lecture for James Snead. *Critical Quarterly*, 33, 1–19.

Chapter 5
Walking Out of Colonialism One Classroom at a Time: Student Walkouts and Colonial/Modern Disciplinarity in El Paso, Texas

Antonio Reyes López

Q: Why is there so much structure in the American educational system?
A: Cause they want to control you. Structure is Powa [sic] and they want you to stay in the boundaries of their powerfulness and your powerlessness (Yapundzhyan, 2007).[1]

> KRS-ONE
> Welcome to El Paso, Mexico
> Poster Held During Walkouts

5.1 Introduction

On the morning of March 31, 2006, thousands of high school and middle school students walked out of their schools and filled the streets of El Paso, Texas. Holding signs and protesting in both Spanish and English, the students marched excitedly through the city, stopping traffic on their way to the San Jacinto central plaza in downtown El Paso. For many students, some of whom walked from schools more than 20 miles away, the walkouts were the opportunity to join the immigrant-rights marches organized to influence congressional debates over House Bill 4437.[2] Despite threats from teachers and administrators, students left their schools on this final day of the 4-day walkouts to demonstrate solidarity with friends and family members who negotiate the difficulties and fears of living without papers in the United States.[3] One student explained: "This is about my grandmother who came, who worked, who raised us but who has no papers. Now they want to make her a felon" (Fonseca-Olivas 2006). Though some students found the series of marches the occasion to meet with friends or miss assignments and classes, the student activists who participated in the walkouts were an inspirational reminder that many young people are highly political actors that recognize the boundaries of their powerlessness.

In this chapter, I draw on the ideas of disciplinarity, hegemony, and coloniality/modernity to explain the significance of the student walkouts in El Paso, Texas. These concepts provide the analytical tools to challenge linear narratives of progress and explain how oppressive groups maintain power in colonial/modern social formations. Unlike most local debates over the walkouts that centered on ethnicity, nationalism, or immigration reform, I argue that the student walkouts in El Paso unveiled the persistence of racial power and coloniality/modernity in the city. To demonstrate how the marches exposed coloniality/modernity in El Paso, I first comparatively examine the techniques of disciplinary power used by Spanish missionaries, Indian boarding schools, and Americanization efforts in El Paso, and outline the discursive regime that silences US colonialism in the region. Turning to the events of the student walkouts in El Paso, I explain that youth activists forced many El Pasoan's to express an anxiety over the loss of social control in the city. Their racialized discourses and coercive actions intended to contain student dissent revealed the persistence of coloniality in El Paso and the role of schools as disciplinary institutions in the region. As such, the marches were remarkable acts of anticolonial resistance.

5.2 Colonial/Modern Disciplinarity in the US–Mexico Borderlands

During the series of walkouts, several students described their schools as authoritarian institutions where instructors failed to teach them about issues important to their community. One student organizer from Austin high school explained:

> At the protest I learned more about Cesar Chavez. At school they hardly teach us anything about him. They hadn't taught us anything about the HR4437 law at school either. That's what I don't like about the system. They don't prepare you for the real world. They don't teach us about our leaders, our culture, our roots. They only teach us what they want, how to obey the government.[4]

Social histories of US–Mexico borderland communities support these sentiments by revealing that indigenous and Mexican youth were targets of Spanish and US colonial projects that sought to discipline their loyalty. As the principal directors of the Spanish colonial project in northern Mexico, Catholic missionaries established power in indigenous communities by converting native children to Christianity. A number of historical studies explain that indigenous children were removed from their parents and communities as infants, baptized, and brought up under missionary guidance. These children were eventually appointed as community leaders and positioned strategically as decision-makers by the missionaries (Hackle 1997). In a discussion of the conversion strategies of Franciscan missionaries in New Mexico historian Ramón Guttiérrez (1991) explains the divisive intentions of Catholic missionaries. Guttiérrez notes:

> The Pueblo youth were the image of Godly innocence to the Franciscans. Snatched from the devil through baptism, their sexual purity still intact, these juveniles, they hoped, would become the saviors of society. The friars knew that if they could turn sons against their fathers and simultaneously win the youth's loyalties by convincing them that the paternity the padres offered was of greater value, a formidable cadre with which to extirpate idolatry and propagate the faith would have been forged. (p. 75)

Guttiérrez's description of conversion practices in New Mexico is consistent with the research of other borderland communities that discuss gendered and racialized forms of colonial disciplinarity in the borderlands.[5]

Several scholars also use a gender analysis to study colonial projects in the region and explain that gender roles, sexual practices, and marriage customs were critical to social control (Castañeda 1993; Alonso 1995; Martin 1996; Bouvier 2001). According to the historian Antonia Castañeda (1993):

> A key element in the missionaries program of conversion to Christianity included the restructuring of relations between the sexes to reflect gender stratification and corollary values and structures of the patriarchal family; subservience of women to men, monogamy, marriage without divorce, and a severely repressive code of sexual norms. (p. 29)

To achieve the goal of reversing indigenous gender relations, space was organized within the missions to seclude young indigenous women, to prevent children from communicating with their parents, and to train young native women to fulfill domestic duties (Sánchez 1995; Bouvier 2001; Hackle 2005). The body was also a focal point of mission disciplinarity. By confining young women, missionaries sought to control the sexual practices and reproductive patterns of native peoples. Resistance to these measures, and the sexual advances of missionaries, could bring whippings, mutilation, and even death (Guttiérrez 1991; Castañeda 1993). Though indigenous communities resisted missionization in a variety of ways, those that voluntarily or involuntarily entered the missions confronted a colonial space of disciplinarity that produced generational and gender divisions in native communities through the cultural transformation of children. These techniques of disciplinary power continued to be used during the US occupation of the region and were critical to the consolidation of white supremacy in the late nineteenth century.

Euro-American settler colonists in the US–Mexico borderlands also first viewed people and nonelite Mexican populations as savage and racially inferior. Like the Spanish missionaries, they also used gender differences to racialize populations, and targeted indigenous and Mexican youth for cultural transformation (Deutsch 1987; González 1999; Chávez-Garcia 2004). The most profound example of the coercive cultural transformation of colonized youth in the borderlands is the Indian boarding schools that emerged during the 1870s. In the decades that followed, thousands of indigenous children were forcibly removed from their parents and enrolled in off-reservation and reservation boarding schools. Many were transported to schools hundreds of miles away from their communities to prevent contact with parents, or escape. The boarding schools functioned as a space of colonial/modern disciplinarity as Euro-American teachers inculcated colonial notions of "civilization" and policed indigenous cultural practices (Stoler 2001).

Within the boarding school colonialist classroom the body occupied a central role in the racialization and disciplining of native children. The disciplinary function of the boarding school and focus on the body in the classroom are summarized by the historian Pablo Mitchell (2005). He explains:

> [T]he education of Indian children at United States Indian schools was a critical space of embodiment and racialization. This racialization project, directed at Indian children and their broader Indian communities, centered on Anglo assertions of the supposed inferiority

of Indian culture, and the corresponding superiority of Anglo culture, and depended on bodily comportment. Anglo teachers and administrators emphasized both sexual contagions (miscegenation, adultery, fornication) and more general bodily pollutions and incoherences (language and speech, hair length, clothing, alcohol consumption, dancing, use of medicine, student's comportment in and out of the classroom) as typical of Indian culture. (pp. 27–28)

Mitchell documents how the imposition of "proper" gender roles, the English language, hygiene, and "American" moral standards reflected colonial understandings of modernity, prevailing ideas of race, and the missionary attitude carried by Euro-American teachers into the region.

5.3 The Colonialist Classroom in El Paso

Children of Mexican descent in El Paso were also targeted by the US colonial project and were subjected to traumatic experiences of coercive cultural transformation.[6] In south El Paso, the segregated section of the city, Americanization projects were enthusiastically pursued by Euro-American teachers following World War I (García 1981; Ruiz 1998; Ramírez 2000). Americanization projects were so prominent in south El Paso during this era that Dr. P. W. Horn (1924), president of the West Texas Technological College wrote to the El Paso Herald Post on September 5, 1924:

> El Paso schools are doing some of the finest Americanization work of the nation. Thousands of Spanish-American children are taken into the public schools, taught to speak English and to think in the American way. I know of no greater piece of work done anywhere and I want to congratulate El Paso's schools. (p. 15)

Horn's favorable evaluation of nation-formation projects demonstrates that Euro-American teachers were central agents in ending the "ethnic isolation" and "cultural backwardness" of Mexicans in south El Paso.

Oral testimonies reveal that as in the boarding schools, proper hygiene, English-only mandates, the imposition of traditional gender roles, and rituals of loyalty and patriotism to the United States characterized the "education" students received. In a 1976 oral history, Ramona González (1976), remembered that at Lincoln elementary school, "we weren't allowed to speak Spanish, because we would get punished. They said that we wouldn't learn English if we talked Spanish." She also recalled an incident on Mexican Independence Day that reveals the will of Euro-American teachers to culturally transform students but also conveys a sense of resistance among ethnic Mexican children in south El Paso during the interwar years. As a joke, González and her classmates asked their principal Miss Stansfield if they could sing songs in the recreation hall of the school. Instead of singing in English they began to sing the Mexican national anthem. González remembered that when Miss Stanfield found out what they were singing, she immediately demanded that "[a]ll you children stand up and sing 'My Country Tis of Thee.'" Her memory of this event captures the way that Euro-American educators countered the resistance of youth in segregated south El Paso with nation-formation projects.

Others also remembered that Euro-American teachers in El Paso were committed to creating "good Americans" out of children of Mexican descent. Hector Bencomo (1975) thought back in a 1975 interview to one occasion when he was slapped by a teacher for not understanding English. According to Bencomo, there was "a lot of resentment on the part of teachers for speaking Spanish." Likewise, Estela Vega (1977), mentioned that there were no Mexican teachers and no cultural events that promoted anything Mexican at Beall school, where she attended.

Oral testimonies and critical social histories in borderland communities highlight that disciplining Mexican and indigenous youth was central to the advancement of Spanish and US colonial projects in the borderlands. Working to produce ideal citizens, or citizen subjects, loyal to the colonial state,[7] both Spanish and Euro-American colonial projects aimed to train colonized children to adhere to colonial power relations. This history of colonialism was not lost to many of the student activists. On Cesar Chávez Day and the last day of the marches, students held signs that exclaimed "We Didn't Cross the Border the Border Crossed Us," and "Stop Making Me Feel Illegal in My Native Land." Through the historical memory of conquest and coloniality in the region these students challenged the silencing of colonial power relations in the city. In doing so they directly confronted a powerful discursive regime that apologizes for US colonialism in the region.

5.4 Historical Memory and US Colonialism

Despite the publication of numerous well-researched social histories of the US–Mexico borderlands that challenge the narrative of American westward expansion, a popular and scholarly discursive regime continues to silence the historical and current impact of coloniality in the region. In the "Politics of Disidentification and Recuperation," historian Deena González (1999) comments on the silencing of US coloniality. She notes:

> The language of domination and takeover pervades the American west today, but it also marked the attitudes and reflections of Euro-American sojourners a century ago, and ignoring it can be as much of a barrier to thoughtful analysis as the mountains and canyons were to westering pioneers and conquerors. (p. 117)

Likewise, theorist and historian Emma Pérez (1999) criticizes Chicana/Chicano historians that also reproduce hegemonic understandings of history in their writings. She explains:

> To learn history, we categorize time linearly, and map regions geographically. Historians assign names to epochs and regions that reflect spatio-temporal characteristics: The Trans-Mississippi West, the frontier, the Renaissance, the Progressive Era, the Great Depression, the sixties. Within these categoric spaces, we continue to conceptualize history without challenging how such discursive sites have been assigned and by whom. … Chicano/a historiography has been circumscribed by the traditional historical imagination. This means that even the most radical Chicano/a historiographies are influenced by the very colonial imaginary against which they rebel. The colonial imaginary still determines many of our efforts to write history in the United States. (pp. 4–5)

González and Pérez articulate how colonial/modern temporal understandings of progress, and spatial constructions of the region derived from the colonial gaze continue to distort theoretical and methodological frameworks in borderlands and Chicano history.

Discourses of US benevolent imperialism are also used by writers to silence the historical and contemporary impact of coloniality. Myths of benevolent rule are buttressed by the idea that the United States was not a traditional colonial power but a benevolent ruler that spread democracy and civilization, freed native inhabitants from despotic rule, and put the land to productive use (Lafeber 1963; Acuña 1972; Pérez 1984; González 1999; Jacobsen 2000). For example, narratives of the "bloodless" conquest of New Mexico and the welcoming of Euro-American colonizers by ethnic Mexican communities are exemplary of hegemonic national history (González 2000, pp. 3–4). Combined with popular "Western" representations of the US–Mexico borderlands and "the border," scholarly writings function through a variety of ways to naturalize hegemonic interpretations of US and Western history (Ortíz-González 2004). In this respect, research in borderland communities confirms, in the words of political scientist Claire Jean Kim (2003), that "most scholars are not independent observers of racial conflict as much as they are active contributors to and borrowers from dominant racial discourses that circulate among the academy, officialdom and the mainstream media" (p. 4). It is exactly this powerful discursive regime that was disrupted by the student walkouts that took place between March 27 and March 31, 2006.

5.5 Walking Out of Colonialism and the Strategies of Containment

Signs held by the students that pronounced "Welcome to El Paso, Mexico," "We didn't Cross the Border the Border Crossed Us," "Stop Making Me Feel Illegal in My Native Land," "Bush, Go Back to Gringolandia," and "Contra Los Gueros Razistas" exemplify the discursive struggle waged during the walkouts. Denouncing whites as racists and the construction of another wall as a reflection of racist attitudes towards Mexicans, the students questioned the hypocrisy of American exceptionalism and liberal discourses of color blindness. One student proclaimed, "I don't think that it's fair that the government is doing this. They say this is the land of the free and that's why we're fighting in Iraq. But here we're fighting against our own people" (Acosta 2006). Clearly, the student's outrage at HR4437 was not only a call for immigration reform, as many denounced the racialized criminalization of US–Mexico border crossers.

One female student from Irvin High School explained: "This is more than just pride. They want to make people like us who immigrated to the US criminals. That's not fair" (Acosta 2006). Another student activist was more direct stating, "It's irrational. They worked to take down the Berlin Wall and now they are working to build a wall here" (Gilot 2006a). A student from Ysleta High School echoed her counterparts saying, "[t]he wall they want to build is a disgrace to all of us … immigrants should not be considered criminals since we are an important base of the economy"(Meritz 2006). Ignoring the significance of these remarks news reports during the marches dismissed the student's grievances with racial injustices in the city and the colonialist classroom.

Except for a few writers from alternative media sources who applauded the actions of the student activists, the majority of public reaction to the walkouts expressed in the city's media sources was highly critical of the students.[9] On each of the days of the marches mainstream media coverage represented the walkouts as chaotic, dangerous, and costly to schools. Students were portrayed as politically passive, unaware of the immigration legislation they were protesting, and only wanting to get out of their classes.[10] The words of one commentary exemplify the discourse reproduced in many of the local news reports:

> These kids don't even know what the bill is for or all about, hek they don't even know what they're about for that sake. If the people who participated in this walk out or their parents for that matter are so proud of Mexico they should go live there. We have to protect our country "The United States of America," for those that have forgotten where we live.[11]

By misrepresenting the ethnically diverse student activists as disloyal Mexicans, and deeming the student protests as illegitimate, irrational, and unpatriotic, negative commentaries on the walkouts ignored the frustrations students clearly voiced about the educational system in El Paso and racial power in the city. One *El Paso Times* newspaper reporter, for example, clearly overlooked students' charges of racism noting that, "[w]hile many students cited race as the ultimate reason they had chosen to skip class in protest, a few focused their attention on specific reform proposals – as well as their effects on American society."[12] Implied in this statement is that only the few students who identified HR4437 as their reason for walking-out were legitimate actors while the majority of those that spoke of racism were "playing the race card" and confusing a very straightforward debate about American society.

What is instructive about the widespread public reaction to the student walkouts that focused on student views of HR4437, or their waving of Mexican flags, is that they functioned as a strategy of containment that silenced the anticolonial critiques of El Paso power relations. In other words, the attention paid to seemingly national issues of immigration reform and citizenship rendered the local critiques of racial power voiced by many of the students mute.[13] For example, one letter to the editor entitled "This is America" exclaimed:

> I am an American of Mexican descent. My father was born American and my mother immigrated from Mexico. The key word here, folks, is "legally." … For all of you protesting out there waiving the Mexican flag, please go back to Mexico. Waive it proudly over there. (Limon 2006)

Another Euro-American business owner explained:

> I heard a loud ruckus outside of my business, and when I peered out the front door, I saw a mob of kids who were chanting "Viva Mexico!" I personally find that offensive. … I don't have a problem with immigration – I don't even have a view on the issue – but I am a proud American so I went outside and held out the American flag. (Torres 2006)

Euro-American mayor John Cook chimed in on the controversy over the student's use of the Mexican flag. Mayor Cook wondered: "When I see young people wrapped in a Mexican flag I wonder which side of the border they are really from" (Renteria 2006). These comments can be read in disparate ways. On the one hand, they can be read as nativist interpretations of the marches that viewed the Mexican flag waiving of the student activists as a threat to the nation. On the other hand, we can read these nativist reactions, which contain no reference to the antiracist local critiques of the student activists, as serving to obfuscate the coloniality of power in El Paso. Interpreted in this way, the calls for national loyalty should be conceptualized as a strategy of containment that worked to neutralize the anticolonial local critique voiced by the students.

Public commentary, reactions by local political officials, and representations of the walkouts by the mainstream media also revealed an intense anxiety over the ability of students to breach a central space of colonial/modern disciplinarity by leaving their schools. Participant descriptions reveal how the walkouts exposed El Paso's middle schools and high schools as coercive spaces of colonial/modern disciplinarity and how many educators viewed the walkouts as a major threat and coercively prevented students from leaving their schools. Student accounts of the walkouts captured in Romo's (2006) "New Voices of Dissent" vividly describe how the walkouts triggered profound reactions by teachers, administrators, and the police and as such deserve to be cited at length. According to one student leader at Austin High School,

> I first found out about the anti-immigration law and the student walkouts by reading about them on the internet. When 700 Jefferson students staged their first walkout (On Monday, March 27) it blew me away. Two days later we were all in class when we heard a whole bunch of noise. There were about 250 students from Chapin and Irvin outside of our school calling us to join their protest. I got out of class but there were teachers and security guards in the halls and the gates were locked. About five of us tried to climb over the fence anyway but the police stopped us. The next day, about 30 of us walked-out. We climbed out through the windows before they could stop us. ... We passed by El Paso High and it was on lockdown. The students were shouting "Let us go!" but the security guards wouldn't let them out. Only three managed to escape and join us. The police rode their motorcycles up to the students to push us back. I and another guy got hit in the legs by a motorcycle. We marched to El Paso Del Norte school and about ten people from there joined us. Then to Cathedral. No one joined us from Cathedral. The students locked arms, made a chain and began shouting "Wetbacks! You don't belong here." Most of them were gringos and a few hypocritical Mexicans who've forgotten where they came from. Just because they have money they think they're better than us. The teachers were watching the whole thing. Many of them were laughing. When we got to the Santa Fe Bridge the U.S Customs agents started yelling at us to "Go back to Mexico" and calling us "wetbacks." One migra got off his car and started yelling all kinds of racist stuff and the students by then were angry and started throwing water bottles at him.

Another student leader form Sam Bowie High School in South El Paso recalled similar experiences during the days of the walkouts:

> The first day of the walkouts, on Monday March 27th about 700 people from Jeff and Burgess were outside the gates shouting "We Want Bowie!" The teachers cautioned us not to leave class. The administration, the security guards and the principal were outside the school grounds making sure nobody left. I was kind of depressed and angry that they didn't let us join them. But then the leaders from Austin called us to plan the walkout on Friday.

They showed up early to lock the gates open so that the administration couldn't lock us in. The cops had spent the night at Bowie to try to stop us, but that morning we walked out.

Finally, the description of the walkouts by a Spanish language teacher at Austin High School is particularly insightful as she reveals the administrative perspective of the walkouts and their efforts to penalize student activists and sympathizers:

> [The principal] instructed me not to let my students download any information about the HR4437 bill or talk about immigration in any way. I told him that I was on chapter three of my Spanish for Native Speakers, Sendas Literarias, that deals with the discrimination immigrants face in this country. He instructed me to teach something else that week. ... The administration tried to do everything they could to prevent the students from walking-out but they couldn't. The next morning, Channel 1 – the school channel – showed clips of the walk-outs in Los Angeles, Austin and Dallas and the students went wild. The administration quickly got on the intercom instructing the teachers to turn off the television. But by then it was too late. The teachers were instructed to form a huge chain and surround the school. But the students managed to get out anyway. One student started running out of the classroom and a substitute teacher slammed the door in her face. The student showed up the next day with a large bruise on her face. Another girl student was pulled back roughly by another teacher when she tried to climb out of the window. ... The school administration has done everything to repress the students who are protesting against the immigration law. Many of them were threatened with not being allowed to graduate. Truancy officers showed up at their homes. One student on parole who walked out was threatened with jail. There's a lot of fear in the school. ... The principal of Austin ... sent me a letter saying that I am under investigation for disrupting school activities. The letter says that I have been accused of urging my students to walk-out of school to protest the immigration law. If I'm found guilty I will be charged with a Class C Misdemeanor.

Participant accounts of the walkouts reveal a range of techniques of power aimed at preventing student resistance and restoring social control. The reactions of educators, administrators, and police officers unveil El Paso's schools as coercive spaces of disciplinarity and convey an anxious desire to restore a disciplinary order that was disrupted by the decision of students to leave their schools. More importantly, negative public reactions to the walkouts that silenced the anticolonial critique of the students, and the coercive actions of teachers, administrators, police, and border patrol agents worked in tandem to manage youth dissent.

5.6 Conclusion

As I walked among the thousands of high school and middle school students towards the San Jacinto Plaza in downtown El Paso on Cesar Chavéz Day I found inspiration in the powerful expressions of disapproval to HR4437 voiced by the students. Indeed, I shared their anger and frustration that an immigration policy would further criminalize US–Mexico border crossers and intensify the militarization of the US–Mexico border. As I looked at the signs the students held, listened to their protest slogans, and talked with angry student activists, it became obvious that the walkouts were much more than a response to HR4437. Many students were also tired of the racism and exploitation that Mexican immigrants continue to confront in El Paso and in the United States. Others took the opportunity to call the American Dream hypocrisy with one student in particular holding a sign that read "American Nightmare." After the protestors listened to a variety of speakers discuss the significance of HR4437 and the legacy of Cesar Chávez many grew angry that their schools failed to instruct them in such important issues. Recognizing that their schools were, in the words of KRS-ONE, "boundaries of their powerfulness and your powerlessness," the students took pride in leaving their schools. When asked why the students felt it necessary to walkout, one student observed: "They notice us when we walk and they can read our signs" (Gilot 2006b). Unfortunately, many dismissed the student walkouts as irrational and failed to acknowledge the voices of the youth in El Paso. Their reactions exemplify the coercive, discursive, and spatial techniques of colonial/modern disciplinarity that work so effectively to control dissent in US–Mexico border communities.

Notes

1. "Ani vs. KRS-ONE," www.daveyd.com
2. Also known as the Border Protection, Antiterrorism, and Illegal Immigration Control Act of 2005, House Bill 4437 included numerous measures that would further criminalize undocumented US–Mexico border crossers as felons and also result in the construction of a 700-mile fence. Many of the students who participated in the student walkouts in March later protested outside the Chamizal National Memorial in El Paso during a conference on immigration and border security in which James Sensenbrenner, the Republican Representative sponsor of HR4437, was present.
3. I thank David Romo for his excellent interviews with a number of the student leaders. I am especially grateful to the students who participated in the El Paso marches that I encountered informally and in my classes. They openly shared their experiences in El Paso's public and private schools with me and also taught me a great deal about the dehumanizing processes that undocumented border crossers and their families endure. I have decided not to use the names of student activists as some remain in school and could face repercussions for their participation in the walkouts.
4. "New Voices of Dissent," www.newspapertree.com
5. It is important to note that El Paso was part of New Mexico at this time. In 1659 Misión Nuestra Señora de Guadalupe de la Villa de El Paso del Norte y de los Mansos was established by Fray García de San Francisco, a Franciscan missionary previously assigned to northern New Mexico. Located on the south side of the Rio Bravo, El Paso remained a part of New Mexico until Mexican Independence in 1821 when it was included in the state of Chihuahua. El Paso del Norte was renamed Ciudad Juárez in 1888.
6. Efforts to culturally transform Mexican youth symbolize how the racial hierarchy imposed by the United States after the War of 1848 categorized most nonelite ethnic Mexicans as "Indians" racially. For a discussion of the racial positioning of ethnic Mexicans in the region see, Martha Menchaca, (August, 1993) Chicano Indianism: A historical account of racial repression in the United States. *American Ethnologist* 20(3), 583–603.
7. I borrow the concept of citizen-subject from Nayan Shah. In *Contagious Divides* (2001). Shah explains:
    The concept of citizen-subject combines the political status of liberal democracy with the social practices of modern disciplinary institutions. ... The objective of liberal governance is to

cultivate citizen-subjects who can govern themselves. ... Liberal strategies of governing have emphasized ruling at a distance – that is, granting authority to professionals who are licensed and empowered by the state to create norms of individual conduct, make judgements and administer policies. (pp. 7–8)
9. The online coverage by *The Newspaper Tree* and the Spanish language newspaper *El Diario* provided favorable representations of the student walkouts. The *El Paso Times* included some favorable reaction to the marches but those were consistently juxtaposed with negative reactions and representations of the marches. It must be said that many university students, faculty members, community activists, and family members joined the students on all of the days of the walkouts.
10. During the days of the marches the *El Paso Times* ran headlines such as "Students Marches Keep Law Enforcement Busy," "Teens Walk Farther, Get a Little Rowdy," and "Demonstrations Spread Police Force Thin." Televised news reports continuously ran interviews with students who were not as conversant on the issues of HR4437, focused on one incident when a few students were arrested for drinking alcohol, and interviewed drivers frustrated by the traffic caused by the marches.
11. "ABC-7 Listens: Your Comments on the Student Walkout," March 31, 2006, http://www.kvia.com/global/story.asp?s=4708610&ClientType=Printable. This commentary is taken from an online message board setup by the local ABC affiliate KVIA. The televised news report asked the public for their reactions to the walkouts which could be sent to the station via the message board and read in a later telecast. Of the 129 responses posted to the message board the overwhelming majority were negative reactions to the marches and many of those included blatantly racist remarks. I chose to include this specific message because it is exemplary of the discourse reproduced in many of the televised news reports on all of the mainstream English-language television networks. It is by no means the harshest reaction posted to the message board which included numerous representations of the students as "wetbacks," "punks," "illegal aliens," "lawbreakers," "shameful Hispanics," "gang members," "foreigners," "childish," and "disgraceful." It is important to note that many of these postings were by self-identified "embarrassed Hispanics" and "ashamed Mexican Americans."
12. Ibid.
13. I follow Claire Jean Kim's definition of racial power in *Bitter Fruit* as "the systemic tendency of the racial status quo to reproduce itself" (p. 9).

References

Acosta, G. R. (March 31, 2006). Teens walk farther get a little farther. *El Paso Times* sec. 2A.
Acuña, R. (1972). *Occupied America: the Chicano's struggle towards liberation*. New York: Harper Collins.
Alonso, A. M. (1995). *Thread of blood: colonialism, revolution and gender on Mexico's northern frontier*. Tucson, AZ: University of Arizona Press.
Bencomo, H. (August 7, 1975). Personal Interview. Institute of Oral History, University of Texas at El Paso, No. 171.
Bouvier, V. M. (2001). *Women and the conquest of California, 1542–1840*. Tucson, AZ: University of Arizona Press.
Castañeda, A. (1993). Sexual violence in the politics and policies of conquest: Amerindian women and the Spanish conquest of Alta California. In Adela de la Torre and Beatríz M. Pesquera (Eds.) *Building with our hands: new directions in Chicana studies*, (pp. 15–33). Berkeley, CA: University of California Press.
Chávez-García, M. (2004) *Negotiating conquest: gender and power in California, 1770s to 1880s*. Tucson, AZ: University of Arizona Press.

Deutsch, S. (1987). *No separate refuge: culture, class, and gender on an Anglo-Hispanic frontier in the American southwest, 1880–1940*. Oxford/New York: Oxford University Press.
Fonseca-Olivas T. (March 31, 2006). Elected officials call student action effective. *El Paso Times* sec. 12A.
García, M. (1981). *Desert immigrants: the Mexicans of El Paso, 1880–1920*. New Haven, CT/London: Yale University Press.
Gilot, L. (March 29, 2006a). As poll shows immigration outcry, EP has protests planned. *El Paso Times* sec. 2A.
Gilot, L. (April 1, 2006b). 'Real Thing' teaches teens how to protest. *El Paso Times* sec. 2A.
González, D. (1999). *Refusing the favor: the Spanish-Mexican women of Santa Fe 1820–1880*. Oxford/New York: Oxford University Press.
González, R. (May – July 1976). Personal interview. Institute of Oral History, University of Texas at El Paso, No. 334.
Guttierréz, R. (1991). *When Jesus came the corn mothers went away: marriage, sexuality, and power in New Mexico, 1500–1846*. Stanford, CA: Stanford University Press.
Hackle, S. (1997). The staff of leadership: Indian authority in the missions of Alta California. *The William and Mary Quarterly* 54(3), 347–376.
Hackle, S. (2005). *Children of coyote, missionaries of Saint Francis: Indian-Spanish relations in colonial California, 1769–1850*. Chapel Hill, NC: University of North Carolina.
Horn, P. W. (September 5, 1924). Little interviews and letters to the herald. *El Paso Herald Post*, p. 15.
Jacobsen, M. F. (2000). *Barbarian virtues: the United States encounters foreign peoples at home and abroad, 1876–1917*. New York: Hill and Wang.
Kim C. J. (2003). *Bitter fruit: the politics of black-Korean conflict in New York city*. New Haven, CT/London: Yale University Press.
Lafeber, W. (1963). *The new empire: an interpretation of American expansion, 1860–1898*. Ithaca, NY: Cornell University Press.
Limon, B. (March 31, 2006). This is America. *El Paso Times* sec. 8B.
Martin, C. E. (1996). *Governance and society in colonial Mexico: Chihuahua in the eighteenth century*. Stanford, CA: Stanford University Press.
Meritz, D. (March 31, 2006). 300 students from Del Valle, Ysleta run into resistance. *El Paso Times* sec. 13A.
Mitchell, P. (2005). *Coyote nation: sexuality, race, and conquest in modernizing New Mexico*. Chicago, IL/London: University of Chicago Press.
Ortíz-González, V. M. (2004). *El Paso: local frontiers at a global crossroads*. Minneapolis, MN: University of Minnesota Press.
Pérez, E. (1999). *The decolonial imaginary: writing Chicanas into history*. Bloomington, Indianapolis, IN: University of Indiana Press.
Peréz, L. (1984). *Cuba between empires,1878–1902*. Pittsburgh, PA: University of Pittsburgh Press.
Ramírez, M. B. (2000). El pasoans: life and society in Mexican El Paso, 1920–1945. Dissertation, University of Mississippi.
Renteria, R. (March 31, 2006). Mexican flag gets negative attention of protest critics. *El Paso Times* sec. 12A.
Romo, D. (May 15, 2006). New voices of dissent: walkouts and other protests. *Newspaper Tree*, http://newspapertree.com/features/926-new-voices-of-dissent-walkouts-and-other-protests.
Ruiz, V. (1998). *From out the shadows: Mexican women in twentieth-century America*. New York/Oxford: Oxford University Press.
Sánchez, R. (1995). *Telling identities: the Californio testimonies*. Minneapolis, MN: University of Minnesota Press.
Shah, N. (2001). *Contagious divides: epidemics and race in San Francisco's Chinatown*. Berkeley/Los Angeles, CA/London: University of California Press.
Stoler, A. L. (2001). Tense and tender ties: the politics of comparison in North American history and (post) colonial studies. *Journal of American Studies* 88(3), 829–865.
Torres, Z. (March 31, 2006). Passers-by ridicule 200 Canutillo students. *El Paso Times* sec. 12A.

Vega, E. D. (November 18, 1977). Personal interview. Institute of Oral History, University of Texas at El Paso, No. 308.

Yapundzhyan, A. (December 10, 2007). Ani vs. KRS-ONE: the lost interview. *Davey D's Hip Hop Blog*. http://blog.myspace.com/index.cfm?fuseaction = blog.view&friendID = 15116190&blogID = 336748662.

Chapter 6
Indigenous Peoples and Black People in Canada: Settlers or Allies?

Zainab Amadahy and Bonita Lawrence

6.1 Introduction

This chapter has been created as the starting point of what will hopefully become an ongoing dialogue, between Black peoples and Native people in Canada, about relationships to this land, as Indigenous peoples and those who have experienced diaspora and settlement here. Its purpose is to clarify what the bases of relationships entail, in the interests of a deeper solidarity. This is particularly important in view of the ongoing struggles relating to the presence of Black citizens within Indigenous nations that have developed in different Native communities in the United States, struggles which represent only one site in which Native–Black relations are taking place globally.[1] This chapter will, hopefully, offer some points of connection, and above all, be read with a good heart.

It is important, in focusing on this subject, to consider specificity of context – that Canadian policies toward Indigenous peoples and toward diasporic racialized communities have been distinct from those in the United States. At the same time, we are mindful that claims to Canadian specificity and difference from American contexts are primary ways in which Canadians deny the prevalence of anti-Black racism and the virulence of colonial relations toward Indigenous peoples in this country. However, the legacies of Indigenous genocide and slavery – how deeply both processes have shaped relations between Black people and Native people in the United States – have had a different shape in Canada, for a number of reasons. We therefore begin by clarifying certain Canadian contexts. Later in the chapter, however, we will also refer to how American discourses of both antiracism and Indigeneity have penetrated and influenced Black–Native relations north of the border.

In this chapter, we also wish to break through and deconstruct postures of innocence – the ways in which both Black and Indigenous people may insist that the primacy of their own suffering and powerlessness is so unique and all-encompassing that it erases even the possibility of their maintaining relationships of oppression relative to another group (Razack 2004, pp. 10, 14). It is particularly important to talk about postures of innocence when referencing Black–Native relations because both Black and Indigenous peoples have experienced unique global levels of devastation as races. Genocide in the Americas[2] represents the largest holocaust that the world has ever known, which destroyed almost one quarter of the earth's population within 150 years (Todorov 1984, p. 133), and in the ensuring 400 years successfully changed the face of two entire continents; today's survivors have descended from the 2–5% of Indigenous peoples who survived (Churchill 1995, p. 41). Moreover, the gold and silver claimed during the initial sixteenth-century genocidal plunder provided Europe with the finance capital necessary to mount the expeditions to the Far East, and to build the ships that made global mercantilism possible, particularly the triangular trade of slaves and goods between Africa, the Americas, and England.[3] The Atlantic slave trade, meanwhile, was unique in its global scale; the manner in which it harnessed chattel slavery to industrial production, thereby bankrolling the industrial revolution; the global relations of imperialism it shaped; and the diasporic Black realities it created.

Perhaps most important, however, is the fact that these unique experiences *still* shape the lives of Native and Black peoples today in particular ways. Indigenous peoples are still being targeted for physical and cultural destruction and are widely assumed to have already "vanished". Erased from history as viable nations, their lands therefore continue to be seen as "there for the taking," either as ongoing sources of resource theft or as real estate for the world's wealthy migrants. In this context, Indigenous peoples globally are still relentlessly being pushed toward extinction, as peoples. Meanwhile, Black diasporic peoples today continue to be uniquely racialized by a discourse created through slavery, whereby everything from standards of beauty to notions of criminality hinge on degrees of phenotypic blackness. Furthermore, globally, the legacy of 5 centuries of slavery, and the rape of Africa that it enabled means that the Black-led nations of the world, while nominally recognized as nation-states, are still the poorest and most disenfranchised of nation-states.

Because of the specificity and intensity of historical and contemporary disempowerment that both Black and Indigenous peoples in the Americas have experienced, claims to innocence for both groups are particularly potent and can be (and in some cases are being) used to cancel out any form of criticism of one group's behaviour toward another group. In this chapter we wish to both acknowledge and avoid this posturing of innocence, by exploring the grounded realities that may help to clarify relations. As part of this process, it is important to consider what we mean in this context when we refer to "Indigenous" peoples and "settlers".

The claims of Indigenous peoples have been hotly contested globally, and perhaps this is reflected in the confusion of definitions that arises when the term "Indigenous peoples" is used. Because of this we have chosen the definition used by the United Nations Working Group on Indigenous Peoples:

> Indigenous communities, peoples and nations are those which, having a historical continuity with pre-invasion and pre-colonial societies that developed on their territories, consider themselves distinct from other sectors of societies now prevailing in those territories or parts of them. They form at present non-dominant sectors of society and are determined to preserve, develop and transmit to future generations their ancestral territories, and their ethnic

identity, as the basis of their continued existence as peoples, in accordance with their own cultural patterns, social institutions, and legal systems. (Maaka and Fleras 2005, pp. 30–31)

While the term "Indigenous" has been contested and challenged, it is perhaps telling that there is little attention paid to the definition of a "settler." The term is intrinsically linked to the complex relations of the post-Columbian White colonialist project globally. As Linda Tuhiwai Smith clarifies, however, settlers are only one part of an intricate apparatus of colonial control that must be in place for settlers to be able to truly usurp the land:

> [A]fter figures such as Columbus and Cook had long departed, there came a vast array of military personnel, imperial administrators, priests, explorers, missionaries, colonial officials, artists, entrepreneurs and settlers, who cut a devastating swathe, and left a permanent wound on the societies and communities who occupied the land named and claimed under imperialism. (Smith 1999, p. 21)

From this perspective, for groups of peoples to be forcibly transplanted from their own lands and enslaved on other peoples' lands – as Africans were in the Americas – does not make the enslaved peoples true "settlers." Even in situations in Canada where Black people, after slavery, attempted settlement as free peoples, the process has been fraught with dispossession and denial of access to land. The reality then is that Black peoples have not been quintessential "settlers" in the White supremacist usage of the word; nevertheless, they have, as free people, been involved in some form of settlement process. What seems more important than the semantics about whether or not individuals should be called settlers is the question of the relationships that Black "settlers" have, by virtue of their marginality, with those whose lands have been taken, and what relationships they wish to develop, *at present*, with Indigenous peoples. In writing this chapter, we will look both at what relationships have been envisioned and what possibilities exist. We will begin, however, by starting with the specificities of our own locations.

6.2 Our Different Places in the Story...

6.2.1 Zainab's Location

I was born in New York City, to a White mother and a Black Indian father. Measuring Indigenous blood quantum on my father's side of the family has always been an inexact science. Measuring African blood quantum was never an issue since we have always grudgingly accepted the one-drop rule (one drop of African blood makes you Black/African-American) imposed by the US context in which we lived.

Suffice it to say that both my father's parents were mixed race with African, Indigenous, and European ancestry and it is unlikely that anyone from my great-grandparents downward knew the exact percentages of any of it. Being enslaved can do that to a family. My father's parents died when he was young so his paternal Cherokee grandmother raised him and his siblings in a small Black community outside of Staunton, Virginia. She was over 100 years old when she passed on and I was 6 when I last saw her.

My great grandmother had been enslaved since birth alongside Blacks, Indians, and Black Indians on the Reynolds tobacco plantation and had experienced emancipation as a child. She was aware of her Cherokee heritage but not connected to any Indigenous community, as was the case with most of the Black Indians in Staunton – and there were many. She raised my dad as a Baptist, although various gems of what I now recognize as Indigenous wisdom permeated her parenting, whether from the African or Cherokee traditions, I couldn't say.

I, however, was raised in an urban environment at the height of both the Civil Rights and American Indian movements. I spent several summers at my great-grandmother's home outside of Staunton, not the most isolated location, but rural enough for a city girl to gain some land-based teachings.

While I was raised to be aware and proud of my Indigenous heritage, it was never presented to me as my primary cultural identity. My parents encouraged me to embrace my multiracial background; a task that would have left me friendless in a terribly segregated society then governed by Jim Crow laws and an official policy of genocide toward Indigenous peoples. Indeed, what I learned of Cherokee and Indigenous peoples generally came first in books – liberal and sympathetic yet written from a Eurocentric worldview.

In the meantime I lived an urban lifestyle in segregated Black or Hispanic neighborhoods of New York City and Philadelphia. Most Black and Hispanic people I knew acknowledged Indigenous heritage, but it never formed the core of their cultural identities, clearly a testament to the effectiveness of the genocide project perpetrated in the Americas. In fact, when I was growing up, identifying as "Black Indian" was often seen as an attempt to claim some sort of light-skinned privilege. With the Black Power movement at its height, I identified simply as Black in my high school years. Though when it came up I never denied Indigenous ancestry and felt pride in it. However, I was never presented with an opportunity to embrace the culture or connect with an Indigenous community or develop a relationship with the land.

Today I really wonder how Indigenous I can claim to be given that I am clanless, my Indigenous family history – African and Cherokee – has been lost in the colonization process and I do not have any familial relationship with the land. I have come to understand that this self-doubt is common to urban Indigenous people whether with White or African ancestry. It is a consequence of genocide.

Though raised in a Protestant tradition, my mother converted to send me to Catholic school because the academic standard was higher than in New York City's public schools. She also regarded Catholic schools as "safer," though I have never before or since experienced anti-Black racism as vicious as I did in the predominantly White Catholic school from students, teachers, and parents alike.

I was in the public system by the time I went into high school, being bussed from a Black community outside Philly in an effort to integrate into a formerly all-White suburban school. Let us just say it was another traumatizing yet character-building experience. It was in this phase of my life that I made a commitment to political activism, mostly to the civil rights/Black power movement.

These movements shaped my framework of analysis when it came to studying Indigenous history and culture in my later years. My familiarity with the American Indian Movement (AIM) was a long-distance one (fund-raising and information-sharing) and I cannot say that I thoroughly understood the fundamental struggle. Even if I did, I would have still been positioned as an outsider to it. I was generally supportive but in terms of concrete activism there was just nothing going on where I lived that provided me with the opportunity to become seriously involved in the parallel processes of decolonizing my worldview as I engaged in activism. In university I was politically active in solidarity work with Central American struggles (a manifestation of Indigenous resistance to the genocide there) and the South African antiapartheid movement.

In 1980s Toronto, I went through 6 years of university without encountering a single student who identified as Indigenous. Genocide will do that to a people. There were no Aboriginal campus groups and I tended to identify and hang out with other racialized students. It was in this context that I was introduced to marxism and developed an antiracist, feminist, class analysis. This academic, Eurocentric framework shaped my early understanding of Indigenous struggles. I came to work within "The Left," though I was never entirely comfortable with it, but lacking a connection to anyone or anything Indigenous, I was unable to develop an analysis of something that just didn't "feel" right.

It wasn't until my mid-thirties that I put concerted effort into absorbing oral histories, songs, and teachings of Elders. Thus, I was finally able to put a name to my political framework of analysis: "Indigenism." I have been active in Toronto's Aboriginal community ever since. Initially I was resistant to identifying as a "Cherokee," despite pressure from many of my friends and colleagues to do so. I compromised with the term "Black Cherokee," which most people accept, even though there is no common understanding of the term.

As an Indigenist activist I cofounded the Coalition in Support of Indigenous Sovereignty in 2003 and currently work with an Indigenous caucus. The Indigenous community in Toronto, as most urban Aboriginal communities, is comprised of alienated, traumatized, and disconnected mixed-race people from a variety of backgrounds and experiences, all of which have left them struggling to come to terms with their cultural identities. It is a community in which I fit quite nicely. The fact that I am not dark-skinned, as Black Indians go, probably helps me fit in even better, since I have heard from other mixed-race people that the more "Black" you look, the less acceptance you find.

Identifying as Black has been even more problematic, as most Black people who will talk to me about the topic don't see me as Black, in terms of my appearance, my mannerisms, or my politics. Certainly I am no longer connected to any "Black" community and my Indigenist worldview makes it difficult to work out of any other framework.

Today, though more experienced and, theoretically, wiser I struggle as much with identity issues, personal and political, as I did when I was 15. My Indigenous worldview makes it difficult for me to interact as an intimate in urban Black communities. My lack of connection to a landed Indigenous community makes it difficult for me to find a complete sense of belonging in Indigenous circles. I constantly grapple with the implicit responsibilities of having Indigenous ancestry from both Turtle Island (North America) and Africa, as well as coming to an understanding of Indigenism through intellectual processes, oral teachings, and occasional ceremony rather than lived experience on the land.

In general, I see my journey as one of many Indigenous stories lived out in the context of colonialism and genocide. There are similar and not so similar stories out there but I see them all as parts of the Indigenous experience on Turtle Island. I share the concerns of many in Black, Indigenous, and Black Indian communities and am personally invested in seeing those communities come to terms with their own indigeneity as we struggle against colonialism, genocide, racism, and other aspects of globalization as it manifests in the twenty-first century. If there is one truth I have come to with age, it is that Indigenism has great potential to heal ourselves, our communities, and the land. It is for this reason that I decided to coauthor this chapter.

6.2.2 Bonita's Location

I come to this chapter from a history of "marginal Indianness." My ancestors on my mother's side were New Brunswick mixed-bloods, Mi'kmaq on one side, Acadian on the other. Our ancestry is unclear – while my grandmother appears to have connections to Lennox Island, she was born in the 1870s, shortly after the reserve was created, so it is unlikely she ever was a band member. By the time my grandmother was born, Mi'kmaq population collapse had reached the point where there were less than 1,500 left (out of a precontact population of 300,000), and a silence around Mi'kmaq identity, for those who were off reserve, became intense, particularly during my mother's generation so that most of her siblings – landless, brown-skinned, predominantly French-speaking, and silent about their identities – were scattered away from the Maritimes in search of work, mostly in the United States. The men worked in factories, the women were cleaning ladies; one uncle, hopelessly alcoholic, remained in New Brunswick and spent most of his adult life in prison. In the postwar proliferation of "new" identities, they mostly married immigrant "ethnic" Whites, so that among my generation, Indianness became a precarious identity. The older aunts and uncles still understood Mi'kmaq, but the younger siblings, like my mother, only occasionally heard Mi'kmaq and did not understand it; they spoke only French (and later, English). And all of them maintained a contradictory stance toward their own identities: too Native to be White, too White to be "really" Indian; if pressed they said they were Acadian.

When my mother married an Englishman and moved to Montreal, we entered into the fiction of being a British family, entailing a complete suppression of my mother's identity until I was 7, when the marriage ended. With my father gone, my mother experienced a defiant reclaiming of being dark-skinned; the darker we got in the sun each summer, the more pleased with us she was. Successive waves of

Indigenous militancy, in the 1970s, 1980s, and 1990s made my mother more open about her heritage and brought our nativeness closer to the surface. The reality, however, is that without Indian status, without our language, without connections to Mi'kmaq territory, and living in a society embroiled in a Quebec sovereignty movement which claimed my mother as "French" but further silenced her Indianness, there has been a significant confusion in my family about Native identity. When we were children, largely surrounded by Whites, we were considered "too dark"; with the advent of significant immigration of people of color, particularly as my family members relocated to Toronto, most of my siblings and nieces and nephews are now mostly considered far, far too White to be "real Indians." Nevertheless, the heritage of oppression that my family carried was replicated in my generation (and that of my nieces and nephews). I come to this chapter, therefore, with a strong awareness of the different levels of racialization and privilege that come from being intermarried with White rather than intermarried with Black, and yet with the knowledge that even with White intermarriage, violence is the legacy that Indigenous families seldom escape.

The struggles around Indigeneity that Native students encounter, and the colonialism they navigate, are also not dependent on the color of their skin. Being one of six Aboriginal students pursuing a doctoral degree at OISE in the late 1990s highlighted this reality. In a university with no Aboriginal professors, I was nevertheless part of a faculty that considered itself highly cutting-edged and equity-minded – where a number of faculty of color taught powerful courses on antiracism which, with a few exceptions, were silent about Indigenous presence, where we were taught postcolonial discourse which ignored ongoing colonization in the Americas, and where the devaluation of Indigenous knowledge was virtually complete. In doing my Ph.D., I was therefore required to assimilate several bodies of knowledge at the same time – not only the standard body of graduate-level sociological knowledge, and the "critical" postcolonial framework which critiqued this standard body of sociological knowledge – but a counter-discourse of resistance to BOTH the previous discourses, composed mostly of Mi'kmaq language classes and elders' critiques of what we were learning in school, supplemented by unpublished essays or occasional articles by Indigenous writers challenging postcoloniality and other antiracism discourses which excluded Indigeneity. The winter that welfare rates were cut by 20% meant that huge numbers of marginal Native people – including my Mi'kmaq language instructor – were forced out onto the street. The exclusion of Native realities and Indigenous epistemologies in postcolonial and antiracist theory was never so contradictory to me as it was that winter, on a daily basis walking by Indigenous bodies huddled on the pavement outside the university.

Several years later, the ongoing erasure of Indigenous presence, particularly within academic, postcolonial, and antiracism theory caused me to coauthor, with Enakshi Dua, the paper "Decolonizing Anti-Racism". In this paper, we asserted that Canadian antiracist theorists, by ignoring the Indigenous peoples whose land they were on, were furthering the colonial project that Canada continues to be engaged in. Dua, in particular, stated unequivocally that peoples of color in Canada should be considered "settlers" on Indigenous land.

In presentations of this paper, the most vociferous criticism has come – and continues to come – from Black people, who have challenged the use of "settler" when speaking of their relationship to Indigenous peoples in Canada, the United States, and the Caribbean. My purpose in undertaking this paper, therefore, is to explore in a deeper and more thoughtful manner the specific relations between Black and Aboriginal people, to more clearly articulate what constitutes a settler relationship, and to explore what might be needed to strengthen connections between Black and Indigenous communities. Having had the opportunity to teach courses which addressed both global and local colonialism has highlighted to me, above all, that there are strong interconnections between Black and Aboriginal peoples, globally and locally. This has led to my desire to work with Zainab Amadahy to address these issues.

6.3 Historical Context: Colonization and Settlement in Canada

In the United States, expressions of overt antipathy between Black and Native people are rare; the lines of tension are situated primarily within the context of their tribal interrelations and/or intermarriage – the existence of Black Indians and/or Black tribal citizens, frequently ignored by Black people, and fraught with tensions for Native people. Contemporary conflicts over the "Indianness" of Black tribal citizens in the United States came to a head in March 2007, when a minority[4] of the Cherokee Nation of Oklahoma successfully voted to expel their fellow Cherokee citizens of Black ancestry, historically known as "freedmen."[5] However, other, less well documented, conflicts have arisen in the other Indigenous nations whose lands were displaced by White slave owners and whose own ranks were therefore divided between slaveholders and those who rejected slavery – for example, the Choctaws (Collins 2006), the Creeks (Chang 2006; Saunt 2005), the Chickasaws (Krauthamer 2006), and the Seminoles (Micco 2006). Still other complexities are taking place within the nations of the eastern United States who, after being overwhelmed by settlers for centuries and intermarrying with both Black and White settlers, are struggling for federal recognition as tribes.[6] In all these cases, slavery, segregation, and the regulation of racial and tribal identities have overdetermined how Black Indians are seen, and have shaped the complex relations between Black Indians or freedmen tribal citizens, and non-Black tribal citizens. There are additional pressures among many Native peoples in the south, particularly those who are struggling for federal recognition as Indians, to be silent about the manner in which anti-Black racism may have entered their communities (Klopotek 2007). As Robert Keith Collins notes, however, one reason why this subject is capable of raising such controversy among Native people is that very little of the discourse about Black Indianness is actually grounded in the lived realities of Black–Native tribal members, including their knowledge of Indigenous languages, and other aspects of cultural knowledge

(2007). Black Indianness therefore can become a lightning rod highlighting Native Americans' most tremendous fear – of ceaseless cultural dilution by those who are perceived as "outsiders," until nativeness, after centuries of genocidal policies, ceases to exist altogether.

Having outlined some details of the complexities of Native–Black relations in the United States, we will now proceed to introduce some of the differences between Canadian and American policies toward Native and Black people, by way of introducing the Canadian contexts in which Native–Black relations take place. While slavery and regulation of Indigenous identity have proceeded in the Canadian context, it has, for the most part, taken different forms with different implications.

Historical policies toward Indigenous peoples in Canada have varied throughout the colonization process – from eighteenth-century policies of outright physical extermination on the east coast toward the Mi'kmaq, coupled with wartime allegiances and fur trade partnerships further west with the Iroquois Confederacy and the Three Fires Confederacy; to nineteenth-century treaty-making and ultimately subordination in central and western Canada with the Cree and Blackfoot peoples; to the "terra nullius" policies toward west coast Native peoples in the nineteenth and early twentieth century; to modern and ongoing resource rape and dispossession in the north, toward the Inuit. On the whole, though, control of most Indigenous communities has been maintained, since the 1870s, through a centralized body of legislation known as the Indian Act, which controls "Indian" identity and entitlement to land, as well as most other aspects of existence for those recognized "Indians" who come under its policies.

Differences between federal regulation of Indianness in Canada under the Indian Act, and the reliance on "blood quantum" in the United States, are on one level, minimal, and on another, profound. While both regimes have focused on drastically supplanting Indigenous ways of identifying relationships (and in the process minimizing numbers of registered "Indians" and maximizing land theft), the Indian Act has functioned less to quantify "degrees" of Indianness than to draw absolute divisions between status Indians and all other Native people.[7] Blood quantum measurement in the United States, however, has specifically mediated Indigenous identity as being solely about "blood," in potentially shaping who will be recognized as a tribal citizen and who will not, among Indian nations.

What is perhaps unique about colonization history in Canada, as compared to that of the United States, is the more overtly colonial framework that Britain was capable of exercising in its Canadian colony, which is highlighted by the formidable nature of the Indian Act as a weapon of legal oppression, which enabled the formal fragmenting of Indigenous nations into tiny "bands" with very few having over 1,000 members. Most bands in Canada only won a very limited degree of control over their membership in 1985, and continue to have governance powers that at best are equal to municipalities; meanwhile, land theft in Canada has been so extreme that all the lands reserved for Indians in Canada would fill less than half of the Navajo nation in Arizona (St. Germain 2002, p. xix). In such a context, the control that the larger federally recognized tribes in the United States can exercise over their-citizenship, whether Black or not, has not been possible for Canadian bands to exercise.

In 1969, in a document entitled "Statement of the Government of Canada on Indian Policy, 1969" (popularly known as the White Paper), Canada attempted to formally divest itself of historic treaty obligations to Native peoples, while holding on to the land which is its basis of power, and privatizing the remaining reserves still left in Native hands. This formed the backdrop to a terrain of ensuing struggle, whereby the Indian Act has become the vehicle through which claims are made ON the state, and where those historically excluded from the Indian Act (and those who continue to be excluded through highly restrictive identity legislation) are divided from those with Indian status and are seen as not only as competitors for state funding but as those whose claims to Indigeneity are in some respects fraudulent. Indigenous identity, therefore, has become a major terrain of struggle for Native peoples, no less in Canada than in the United States. The extent to which this identity legislation becomes the crucial factor dividing Black Indians from other Native people, as it undoubtedly has in the United States, remains to be seen.

Under the Indian Act, the only people who can gain Indian status in Canada are those whose male ancestors were defined as Indians (the status of Indian women was considered to flow only from their fathers or husbands until 1951), and only those with Indian status have been entitled to live on reserve. If Indian status continues to be the final arbiter of who is "really" Indian, then historic off-reserve intermarriages between Black people and Mi'kmaq people in the Maritimes and Black people and Ojibway people in Ontario will never "count" as *real* Indians in Canada – at least not as far as status Indian communities are concerned; although the ongoing intermarriage between Black people and status Indians in communities all over Canada today means that at present, and in the future, their children, Black Indians, will have Indian status; their band membership will depend on their parent's membership and the policies of band membership on their reserve. Reserves may potentially have significant numbers of Black Indians in the future. For Black–Native intermarriage where the Native parent is non-status, however, being recognized as Black Indians will be considerably more precarious.

In comparing Black–Native relations in Canada with those in the United States, perhaps the biggest difference, however, is in immigration history. While both Native and Black slavery existed in Canada until the early nineteenth century, its limited economic value in a climate too cold for a large-scale plantation agricultural economy has meant that large numbers of enslaved Black people were not brought in to Canada, as with the United States. Indeed, settlement in Canada has, as in Australia, been overwhelmingly on a Whites-only basis. This was maintained through racist immigration policy and legally codified racial discrimination that was stringently maintained until after World War II. With changes to immigration policy at that point, urban centers in Canada have experienced profound demographic shifts, as immigration from the Caribbean, South Asia, East Asia, and Africa changed the face of some Canadian cities. Toronto, and to a lesser extent, Montreal and Vancouver, have become increasingly "brown" cities; however, they are surrounded by smaller communities across the country which are still overwhelmingly White.

In response to such profound urban demographic shifts, in 1971, the Canadian government enacted the policy of multiculturalism, which, in addition to other human rights legislation, affirmed individual racial equality and created space for limited cultural "difference" within the Canadian bicultural (French–English) framework. While debates on multiculturalism are considerable, multiculturalism as a policy can be considered to have had three primary effects. First of all, it has contained insurgent diasporic communities in subordinate positions to the two so-called founding races (British and French). Secondly it has enabled those diasporic communities to make limited claims on the state in the name of multiculturalism, for services and support, and often in the process, to engage in antiracist resistance. Finally, the multiculturalism policy profoundly strengthened Canada's attempts to divest itself of any formal recognition of Indigenous peoples, by creating a playing field where Aboriginal peoples could potentially be reduced to "just another cultural group" within a multicultural mosaic.[8]

There are a number of other by-products of these histories. A crucial one is that the presence of older communities of color – in particular, the communities of Black people who entered Canada between the sixteenth and the nineteenth centuries, as well as west coast East Asian and South Asian communities dating back to the nineteenth and early twentieth centuries – is constantly being erased from the Canadian body politic, by a multiculturalism policy that treats all racialized cultural communities as "new immigrants." Black Canadians in particular face a nation-state which has continuously excluded large-scale Black settlement, and which, despite the existence of centuries-old Black settlements, continues to construct a vision of Canadian nationhood where Black people are forever marginal newcomers, always external to the nation.[9]

What this means is that any acknowledgment of the presence of Black Indians in Canada has been sharply constrained, not only by the colonial control that Britain (and then Canada) has maintained over Indigenous communities, isolating them and subordinating each community, until 1951, under the coercive control of government "Indian Agents" and the Church, but by the profoundly "Whites only" nature of the rest of Canadian society. In such a repressive context, surrounded by hostile Whites, historic Black communities faced continuous pressures to "whiten themselves" culturally. Meanwhile, the intensity of control maintained over Indigenous communities prevented those Black people with Native heritage from turning to Native communities in any large-scale manner for support. The result has been a legacy of silence about Black Indianness in the Maritimes, a silence which has yet to be significantly broken. An even greater silence, about the very existence of Black Ojibways in central Ontario, has also been maintained. In each case, the only communities who have acknowledged the existence of Black Mi'kmaqs or Black Ojibways have been the surrounding Mi'kmaq and Ojibway communities.

Another by-product of this erasure of historic Black (as well as East Asian and South Asian) presence in the massive upsurge of postwar diasporic communities is that the newer and more numerous communities are defining the terms of struggle with the state; these communities, however, have little or no knowledge of the presence of Indigenous peoples in Canada.[10] As a result, particularly in the larger Canadian cities, antiracism has been theorized and articulated solely in the context of diasporic communities, in the process absolutely eclipsing and erasing Aboriginal presence (Lawrence and Dua 2005). On those occasions when antiracist activists attempt to be inclusive of Indigenous contexts, they lack knowledge of the histories of Indigenous communities, their relationships to the land, the spiritual–political processes that maintain Indigenous communities today, and the value which Indigenous peoples place on relationships. It is in the hopes of addressing these absences that we introduce some aspects of these perspectives below.

6.4 Indigenous Ways of Maintaining Relatedness

In seeking to understand ways of working together, we can learn much from the oral histories and stories of Indigenous peoples concerning the framework in which relationships are understood. While the examples below are taken from Indigenous Turtle Island stories and teachings, the values inherent in them are common to all Indigenous cultures from around the globe. Probably the most fundamental principle of many Indigenous cultures is human interdependence with other life-forms in nonhierarchical ways. Creation Stories, for example, emphasize the interdependence of two-leggeds (human beings) with the plants, animals, sun, moon, and the land itself. In the *Rotinosoni* (Iroquois) Creation Story, Sky Woman and the land animals, sea creatures, and winged ones cooperated and had different roles in the formation of Turtle Island and in growing food that sustained the human lives that came afterward.

Indigenous worldviews give us other ways of looking at "cultural pluralism." To illustrate, consider this Cherokee teaching.

> Mother Earth and all her children teach us that diversity is necessary to our health and well-being. You do not see the trees insisting that they all bear the same fruit. You do not see the fish declaring war against those who do not swim. You do not see corn blocking the growth of squash and beans. What one plant puts into the soil, another takes. What one tree puts into the air another creature breathes. What one being leaves as waste another considers food. Even death and decay serve to nurture new life. Every one of Mother Earth's children co-operates so that the family survives.[11]

In *Rotinosoni* communities every gathering – ceremonial, social, or business – is opened with what is known as the Thanksgiving Address, a prayer expressing appreciation to all "living"[12] creatures (plants, animals, waters, stars, sun, moon, etc.) for their contribution to providing two-leggeds with food, clothing, shelter, medicine, and everything else that is required for healthy living.

In *Anishinabe* gatherings the term "All My Relations" is used to honor a concept of family that does not stop with living blood relatives but includes ancestors, the generations to come, and a whole host of "spirit beings" that inhabit another realm, all of whom play various essential roles not only in sustaining life on Mother Earth but in facilitating our spiritual development – collective and individual. It also includes, in a nonhierarchical way, the animal and plant life that are a necessary part of Indigenous survival.

In this worldview, "extended family" takes on a whole new meaning. This concept of family challenges us to evolve beyond philosophies urging tolerance of "otherness" in the expectation that "diversity" or even equity can enrich us in either material or esoteric ways. Inherent in cultivating relationships with "others" we must understand our mutual interdependence, both in terms of our very survival as a species as well as our evolution as spiritual beings (and there is no endpoint to spiritual development).

In this framework, individuals do not and could not exist outside of community or the land. Our past, present, and future relationships define who we are and determine what roles we play as well as responsibilities we have to the community and to the land that sustains it. Likewise, who we are and what we do as individuals impacts that broad sense of community.

The notion that roles and responsibilities are assigned to all beings, genders, age groups, clans, nations, etc. is thematic in Indigenous histories, stories, and worldview. Inherent in this concept is that we need to understand, respect, and celebrate what everyone brings to the circle. Anyone who has ever worked in a team is challenged to respect the notion that individuals bring something unique to the group's work. Likewise, communities, with our particular histories, cultures, and experiences have something to contribute to the human family: indeed to "all our relations."

Consequently, leadership is just another role someone is expected to play in service to community. Leadership opportunities are understood less as privileges that come with perks than they are responsibilities to serve and remain accountable to a community and a set of values that the community aspires to.

As we develop an understanding of these concepts, it is important to realize that they reflect value systems or sets of ideals that have been profoundly damaged by colonialism. And yet, these fundamental values have survived in many contemporary Indigenous communities, and are the source of every successful defense of the land and the life-forms that rely on it. It is easy, from the outside, to romanticize and idealize Indigenous societies (past, present, and future); however, such romanticism prevents outsiders from seeing in real terms the actual strengths and values that contemporary Indigenous communities maintain today. Viewing the world through the lens of Indigenism highlights the fact that Native communities are still here, that they know the histories of their own traditional lands, and that these realities, despite their erasure from the mainstream, need to be taken into account by activists from other communities. More profoundly, it can offer a template to understand how deeper connections can be developed, across our differences, as Black and Indigenous peoples.

How we understand our relationships also shapes and is shaped by what academics write about these issues. It is theory and literature which "train" successive generations in how to think about certain issues, and for that reason, it is crucial to explore this aspect further, as well.

6.5 Another Way of Understanding the Story: The Theoretical Picture of Our Relations in Black Thought

6.5.1 Black Writing in Canada

> *Dry rivers in the valley*
> *The thirst at the banks of plenty*
> *The room at the streetcar shelter*
> *A bus stop bed…*
> *The last postcard you sent was kinda weird*
> *Poor people sleeping at the bus stop?*
> *Surely you don't have that there?*
> *Anyways, I'm dying to come to Canada*
> *I'm a pioneer.*
>
> (Lillian Allen 1989, "Unnatural Causes")

The above spoken-word poem, from the album *Conditions Critical*, by Jamaican–Canadian dub poet Lillian Allen, reflects the ambiguous position of Black people in Canada relative to Indigenous peoples, as portrayed in critical Black writing. In her poetry, Allen encompasses the realities of those who leave (or flee from) homes already devastated by colonialism globally, those who have bought in to the myth of Canada as an empty land where they can remake themselves and their lives, and the violence of racism that all Black migrants encounter at the point of arrival in Canada (whether in the eighteenth century or the twenty-first). For Allen, a politicized vision of Canada's anti-Black racism is highlighted by a gesture toward its colonial relationship to Indigenous peoples, as referenced by the satirical ending "I'm a pioneer."

And yet, this gesture – which a growing number of Black Canadian writers make toward the colonial nature of the Canadian state – is insufficient to address the ongoing erasure of Indigenous realities within critical Black writing. This erasure is neither deliberate nor accidental – it flows inevitably from a theoretical framework that separates racism from colonialism and genocide, and grants priority to racism. It is perhaps not surprising that this approach would dominate in Black Canadian writing; the reality of Black suffering in Canada is mediated through racism – whether it is through the structural realities of poverty, job discrimination, discrimination in housing and in education, or the lived daily realities of police violence and over-incarceration.

By comparison, when Aboriginal peoples, across Canada, address racism, it is in the context of colonialist genocide – the ceaseless targeting of Aboriginal people for destruction *as peoples* in a colonial order – whether through removing people from land and livelihood, or removing children through child welfare agencies (and formerly through residential schooling) – too often resulting in the relentless spirals of alcoholism, drug addiction, family violence, and sexual abuse that are devastating Aboriginal communities. In such a context, the pressures to relinquish culture, language, and identity as Indigenous nations are constant and overwhelming; and the price for those who cannot survive the losses are the highest rates of Indigenous incarceration and suicide in the world (Razack 2002, p. 122), accompanied by such a phenomenal rate of sexual violence against Indigenous women that it has brought international attention to this issue (Amnesty International 2004). Indeed, Andrea Smith, addressing both Canadian and American contexts, has highlighted the role that sexual violence plays in ongoing colonial control, noting that Native women AND Native youths are approximately 50% more likely to experience violent assault than any other racial group, including Black people, and that, unlike any other racialized group, Native women are assaulted more often by White men than by men of their own group: 60% of the perpetrators of sexual violence against Native women are White (Smith 2005, p. 28).

Indeed, when epidemics of diabetes and fetal alcohol syndrome, poor housing, and unsafe drinking water are taken into account, it is very clear that Indigenous communities, in Canada and globally, form the "Fourth World" as described by the late Rodney Bobiwash (2001, p. 12):

> The Fourth World is ... the world of Indigenous people – the original peoples of the Americas and across the globe who have been marginalized on their own lands, excluded from civil society, denied economic opportunity, and stigmatized by the Myth of Conquest and The Doctrine of Discovery – who have fallen off of even the lowest rungs of the false ladder of economic determinism – called progress.

Particularly now, under globalization, the very survival of Indigenous peoples throughout the world is threatened.

In Africa, Indigenous peoples face land appropriation, resource theft, and policies of genocide, often organized by Black African elites, in partnership with colonial or imperial powers, who have internalized colonial values. But whether we are talking about contemporary migration from Africa itself, or the ongoing diaspora of peoples of African descent created by slavery, the reality is that African peoples living in the Americas are living on the lands of other Indigenous peoples. And for all peoples forced to live on other peoples' lands, a crucial question becomes what relationships they will establish with the Indigenous peoples of that land whose survival is so under siege. Ultimately, to fail to negotiate a mutually supportive relationship is to risk truly becoming "settlers," complicit in the extermination of those whose lands they occupy.

What renders the situation more complex, of course, is that peoples of African descent in the Americas are primarily those who are survivors of the holocaust and cultural genocide that is slavery; others are survivors of direct colonial occupation or genocide in Africa. Most peoples of African descent in Canada, whether recently arrived or "old stock" from the seventeenth century, are therefore in a profoundly contradictory relationship to Indigenous peoples here. As racialized people, inevitably positioned as outsiders to the Canadian nation, and survivors of one or another form of genocide, they have much in common with Indigenous peoples. Perhaps this is the reason that most Black Canadian writers routinely make gestures toward Indigenous presence. And yet their very marginality within Canada generally also forces them, contradictorily, to make settler claims as part of challenging Canada's racism.

Rinaldo Walcott, for example, in his work frequently references Indigenous genocide and a subordinated First Nations presence, positioning Black people implicitly as allies to Indigenous peoples. And yet, contradictorily, he also advocates that the eighteenth-century loyalist land grants offered to Black Loyalists, but subsequently denied, should be honoured (1997, p. 36). In so doing, he is erasing not only the reality of the eighteenth-century genocide of Mi'kmaq people[13] that accompanied the loyalist presence in Nova Scotia, but the fact the Mi'kmaq people today have never formally ceded their land to any settlers. In such a context, to urge the "honoring" of Africadian land rights means demanding the right to retroactively participate with Whites in an ongoing illegal land grab. Another contradiction within Walcott's writing, which appears common in most critical Black Canadian writing is the ongoing erasure of Black Mi'kmaq people, by referencing all Maritimers of African descent simply as "Black." He thus deepens an already profound silence about Black Native identity which few Black Native people in Canada have broken, to date.

Indeed, Walcott's work highlights a fundamental contradiction within most critical Black Canadian writing, particularly Black history: even as the writing attempts to reference Canada's subordination of Indigenous peoples, it normalizes relations of colonialism. Joseph Mensah (2002), for example, in *Black Canadians*, restricts his coverage of the presence of eighteenth-century Indigenous people to the fact that the family of Joseph Brant, as acculturated elite Mohawks, historically owned slaves. In this treatment, the eighteenth-century presence of White AND Black people on Indigenous lands is normalized, as if colonial domination and the claiming of Indigenous lands for settlement are inevitable and beyond question. Such treatment is not only inaccurate, given that in the eighteenth century, the European presence in North America was still being consolidated. It also invites the posturing of Black innocence as settlers: if colonization is inevitable and beyond question, the presence of Black settlers on Indigenous lands can be normalized; they are, in fact, not colonizers, but victims, of slave-owning Native people such as Joseph Brant.

If we do not normalize colonization, it becomes clear that Black struggles for freedom have required (and continue to require) ongoing colonization of Indigenous land. While the Underground Railroad frequently ran through the cross-border reserves of Indigenous peoples, it brought Black peoples to Canada to claim land that was newly taken from Indigenous peoples. And yet it is clear that, because of slavery, in this context there was little choice. Moreover, Black settlers, unlike White settlers, were generally forced to proceed without the support of established colonization programs.

We can see these contradictions in the writings of Daniel Hill about Blacks in early Canada. By leaving out the presence of Indigenous peoples, Hill positions Black settlers simply as noble in their fortitude in clearing the land, not as those who are displacing Indigenous peoples in the process. However, his work also demonstrates that while Blacks in Ontario attempted to claim land as Whites did, they were not included in settler programs but were forced to forage out on the land on their own, often clearing bush recently claimed from Indians only to be later displaced by Whites. They were, in a sense, ambiguous settlers, tied to the colonization process not only through a desperate need to survive after slavery, but by Christian beliefs that land must be cultivated to do God's work and by their acceptance that the land would be theirs if they could claim it. Hill demonstrates these contradictions in the writing of John Little, a Black refugee from North Carolina, who settled in the Queen's Bush with his wife, in 1840:

> We had not a second suit of clothes apiece; we had one bedquilt and one blanket, and eighteen dollars in money. I bought two axes in Hamilton, one for myself and one for my wife; half a dozen plates, knives and forks, an iron pot, and a Dutch oven; that's all for tools and furniture. For provisions I bought fifty weight of flour and twenty pounds of pork. Then we marched right into the wilderness, where there were thousands of acres which the chain had never run around since Adam. At night we made a fire, and cut down a tree, and put up some slats like a wigwam. This was in February, when the snow was two feet deep … the settlers were to take as much land as they pleased when it should be surveyed, at various prices, according to quality. Mine was the highest price, as I had taken the best land. It was three dollars seventy-cents an acre. I took a hundred acres at first, then bought in fifty. (Little in Hill 1992, p. 52)

Careful reading of this text demonstrates what else is left out when Indigenous peoples' presence is ignored: we do not get to even consider what the range of relationships might have been between early Black settlers and Indigenous peoples. For example, while it is not clear whether Little and his wife are Black Indians, the fact that they build wigwams at night to survive, and that, after escaping from North Carolina, know how to survive in the Ontario bush in February, suggests that they have been close enough to Native people in Canada to have learned survival skills from them. However, the overprint of Christianization separates them from so-called savages, as they refer to the bush as "a wilderness … which the chain had never run around since Adam."

Hill's silence around Indigenous presence is not unique. Most accounts of early Black settlement in Canada ignore Indigenous peoples, and their relationship to Black settlers. Therefore, not only is the colonial context of settlement ignored, but also the possible anticolonial framework of Black–Native alliances of the time, which undoubtedly took place during the difficult times of Native dispossession and Black marginalization. Nowhere is the presence of Black Mi'kmaqs in the Maritimes, and Black Ojibways in central Ontario even mentioned in Black histories of early Canada. A question which therefore must be asked is the extent to which Black historians may need to revisit the past to examine whether their portrayal of Black people as settlers in early Canada truly reflects the reality of Black–Indigenous connections.

Although Black historians ignore Indigenous presence, it is a hallmark of the more critical Canadian Black writing that it at least obliquely references Canada as a settler nation by invoking a contemporary Indigenous presence. By comparison, in African-American writing the reality of the United States as a settler nation has been absolutely invisible. And we cannot deny the hegemonic influence of African-American writing on anti-oppression writing within Canada; nor can we deny the presence, within that body of theoretical work, of a significant erasure (even a conscious displacement) of Indigenous presence by Black presence.

6.5.2 Black Writing in the United States

When Toni Morrison stated, in an interview with Paul Gilroy, that "modern life begins with slavery,"[14] she articulated the parameters of a discourse whereby slavery is seen almost as the defining moment creating the (North) American experience. Indeed, in other work, Morrison has stated that the major characteristics of American national literature are all responses to a "dark, abiding, signing Africanist presence," and that the very existence of an American literature is rooted in this "unsettled and unsettling" population (Morrison 1993, pp. 5–6). In other words, its literature marks America as being fundamentally about White and Black people; all others are irrelevant to the dynamic.

I do not want to imply that Toni Morrison created such a trend; indeed, from the moment of emancipation, when "unowned/disowned" slaves[15] began a relentless struggle for a toehold in American society, it would have been inevitable that Black people would need to define themselves in relationship to White America – and therefore as central, in some ways, to what America *means*. But the problem has been that almost overwhelmingly, both the theoretical and literary writing coming out of Black America positions Black people as being at the core of racial oppression and marginality in the United States, in ways that exclude the possibility of an Indigenous presence fundamentally *mattering*. It is as if, in African-American writing, White settlers landed in empty lands, bringing with them the African slaves who would represent the *other* America to the world. This erases the reality of colonization, and that the agenda of settler nations across the Americas is still to destroy all remaining Indigenous peoples, if not directly through murder then through forced assimilation (Churchill 1995, p. 34). It also erases the generations of Native American slavery that preceded and accompanied Black slavery (Gallay 2002), and the powerful bonds that this created between African-Americans and Native Americans – the reality of generations of intermarriage so that, according to Jack Forbes, African-Americans, particularly in the south, should be viewed as actually being "Red–Black people" (Forbes 1988).

The existence of Indigenous peoples in White settler nation-states is *inevitably* central to the identity problems at the heart of these nation-states (Churchill 1992, pp. 17–29). In referencing the massive proliferation of images of Indianness which exist across North America, the late Vine Deloria Jr. wrote:

> [T]herein lies the meaning of the whites fantasy about Indians – the problem of the Indian image. Underneath all the conflicting images of the Indian one fundamental truth emerges: the white man knows that he is alien and he knows that North America is Indian – and he will never let go of the Indian image because he thinks that by some clever manipulation he can achieve an authenticity which can never be his. (Deloria 1980)

White images of Native people are so far embedded in the vernacular of America that even Toni Morrison, in *Playing in the Dark*, in referring to how Ernest Hemingway constantly creates subordinate Black characters who exist solely to provide a range of services for White men, speaks of these servile or sullen Black characters as being "Tontos" to Hemingway's White "Lone Rangers" (1993, p. 82). Amazingly, Morrison does not register any awareness of the oddness of utilizing a terminology based on an already-existing relationship of colonialism to ascribe slavery and not colonialism as the defining moment shaping meaning in American literature.

It is equally important, however, to note that as White settlers in Canada consolidated their hold on the nation and maintained a century of Whites-only immigration, a powerful body of racist images harnessed by Black slavery was utilized to promote a sense of White racial superiority and ownership of the land among new European settlers.[16] Even today, in the western United States, where the predominant racialized other is Native American, a common racist term for them is "bush nigger."

We must therefore see this as a two-way process – that if White images of Indians are so deeply embedded into the vernacular of American (and Canadian) society that they are capable of evoking fundamentally demeaning relationships, a body of demeaning images of Black people originating in slavery has also become a potent tool of White identity formation as part of the colonial process, in Anglo North America. Nor should the centrality of *both* Native and Black imagery in White identity formation be a surprise to us. As Comanche activist Paul Smith has written, about the United States: "The essence of this country is bound up in Indian land and African slave labor" (Smith 1992, p. 23).

Unfortunately, in the United States, it is more common for American Indians and African-Americans to adapt mutually exclusive views. However, Native Americans are less than 1% of the population, and are still far more commonly written about than the ones shaping the discourse defining them. They remain far less visible within the mainstream than African-Americans. And at present, most African-American writing still decenters a Native American presence, and therefore contributes to their ongoing invisibility.

This is doubly problematic considering the hegemonic role that theoretical work by African-Americans has played internationally within anti-oppression writing. An entire generation of academics from other White settler nations, particularly Canada, have taken up African-American writing as "the canon" of antiracist thought, in ways that have contributed to displacing and silencing of local Indigenous activists. Cree Metis academic, Emma LaRocque, for example has described how in Canada, Indigenous writers attempting to call Canada on its genocidal history toward Native people were pathologized and accused of "blustering and bludgeoning" society, while writings by African-Americans describing their oppression were taken up willingly by White liberals (LaRocque 1993, p. vii).

It is, in fact, highly instructive to see how eagerly an African-American discourse which positions Blackness as the quintessential racial "other" has been taken up by "progressive" Whites from other settler nations and reproduced to further erase local Indigeneity and ongoing colonization. For example, the Australian film *Black Soldier Blues*[17] valorizes African-American soldiers stationed in Australia during World War II, and therefore positions White Australians as free of racism by virtue of their positive views of African-American soldiers. This can only be accomplished, however, if the presence of Indigenous Australians is erased: White Australians are not settlers then, just "good" antiracist Whites. What gets erased here is not only Australian Indigeneity, but a truer picture of the complex racial dynamics in colonized Australia at a specific historical moment; this might have also taught us something about the complexity of racial dynamics in contemporary colonized America. Another example, from Brazil, where many Indigenous peoples are also of African heritage but are frequently positioned within the mainstream as being "really" Black (Warren 2001), concerns the manner in which an African-American discourse of antiracism is being imported by White progressives to eradicate racism against "Black" people; in the process erasing them as Native people.[18]

A minority vein of Black writing in the United States has attempted to resurrect the reality of powerful and sustaining relations between Black and Native peoples under colonization and slavery. The first efforts came from bell hooks (1992), who has emphasized not only the shared resistance but the shared value systems of Africans and Native Americans. Hooks also speaks of the manner in which many Black people, as they left the south, willfully silenced themselves about their Native ancestry – sometimes because of the racism they faced as Black people, and sometimes because of pressure from other Black people who viewed those who identified with Native Americans as being race traitors.[19] Meanwhile, Carol Boyce Davies has utilized Native American theoretical models to affirm and strengthen Afro-Caribbean and African modes of thought through the writing of Laguna Pueblo writer Leslie Marmon Silko. She also references how Indigenous peoples "made possible the emergence of African-Americans" (Davies 1994, pp. 9, 162). For hooks and Davies, as well as novelists such as Alice Walker, Indigenous thought and spiritual frameworks are a means to unify the fragments of an African heritage torn apart by slavery and diaspora. Indeed, there are signs that Toni Morrison is also moving in this direction, in her most recent book, which references Native American as well as African presences in early America.[20]

In examining this more recent trend in African American writing, it seems clear that Black peoples of Native heritage have suffered a double loss – not only the suppression of their knowledge of their North American or Caribbean Indigeneity, but the shattering of an African Indigeneity that can neither be affirmed as whole nor entirely relinquished. The powerful yearning for reconnection with ancestral roots felt by many diasporic Black peoples, and the strong affinities between North American Indigenous knowledge and spirituality and African Indigenous knowledge and spirituality suggests that building connections between Black and Indigenous communities, in the Americas and Canada may be a crucial source of empowerment for Black people. However, for the most part, when Indigeneity is raised, among Black activists and writers, overwhelmingly it is in a context which takes colonialism and genocide to be a tragedy of the past – so that ongoing colonialism in the present is taken-for-granted as normative, inevitable, and, indeed, invisible. It is an important step for African-Americans to begin to celebrate their Native roots. The next step, however, is for Black people to begin to interrogate how "stolen people on stolen land" can situate themselves in relation to today's existing Native peoples who are *still* struggling to reclaim stolen lands.

6.6 Racial Classification and Its Effect on Indigenous–Black Relations

The failure of many African-American writers to critically interrogate their positioning when they assert the primacy of slavery over Indigenous genocide may be connected to the manner in which some Native American groups are powerfully threatened by the notion of a Black Indigenous presence. However, the divisions of colonialism and racism are powerful enough to undermine most attempts by individuals from both sides to critically embrace Black Indigeneity. As Eva Marie Garroutte, in her study of Native American identity, has noted, the differences in racial categorizing (and the corresponding racial identity formation) for Black people and Native Americans has been huge. Racial classification of Blacks has hinged on the notion of hypodescent – that "one drop" of Black "blood" constitutes a Black identity. In some cases, up until the 1970s, anybody with more than one-thirty-second parts "Negro blood" was legally classified as Black. Native Americans, on the other hand, are required, both by law and by public opinion, to establish rather high blood quanta for their claims to a distinct racial identity to be accepted as meaningful. Quoting Jack Forbes, Eva Marie Garroutte notes that "modern Americans are always finding Blacks and losing Indians" (Garroutte 2003, pp. 45–48). This destructive manner of measuring Native American identity according to degrees of Indian blood, with an established cut-off point where Native Americans will cease to be recognized as Indians, has been internalized by many Native Americans and has been highly detrimental to their ability to *see* Black Indians as Indians. It has also been central to the struggles within the five tribes – the Cherokees, Creeks, Choctaws, Chickasaws, and Seminoles – who formerly held African slaves (and who also had Black allies, in the case of the Seminoles), about expelling those Black freedmen citizens who cannot prove their degree of Indian blood. This, however, is taking place on top of another legacy – the pervasiveness of anti-Black racism within American society and its reproduction in many southern Native communities.

The reality is that in both the past and the present, in Canada and the United States, Black people and Native people have been subjected to different forms of racism and racial categorization by Europeans and their descendants, in the interests of exploiting both peoples. This is most obvious with racial classification in the United States, but the peculiarities of Canada's "Whites only" immigration system, its pervasive anti-Black racism, its Indian Act, and its constant erasure of Black presence may wreak havoc on Black–Native relations in different ways in the future.

6.7 Where Are the Struggles Today and What Are the Implications?

For the increasing numbers of people in Canada who are not only from historic Black Mi'kmaq or Black Ojibway communities but are the product of contemporary intermarriage between Caribbean or African peoples and Native people in Canada, as well as numerous Black people of Caribs or Taino descent from the Caribbean, relations between Black and Aboriginal peoples are complex, but not inherently contradictory. The strength of the historic connections between Black and Native people has been weakened by exclusionary racial classification, by anti-Black racism among Native people and a profound ignorance on the part of many contemporary Black people about Indigenous presence, nevertheless, it appears that there will be growing movements of Black–Native people across both Canada and the United States to reclaim Indigeneity – not only to lost African roots but to contemporary Native realities in Canada.

Black people without known Indigenous heritage, however, exist in a profoundly contradictory relationship to Indigenous peoples. Despite both groups having distinct histories of cultural genocide, and sharing present marginality, Black peoples at present have little option but to struggle for power as settlers in Canada. This overwhelmingly speaks of a failure among Indigenous leadership to provide an alternative vision for those racialized peoples who may have little real allegiance to the Canadian settler state but have no option for their survival but to fight for increasing power within it.

There is also the reality that Black peoples have been profoundly changed through processes of struggle for racial empowerment. Throughout days of slavery, Africans and Indigenous people were enslaved together on plantations in the United States as well as in various parts of Latin America and the Caribbean. Throughout this history there have been alliances between groups and the formation of community as a form of resistance.[21] The crucial difference was that these alliances took place within strong and viable Indigenous cultures whose vitality had not been attacked and usurped through physical extermination and cultural genocide.

In "Canada," Indigenous communities such as the *Rotinosoni* adopted runaways into their clans and their communities. There was an Underground Railway not generally taught about in schools, run by *Rotinosoni*, where renowned Tuscarora guides risked their lives at a time when Indigenous people could have been enslaved, killed, or dispossessed of their land for helping runaways. Once "adopted in" runaways became *Rotinosoni*. They became Bear, Wolf, or Turtle clan members, etc. Elders describe processes where the Clan Mothers would decide which clans needed more people and they assigned runaways to the neediest. So Africans, both in Canada and the United States, did not live as Whites or even as African settlers in these communities. They lived under the laws and the social dictates of the Indigenous nations into which they were adopted.

The reasons as to why Blacks and Indigenous people got along so well in this early phase of colonial expansion had to do with cultural similarities. Both peoples had a spiritual worldview, land-informed practices, and were held together by a kinship structures which created relationships that allocated everyone a role in the community. These commonalities helped Africans and Native Americans to maintain good relations but, of course, there was also a common cause: the colonial project threatened the very existence of both Black and Indigenous peoples. With minor exceptions, African runaways were not enslaved in Indigenous communities located in what we now know as Canada. Indigenous communities looked to African newcomers as people who could inject new life, new blood, and new ideas into nations threatened with extinction by European disease and genocidal policies. Africans who spoke the languages of the settlers and knew their battle tactics were an asset to many communities defending themselves against or negotiating European aggression.

Today, at the risk of generalizing, the struggle for an equitable distribution of resources within or among nation-states that form a part of antiracist and diasporic struggles of Black peoples can be critiqued from Indigenist points of view for internalizing colonial concepts of how peoples relate to land, resources, and wealth. There is no indigenous framework around which such struggles are carried out.

Diasporic Black struggles, with some exceptions, do not tend to lament the loss of Indigeneity and the trauma of being ripped away from the land that defines their very identities. From Indigenous perspectives, the true horror of slavery was that it has created generations of "de-culturalized" Africans, denied knowledge of language, clan, family, and land base, denied even knowledge of who their nations are. Moreover, while many African diasporic peoples took up Christianity as a theology of liberation and "racial uplift"; there are tenets of Christianity that are profoundly anti-Indigenous, which equate Indigeneity (both North American and African) with savagery. Whether or not Christianity is responsible, to put it bluntly, Black activists in the Americas have internalized colonial, imperial, and Eurocentric values at the same time that they decry them. What many Black struggles tend to be centered around is how the legacy of racism and slavery rationalizes their inequality and hampers their ability to compete for power, wealth, and opportunities in colonial, settler states or the global economy.

Even socialist-oriented movements are not framed around, nor are they inclusive of, Indigenous struggles, even when integrating an antiracist framework. Socialist discourse maintains a perspective on spirituality that ranges from antagonism to ridicule. Identification with a "national" identity is seen as some sort of proto-fascism. Indigenous economics have never been well understood in the scholarly work of self-identified socialists or Marxists. John Mohawk (Seneca) illustrates how Indigenous activists and academics regard these philosophies:

> Let's say you have three people approach a tree. One's a socialist materialist, one's a capitalist materialist and one's a traditional native person. The capitalist materialist will explain to you that he has to cut the tree down because this is the best interest not only of himself but also of society; that it is a kind of destiny; that by cutting the tree down he will rationally distribute the materials from the tree and he'll do the most good for the people. A socialist person approaching the tree will also tell you to cut the tree down, because after cutting the tree down you can distribute it equally to everybody and it's going to do

the most good for the world that way. But a native person looking at the tree will say that the tree, in its unharmed, original form, has a value that's greater than anything the others are proposing. (Mohawk 2006, p. 26)

While this is an oversimplification, because we know that environmental concerns sometimes impact materialism and that Indigenous people sometimes cut trees down (albeit for the purpose of subsisting), Mohawk's point is well taken. Indigenous academics and activists regard both capitalism and socialism as Eurocentric materialist ideologies. The majority of diasporic Black struggles are equally materialist. The Civil Rights movement in the United States focused on "equal rights and opportunities." Today the ultimate vision driving Black struggles in Canada (with some notable exceptions) is much the same: Black people want equity within the laws, economy, and institutions of the colonial settler state.

However, in looking at recent Native activism, we can see another role that racialized activists, including Black people, are beginning to take. The proximity of Six Nations and Tyendinaga to the urban centers of Toronto, Hamilton, and Montreal have enabled racialized activists to provide material and moral support to these besieged communities to a level not previously experienced in the last century and a half of the Indigenous movement on Turtle Island. In the process these groups and individuals are beginning to explore the implications of Indigenism to both Indigenous and non-Indigenous struggles. However, the situation on the ground changes rapidly and we have witnessed significant evolution of solidarity and activism work since March 2006, when members of the Six Nations of the Grand River community began a land reclamation near Caledonia, Ontario.[22] Many groups across Canada have mobilized to lend support to this struggle. This support consists of fund-raising efforts, providing food and supplies as well as working at the camp doing a variety of jobs that include cooking, woodcutting, and taking security shifts.

At Kanenhstaton there is a discourse that seeks to prove ownership of the Haldimand Tract under Canadian law. In her July 1, 2006 *Update from Grand River* Confederacy spokesperson Hazel Hill wrote: "The Six Nations people have a legitimate claim, and will continue on a peaceful path to bring awareness to the world of how corrupt the government has been with respect to the sale of lands to which they hold no title, all along the Grand River. As I've stated before, Canada is guilty of the biggest white collar crime in the history of their people." On November 16, 2006, Hill recounts what happened in a negotiation session: "Clearly, the Six Nations presented a full and complete history not only of how the Crown had frauded our lands away, but also how they had usurped the authority of our Traditional Government, imposed their laws on our people which is a violation of the ancient agreements between us, but far more concerning, a Direct Violation Against Creation." [sic]

However, in a parallel discourse, the Clan Mothers, Elders, and Confederacy supporters constantly remind us that the seizure of this land and the negotiations they have entered into with the province and the federal agencies are not about contesting Eurocentric concepts of ownership. The Confederacy and its supporters have made a decision that is perfectly legal under Rotinoshoni Law to prevent further development of the land in order to protect it for generations to come, whether those generations are Onkwehonwe (Indigenous) or not. Hazel Hill's July 12, 2006, update speaks of this.

> It is an issue of Sovereignty that runs far deeper than a simple issue of a land claim, and one that reaches deep into the hearts and souls of our people. It is the very essence of who we are, and the strength that comes from believing in the Kaienerekowah,[23] and upholding our responsibilities to our Great Law. We would be negligent if we did nothing to ensure that our future generations didn't have the same strong foundation that our ancestors laid out for us.

What many non-Indigenous supporters initially assumed was a struggle for a piece of the colonial pie or even a recognition of territorial boundaries negotiated with the federal government is now coming to be understood as a call to everyone on Turtle Island to shift their ideological frameworks, values systems, and conceptual understandings of how humans relate to land and the resources within it. As Hill's September 22, 2006 update states: "We dare to uphold our obligation and responsibility that was given to us not only for our own good, but also for the good of all of Creation, including all of the other races of the world."

This is the issue that Indigenous and non-Indigenous activists (many of them Black) have put their lives on the line to defend. Individual as well as organizational (community support) is evident. For example, Palestine House, the Coalition Against Israeli Apartheid, and No One is Illegal are organizations comprised primarily or entirely of racialized people that have raised funds, worked on the site, and transported supplies to Kanenhstaton. On May 17, 2006, the Canadian Islamic Congress issued a media statement entitled "Islamic Congress Supports Six Nations Land Reclamation." The following excerpt illustrates one aspect of the connections that are starting to be recognized:

> Many of Canada's 750,000 Muslims have strong emotional ties to this situation, in which aboriginal peoples are systematically being denied their birthright. Palestinians are being robbed of their native land in similar ways by the Israeli occupying power that denies them justice through unilateral expropriations and by refusing to negotiate in good faith with their elected representatives.

The Black Action Defense Committee's (BADC) office in Toronto proudly flies the Hiawatha Flag, the banner of the Haundenosaunee. BADC has developed programming such as Freedom Cipher Youth that enables urban racialized youth to interact and collaborate with Six Nations youth around arts and cultural activities. On several occasions over 2007/08 BADC brought urban youth from Toronto to cultural events on Six Nations territory. Six Nations youth were hosted at a BADC event in June 2007 to share their experiences. Chris Harris, a youth programmer at BADC, has spoken publicly on several occasions about his organizations work at introducing Black and other urban youth to Indigenous solidarity activities. Six Nations hip-hop activist Shiloh and youth involved with Freedom Cipher spoke on a June 30, 2007, CKLN radio show about the need for Black–Indigenous solidarity and the use of hip-hop to educate youth about anticolonial resistance. Former CKLN radio personality Norman Otis Richmond, a veteran Black community activist, spoke out several times on his radio program about the need for the Black community to support Indigenous struggles. Richmond also provided space for invited guests from Indigenous communities or Black activists who worked in solidarity with Indigenous struggles to discuss topical issues on his program.

Another development worth mentioning has been the fall 2006 formation of a Toronto chapter of INCITE[24] comprised of Black and Indigenous women devoted to exploring relationships between the two communities on Turtle Island. Up to now their discussions have been internal but it will be interesting to see how the group evolves and how its activism will be impacted.

At an April 2007 gathering of the Coalition in Support of Indigenous Sovereignty, activists representing the Coalition against Israeli Apartheid, the Ontario Coalition Against Poverty, No One is Illegal as well as unaffiliated activists, from a variety of ethno-cultural backgrounds began a process of "decolonizing our mindsets" and looking seriously at what it means to be an ally to Indigenous struggles, which means being an ally to the land. This work took place under the tutelage of an Indigenous caucus, also admittedly in a process of internal decolonization. All parties have committed to a long-term process aimed at exploring the implications of Indigenous solidarity work as well as the impact of Indigenism on various settler struggles. This and future gatherings will discuss the question of expectations we have of each other and how we hold each other accountable.

One of the questions that emerge from the work described above must be posited to Indigenous peoples: Where do racialized settlers fit in the vision of Indigenous sovereignty? For the purposes of this chapter we need to ask where Black people fit into the vision.

This is a huge question. If Indigenous sovereigntists expect Black community support of nation-to-nation negotiation processes regarding land, resources, and reparations, we have to recognize how Blacks become completely disempowered in that process. Through such a process, Indigenous nations inherently (and begrudgingly) acknowledge Canada's nationhood. But Black people have no power or even validity in the Canadian nation state.

This leaves Blacks who do not identify or are not accepted in whole or part as Indigenous North Americans in a kind of limbo, waiting for a colonial state and Indigenous nations to "work out" a relationship while they continue living in a land that denies their contribution to "nation building," whether that contribution was forced, coerced, or willful. Worth remembering here is the fact that many Blacks historically contributed to sustaining the Indigenous communities such as the Rotinoshoni that helped them achieve freedom from slavery.

Settlers working in solidarity with Indigenous struggles have pointed out that they have a particular responsibility as "Canadians." As legal citizens or residents of Canada they must hold the state accountable to recognizing sovereignty and negotiating in good faith with the true leadership of Indigenous communities. Though this might be a perfectly moral stand, the reality is that Blacks, and other racialized settlers combined, do not have the political clout to make a significant impact in this regard. Furthermore, on the face of it, they cannot be sure they will survive such a political stand, particularly when one takes into account the racism that Indigenous communities have internalized as a result of colonization.

This challenges grassroots Indigenous leadership to develop a vision of sovereignty and self-government that addresses the disempowered and dispossessed from other parts of the world who were forced and/or coerced into being here on Turtle Island (a global phenomenon in which Canada shares culpability). How much support should be expected from communities when there are glaring examples in our midst, such as the expulsion of Black Cherokees in Oklahoma, that there is no guarantee that Black Indians and Black people who lend their support to Indigenous communities will have a place in or beside them?

Further questions emerge regarding the framework of the Two Row Wampum, often referred to as the agreement that sets out how settlers and Indigenous people are supposed to coexist on Turtle Island. The wampum belt depicts two parallel rows of lavender beads running the belt's length. Elders tell us this symbolizes that White settlers and Indigenous people agreed to sail in their canoes or boats down the waterway respecting and not interfering with each others' progress nor interfering with each others' communities (another "treaty" not kept). The notion that Indigenous nations can coexist with the Canadian state, whose ideology, values, and institutions lead to the poisoning of the air, water, and land that we all depend on; that forms the basis of our identities and cultures, is increasingly coming into question.

Indigenous Elders and oral historians at Six Nations and elsewhere are appealing to settlers to modify their values systems, worldviews, and practices to enable the original vision of the Two Row; to understand that the mutual respect agreed to in the Two Row requires settlers to reimagine their analytical frameworks, belief systems, and behaviors.

Having posed these challenges it is important to recall that the fundamental framework for how Indigenous peoples relate to non-Indigenous peoples is laid out in our histories, stories, and spiritual tenets, as we saw earlier in this essay. Whatever emerges from relationship-building between Black and Indigenous communities should take place within this framework as opposed to competitive materialistic ones, which to date have not served either people.

We also want to acknowledge that Indigenous communities are consumed with simply trying to stay alive, waging struggles that must address youth suicides, violence against women, the rapid spread of HIV/AIDS, housing shortages, contaminated drinking water, mining and deforestation on their lands, the loss of language and ceremonial knowledge, etc. Thus, there is limited capacity to drop these struggles to "develop a vision" on how racialized settlers and Indigenous people can coexist on Turtle Island. Black communities are also waging significant struggles with life-and-death implications. The colonial system benefits greatly from the fact that our communities are in a perpetual state of crisis. But do we not owe it to the coming generations to find a way of supporting each other and the land that sustains us all?

Notes

1. While the myriad complexities of Black–Native identities and alliances in the Caribbean, as well as parts of Central and South America have taken a very different turn from the polarized and contradictory situation in some regions of the United States, the hegemony of the United States not only in influencing how Black–Native relations are perceived, but also in shaping how "race" is understood in Canada has required us to focus primarily on the American context in order to begin to delineate the Canadian situation at all.
2. Indigenous peoples globally have experienced *and continue to experience* the brutality of colonization, land theft, and being targeted for extermination. In emphasizing historic Indigenous American genocide, we do not wish to detract from a recognition of ongoing Indigenous holocaust globally, only to highlight the historic scale of depopulation in the Americas and the global imperialist system that the sack of Indigenous America helped to create.
3. Between 1493 and 1800, 85% of the world's supply of silver, and 70% of the world's supply of gold came from the Americas. Without this gold and silver, the mercantile system would not have been able to expand the way it did. Gold and silver were the primary currencies; with the flood of gold and silver into Europe a huge global expansion in commercial transactions became possible (Weaver 2002, p. 21).
4. Of approximately 270,000 members, 8,700 voted; of those, 76.6% voted to amend the tribal constitution to limit citizenship to those tribal members whose "Indian" blood quantum could be proven (BBC News, March 7, 2007).
5. The list of descendants stems from the Dawes Commission, established by Congress more than 100 years ago. It created what are known as the final rolls, establishing different categories including "blood" Cherokee, Cherokee freedman (of African descent), Cherokee by intermarriage, and Delaware Cherokee (BBC News, March 7, 2007).
6. In communities that are currently struggling for federal recognition as tribes, such as the Mowa Choctaws of Alabama, the Golden Hill Paugussetts of Connecticut, and the Ramapough Mountain Indians of New Jersey, a significant problem they face with the Bureau of Indian Affairs' Branch of Acknowledgement and Research (BAR) is that too much "black blood" is seen as a contaminant for Indian authenticity and can result in a failure to be federally recognized, while "white blood" is seen as more neutral and less problematic (Cramer 2005, p. 60).
7. From 1869 to 1985, women registered as Indian were designated non-Indian if they married non-Indians, as were their children. In 1985, women who lost their status had it reinstated; in the process, a new system of "half-status" was implemented to provide Indian status for their children. Those with half-status who marry non-Indians will have children designated as non-Indians. Meanwhile, those designated "half-breeds" in western Canada during the treaty process, and those who were left out of the treaty process in eastern Canada were classified as non-Indian; they were not recognized in law as Native peoples until 1982. However, at this time they were recognized only as "Aboriginal", and the treaty rights accruing to their status Indian relations are denied to them.
8. M. Nourbese Philip's critique of multiculturalism encapsulates the pain manifested by racialized peoples for the false sense of equality it evokes, by emphasizing cultural equality and belying the deeply embedded racism within Canada (Philip 1992, pp. 181–186). However, Himani Bannerji takes the more complex role of challenging the liberal framework of equality talk in general that is enabled by the multiculturalism policy. She notes above all the role that multiculturalism plays in enabling Canada to maintain the facade of being a liberal democracy while maintaining itself as a colonialist nation for Indigenous peoples (Bannerji 2000, pp. 8–11).
9. As Rinaldo Walcott notes, there has been a deliberate and ongoing erasure of Black historical presence in Canada, accomplished through the constant razing of old Black settlements and the changing of their names, coupled with the linking of contemporary Blackness solely to Toronto, to Somali youth, and illegal immigration, or to "Jamaicanness" and crime. The result is that Blackness in Canada is situated on a continuum that runs from the invisible to the hypervisible (Walcott 1997, pp. 36–37, 39, 118).

6 Indigenous Peoples and Black People in Canada   133

10. It is important to recognize that their lack of knowledge is part of deliberate policy. In those areas of Canada where there are large numbers of Indigenous people, ongoing segregation maintains a distance between Native people and the Canadian public. Meanwhile, Canadian schools continue to be places where a colonialist mind-set is cultivated, and the media reflects colonialist biases. In such a context, for non-Natives to have knowledge of Native peoples is highly unusual.
11. Paraphrased by Zainab Amadahy from a variety of oral teachings.
12. Aboriginal concepts of "life" are more inclusive than Eurocentric definitions and are based in a spiritual ideology that provides a conceptual framework for understanding and interpreting the world.
13. After over a century of sporadic wars with the English, the combined onslaught of being hunted for their scalps by bounty hunters, and burned out of their villages by British soldiers decimated Mi'kmaq populations in the years immediately prior to the Loyalist settlement. Furthermore, as loyalists took their lands, no reserves were set aside for them for almost a century. Homeless and destitute, Mi'kmaq misery was so extreme that in New Brunswick in the early 1800s it is reported that some parishes auctioned Mi'kmaq paupers off to those willing to provide for their care (Twohig 1996, p. 338). In the 1830s, cholera devastated a starving population, and by the 1850s, tuberculosis reached epidemic proportions. Among settlers, the generalized belief was the Mi'kmaq population was going to go extinct (indeed, the population finally stabilized at just under 1,600 from 20,000 a century earlier, and an estimated 300,000 at time of contact (Paul 2000, p. 184).
14. Gilroy (1993, p. 221).
15. Williams (1991, p. 21).
16. Minstrel shows, with Whites in blackface, were performed regularly across Eastern and Central Canada from the 1840s in the East and the turn of the century in Western Canada (Le Camp 2005, 350–361).
17. Written and produced by Veronica Fury and Nicole McCuig.
18. Personal communication with Jonathan Warren, August 2007, at "Who is an Indian" conference, Montreal.
19. One reality which hooks perhaps overlooks is that one's Indigenous identity and culture inevitably transforms when separated from the land. Indigenous identity is difficult to maintain when the relationships with other life-forms on the land are lost. It is perhaps inevitable that Black Indians would cease to identify as Indian as their connections to land and community were ruptured.
20. Morrison (2008). *A Mercy*. Alfred A. Knopf.
21. Since the beginning of European arrival there are historical accounts of the Algonquin Confederacy, the Natchez, and other nations raiding colonial towns to free African slaves. The Seminoles of Florida raided the plantations of neighboring states in Georgia and Alabama, freeing slaves and bringing them home to their communities. Thousands of runaways found homes with the Mi'kmaq, the Wampanoag, and other nations, and then fought side by side with their adopted brothers and sisters to ward off European incursion. Runaways formed maroon colonies in places like Jamaica and Florida. In Brazil these maroon colonies were called *quilombos*, the most famous of which is Palmares, where generations of Africans, Indigenous, and mixed-race peoples lived side by side, grew crops, raised their children and fought off several Portuguese military campaigns aimed at wiping them out.
22. This tract of land is a small portion of what was granted under the Haldimand Deed in 1784. In early 2006 the US-based Henco Corporation began construction on the territory for the purpose of building a residential complex. Henco proceeded to remove the topsoil, fill in the creek flowing through the property, and construct homes. No traditional or elected leader at Six Nations gave permission for this land to be sold or developed. In addition, this territory is currently included in an unresolved land claim and under federal law cannot be sold, leased, or developed. The case is in abeyance, as are many land claims.
    Consequently, after many attempts through letters and phone calls to persuade local and federal authorities to halt construction, the Six Nations community peacefully reclaimed the site on February 28, 2006. Rather then deal with the issue politically, the government decided to

move in with police and on April 20, 2006 the OPP attacked the camp, armed with tasers, pepper spray, and automatic weapons. Some members of the community were injured, 17 were arrested, and over 50 are facing criminal charges. Astonishingly, the community was able to peacefully reestablish the camp. They subsequently blocked all roads leading into the tract of land in an act of self-defense.

Negotiations are currently underway between members of the Six Nations Confederacy (traditional government) and the federal and provincial governments. All roadblocks were removed in May 2006 as a show of good faith by the community of Six Nations. Meanwhile, the site has been renamed Kanenhstaton (the Protected Place) and it continues to be peacefully occupied by the Six Nations community.

23. Great Law of Peace.
24. INCITE! Women of Color Against Violence is a US activist organization of radical feminists of color advancing a movement to end violence against women of color and their communities through direct action, critical dialogue and grassroots organizing (http://www.incite-national.org/about/index.html).

References

Amnesty International. *Stolen Sisters: A Human Rights Response to Discrimination and Violence Against Indigenous Women in Canada*. London, UK: International Secretariat, October, 2004.

Bannerji, H. (2000). "Introduction" in *The Dark Side of the Nation: Essays on Multiculturalism, Nationalism and Gender*. Toronto: Canadian Scholar's Press.

Bobiwash, R. (2001). *The Fourth World: Site of Struggle and Resistance in the Fight Against Global Capital*. Statement to the World Social Forum, Porto Allegre, Brazil.

Chang, D. (2006). "Where Will the Nation Be at Home? Race, Nationalisms, and Emigration Movements in the Creek Nation" in T. Miles and S.P. Holland (Eds.), *Crossing Waters, Crossing Worlds: The African Diaspora in Indian Country* (pp. 80–99). Durham/London: Duke University Press.

Churchill, W. (1992). *Fantasies of the Master Race: Literature, Cinema, and the Colonization of American Indians*. Monroe, ME: Common Courage Press.

Churchill, W. (1995). *Since Predator Came: Notes from the Struggle for American Indian Liberation*. Littleton, CO: Aigis Press.

Collins, R. (2006). "Katimih o Sa Chata Kiyou/Why Am I Not Choctaw?" Race in the Lived Experiences of Two Black Choctaw Mixed Bloods in T. Miles and S.P. Holland (Eds.), *Crossing Waters, Crossing Worlds: The African Diaspora in Indian Country* (pp. 260–272). Durham/London: Duke University Press.

Collins, R. (2007). "On the Black Part of Being Indian: Evidence from Choctaw Life Histories" at the panel *What Is This "Black" in Studies of American Indian Culture?* Native American Studies Conference, University of Oklahoma, Norman, Oklahoma, May 3–5.

Cramer, R. (2005). *Cash, Colour and Colonialism: The Politics of Tribal Acknowledgement*. Norman, OK: University of Oklahoma Press.

Davies, C. B. (1994). *Black Women, Writing and Identity: Migrations of the Subject*. London/New York: Routledge.

Deloria, V., Jr. (1980). "Forward: American Fantasy" in G. Bataille and C. Silet (Eds.), *The Pretend Indians: Images of Native Americans in the Movies* (p. xiv). Ames, IA: Iowa State University Press.

Forbes, J. (1988). *Black Africans and Native Americas: Color, Race and Caste in the Evolution of Red-Black Peoples*. London: Basil Blackwell.

Gallay, A. (2002). *The Indian Slave Trade: The Rise of the English Empire in the American South 1670–1717*. New Haven, CT/London: Yale University Press.

Garroutte, E. (2003). *Real Indians: Identity and the Survival of Native America.* Berkeley, CA: University of California Press.
Gilroy, P. (1993). *The Black Atlantic: Modernity and Double Consciousness.* Cambridge, MA: Harvard University Press.
Hill, D. (1992). *The Freedom Seekers: Blacks in Early Canada.* Toronto: Stoddard.
hooks, B. (1992). *Black Looks: Race and Representation.* Toronto: Between the Lines Press.
Klopotek, B. (2007). "Of Shadows and Doubts: Indians and Blacks and the Legacy of Jim Crow". Presentation at panel *What Is This "Black" in Studies of American Indian Culture?* Native American Studies Conference, University of Oklahoma, Norman, Oklahoma, May 3–5.
Krauthamer, B. (2006) "In Their 'Native Country': Freed People's Understandings of Culture and Citizenship in the Choctaw and Chickasaw Nations" in T. Miles and S. Holland (Eds.) *Crossing Waters, Crossing Worlds: The African Diaspora in Indian Country* (pp. 100–120). Durham/London: Duke University Press.
LaRocque, E. (1993). "Preface – or 'Here Are Our Voices – Who Will Hear?'" in J. Perreault and S. Vance (Eds.), *Writing the Circle: Native Women of Western Canada* (pp. xv–xxx). Edmonton: NeWest Publishers.
Lawrence, B. and E. Dua. (2005). "Decolonizing Anti-Racism." *Social Justice: A Journal of Crime, Conflict and World Order,* 32(4), 120–143.
Le Camp, L. (2005). *Racial Considerations of Minstrel Shows and Related Images in Canada.* Unpublished Ph.D. dissertation (pp. 350–361). Toronto: Ontario Institute for Studies in Education/University of Toronto.
Maaka, R. and Fleras, A. (2005). *The Politics of Indigeneity: Challenging the State in Canada and Aotearoa New Zealand.* Dunedin: University of Otago Press.
Mensah, J. (2002). *Black Canadians: History, Experiences, Social Conditions.* Halifax: Fernwood.
Micco, M. (2006). "'Blood and Money': The Case of Seminole Freedmen and Seminole Indians in Oklahoma" in T. Miles and S. Holland (Eds.), *Crossing Waters, Crossing Worlds: The African Diaspora in Indian Country* (pp. 121–144). Durham/London: Duke University Press.
Mohawk, J. (2006). "Subsistence and Materialism" in V. Tauli-Corpuz and J. Mander (Eds.), *Paradigm Wars: Indigenous Peoples' Resistance to Globalization.* Los Angeles, CA: Sierra Club Books and University of California Press.
Morrison, T. (1993). *Playing in the Dark: Whiteness and the Literary Imagination.* New York: Vintage Books.
Paul, D. (2000). *We Were Not the Savages: A Mi'kmaq Perspective on the Collision Between European and Native American Civilizations.* Halifax: Fernwood Press.
Philip, M. N. (1992). *Frontiers: Essays and Writings on Racism and Culture.* Toronto: Mercury Press.
Razack, S. (2002). *Race, Space and the Law: Unmapping a White Settler Society.* Toronto: Between the Lines.
Razack, S. (2004). *Dark Threats and White Knights: The Somalia Affair, Peacekeeping, and the New Imperialism.* Toronto: University of Toronto Press.
Saunt, C. (2005). *Black, White, and Indian: Race and the Unmaking of an American Family.* Oxford/New York: Oxford University Press.
Smith, A. (2005). *Conquest: Sexual Violence and American Indian Genocide.* Cambridge, MA: South End Press.
Smith, L. (1999). *Decolonizing Methodologies: Research and Indigenous Peoples.* Dunedin: Zed Books and University of Otago Press.
Smith, P. (1992). "Lost in America." *Border/Lines* 23(Winter), 17–18.
St. Germain, J. (2002). *Indian Treaty-Making Policy in the United States and Canada, 1867–1877.* Toronto: University of Toronto Press.
Todorov, T. (1984). *The Conquest of America: the Question of the Other.* Translated by Richard Howard. New York: Harper & Row.

Twohig P. (1996). "Colonial Care: Medical Attendance Among the Micmac in Nova Scotia." *Canadian Journal of Medical Health*, 13, 333–353

Walcott, R. (1997). *Black Like Who? Writing/Black/Canada*. Toronto: Insomniac Press.

Weaver, F. (2002). *Latin America and the World Economy: Mercantile Colonialism to Global Capitalism*. Boulder, CO: Westview Press.

Williams, P. (1991). *The Alchemy of Race and Rights: Diary of a Law Professor*. Cambridge, MA: Harvard University Press.

Chapter 7
Resistance from the Margin: Voices of African-Canadian Parents on Africentric Education

Paul Adjei and Rosina Agyepong

7.1 Finding Our Voices: The Rage at the Margin

Almost a decade ago in New York City, a middle-class, White male was kidnapped and held against his will for several days by Spanish-speaking kidnappers. After 7 days of searching, the authorities finally found him in a hole in the ground. According to the official report, the man was found "wild" and his demeanor suggested disorientation (cited in Asante 2003). When he was asked the most difficult part of his experience, the man answered: "I thought I was losing my mind. I felt helpless. People were speaking in a language that I could not understand, but I know they were speaking of me. It angered me that I had been caught in this situation. The worst thing was the possibility that I would actually lose my mind and never be found" (Asante 2003, p. 100).

This is the mood at the margin as we write this chapter. We know the media and the general public are talking about the education of Black youth, yet they are speaking in a language we do not understand and it enrages us. It enrages us because somebody is telling us to pretend that the current education system is indeed desegregated and that those proposing Africentric schools are fermenting segregation (see Brown 2007). The mood at the margin is naked rage, because those quick to accuse us of anything that goes wrong in Canada, and who have charged us to put our house in order are the very people telling us we cannot have a school that would address our concerns. Our demeanor, today, suggests disorientation, and we are afraid we might lose our minds because the inner-city neighbourhoods (ghettos) occupied by Black bodies have become the glorified "modern-day concentration camps" (see Monroe 1998, p. 281). Our future doctors, engineers, lawyers, teachers, nurses, accountants, and other professionals are being slaughtered on the streets of Toronto, while those lucky enough to escape early death end up in prison. Yet, these realities are not what concern these "moral educators," but a proposed school to correct these unfortunate developments (see Radwanski 2007).

Black communities at the margin have lost patience and are indeed enraged, because the Toronto District School Board (TDSB) has failed them. Today, for every ten Black youth the TDSB undertakes to educate, at least four of them "drop out" or get "pushed out" before they complete the program (see Palmer 1997; Solomon 1992; Dei et al. 1997, 2000). The remaining six are taught 60 ways to despise themselves, their culture, history, and worldview, thereby perpetuating this false sense of inferiority, while the White students are taught 134 ways to adore themselves, their cultures, their values, histories, and worldview – all serving to reinforce a false sense of superiority. As King (1967, 1992a) argues about this (mis)education: "[E]ven semantics have conspired to make that which is black seem[s] ugly and degrading. In Roget's *Thesaurus* there are 120 synonyms for blackness and at least sixty of them are offensive, for example, blot, soot, grim, devil, and foul. And there are some 134 synonyms for whiteness and all are favorable, expressed in such words as purity, cleanliness, chastity, and innocence" (pp. 170–171). Moreover, many Black youth get their first taste of prison life through the zero tolerance policy of the TDSB. Indeed, the school system has breached its contract with Black community. To borrow the words of Dr. King Jr., the Black community has been offered a raw deal:

> So we've come here today to dramatize a shameful condition. In a sense we've come to our nation's capital to cash a check. When the architects of our republic wrote the magnificent words of the Constitution and the Declaration of Independence, they were signing a promissory that all men and women, yes, black men/[women] as well as white men/[women], would be guaranteed the unalienable rights of life, liberty, and the pursuit of happiness. It is obvious today that America has defaulted on this promissory note in so far as her citizens of color are concerned. Instead of honouring this sacred obligation, America has given the Negro people a bad check; a check which has come back marked "insufficient funds." We refuse to believe that there are insufficient funds in the great vaults of opportunity of this nation. And so we've come to cash this check, a check that will give us upon demand the riches of freedom and the security of justice. (King 1963, 1992b, p. 102)

Thus, the call for Africentric schools is our way of dramatizing the shameful condition in the current education system and the breach of contract by the school system in Toronto. In 1773, Phillis Wheatley became the first African-American woman (and the second woman in America) to publish a book in America. A controversy ensued as to whether she could be the author of the book. Phillis Wheatley had to settle this controversy by reading to a panel of White men before she was assigned a copyright (Asante 2003). It is a pattern in Euro-American society that Blacks have to explain and justify every move we make to others. And many people also appear to reinforce their sense of superiority through their ability to pass judgment on the Black community and everything we do or fail to do. So, after the Lawrence forum,[1] we once again were summoned before a jury to explain why we need an alternative approach to education system. Our first literary breakthrough (the case of Phillis Wheatley) needed a White panel to approve it. After 124 years, we still need another panel to approve an alternative approach to education for our children. It appears our fate is always decided by a panel, and those of us at the margin are saying enough is enough. We cannot sit at the margin and leave the issues affecting our children and future to others who do not speak the language we understand or share our concerns. This is the mood at the margin and it is within this mood that we write this chapter.

The "we" in this chapter is two doctoral students (a male and a female) of African descent currently pursuing their doctoral education at the University of Toronto, Canada. We both received our initial education (from grade one to undergraduate level) in Ghana, and the schools we attended were attended, taught, and managed by Blacks. Thus, it came as a surprise to us when an impression was being created in the media in Toronto that a school designed and managed by Blacks cannot function without the support of non-Blacks. Again, we were taken aback with this distorted idea that students who attend Africentric schools cannot fully integrate into the larger society when completing the program. This position cannot be accurate because there are at the moment many privately owned and managed Africentric schools in Toronto, and students who attend these schools do not have any problem integrating into the larger society. It is with these distorted stories coupled with our own individual experience, to some extent, with an Africentric school that we write this chapter to protest against this distorted narration and set the record straight. In the next section, we articulate the theoretical underpinnings of the chapter.

7.2 Mapping Anticolonial Terrain for Africentric Schools

There is a saying that whenever Joseph Goebbles, the former Minister for Public Enlightenment and Propaganda of the infamous Nazi's regime, heard the term "culture," his first instinct was to draw his revolver. The Nazis, the most tragic expression of imperialism, had a clear sense of the values and implications of culture as a resistance tool to colonial domination. Amilcar Cabral (1970) rightly noted that colonial domination cannot function permanently within the domain of the material if it cannot repress the cultural life of the colonized subjects. As long as there still exists some elements of the colonized subjects who are willing to retain their cultural identity, foreign domination cannot remain forever (Cabral 1970, p. 3). A critical review of Cabral's words provides a significant understanding of the relevance of culture in anticolonial analysis. Culture is arguably the most significant aspect of a people's history. Embedded in the culture of the people are the values, worldviews, knowledges, languages, and above all, the identity of the people. Thus, to dominate any group of people, the first strategy is to secure their culture. By securing the culture, one can dominate the mind and the identity of that group. The colonizer understands this strategy best; hence, the colonizer takes great interest in the education of the colonized subjects. Thus, the process of producing and validating what is knowledge in the academy has become a colonial exercise. Rather than heralding knowledge that allows learners to develop a counter culture, the current education system actually rewards the knowledge that allows learners to reproduce colonial structures and practices (Dei and Asgharzadeh 2001). So, when Said (1994) talks about the West "doing something about indigenous residents" in order to access and control their territory, he is invariably talking about the act of cultural genocide that denies, devalues, and debases the cultural knowledge of the colonized subjects through colonial education. Thus, whether through the colonial education in Africa (Wa Thiong'O 1986), or forced residential schools in Canada (Henry and Tator 2006), the interest of the colonizer remains the same: removing the local learners from their culture, history, and identity.

Just as an education system embedded in the cultural knowledge of the colonizer corrupts and disrupts the identity, values, and worldview of the colonized subjects; by the same token, an education system grounded in the cultural knowledge of the colonized subjects can generate oppositional and resistance-oriented knowledge to colonial domination. Graveline (1998) supports this argument with the proposition that centering the traditional worldviews, cultures, and values in education is the steadfast way of challenging the Western paradigms that guide today's educational system. Dore (1976, p. 8) argues that the effect of schooling, the way it alters a person's capacity to behave and to do things, depends not only on what is learned, but also on how, why, and where it is learned. Thus, in mapping an anticolonial terrain for Africentric schools, the discussion should not be limited to what is learned in this type of education, but also, how, why, and where it is learned. Within this chapter, we outline a few pedagogical approaches for Africentric schools based on anticolonial thinking.

First, an Africentric classroom needs to accord a discursive integrity and authorial control to the subjective accounts (voice/words/languages/experiences) of learners. Palmer (1999) noted that the current education system is wedded to the notion that higher education can stock people's minds with facts and theories and train them in skillful means; however, it cannot help them grow larger hearts and souls. Thus, in the quest for an alternative education paradigm for Black students, it is critical that learners are taught to reclaim their own voices and subjectivities. After all, when the academic discussion is over, it is our subjective worldviews that matter (Todd 1992, p. 78). This means the pedagogic framework of Africentric schools needs to recognize the knowledges students bring with them to the classroom. Students do not come to school as empty vessels waiting to be filled by "all-knowing teachers." Students come with cultural and experiential knowledges which can and should enrich teaching and learning. Thus, teachers need to create a conducive atmosphere where learners' knowledge, experiences, and voices can be nurtured and used in teaching. As noted (Adjei 2007, p. 8), "it is only when teachers see learning as a process of sharing, and not necessarily giving, that local learners could also have confidence to ask critical questions concerning the conspicuous absence of certain forms of knowledge while others are constantly glorified."

Second, an Africentric classroom needs to interrogate institutionalized power, privilege, and the accompanying rationale for dominant production of what is considered "legitimate" knowledge, culture, and language (Dei 2002). Shahjahan (2005) notes that the reproduction of only dominant knowledge has the power to strip the identity, culture, and values of racialized students in the classroom:

> Western knowledge systems in the academy, as derivatives of colonialism, to the extent to which we can internalize them, can strip off the spirituality, [culture, language and identity] of people like myself, so that our [knowledge], spiritual worldviews, and our histories are disfigured and destroyed. We are in turn left with emptiness and a fragmented life devoid of higher meaning and purpose within the academy. (2005, p. 694)

Thus, an Africentric classroom should be a decolonized space. By decolonized space, we imply an academic space, where Indigenous cultures, languages, values, and worldviews of learners are reclaimed from the margin to the center of learning. It is also a space, where teachers facilitate the internalization of value systems useful in transforming learners from a state of psychological, social, political, and spiritual disempowerment to one of awareness and spiritual empowerment for change (Murtadha 1995). hooks (1994) sees a decolonized classroom as a space where learners reject ways in which the reality and experience of colonized subjects are shaped by the hegemonic cultural discourses. The Africentric classroom should encourage knowledge that will challenge the historic inferiorization of Black students' experience and rich cultural knowledges. Learners in an Africentric classroom should not accept knowledge simply because it emerges from a text or a teacher but should critically analyze all knowledge before accepting it. It is only when the knowledge makes sense within local realities that learners can be prepared to work with it.

Finally, an Africentric school should make identity reconstruction of blackness its priority. Dei (1996) noted that within Euro-American contexts, the social construction of "blackness" and "whiteness" has serious implications for schooling and education of all students but particularly, for students of African descent. George Dei's observation is grounded on the reality that both electronic and print media have never ceased to show or carry stories in which there are Blacks, either in trouble with the law or involved in some form of illicit activity. Thus, there is no doubt that the media distortion of blackness has produced a false sense of inferiority among many Black students in North America. A student articulated in the research conducted by George Dei at a school in Toronto: "Sir, it is not that we Black students do not have self-esteem, but the truth is that we are trying to keep it" (Dei et al. 1997). The South African writer and activist, Steve Biko (1997) in his book *I Write What I Like* argued that identity is not simply a question of skin color, gender or class but an issue of mental attitude. Steve Biko and his friends noted that any change that could end apartheid in South Africa needs to defeat the one main element in politics that was working against Blacks: a psychological feeling of inferiority which was deliberately cultivated by the apartheid system as one of the strategies to ensure White domination in South Africa. Consequently, Steve Biko and his fellow students developed a black consciousness movement to rebuild strong self-identity of Blacks in South Africa. Nelson Mandela, speaking on the occasion of the commemoration of the 20th anniversary of Steve Biko's death, recalled with nostalgia the effects of Steve Biko and his students' organization in reconstructing blackness in South Africa: "It was a time when the tide of Africa's valiant struggle and her liberation, lapping at our own borders, was consolidating black pride across the world and firing the determination of all those who were oppressed to take their destiny into their own hands" (1997, p. 1).

The success story of Steve Biko and his students' organization should serve as a reference point for Africentric education. The curricula in Africentric schools should affirm the values, cultures, history, worldviews, knowledge, and identity of blackness in society. However, in reconstructing and reaffirming Black identity, we should be cautious of paralyzing questions such as: who or what is black? Such questions are often posed to conveniently deflect and deny accountability and responsibility. How can we even discuss the question of "who and what" is Black when it is obvious which bodies get marked for discrimination and punishment. Howard (2006) rightly asks:

> When one looks at the appalling realities of anti-Black racial profiling by criminal justice, employment, and education systems here in Canada – the statistically demonstrated existence of the driving while Black charge (e.g., Rankin et al. 2002); that the employment rates for Black university graduates equals that of White grade ten dropouts (e.g., Solyom 2001) ... – what, indeed, is the purpose of trying to micro-analyze who/what is Black and/or who/what is White when this is so clear with respect to the distribution of privilege and punishment at the systemic level? (p. 49)

Nobody is denying the fact that the Black community is heterogeneous. Indeed, the Black identity is further complicated by class, gender, sexuality, ethnicity, disability, and religion. Therefore the experience of one Black person cannot represent the whole community. Thus, we agreed with Toni Morrison, when she warned us some years ago that the task is not "to alter one hierarchy in order to institute another" (1992, p. 8). There is no point in subverting Eurocentric identity if we are going to replace it with another hegemonic identity that does not represent everybody. Thus, there is validity in complicating Black identity. However, we should not pay much attention to those questions intended to construct a fractured and disjointed community in order to deny responsibility and accountability. The next section deals with how the data used in this chapter were collected and analyzed.

7.3 Methodology

This research is a qualitative study of 20 African-Canadian parents purposively selected from diverse backgrounds (class, ethnicity, gender sexuality, religion, and ability) in the Greater Toronto area. The questions and interview settings were organized in a way that allowed open and frank discussion on issues affecting Black youth education. The interview questions were meant to draw out open-ended stories and responses, and where necessary, follow-up questions were posed for further clarification.

The interviews were guided by the following questions:

1. How do African-Canadian parents conceptualize Africentric schooling?
2. Is the school doing enough to make attending school worthwhile for the children of African-Canadians?
3. Why is an alternative education like an Africentric school necessary for Black youth in Toronto?
4. Do African-Canadian parents consider absence of parental involvement a major issue for the poor performance of Black youth in education?

5. Is the call for Africentric education not the same as the segregation of the past?
6. What are the risks, perils, and limitations of having Africentric schools as alternative education for Black youth?

Each interview lasted for one hour and was audiotaped. Transcripts were carefully read and analyzed for recurrent or dissenting themes. Through triangulation, we compared individual narratives and how they show general or distinct trends. We then formulated common themes that answer the research questions. Our final analyses and interpretation of the data were significantly informed by the stories and narrations of our research participants. In the next section, we outline some of the emerging themes from the interviews.

7.4 The Sensation of Moving While Still Standing: The Education of Black Youth in Toronto

When Sidney W. Mintz (1989) used these words "the sensation of moving while standing still" to describe the choppy relations between an ethnographer and an informant in research, little did we know that such an interesting phrase would be relevant for academic discussions in 19 years to follow. No phrase, however, better captures the conditions of Black youth education in Toronto than the words of Mintz. While the reality suggests that schools in Toronto, over the years, have become more racially diverse as more immigrants from Europe, Latin America, Africa, and Asia settled in Toronto, the school curricula in Toronto are still White. In spite of the numerous calls by parents, educators, and researchers for the curricular and pedagogical practices to change to accommodate the new reality in Toronto (see Daenzar 1983; Solomon 1997; Dei 1996; Fine 1991; Wane 2004; Foster 1997; James and Brathwaite 1996), the TDSB is reluctant to embark on any overhauling exercise that will achieve the required transformation. So is it any wonder that the education of Black youth in Toronto today looks like the proverbial octopus on dancing skates: it is moving alright, but still standing where it started. In our research, African-Canadian parents who were interviewed could not hide their disappointment with the school system for failing to do enough to address the needs of Black students. According to Lisa, an educator and African-Canadian parent originally from South Africa, the school system is failing Black students because the curricula are not preparing them for the world out there:

> I don't think school actually is worth attending, for the most part, for our children. This is because I think the curriculum is lacking in so many ways. It doesn't engage the children, emotionally, culturally, spiritually and intellectually. The children are not really challenged to become critical thinkers. They are just supposed to be these machines who only regurgitate what the teacher wants them to know. They are not supposed to have opinions on their own. They don't seem to be able to relate what happens in the classroom to what happens in their lives or in the broader society. I think the schools really seem to be extremely disconnected from what children should be learning and for what children should be preparing themselves for in terms of the kind of world we live in. [Transcribed file 21/06/07]

The issue of curriculum and how it is failing to connect to the lived realities of Black youth was further echoed by David, a medical technologist and African-Canadian parent originally from Ghana:

> From what I have seen, I think they can do a little bit better. Depending on the issues that they come across probably, they can change the curriculum to suit minorities. By this I mean that they can teach the children more about different races. It looks as if the teaching is based on the North American or Caucasian system. I am not trying to be too biased. Where I come from they are very broad minded and at school they teach only black students, [yet] they try to cover or teach about all races. Before I came to Canada, I knew about North America and Canada. I even knew about the presidents before and after. I also knew the geography. But here ... will you believe that if I ask my children about Ghana they don't seem to know anything. They don't even know the capital of Ghana or the head of state and that is where they come from. To me that is very embarrassing. [Transcribed file 27/06/07]

Matilda, an African-Canadian parent originally from the West Indies sees the problems facing Black students' education beyond the curricular. According to her, the negative attitude of teachers is a major reason why Black youth are dropping out of school:

> There are so many reasons why many black youth drop out of school. One of them is the teachers give the children attitudes for no reason at all even though they do not know these children. They look at them; maybe there is a situation and they talked to them or something and then they gave them attitude. The teachers are disrespectful and rude towards the black children. They do not treat them as human beings. Some teachers are harsh. I agree there need to be discipline in schools. You need rules and regulations but they are human beings as well. They need to know where they stand. They need to know that they are being treated fairly. They need to know whether if their white counterparts did the same thing they would be treated the same as they are getting and they don't see that. They feel that they are ostracized. I also find that there are some principals who do care but many of the time it is not that way. The kids are frustrated in the schools. [Transcribed file 20/06/07]

Francis, a retired teacher of TDSB and a father of four, also sides with what Matilda is saying. According to him, some of the teachers within TDSB not only have a negative attitude, but also are biased toward Black students:

> I have come to the realization that teaching is no longer a profession that people do because they love children or love to teach. It has become a place where people go to earn a living and for me that is a problem. Why will kids not drop out of school when they are not comfortable? For 365 days kids are at school more than they are at home with their parents. If you go to a place where you are not accepted or you don't feel comfortable; everybody wants to go to a place where people know you by your name and call you by your name and make you feel at home. These kids are sensitive. To ignore this is to give the impression that the kids are not smart. They see through all these things at a very early age. I don't know but I think that is the reason. They are not welcome. The kids are not made to feel at home. Teachers have pets in the classroom. These are kids who look like them and go "score free" when they misbehave. These black kids also misbehave and they are in trouble. I have another example. A teacher said to my son or the class not to use certain words in the class. I do not know if he had used it himself and gotten himself into trouble. One day in class a girl used the word the teacher had specifically asked them not to use. This happened to be the teacher's pet and my son said "teacher did you hear what so and so said," she ignored my son. So my son asked her "Are you going to do something about it?" The third time my son drew her attention to that she got angry with my son so my son became a problem for her. From that day my son saw that his teacher was not fair. Again

when you are getting yourself into trouble for trivial things you don't want to go to such a place. You are human and even animals won't do that. [Transcribed file 26/06/07]

As noted from the responses of Lisa, David, Matilda, and Francis, the absence of conditions that make learning convenient for Black students seems to drastically impose a critical limit on the number of Black students willing or able to enter and remain in school to complete their education (also see Callender 1997; Dei 1996; Dei et al. 1997). These responses clearly show that Black students are often confronted with different conditions that frustrate and influence their "dropout" from school (also see Palmer 1997; Dei et al. 1997; Fine 1991). The *Akan* culture of Ghana has a saying that "every animal searches for food and sleeps in areas it finds peaceful and comfortable." Thus, Black students, like all humans, are hesitant to stay and study in a school environment in which they are not welcome. According to Dei et al. (1997), lack of representation in the curricula does not only produce a sense of invisibility for Black students, but also reinforces the power of Whiteness and the colonizing agenda of Euro-American society. Thus, rather than associating Black youth's dropping out with a lack of self-esteem or interest in education, it should be argued that dropping out is a way some Black students register their disapproval and displeasure to the current arrangement in the TDSB. Although dropping out should not be an acceptable excuse, we as educators cannot dislodge the lived experiences of Black students when we are discussing the school system in Toronto. The frustrating part of what our research respondents are saying is that *none* of this is news to the TDSB. The board is fully aware of these issues. Although the occasional commissions and committees set up by TDSB to investigate issues of schooling in Toronto often come out with reports that articulate similar concerns, yet the TDSB in many cases manages to "appear" concerned while doing nothing. Thus, we argue in this chapter that the call for alternative approach to educating Black students in Toronto is the responsible choice for the Black community at this historical moment.

7.5 Issues of Parental Involvement: Dispelling the Myth

The most common alibi used by the TDSB to deny responsibility and complicity in the poor performance of Black students is the absence of African-Canadian[2] parent involvement in their children's education. Parents, clearly, have a role to play in their children's education. Indeed, education is too important to be left in the hands of teachers and administrators alone. Parents, community members, and government all have crucial roles to play in the education of Black students. For instance, while we expect teachers and government to do their parts, they cannot be at homes to switch off television when children are supposed to go to bed in time. They cannot take the video games away from children when they are supposed to do their homework. Teachers and government cannot be at various homes to help children read books and ensure that they appear at school on time. Black parents need to do all these things. They need to be responsible by taking care of their children and also playing a central role in their children's education. In fact, Dei et al. (1997) noted in their research that almost all Black students who participated in their research saw home support as an integral part of their educational success: "Almost all of the students interviewed said that parents should show interest in their children's education, especially by giving them moral support and encouragement" (Dei et al. 1997, p. 190). Thus, our intent is not to offer any excuse for Black parents who fail to keep up their end of the bargain. However, there is still danger in limiting Black youth's school disengagement to only the "family" explanation. While African-Canadian parents we interviewed unanimously agreed that parent involvement is central to Black youth education, they warned that an active involvement does not guarantee that one's children will not face problems at school. Francis prides himself on being an active parent in his children's education:

> If you are looking at someone who is involved in their children's school then I am the one to look for. I am always there. As soon as they call me, in five or ten minutes I am there. Even when I am teaching I find time to come. So, every step of the way I am there. I have listened to the teachers. I have shared ideas with them. I have done what a reasonable parent will do. So, I am very much involved in my children's education. I also go with them on trips and I have conferences with the teachers even before the parent teacher interviews. Sometimes, I go there just to find out how my children are doing. So in terms of involvement I have involved myself with the schools. [Transcribed file 26/06/07]

Yet, in spite of his active involvement, Francis has the following to say about his children's education:

> None of my children have dropped out of school because I will not let them. My older son in particular shows signs of a child who will want to drop out if I let him. The moment my son wakes up in the morning, he is angry and this is not the son that I took to the school system. … You see this is what the school system does to the black kid. It is gradual process but in most cases it works. Another example, my daughter, my oldest child, she was a very brilliant girl. When she was in grade four, she was doing very well. Any work the teacher gave her, she would do it very well. I think the teacher was surprised at the way she was doing well. I don't know if the teacher was being candid or stupid. The teacher told me that she thinks somebody was doing the work for her. You know what? My daughter was the only black kid in the class, so who was doing the work for her? If it were home work you can say the parents were doing the work for her, but in class who would be doing the work for her? So, then, it implies that my daughter was cheating or copying another white kid. Nobody gives the black kid the benefit of the doubt. Nobody has any expectations for these kids. If there are any expectations it is the low expectation. They don't think the black kid is capable of anything. They are not just saying it but they are doing it. I decided to go over every work that my children bring home and discovered that some of her work was marked wrong but they were right. So I went to the teacher and his reply was that my child should bring the work to him early otherwise he would not give him the mark. This is a mark of incompetence on his part. I made the principal aware of what had happened but it did not go anywhere. The kids in the school have their own peers to contend with and then the teachers. When it comes to peer versus peer the teacher is lurking somewhere, seen or unseen. When it comes to the teacher and the two groups of kids, the black kid is always at fault. [Transcribed file 26/06/07]

Lisa also talks about her dedication as a parent to her son's education and how she has always been there to support her son's school:

7 Resistance from the Margin 147

> I have been very involved in my child's school. Over the years I have been a member of the parents' council. I have volunteered in a number of capacities. I go on trips and I help out with school events. You know, on the parent council we do everything from fund raising, to planning events to organizing various events throughout the year and working with teachers and principals. [Transcribed file 21/06/07]

Lisa also has a painful story to tell about her own son's education and how he is very much disengaged from schooling:

> My child has not dropped out of school. He is only twelve but I can see he is already disengaged and by high school he will be ready to drop out. I think I am very much in that space. I write about these issues myself. I give support to parents whose children are dropping out or have dropped out. I don't think he will drop out per se but I think that I can already see signs of him disengaging based on the personal experiences that he has had, and also the school's curriculum and lack of care. … All of these together [including his recent experience of assault from a teacher] have seriously impacted him in many, many ways. Emotionally he has lost confidence in himself and it has affected his self-esteem. He also doesn't believe in doing well or he has started to believe that who cares if you are doing well because if you are smart, you get punished for being smart. So he dumps himself down. You know. For a while during the assault he was so afraid. He wasn't eating. He was developing skin rashes. He wasn't sleeping. He was afraid to go to school. We had to spend fifteen minutes every day to make him comfortable. [Transcribed file 21/06/07]

These two examples, like many other stories shared in the interviews, clearly indicate that there is more to Black students' school disengagement and dropouts than the simple explanation that their parents do not get involved. We do admit that for some Black students the absence of home and community supports do exacerbate the effects of the systemic and structural failures of the school system on them. However, we question this pathological location of the family or home environment as the source of problems for Black students' abysmal performance in the school system. Such explanations are evoked to divert attention from the social-economic consequences of systemic racism. We strongly argue that those who take credit for students' academic success must also be prepared to accept responsibility when success is not achieved. Teachers and administrators always take pride and credit when their students are successful. However, when a student becomes a failure, somehow, parents get the blame. Moreover, we have to put parental involvement in a broader context. The idea that parents are only involved when they show up in the school council meeting or become part of the fund-raising committee or volunteer their time at the school is very narrow and obscures other forms of involvement. Furthermore, the narrow definition of parental involvement does not capture the lived experiences of many racialized, working class, immigrant parents. These individuals face a parallel series of hurdles which operate along and within the same tropes of dominance as those structuring the educational lives of Black youth. For example, many African-Canadian parents are involved in low-income jobs; thus, many have to work for more than 12 hours a day in order to raise enough income to cater to their family needs (Galabuzi 2008, 2006; Swanson 2002). In view of that, many of them cannot perform the White, middle class female's definition of "parental involvement" (showing up for school meetings, participating in school fund-raising, and attending in school council meetings). This does not imply that these parents do not care about their children's education. They do care. For instance, Cynthia, an African-Canadian parent, shared her story of trying to combine a full-time job and with getting actively involved in her child's education:

> You have to know what is going on. You have to be in their faces and I have lost my job because I wanted to spend time with my kids. It is a problem for me now because you have to put in that much time into showing people how to do their work and you spend all that time investing in your kids and you get penalized at your job. So it's a vicious cycle. You need to take time off for this meeting. You need time off for that meeting to see the teacher because you can only do that between 9–4 p.m. because that is the only time the teachers work and that is the time you need to work if you are working at your regular day job. They turn around and think that you don't have it all together. You can't be here on time. My holidays are spent talking to teachers, going to meetings. It is gruelling. You need to be very strong because of the talk down and you feel you are at a losing battle. [Transcribed file 29/06/07]

So, if Black students whose parents are actively involved are also facing the threat of school disengagement and dropout, then we need to look at challenges facing the education of Black youth beyond parental involvement. In addition, it appears the discourse of parental involvement is at the moment, racialized, gendered, and classed to the extent that it literally excludes what some African-Canadian parents have been doing.

7.6 In Search of an Alternative Approach to Schooling: Black Students and Learning

As already noted, some Black students within the TDSB have to constantly endure low expectations of some teachers, negative and biased attitudes of some teachers, school curricula that are not inclusive, and unnecessary surveillance by some teachers and administrators. All these factors have become barriers that impede the progress of Black students in the education system in Toronto. In spite of numerous calls and appeals from parents, educators, researchers, and the TDSB's own committees' reports, the TDSB has done nothing concretely to address these concerns. Thus, the search for an alternative approach to educating Black youth cannot be postponed any longer. In this study, we asked our participants whether the call for an Africentric school as alternative education for Black youth was justified. Most of our respondents (95%, 19 of 20) were of the opinion that Africentric schools as alternative education for Black youth is long overdue. Janet, a teacher with TDSB, and an African-Canadian mother of two, who originates from Nigeria, sees Africentric education as a relevant alternative school that will teach Black students to see the world through an Africentric lens:

> I think black children who will go to an institution which teaches from an Africentric perspective will identify and feel very comfortable. The school will be sensitive to their needs and address certain issues that they want to see addressed. Most of the things they will be taught in the school will incorporate their spirituality. The learning will be holistic.

> Every child has something to say and they are listened to because it is not just adults who have something to say. The children will also contribute to the learning. They will feel more comfortable seeing black teachers that they can reckon with. One of the things that these children are missing in the mainstream is that there are no role models that they see among the school administration, teachers and staff but in the Africentric school they are going to see lots of role models and the children will feel represented. They will be valued, respected and this will make them feel at home. [Transcribed file 28/06/07]

The term "centric" refers to how the individual learner's culture, values, knowledge, and worldviews become the lenses through which she or he sees the world. There are several "centrics": *Eurocentric, Asiancentric, Africentric,* and *Aboriginalcentric.* The unfortunate challenge we have in contemporary education is that Eurocentric continues to present itself as the only way of seeing the world. Thus, any other center from which to generate, disseminate, and reflect in knowledge is pushed to the margin of knowledge production, validation, and dissemination. So in today's academy, every learner – no matter where she or he originates from – is forced to see the world through White, middle class, European perspectives (see Scheurich and Young 1997). Africentric education is a way for learners of African descent – whether born in the continent of Africa or in the diaspora – to view the world through their African culture, values, and worldviews. Africentric education works with the assumption that because many Black students have suffered identity crises in the Eurocentric classroom, shaping school curricula to help Black students rediscover their African philosophies, culture, worldview, values, and knowledge holds the promise of cultural transformation (Karenga 1986; Asante 1987, 1991; Dei 1994). Murrel (2002) argues that because racism is an ideology that positions Whites as superior and non-Whites as inferior, the pedagogy developed for African-Canadian children should confront and also inoculate them from internalizing this racist ideology. Africentric education has the potential to build the ethnic pride of Black students; strengthening the knowledge associated with their history, values, and culture and fostering their worldviews to value community; and being in harmony with themselves, others, and nature. It is within this context that Janet lauded and welcomed Africentric schools. Francis also wants Africentric schools because he is tired and fed up with the lukewarm attitudes and lack of concern for the needs of Black students within the TDSB:

> We are not the only parents complaining. There are lots of other black parents too complaining. Every single day these teachers have problems about our children. They kept on telling us about how our kids are behaving or not behaving. This must be the reason why we as black people must have our own school or institution manned by our own people who understand these kids. People who can see through and understand how they feel and love them. It is enough. I am not saying that all white teachers are bad. That is not what I am trying to say. But it is difficult because after having so many of them treats your children this way, you tend to think that all of them are like that. But that is not a fact. You can find some of them who understand, want to do something, have good hearts and are good teachers. [Transcribed file 26/06/07]

However, not all our respondents support Africentric schools, although they do recognize that the existing school is not working for Black students. For example, Georgina, an African-Canadian parent, who works with Statistics Canada, thinks that an alternative school is a waste of resources. Instead, she explains, the resources should be channeled into the existing system to make it work:

> I don't see the Africentric school as an alternative at all. What I think should be done is to put all those resources in the mainstream because if they do that they will be more or less killing two birds with one stone. At the same time that you are attending to the needs of these children, their counterparts who are not black also have the opportunity to learn in the same process. It will create an atmosphere that will encourage the students to understand each other and get along better than they do now. [Transcribed file 29/06/07]

Georgina's position on Africentric schools raises interesting issues for critical analysis. Indeed, the call for Africentric schools is due to the failure of the TDSB to positively respond to years (20 years or more) of protest by educators, researchers, and African-Canadian parents against the current education system and how it is not working for Black students. So, why will Georgina suggest that we keep waiting for the TDSB to effect the needed changes when it is clear such a time will never come? If the current system is not working, why is Georgina against the alternatives? Answers to these questions can be found in Georgina's later statement:

> Now if they have this Africentric school, my fear, my fear is that they may not necessarily divert a lot of funding to this school. The other schools who are already in existence might take priority over this school and that will affect the school in more than one way which might not necessarily help in achieving the goals that were originally set. A school that does not have funding to purchase the things that students need is not going to progress in anyway. If a school is not going to be funded, the performance of students is not going to be good anyway. Another thing I want to mention is that ... [i]f you study in that school [Africentric school] for three or four years and come out just like somebody in the mainstream, but at the employment level you [will be] judged differently. This might even enhance racism all the more. So I believe that those things need to be looked at very carefully. The only thing that will be good if an Africentric school is established is when the school produces students with average grade points that are higher than the mainstream then we will achieve something. If not it will be worse than it is now. [Transcribed file 29/06/07]

In the opinion of Georgina, given the existing racist and discriminatory practices against Black people, an Africentric school will be an easy target for discrimination and racism, which will further exacerbate the existing challenges facing Black youth in Canada. While there is cause for Georgina to be concerned, we need to put her fears in a broader context. In the first place, Blacks are not performing incredibly well in the job market. According to Solyom (2001) the employment rates for Black university graduates are equal to that of White grade ten dropouts. Second, whether we have an Africentric school or not, racism will continue to exist in Euro-American society. Racism is not a recent phenomenon that emerged only after the arrival of immigrants of color in North America. In fact, both Canada and America were founded on racist ideologies and practices. These ideologies and practices informed the physical, cultural, and spiritual violence committed against Aboriginal people, and against Africans who were later brought to North America to be slaves (Churchill 2004; Henry and Tator 2006; see also Scheurich and Young 1997). Moore (1994), Montague (1974), and Stepan (1982) have rightly observed that racism was used historically in Euro-American society to organize human groups into series of hierarchies in order to exert White power and privilege. Thus, this chapter sees the struggle against racism as not simply a task against a few racist lunatics on the fringe, but rather the struggle to de-racialize micro and macro social formations left to us through slavery and colonization that continue to affect and shape the lives of racialized groups in Euro-American society (see Adjei 2008). The Black community cannot continue to let Black students fail and drop out from schools because we fear an alternative school will not be welcomed by the dominant. If anything, we need an education system that will teach Black students how to live with, and navigate through, this complex world of racism. Finally, the question of funding cannot be ignored. It is a relevant issue that requires further discussion. The TDSB should not give the Black community an Africentric school, if the intent is to set the school up for failure. If the required funding for the successful implementation of an Africentric school is not going to be provided, then the school should not be set up. But if members of the Black community pay taxes like any other groups, then, the state providing funding for such a program is not a favor. The Black community, like any other group in Canada, deserves a well-funded school for its children.

7.7 Much Ado About Segregation in Africentric Schools and Issues of Re(Segregation)

Segregation was fermented in the United States after a legal tussle between Homer Adolph Plessy and the State of Louisiana which ended up at the Supreme Court of the United States in 1896. On June 7, 1892, 30-year-old Homer Adolph Plessy, a person of color, was jailed for sitting in a "Whites only" car in the East Louisiana Railroad. Homer Plessy was only one eighth Black and seven eighths White, but under Louisiana law, he was still considered a Black person and therefore required to sit in the cars meant for persons of color. Homer Plessy went to court and argued in *Homer Adolph Plessy v. The State of Louisiana* that the *Separate Car Act* violated the 13th and 14th Amendments of the Constitution of the United States. The judge at the trial, John Howard Ferguson, found Plessy guilty as charged for refusing to leave a car meant for only Whites. Plessy appealed to the Supreme Court of the United States against the ruling. The Supreme Court heard *Plessy vs. Ferguson*'s case in 1896 and upheld the ruling. This ruling became the determining factor that cemented segregated relations between Blacks and Whites in the United States. This "separate but equal" doctrine was further extended to cover many areas of public life such as the use of restaurants, theatres, restrooms, and public schools. It was not until *Brown v. Board of Education*, which started in 1951 and ended at the Supreme Court on May 17, 1954, that the practice of segregation in public schools was made unconstitutional in the United States. And it even took the civil rights movement more than a decade to achieve some amount of "desegregation" in the South.

Although Canada has done a lot to cover and deny its history of segregation, many writings (Bolaria and Li 1988; Winks 1971, 1978; Shepard 1991; Troper 1972, and others) point to an explicit history of segregation in Canada. For instance, Winks in his book *The Black in Canada: A History*, noted that Blacks who remained in Canada lived in largely segregated communities in Nova Scotia, New Brunswick, and Ontario. Perhaps, the most celebrated case of segregation in Canada was when in 1931 a Black customer was denied services at a Montreal tavern. The case was heard at the Supreme Court in Canada in 1939, and the highest Court of the land ruled that racial discrimination was legally enforceable (Walker 1985). In fact, the legislature supporting segregation in Ontario existed in the legal books until 1964. It was not until Professor Harry Arthurs drew attention to it in a note to the Canadian Bar Review that the segregated law was finally removed (Arthurs 1963). Thus, given the long history of segregation in Canada, it is only those who are informed by historical amnesia or have vested interest in defending the illusion of an idealized democratic, multicultural, and desegregated society that will accuse proponents of Africentric schools of fermenting (re)segregation. For instance, there are many people in Toronto today who have racially monolithic social encounters: They live in de facto White only or people of color only (or predominantly White or people of color) neighborhoods, their children go to "white only or people of color only" (or predominantly White or people of color) schools, and have friends who are only White or only people of color. These are not simple personal choices; they are political choices that cumulatively entrench segregation. But Blacks are supposed to accept this de facto segregation because Canada needs to appear integrated, at least to the uninformed mind. So, today, integration has become the new erotic, exotic, and sugar-coated term for assimilation. When they tell us to integrate, they are invariably telling us to assimilate White, middle-class, male values. Not surprisingly, integration has been elevated to the level of an intrinsic moral value that ought to be respected at all costs. Integration is no more a means to an end; in fact, it is an end in itself. Not that this chapter is against integration, but when integration is rooted in vigorous pursuit of equity, fairness, and social justice, we are simply working to maintain the status quo. The fundamental question to be asked is not "whether all races can integrate?" but rather, "what are the ground rules for integration?" "Who are those being called upon to integrate?" and "Integration should be accepted at whose expense?" We cannot pursue integration when the current arrangement clearly favors one racial, gendered, and classed group. In our research, we asked research participants whether they consider an Africentric school as a form of segregated school. Francis does not think of an Africentric school as a segregated school. In fact, he finds it hard to understand how people can equate an Africentric school with a segregated school, when the actual segregation existing in the Greater Toronto area is there for all to see:

> They are talking about segregation; go to Barrie or Newmarket and you will see what segregation is about. Everybody is moving away because we [Blacks] are coming close to them, but the teachers are still here. The teachers come from Barrie and New Market to Jane and Finch to teach and go. You said we want community schools where kids attend

7 Resistance from the Margin 153

> schools which are in their neighbourhood that is a good idea. Then community schools must have community teachers who live in the community and know what is going on in the community. ... I have taught in a class in high school and a kid tells me "you are the first black teacher I have encountered." This was in Scarborough [a place dominantly occupied by racialized bodies]. ... An Africentric school is not a school meant for only black kids. What is taught there, the prism from which curriculum is taught is from a black prism; a black person's prism. The teachers there understand the black kids and the purpose of it is to make the black kid successful. [Transcribed file 26/06/07]

Francis is right in his observation that an Africentric school is defined by what is taught and practiced there, rather than who goes or does not go there. While an Africentric school may have Black students in mind, the school will be open to everybody irrespective of his or her race, gender, ethnicity, class, and religion. In any case, there are several focused schools in Toronto. We have gender-based schools, faith-based schools, and in some cases, certain schools located in White neighborhoods have more than 98% White students. So, why are people singling out Africentric schools as if that is the first focused school in Toronto? Besides, Canada and the Unite States have a history with Africentric education. So, this is by no means an untested approach to this region or country. For example, there are three Africentric schools (although they are private) in Toronto at the moment.

Lisa, recalling her experience as a Black student in South Africa during the era of apartheid, argues that her concern is not how the school is branded by the media or any section of the general public. In her opinion, an Africentric school is not a segregated school. However, even if it were, and will reaffirm the identity of Black students and give them a better future, the Black community would owe no one an apology:

> Well I think bell hooks writes about schooling during the times of segregation. I grew up in apartheid South Africa and so we grew up in segregation. While we recognized that there are so many problems in our communities we were together. I never went to school scared that the teacher would not understand where I came from or did not understand that I experienced racism; had no cultural contexts. So even though we were segregated we thrived in so many ways because we were intact. We took care of ourselves spiritually, knowing that white people did not want to be anywhere near us because we were savages. When we were together, we affirmed our identities in so many ways that we actually did well in school because teachers generally cared about us. We were taught to be survivors because of what we would face in the world and I think that kind of work has stopped happening because we assume that we live in a multicultural society now. We were programmed to believe that everybody loves each other now and everybody is equal. We see the lies of that every single day; you know, because Eurocentricism is still centered within the notion of multiculturalism. Multiculturalism does not acknowledge racism or the need for antiracism education. It does not do any good thing for any black children except white children. They still know that we conquered all these cultures and that is why we can appropriate them at will. So we do not have to respect them. We still don't have to learn about them, you know. It just promotes this superficial nature of this society so we desperately need African-Centered Schools. We should not feel guilty or be made to feel that we have to apologize for wanting schools that represent us and want the best for us. So it says something about the society when they choose you as being segregationist for wanting to create opportunities for yourselves. This is a choice but they make it sound like it is slavery. And that they will have to go to jail or something if their children don't go to these schools. [Transcribed file 21/06/07]

We agree with Lisa. To think of someone as a slave but not treat him or her that way is neither a noble nor gracious gesture of which one can be proud. An education system that insists we are always welcome, and yet constantly ignores our presence by refusing to include our experience, culture, knowledge, values, identity, and history cannot be desegregated education. So, rather than wasting time explaining ourselves to people who deliberately engage in the politics of selective forgetting and remembering to protect White privilege and power in Euro-American society, proponents of Africentric schools should focus on ways an Africentric school can address the challenges facing the education of Black youth in Toronto. If Africentric schools will better affirm the identity of Black students and prepare them for a better tomorrow, who really cares if such a school is viewed within the imagination of the media and a section of the public as a segregated school?

7.8 Discussions and Conclusion

In any free and democratic society, the welfare of its citizens is developed based on the ability to make choices. The right to choose should equally be integrated into the educational objective of this country. Many African-Canadian parents interviewed in our research insist that they deserve the right and freedom to make a choice between the current education system and an alternative education like an Africentric school. Dei (1996) rightly notes that our ability as educators, parents, community members, and policymakers to create choices for youth to succeed in their academic pursuit should not be politicized. The call for Africentric schools is dynamic and revitalizes the African-Canadians' self-definition and empowerment. Our research shows that the establishment of an Africentric school is a way to create a collective consciousness, which can lead to empowerment and respect for Black communities (see Kenyatta 1998; Dei et al. 1997).

However, the implementation of Africentric schools will not be without challenges. For instance, the establishment of an Africentric school may shift attention away from the existing fight to ensure equity and justice within the current TDSB. This could be a problem as some Black students will still want to remain in the mainstream school system. Thus, the advocacy for inclusive curricular and pedagogical practices within the TDSB should not be stopped after the establishment of an Africentric school. If anything, successful stories from Africentric school should be transferred into the TDSB. Finally, an educational paradigm built on Africentric schooling places a huge responsibility on teachers who are themselves products of Eurocentric education. This means that teacher training programs will need to both use and impart an Africentric framework to equip teachers with the necessary skills to work effectively within an Africentric school.

For those who insist that the Black community should not rush for an alternative school but should wait for the TDSB to put its house in order, we offer the words of Dr. Martin Luther King Jr. "This 'Wait' has almost always meant 'Never.' It has been tranquilizing thalidomide, relieving the emotional stress for a moment, only to give birth to an ill-formed infant of frustration. We must come to see with the distinguished jurist of yesterday that justice too long delayed is justice denied" (King 1992c, p. 88). We have waited for more than 20 years for something obvious to the Ontario Royal Commission on Learning (RCOL), the Organization of Parents of Black Children (OPBC), and many researchers and educators such as Solomon (1992), Palmer (1997), Dei et al. (1997, 2000), Fine (1991), and James and Brathwaite (1996) - it is time for an Afrocentric school.

It is easier for those who have not experienced what Lisa, Francis, and Cynthia have gone through in their children's education to say "we should wait for the TDSB to put its house in order." But, when you have been called during the day from work to bail out your child, who you knew was at school, from jail because of the "zero tolerance policy" of TDSB; when your son is not eating or sleeping because he is afraid to go to school the next day to meet teachers and administrators who hate him (like the case of Lisa's son); when you have to give up your job so as to keep up the number of times you can answer calls from your children's school (like Cynthia); when your child has been slapped in your presence at school and is still suspended because she is Black (as in the case of Francis's daughter); when your daughter is ill-advised by the school guidance counselor to choose a course that will affect what she wants to do at college (like Janet's daughter); when your first child has been killed on the street after dropping out of school, and your second child is also feeling disengaged and wants to dropout; then you will understand why those in favor of Africentric schools find it difficult to wait. "There comes a time when the cup of endurance runs over, and men and women are no longer willing to be plunged into an abyss of injustice where they experience the blackness of corroding despair" (King 1992c, p. 89). We hope those who want us to wait will understand our legitimate and unavoidable impatience.

7.9 Postscript

At the time we were concluding the research, the TDSB board of Trustees, by majority decision, voted to set up an Africentric school in TDSB. Although this is a welcome development, the mainstream media, a section of politicians in Toronto, and a section of the general public have not backed away from their misinformed views of Africentric school. Such individuals are waiting for the experiment to fail and then to cry out loud: "We told you so." This chapter has been written both to make a case for Africentric schools and also to educate those who still have misinformed views about on Africentric schools. We want to conclude that when we see the number of Black youth killing each other on the street every day, we cannot but pray that this school succeeds. For us, anything that will stop Black youth from killing each other, ending their careers in jails, and engaging in drugs should be welcomed by any individuals that have concern for the future of the Black community.

Acknowledgments We dedicate this work to Professor George Dei of the University of Toronto, who took so much heat and threat for calling, and pushing for, Africentric schools. Nana Sefa Atweneboah, your dedication to educational and community activism is an example from which to learn. The raw data in this chapter are from the doctoral thesis of Rosina Agyepong, coauthor of this chapter. Paul Banahene Adjei is most grateful to her for allowing the use of part of her research interviews to write this chapter. Rosina Agyepong, thank you very much.

Note

1. It was a forum organized by the Black community in February 2005 to identify some of the issues facing Black youth education in Toronto. Among the recommendations at the forum was the need for the TDSB to experiment with an Africentric school.
2. Within this chapter, the term 'African-Canadian Parent(s)' when used in general reference to a group of people refers to all parents raising African Canadian children, not just to those of African-Canadian ancestry.

References

Adjei, P. B. (2007). Decolonising knowledge production: the pedagogic relevance of Gandhian satyagraha to schooling and education in Ghana. *Canadian Journal of Education, 30*(4), 1046–1067.
Adjei, P. B. (2008). Unmapping the tapestry of *Crash*. In P. Howard and G. Dei (Eds.), *Crash Politics and Antiracism: Interrogations of Liberal Race Discourse* (pp. 111–130). New York: Peter Lang.
Arthurs, H. (1963). Civil liberties and public schools: segregation of Negro students. *Canadian Bar Review, 4*, 453–457.
Asante, M. (1987). *The Africentric Idea*. Philadelphia, PA: Temple University Press.
Asante, M. (1991). The Africentric idea in education. *Journal of Negro Education, 60*, 170–179.
Asante, M. K. (2003). *The Survival of the American Nation: Erasing Racism*. Amherst, NY: Prometheus Books.
Biko, S. (1997). *I Write What I Like: A Selection of His Writings*. Randburg: Ravan Press.
Bolaria, B. S. and Li, P. (1988). *Racial Oppresion in Canada*. Toronto: Garamond Press.
Brown, L. (2007, November 9). *Majority at grassroots gathering support concept of African-centred learning to curb dropout rate*. Retrieved June 3, 2008 from http://www.thestar.com/article/275059.
Cabral, A. (1970, February 20). *National Liberation and Culture*. Paper presented at the The 1970 Eduardo Mondlane lecture, Program of Eastern African Studies of the Maxwell School of Citizenship and Public Affairs, Syracuse University.
Callender, C. (1997). *Education for Empowerment: The Practice and Philosophies of Black Teachers*. Wiltshire, UK: Cromwell.
Churchill, W. (2004). *Kill the Indian, Save the Man: The Genocidal Impact of American Indian Residential Schools*. San Francisco, CA: City Light Books.
Daenzar, P. (1983, March 10). How structural racism is reinforced by Canadian educational institutions. *McMaster Courier, 2*(4).
Dei, G. S. J. (1994). Africentricity: a cornerstone of pedagogy. *Anthropology and Education Quarterly, 25*(1), 3–28.
Dei, G. J. S. (1996). *Theory and Practice: Anti-racism Education*. Halifax: Fernwood.

Dei, G. J. S. (2002). Rethinking the role of indigenous knowledges in the academy. *International Journal of Inclusive Education, 4*(2), 111–132.
Dei, G. J. S. and Asgharzadeh, A. (2001). The power of social theory: the anti-colonial discursive framework. *Journal of Educational Thought, 35*(3), 297–323.
Dei, G., Mazzuca, J., McIsaac, E., and Zine, J. (1997). *Reconstructing "Drop-Out": A Critical Ethnography of the Dynamics of Black Students' Disengagement from Schools.* Toronto/Buffalo/London: University of Toronto Press.
Dei, G. J. S., James, I. M., Karumanchery, L. L., James-Wilson, S., and Zine, J. (2000). *Removing the Margins: The Challenges and Possibilities of Inclusive Schooling.* Toronto: Canadian Scholars press.
Dore, R. (1976). *The Diploma Disease: Education, Qualification and Development.* London: George Allen and Unwin.
Fanon, F. (1963). *The Wretched of the Earth.* New York: Grove Press.
Fine, M. (1991). *Framing Dropouts: Notes on the Politics of an Urban Public High School.* Albany, NY: State University of New York Press.
Foster, M. (1997). *Black Teachers on Teaching.* New York: The New Press.
Foucault, M. (1980). *The History of Sexuality: An Introduction.* New York: Vintage.
Galabuzi, G.-E. (2006). *Canada's Economic Apartheid: The Social Exclusion of Racialized Groups in the New Century.* Toronto: Canadian Scholars Press.
Galabuzi, G.-E. (2008). *Changing the Canvas.* Toronto: Canadian Labour Congress.
Graveline, F. J. (1998). *Circle Works: Transforming Eurocentric Consciousness.* Halifax: Fernwood.
Henry, F. and Tator, C. (2006). *The Color of Democracy: Racism in Canadian Society.* Toronto: Thomson Nelson.
hooks, b. (1994). *Teaching to Transgress.* New York: Routledge.
Howard, P. (2006). On silence and dominant accountability: a critical anticolonial investigation of the antiracism classroom. In G. Dei and A. Kempf (Eds.), *Anti-Colonialism and Education: The Politics of Resistance.* Rotterdam/Taipei: Sense publishers.
James, C. and Brathwaite, K. (1996). The education of African Canadians: issues, contexts and expectations. In K. Brathwaite and C. James (Eds.), *Educating African Canadians* (pp. 13–31). Toronto: John Loriner.
Johal, G. S. (2005). Order in K.O.S.: on race, rage, and method. In G. S. Dei and G. S. Johal (Eds.), *Critical Issues in Anti-racist Research Methodologies* (pp. 269–290). New York/Washington, DC/Baltimore, MD: Peter Lang.
Karenga, M. (1986). *Introduction to Black Studies.* Los Angeles, CA: University of Sankore Press.
Kenyatta, K. (1998). *Guide to Implementing African-Centred Education.* Detroit, MI: African Way Investments.
King Jr., M. L. (1967, 1992a). Where do we go from here? In J. M. Washington (Ed.), *I Have a Dream: Writings and Speeches that Changed the World. Foreword by Coretta Scott King* (pp. 169–179). San Francisco, CA: Harper Collins.
King Jr., M. L. (1963, 1992b). I have a dream. In J. M. Washington (Ed.), *I Have a Dream: Writings and Speeches that Changed the World. Foreword by Coretta Scott King* (pp. 101–106). San Francisco, CA: Harper Collins.
King Jr., M. L. (1992c). Letter from a Birmingham jail (1963). In J. M. Washington (Ed.), *I Have a Dream: Writings and Speeches that Changed the World. Foreword by Coretta Scott King* (pp. 83–100). San Francisco, CA: Harper Collins.
Lorde, A. (1977, December 28). *The Transformation of Silence into Language of Action.* Paper presented at the The Modern Language Association's "Lesbian and Literature Panel," Chicago, IL.
Lorde, A. (1978). *The Black Unicorn: Poems.* New York: Norton, W. W.
Memmi, A. (1965). *The Colonizer and the Colonized, Introduction by Jean-Paul Satre.* Boston, MA: Beacon Press.
Mintz, S. W. (1989). The sensation of moving, while standing still. *American Ethnologist, 16*(4), 786–796.
Monroe, I. (1998). Louis Farrakhan's Ministry of Misogyny and Homophobia. In A. Alexander (Ed.), *The Farrakhan Factor: African-American Writers on Leadership, Nationhood, and the Minister Louis Farrakan* (pp. 275–298). New York: Grove Press.

Montague, A. (1974). *Man's Most Dangerous Myth: The Fallacy of Race*. New York: Oxford University Press.
Moore, B. (1994). Resisting racism through religion education, religious educational. *Journal of Australia, 10*(2), 1–22.
Morrison, T. (1992). *Playing in the Dark: Whitness and the Literary Imagination*. New York: Vintage.
Murrel, P. C. J. (2002). *African-Centred Pedagogue. Developing Schools of Achievement For African-American Children*. Albany, NY: State University of New York Press.
Murtadha, K. (1995). An African-centred pedagogy in dialogue with liberatory multiculturalism. In C. Sleeter and P. L. Mc Laren (Eds.), *Multicultural Education Critical Pedagogy and the Politics of Difference* (pp. 349–370). Albany, NY: State University of New York Press.
Palmer, H. (1997). *Perceptions of Home, School and Community – Related Factors that Contribute to Academic Underachievement Among Incarcerated African Caribbean Male Students in an Urban Residential High School*. Unpublished manuscript. Buffalo, NY: University of New York at Buffalo.
Palmer, P. (1999). The grace of great things: reclaiming the sacred in knowing, teaching and learning. In S. Glazer (Ed.), *The Heart of Learning: Spirituality in Education* (pp. 15–32). New York: Jeremey P. Tarcher/Putnam.
Prah, K. (1997). Accusing the victims – review of in my father's house by Kwame Anthony Appiah. *Codesria Bulletin, 1*, 14–22.
Radwanski, A. (2007, November 6). *Voluntary or not, it's still segregation*. Retrieved March 6, 2008, from http://www.theglobeandmail.com/servlet/story/RTGAM.20071106.WBwbradwanski20071106123702/WBStory/WBwbradwanski
Rankin, J., Quinn, J., Shephard, M., Simmie, S. and Duncanson, J. (2002, October 19). Singled out: Star analysis of police crime data shows justice is different for blacks and whites. *Toronto Star*.
Said, E. (1994). *Culture and Imperialism*. New York: Vintage.
Scheurich, P. and Young, M. (1997). Coloring epistemologies: are our research epistemologies racially biased? *Educational Researcher, 26*(4), 4–16.
Shahjahan, R. (2005). Spirituality in the academy: reclaiming from the margins and evoking a transformative way of knowing the world. *International Journal Qualitative Studies in Education, 18*(6), 685–711.
Shepard, B. (1991). Plain racism: the reaction against Oklahoma Black immigration to the Canadian plains. In O. Mckague (Ed.), *Racism in Canada*. Saskatoon: Fifth House.
Solomon, P. (1992). *Black Resistance in High School: Forging a Separatist Culture*. Albany, NY: State University of New York Press.
Solomon, P. (1997). Race modelling and representation in teacher education and teaching. *Canadian Journal of Education, 22*(4), 395–410.
Solyom, C. (2001, October 26). Black-and-white inequity: pigment matters in Montreal: survey. *The Gazette (Montreal)*
Stepan, N. (1982). *The Idea of Race in Science*. Hamden, CT: Archon Books.
Swanson, J. (2002). *Poor bashing: the politics of exclusion*. Toronto: Between the lines.
Todd, L. (1992). What more do they want? In G. McMaster and L. Martin (Eds.), *Indigena*. Vancouver: Douglas and McIntyre.
Troper, A. (1972). *Only Farmers Need Apply*. Toronto: Griffin House.
Walker, J. (1985). *Race and historian: Some lessons from Canada public policy*. Waterloo: University of Waterloo.
Wane, N. (2004). Experiences of visible minority students and anti-racist education within the Canadian education system. *Journal of Thought, 39*(1), 25–44.
Wa Thiong'O, N. (1986). *Decolonising the Mind: The Politics of Language in African Literature*. Nairobi: East African Educational Publishers.
Winks, R. (1971). *The Blacks in Canada: A History*. New Haven, CT: Yale University Press.
Winks, R. (1978). *The Blacks in Canada: A History*. New Haven, CT: Yale University Press.

Chapter 8
Anticolonialism, Labor, and the Pedagogies of Community Unionism: The Case of Hotel Workers in Canada[1]

Peter H. Sawchuk

> The proposed economic solution of the Negro problem in Africa and America has turned the thoughts of Negroes toward a realization of the fact that the modern white laborer of Europe and America has the key to the serfdom of black folk, in his support of militarism and colonial expansion. He is beginning to say to these workingmen that, so long as black laborers are slaves, white laborers cannot be free. Already there are signs in South Africa and the United States of the beginning of understanding between the two classes.
>
> (W.E.B. DuBois: *The Negro* – 1915, pp. 145–146)
>
> Labour cannot emancipate itself in the white skin where in the black it is branded.
>
> (Karl Marx: *Capital Volume 1* – 1867/1990, p. 414)

8.1 Introduction

In Toronto (Canada) today, hotel workers have turned a new page in their own lives but they may also have begun to turn a new page in the collective life of the trade union movement. They are organizing, and in Canada, these efforts may represent a movement of distinction: at the center of a coalition of largely female and largely immigrant workers of color, an increasingly coherent and effective form of community/labor organizing has moved north to Canada from the United States and taken root.

Here I explore one of a growing number of examples in which the logics of race, gender, and class – so often kept isolated from each other as practical, social, political, and economic questions – converge with rare clarity. It is an example of a moment of undeniable possibility in which, what Raymond Williams (1977) referred to as "commitment" is overcome by powerful "alignments" of subaltern forces (pp. 199–205).

In order to better understand these events and their potential significance, in this chapter I draw on and explore questions emerging from *anticolonial* thought going back to foundational texts in the tradition. The colonization process, in the sense developed in this chapter, describes the lived complex of race, gender, and class reproduction as well as resistance across individual, group, and community practice and eventually broader societal forms. The contradictions of the *colonized experience* and the development it describes, then, are assessed as a potential unifying analytic term for understanding the confluence of specific forms of race–gender–class alienation, exploitation, and oppression but one emerging out of a tradition in which race and racism have particular "salience" to draw on the term used by Kempf in Chapter One to this book. This perspective challenges certain streams within postcolonial thought as either premature and nostalgic: premature or nostalgic in the context of the argument in this chapter in the sense that the colonizing process is viewed as inherent to the functioning of late capitalism rooted in race, gender, and class divisions.

I begin by reflecting on particular elements of anticolonialist thinking, building on the tradition which admits that colonial relations are developed within the nation-state as well as between nation-states and arguing that analysis of collective action must be central. Following this I turn to a detailed consideration of organized labor's uneven past and present in terms of interracial unity: a past that, as we will see, includes active racist overtures, actions, and failures to act as well as significant periods of progressive "alignment" and solidarity. A key, contemporary form of the latter, which I then explore, is a form of union organizing called *community unionism* which may come the closest to (re-)realizing the potential of a anticolonial stance within the Canadian labor movement's present. Following this I introduce, outline, and then discuss the *Hotel Workers' Rising* and Community Benefit Agreement campaigns currently underway (at the time of writing) in Toronto; campaigns undertaken by the workers of color that overwhelmingly make up the hotel services labor force of Toronto. The key question for workers of color and the labor movement is whether community unionism offers a return to the interspersed periods of progressive unity or alternatively represents an under-realized ideal, ratifying the less progressive trajectory of the labor movement's history in which it, not infrequently, served as a type of "middleman" for maintaining race divisions and intra-nation state colonialization. The backdrop of these activities is, of course, the contradictory process of an accelerated economic apartheid supporting the separation of political interests through sectarian recolonization, and its challenger: a pedagogy of anticolonialist social movement building. As I suggest, this is a pedagogy that may contain the potential to invigorate organized labor's progressive impulse, if not the path of its future with regards to questions at the confluence of class, gender, and race. It is a pedagogy through which one of the most potent forces for social change within and beyond capitalism – a racially united union movement – must confront a troubling past, and *learn* and *relearn* an alternative way of constructing itself. It is a pedagogy that, for Toronto hotel workers, necessarily must march from the "*darkened* back stairs" and hallways of the industry, through the fair-skinned lobbies and out into the streets to claim its rightful place in a united house of labor.

Necessarily presumed in this analysis, due to space, is an expansive notion of pedagogy. A pedagogy of anticolonialism for the labor movement entails a broad understanding of learning that takes in the full range of individual and collective developmental practices. Thus, organized educational offerings can be included,[2] though the style of campaign we see amongst hotel workers in Toronto and throughout North America barely draws on it at all. In the case we will explore here, rather the most important pedagogy of all, is "campaign pedagogy": learning in everyday life, amidst new and continuing organizational forms of hotel workers' own doing. Just as important in registering this broad notion of pedagogy, however, is that it inherently rests on the possibility of radical change. In other words, it is not a pedagogy of adaptation, but of transformation. The term pedagogy in this sense is linked to an ontological worldview – i.e., a *dialectical worldview* – that presumes change even where conventional analysis and common sense register stasis; a point that, as we will see, emerges as an important feature defining much anticolonialist thought as well. In this chapter, therefore, we explore the following questions: What might a broader pedagogy of anticolonialism look like in terms of organized labor and community unionism; and, do the Toronto *Hotel Workers Rising* and Community Benefit Agreement campaigns articulate such principles?

In fact, as articulated in the Introduction, the entire volume is based on this more profound ontological claim that change is fundamental to social practice and the organizing and reorganizing of social arrangements. In short, the colonial only emerges in analysis through the existence of the anticolonial. However, if the "breaching" hypothesis of this book is to have value in terms of the content of *this chapter*, it is essential to make a contribution to our understanding by looking at colonialism–anticolonialism as not only a situation or state of affairs but as a specific social mechanism of *inclusion* in relations of domination which begins but cannot end with issues of racialized differences.

8.2 Context

As further context to this chapter, it is worthwhile to take a moment to situate such concerns in the reality of, what in earlier work, I have described as the "evisceration of working-class communities" under advanced global capitalism (Sawchuk 2007). Briefly, at issue is the current status or social health of the diverse working classes, but in particular the segment of the working classes that faces the triple-edged sword of a racialized, a gendered, as well as a viciously classed life. A host of sources have recently documented in agonizing detail the forces of dissolution and fragmentation of working-class communities generally (e.g., Swift 1995, Forrester 1998, Putnam 2000, Ehrenreich 2002), however issues of racialization have figured in such texts in secondary ways. In part, this gap in working-class studies motivates this chapter, and demands a turn toward anticolonialist thought, rooted as it is in the salience of race. My point is that under conditions prevalent in advanced industrialized countries around the globe, it may not be hard to understand that amongst the general declining conditions and atomization that must be considered the hallmarks of advanced capitalism, there is also growing internal divisions rooted in gender, ethnic, and racial differences that play an increasingly determinant role, one of the most obvious recent examples being anti-immigrant sentiment across North America (e.g., Chacón and Davis 2006) and Europe (e.g., Layhay 2004) that implicate the native elites as well as the (white and non-white) native working classes. Taken together, the results are new levels of economic isolation, secured by an internal colonialism, resulting in the social fragmentation of a potentially united, diverse working-class majority.

Solidifying and in turn intensifying racialization as well as gendering processes within working-class community, however, are the institutions of paid work. As Creese (2007) has recently confirmed:

> Pay equity and employment equity legislation, for example, have been enacted in many jurisdictions across the country [yet] racialization remains central to the organization of gendered labour markets, and white men continue to monopolize choice jobs and earn a premium compared to other groups. (Creese 2007, p. 192)

Moreover, racialization processes have an interwoven but distinctive relationship to immigration patterns in Canada, as Creese goes on to say:

> The "imagined nation" of Canada was soon embedded in images of whiteness in spite of the continued vitality of First Nations communities and the fact that immigration always included some people from outside Europe, including, by the late nineteenth century, significant populations whose origins were in Africa and Asia (Li 2003).... By the dawn of the twenty-first century, then, it might be argued that although the imagined nation, with associated material structures of privilege, has been destabilized and complicated by recent trends, it retains a white centre that is evident in the labour market and elsewhere. (Creese 2007, pp. 194–195)

Das Gupta's (1996) work expands this point: "Racism is the effect of rather than the intention to cause deprivation to people of colour" (p. 14). That is, racist outcomes are not simply the result of institutional dynamics of education or the labor market; nor can it be placed neatly on the shoulders of employer and human resource (HR) practices. Each of these play a crucial role (e.g., Henry 1999); however, the effects are cumulative and include the functioning of social networks amongst workers (e.g. Vallas 2001) and dynamics of inclusion–exclusion in and through unions themselves.

Our turn, in this chapter, toward the role of unions and union organizing is both a crucial and under-assessed one. We know, for example, that an analysis of subordination of the working classes within this state of advanced cultural and economic evisceration is incomplete without recognition of the points of resistance. This chapter begins from the idea that the capacities of diverse working-class groups, particularly though not necessarily exclusively unionized ones, can and still do stubbornly resist these forces of evisceration particularly where there remain vestiges of social stabilization (e.g., a strong welfare state, strong labor laws, workers' political parties, and significant social capital in the form of family and community). Practically speaking, at the center of this claim are instances of the accumulation of scarce discretionary time, the pooling of scarce resources, and collective action which positively expresses the mix of subaltern standpoints. Indeed, the hopes of working-class struggle depend on emerging relationships of "alignment," a term flagged earlier, in which all are equal, none are more equal than others, and deep-seated impulses toward economic and social justice inform new structures of solidarity.

8.3 Reading Anticolonialist Thought: Setting the Stage for Understanding Hotel Worker Campaigns

Addressed as a political, psychological, as well as an existential phenomenon, anticolonialist thought is already on solid footing in classical works including those of Fanon, Memmi, Césairé, and possibly Freire as well. However, taking Sartre's introductory comments to Memmi's classic *The Colonizer and the Colonized* (1965) as a case in point, one of the roles of this chapter is to make an invitation out of Sartre's constructive critique: "The whole difference between us arises perhaps because he sees a situation where I see a system" (Sartre in Memmi 1965, p. xxv). True, Memmi's analysis in that specific piece of work does not necessarily lend itself to understanding a social system – if by system Sartre is indicating patterns subject to motion and change – but rather a situation or snapshot of the colonial–anticolonial contract, refracted through experience of a specific space, place, and time.

Having noted this, however, the specific contribution of this chapter lies in continuing to build on, apply, and move out from classical colonial relations of "mother country" and "colony," to embrace the colonization processes actively proceeding within countries across the globe but in particular in advanced capitalist countries such as Canada. This turns our attention toward the general approach advocated in Blauner (1969)[3] in his studies of Black social movements in the United States of the 1960s where he notes:

> [T]he utility of a distinction between colonization as a process and colonialism as a social, economic, and political system. It is the experience of colonization that Afro-Americans share with many of the non-white people of the world. But this subjugation has taken place in a societal context that differs in important respects from the situation of "classical colonialism." … Viewing our domestic situation as a special form of colonization outside a context of a colonial system [explains] some of the dilemmas and ambiguities. (p. 393)

Dilemmas, ambiguities, and, as we will see, historical contradictions of this intrastate colonial project will be explored in terms of the role of the labor movement specifically, but first it is necessary to take a closer look at classical anticolonial literature and its relationship to levels of analysis, collective action, and internal colonialism.

8.3.1 Collective Responses and Alternative Forms of Social Organization

Perhaps the first theoretically articulated breach in the colonial contract is found in pathbreaking works appearing following World War II. And, if there is a particularly defining feature in this regard, it is in the analysis of the relational identities of the colonizer and the colonized. One of the core articulations of Memmi (1965) is that there is no partial escape for the colonizer. There is, in other words, simply no relevance to the distinctions between good, bad, well-meaning, alienated, disenchanted, or disaffected colonizer. That is, on the *individual level* there is no solution to the contradictions of colonialized relations; virtually all individual forms of response feed it, some, in fact most, directly so. Rather, what the classical scholarship shows us is that there is a need to discover, rediscover, articulate, and develop analysis and understanding of the minutiae of *collective responses*, inclusive of, but not limited to, overt revolutionary action. In the case of this chapter, our focus is turned to the collective responses of labor organizing – yet another form of politics carried out by other means – through the lens of re-colonial–anticolonial processes within the advanced capitalist nation-state.

To move deeper into an analysis of "systems" and away from "situations" in terms of the re-colonial moment that marks the ongoing fruition of intra-state or internal colonialism, we must look toward the collective possibilities through which the relational identities of the colonizer–colonized change; identities of not simply workers of color and the ruling elite but those produced in the still disproportionately white, formally organized labor movement as well. But how is this achieved? The focus of this article is on how this was achieved through one particular form of political–economic organizing – unionization. Inherently challenging liberal relativism and regressive forms of identity politics, this argument builds from the basic notion that social standpoints matter, drawing on the marxist perspective that the standpoint of the oppressed, given its lived closeness to the contradictory mechanisms of the social and economic system, offer the greatest potential for claims to truth, where we understand claims to truth as rooted in the experience of interlocking contradictions that drive historical change. Dehumanization is a process that is not, as Memmi (1971) argues in *Dominated Man*, isolated to what can be always best described as the re-colonialization–anticolonization process: dehumanization remains central to class and gender as well as anti-ethnic violence (e.g., anti-Semitism). In this sense, all power relations make use of it for reproduction, and scholars like Memmi, as well as Said, Fanon, Freire, and others, are aligned with the tradition of radical scholarship that shows how the minds of dominator and dominated are intertwined. But it is still worth, once again, pointing out – as a means of situating how traditions of radical feminism and marxism, as well as labor organizing, fit into these concerns – that, make no mistake, it is the anticolonialist critique that has most clearly articulated the racist dimensions of the dehumanization dynamics. The anticolonialist critique points out, for example, the unique possibility of *individual* mobility in class systems given the absence of many of the embodied, racialized differences which tends to restrict the segregationist capacities of a purely class-based system of social hierarchy. That is, individual members of the white, male working class have a unique potential to "pass" and in isolated cases to become a member of the ruling elite; a potential that under patriarchy and colonial systems is denied workers of color; an achievement, in fact, built upon both continued racial as well as class and gender hierarchy.

More generally, it follows here that the standpoint of those suffering multiple oppressions offers the greatest potential of all to generate claims to truth through collective action, and it is this perspective that offers the possibility of the most dangerous forms of praxis. But what should not follow from this is the assumption that knowledge emerges in the absence of countervailing forms of social organization. While certainly the academy, as a whole, may be one of the last places to look for knowledge of this kind, we should not expect to find it where fragmentation reigns and culturally or materially stable communities that positively express subordinate standpoints collectively are absent.

The point here is that if colonialism–anticolonialism is to be understood, in the first instance, as more than the individual contradictions of lived experiences (of both colonizer and colonized), and in the second, as more than a macro political–historical analysis; it is perhaps particularly in the realm of collective practices – that is collective countervailing forces of social organization – that this is to be achieved. Marx's notion, of "ascending from the abstract to the concrete," his 11th thesis on Feurerbach, and Freire's (1970) extrapolation of these dialectical principles of *radical praxis* to the pedagogical process *writ large* may be particularly relevant in this regard. But more to the point, what is needed are the very kinds of analysis available in this collection, and elsewhere, that tailor, select, and apply an approach to reveal the re-colonialization and anti-colonization process of new forms of collective resistance. At subject in this chapter is just one such instance: an attempt at selectively thinking through and applying anticolonial concepts to better understand what Galabuzi (2006) has recently demonstrated to be Canada's own "economic apartheid," a system which his analysis shows is clearly expanding rather than contracting. Like many in this collection, I take it as given that colonialism is defined generally as a system of imposition and domination, though I go on to indicate that a definition cannot stop there: a full definition must also include points of resistance, and in particular it must include countervailing social organization and collective responses to injustice.

8.3.2 Internal Re-colonialization in Advanced Capitalist Countries

As has been understood for sometime, capitalism and colonialism are deeply intertwined. They develop and draw on each other even if, by some definitions (precapitalist), colonial relations are detectable much earlier. Over the last century, however, we can say with confidence that capitalism must maintain its grip in the metropoles, but that it cannot simply leave imperialist outposts as raw (human and material) resource suppliers and must instead draw these former outposts deeper into the direct capital accumulation processes themselves (hence, the growth of sub-Saharan, Southeast Asian, and Pacific-rim manufacturing, for example). So too, in mutually constituting fashion, colonial relations must also continue to expand, to maintain existing colonial relations internationally while exporting and intensifying these relations within the metropoles. Colonialism, in other words, must be expanded and established within as well as between all nation-states, as Loomba's review of the status of postcolonial scholarship (1998) begins to indicate:

> "Colonialism" is not just something that happens from outside a country or a people, not just something that operates with the collusion of forces inside but a version of it can be duplicated from within.... Many people living in both once-colonized and once colonizing countries are still subject to the oppressions put into place by colonialism. (Loomba 1998, pp. 12–13)

Building on this, it seems clear that at least in terms of empirical demonstrations of re-colonialization–anti-colonialization within the heart of Western empire, our understanding is incomplete. And, in furthering such examinations, it is important to continue to return to questions raised in the seminal scholarship of the anticolonial tradition. If, for example, re-colonialism–anticolonialism does not require the formal markers of foreign powers of an imperialist national state, but rather revolves around more generalized notions of legitimate belonging, membership, difference, and superiority (Principe 2004) *within* a nation-state, then it is necessary to rethink the concrete nature of these internal relationships.

In the case of this chapter, the analysis traces this mutually constituting evolution of capitalism and colonialism within Canada. The focus here is on the service sector in Canada which increasingly defines the economic activity of this and other advanced capitalist countries,[4] and more specifically the hospitality sector which also continues to grow. The discussion revolves around workers of color, many newly immigrated, all making among the lowest wages the economy has to offer, delivering services in some of Canada's most luxuriously appointed hotels.

As I have already begun to show here, there is value in regularly returning to foundational scholars in pushing toward new empirical projects, and in this context we can further clarify the work in this chapter. In *The Colonizer and the Colonized* (1965) Memmi outlines: "Colonial racism is built from three major ideological components: one, the gulf between the culture of the colonialist and the colonized; two, the exploitation of these differences for the benefit of the colonialist; three, the use of these supposed differences as standards of absolute fact" (p. 71). We are all a product of our place and time which, in turn, conditions our preoccupations; and hence, according to my own preoccupations in this chapter, I feel it is important to inquire into whether or not and/or to what degree Memmi's original points are relevant for going forward. To take this key example, I will argue Memmi's overall claims remain relevant, though I test them against the context of both twenty-first century, intra-state colonial relations, and more specifically, in terms of the choices facing the Canadian labor movement to either foment its role in our colonial past in relation to workers of color, or alternatively depart toward a potentially new, liberating project of structurally conjoining the political economic tools of unionization to the capacities of communities of color vis-à-vis the model known as "community unionism."

Likewise, going back in history as with Memmi, I ask whether or not and/or to what degree are some key claims of Fanon to be seen as relevant. Turning toward his chapter on national culture in *Wretched of the Earth* (Fanon 1963), for example, we see that he is correct to implicate the importance of the active creation of new political cultures. Cultural history, in this sense, is central in Fanon's approach. However, as others have pointed out generally (e.g., Said 1978), there are important limitations here. In terms of this chapter, we are compelled to expand and apply Fanon's thinking, and for this we can benefit from a specific example summarized by his allusion to the "doctrine of Cartierism." Specifically, we find that such a doctrine can be translated nicely to the *intrastate* colonial relations as well. In Fanon's original presentation of Cartier's dilemma we see a series of relevant questions drawn into view: how much to feed and support the colony, how much to maintain the colonial population balanced against the more primary needs of the so-called mother country?

Applying the questions to the topic of this chapter, we could find ourselves speaking of the Canadian (and Foreign Direct Investment) capital as the "mother country" which must be constantly constructed and reconstructed, materially as well as symbolically, to include largely white, "middle classes" of professional groups and petite bourgeoisie who administer and those segments of the white working-class allies which are essential to splitting its primary opposition. The crystalline examples of internal colonization of aboriginal nations in North America (including Mexico) may be notable in this regard, as will be the equally clear example of the developmental trajectory of the US slave economy from antebellum, reconstruction, and "Jim Crow" through to the present (Genovese 1974; Blauner 2001). But it is just as essential, as I shall try to show here, that the internal colonial project and in particular its breaching finds expression within a discussion of unionization and the development of the labor movement; a matter which becomes as obvious as it ever has been in today's North American "free trade era" where we have seen the impoverishment of all segments of the working classes of not one, not two, but all three of the NAFTA signatory countries (e.g. Chacón and Davis 2006). Clearly, the modern re-colonial project has had to increasingly turn its attentions inward, just as the anticolonial project must as well.

8.4 Organized Labor, Re-colonialism–Anticolonialism: Community Unionism as a Departure?

The focus on union organizing may, in some quarters of postcolonial and anticolonial scholarship, raise eyebrows amongst those who question the capacity to remake the master's house with the master's tools. It may be useful in this regard to preempt questions on the European origins of the organized labor movement as it exists in countries like Canada, by way of engaging in a discussion of the possibility for so noble (and so regularly under-applied) an idea as "universal labor solidarity." There is virtually no avoiding the fact that an adequate account of actual trade union practice historically represents a contradictory trajectory. Clearly, critical labor history in North America has shown the movement to have served both a figurative and sometimes viciously active role as "colonial administrator," deeply intertwined with the reproduction of racism (e.g. Spero and Harris 1931; Jones 1992; Hutchinson 1995; Heron 1996; Horowitz 1997; Brecher 1997; Huntley and Montgomery, 2004). But as Huntley and Montgomery point out: "[U]nions were theaters of conflict *and* of mobilization against racial discrimination" (2004, p. 1). Indeed, Chacón and Davis (2006) indicate that radical opportunities emerged during the first few decades of the twentieth century when both the International Workers of the World (IWW or Wobblies) and newly formed Committee for Industrial Organizations (CIO)[5] were engaged in what would be understandable as serious breaches of the internal, colonial order by organizing effectively across racial lines, though not without considerable resistance from within organized labor which, in effect, reasserted their conservative status as both a source of shock troops (e.g. the Teamsters Union in California in the early twentieth century) and effective contributor to the overall administration of internal colonization:

> Under these circumstances, the Congress of Industrial Organizations (CIO) emerged and split from the paralyzed AFL to transform the militancy of a growing sector of workers into a mass strike movement for industrial unionism, driven by masses of unskilled workers. Communist and socialist workers provided leadership and a class-conscious, multiracial approach to organizing. First- and second-generation immigrants were the backbone of the new movement, a reality reflected by the fact that CIO unions "aimed to meet workers on their ethnic, or racial, ground and pull them into a self-consciously common culture that transcended those distinctions" [Milkman 2000]. Mass militancy, often imbued with socialist ideology, created new confidence among workers to confront and overturn the prejudices of the past. The leading role many immigrants played in the rising union movement – as well as the class consciousness that emerged through workers' collective struggles – smashed the putative segregation that had divided most workers on the basis of ethnic origins. The CIO represented the apex of working-class power, which redefined class relations and shifted the balance of power in U.S. politics. (pp. 273–274)

Indeed, prior to the CIO's rise, there were other key examples in North America: some independent multiracial–multiethnic labor organizations such as the "Japanese–Mexican Labor Association" (circa 1903), but many others linked to the work of the Wobblies, as Hall (2001) notes:

> [The] Wobbly press frequently addressed the commonality of labor experience amongst white, Asian, Hispanic and African-American workers. Whether reporting on the difficult working experience of Mexican construction laborers in San Diego, the exploitation of white, Chinese and Japanese farm workers in California's central valleys, or the plight of impoverished white and African-American loggers in Louisiana's pine forest, the Wobbly press sought to encourage workers to see past race to their common struggle against the employer who controlled the means of production. (pp. 58–59)

Seeing "past race," in these terms, encompassed a change in both white workers and workers of color, but it also meant an additional commitment amongst the latter who faced racism both within the labor movement and within capital–labor relations themselves.

Nevertheless, it was in particular regions, economic sectors, and movements in both Canada and the United States – in the form of CIO and IWW organizing combined with the internal organizing efforts of communities of color themselves, as well as the socialist and communist parties – that notions of "universal labor solidarity" were being both actively constructed, as well as resisted, within union ranks.[6] These were times, as Chacón and Davis (2006) argue, when issues of race, immigration, and the future of organized labor took front-stage, facing-off against the all-too-easily mobilized "nativist" impulses (and resources, including those offered by the state) of the white working, middle, and ownership classes. It was during these periods of collective action that it became increasingly clear racial unity defined the transformative potential of the working class as whole:

> Inter-ethnic and international class solidarity, or lack thereof, has been a determinant of the progression, inertia, or regression of the [labor] movement. When nationalist or chauvinist sentiments are strong, the working class is weak, demonstrating the deep penetration of ruling-class ideology into working-class consciousness. (Chacón and Davis 2006, p. 268)

On this matter, Brecher's historical analysis of racial divisions in the American labor movement in *Strike!* (1997) is even more clear: "[White labor's] sense of 'privilege' – stoked by the prevalent racism introduced into labor relations and immigration policy – fueled an anti-immigration disposition that strangled multiracial solidarity in the crib of early industrialization" (p. 269).

But lest we bury the corpse prematurely, in Canada challenges to the disproportionately white, male labor movement continued (see Lopes and Thomas 2006). First, rooted in changes to (provincial and then federal) legislation, unionization of public sector workers (a sector where there was approximate gender, though not racial, parity)[7] brought about important changes beginning in the 1960s. In this context, white women began to finally experience some success in access to the labor movement including leadership positions. Likewise, beginning in the 1970s and 1980s, we saw the structural conditions for an analogous pressure vis-à-vis the rise of the service sector: the lower tier of which had become the home of a disproportionate number of (both male and female) workers of color. Indeed, over the last 2 decades organizing in this sector has accounted for the stabilization of the union density. As Galabuzi's recent analysis indicates, unionization is a "serious non-governmental option to deal with the income gap between Canadians of colour and those of European origin" (Galabuzi 2006, p. 97). Though workers of color remain underrepresented in unionized jobs,[8] this pattern appears to be changing. And, it is through such changes that organized labor's own internal, colonial contribution, is once again being seriously challenged from among its own ranks as it was in the early twentieth century.

It is relevant to note, however, that the impetus for this change has not been through organized education of existing membership (though this goes on), but through a new pedagogy of organizing and social movement building (e.g. Russo and Banks 1996; cf. de Turberville 2004). The relatively recent emergence of a body of research on labor and community coalitions and "community unionism" speaks to these issues directly, and can be argued to be a new code word for organizing immigrant and nonimmigrant workers of color.

As we see below, generally speaking, the term community unionism has come to be defined as the deep integration of labor union and community needs, strategies, and activities combining traditional work-based issues with issues of community sustainability, as quality of life, and civic engagement. What comes onto the bargaining table, for example, are issues such as quality of work life alongside the quality of community life and social inclusion involving issues of public services such as youth training, transportation, and child-care. These are issues that necessarily require employer and union as well as community and governmental engagement. Beyond this, however, the conceptualization of community unionism becomes quite blurry. In 1998, Tufts, drawing explicitly on research with hotel workers in Toronto in fact, described the concept as "embryonic" (see also Nissen 2004), though in the last 5 years major changes appear to be on the horizon (cf. Tufts 2006a). Two recent efforts have attempted to build an expanded theoretical framework for community unionism; the first, based on comparison between Australia and the United States, is Tattersall and Reynolds (2007); and the second is Frundt's (2005) theoretical synthesis which focuses on the potential for international solidarity. It is worth noting that by far the bulk of the available literature on community unionism is American. This emerges directly out of race relations and a particularly intense sense of crisis in US urban centers. Nevertheless issues of community and union cooperation and community unionism are now rising in importance in Canadian cities as well.

Several community unionism contributions stand out, however, with regards to my interest here in exploring re-colonialism–anti-colonialism. A key starting point in this regard is the historical review offered by Kelley (1999). Community is confirmed as an essential starting point for workers of color for many of the reasons indicated above. Other examples of contemporary research from the United States includes Kemper's (2006) study of relations between Navajo tribes and the Laborers' International Union of North America, whereas Worthen and Haynes (2003) focus on workers of color in the Chicago area partnering with labor and the Chicago Interfaith Committee. Both are supplemented by the work of Needleman (1998). In Canada, Choudry and Shragge (2007) have produced a groundbreaking study in their investigation of community and labor cooperation involving immigrant, migrant, as well as undocumented workers in Montreal. What becomes clear is that labor's mobilization resources and tools may not be well suited at present and that new organizational forms may be required; a point underscored by Cranford and Ladd (2003) who focus on racialized groups working through temp agencies, on contract and unemployed who seem to benefit from community strategies that bare only a faint, familial resemblance to traditional labor movement organizational forms.

This turn toward "community" in "community–labor" coalitions is significant, and in this regard it is essential to recognize that workers of color, if they are to successfully take their rightful place as a leadership component of labor movement, begin from a standpoint of cultural–racial outsiders in a way that whites, though hardly homogeneous themselves, simply are not. This community unionism approach thus entails the question of either cultural assimilation or the building of a fundamentally new culture for labor. In other words, what is at stake is more than simply seeing more black, brown, or yellow faces throughout the structure of the labor movement, although this would obviously signal other important changes. Rather it is about recognizing that the culture of the Canadian labor movement reflects particular racialized communities already, and that a new labor movement must evolve new hybrid cultural forms. And thus, the crucial question becomes whether the labor movement engages in a colonization process of its very own, simply reproducing hierarchical racial relations in new intra-class forms or takes an alternative route. And, in answering this question the basic litmus test here would be to what degree *both* the community and the labor movement engage in mutual change and development.

8.5 The Hotel Worker Rising and Community Benefits Campaigns

Against the backdrop I have developed above, this section provides an introduction to the collective action amidst the ongoing processes and the resultant racial economic apartheid that have produced internal colonialism within Canada today. To understand it in terms of discussions of unionization and organized labor, it is necessary to provide a basic profile of the sectoral context from which it emerges.

The hotel industry forms a major proportion of retail services in both Canada and the United States, and is growing both in profitability and employment levels. The industry has seen accelerated ownership turnover in recent years and has become increasingly dominated by large conglomerates that operate internationally including Marriott, Hilton, Starwood, and Hyatt which, in addition to flagship hotels, run an even broader set of others operating under different names including those familiar in Canadian urban centers, such as Holiday Inn, Embassy Suites, Crowne Plaza, and Sheraton to name only a few. According to *Smith Travel Research*, 2006, in fact, the hotel industry recently broke a record in consolidations in the United States. *The Wall Street Journal* estimated in late 2005 that the coming years would show record profits in the industry, and indeed it has. In 2006, for example, the Marriott group experienced a 100% growth in net income during one of its quarters to lead the pack (though not by much). Fuelling the quarterly gains seen in the industry, however, is not increased consumption, but rather both growing room rates and most importantly, work intensification. The excerpt below gives us a glimpse into the working lives upon which these forms of economic "gain" rest in Toronto specifically.

> Every morning shortly after 6 a.m., Althea Porter leaves her Mississauga home for a trek into the core of Toronto, where she works at a large Holiday Inn whose shape begs comparison to a wedding cake. She makes up 16 rooms each day, and is joined, on busy days, by some two dozen other room attendants. If everything's going smoothly, it should take a veteran attendant like Porter about 30 minutes to get a room ready for the next guest. That means stripping the sheets, replacing the bedding, cleaning the coffee pot and glasses, swabbing the bathroom, collecting the garbage, replenishing the soap, towels and stationery, and generally straightening up the place. If everything isn't going smoothly – if there's a foyer full of conventioneers waiting for rooms or if Porter has to scour the hotel looking for supplies the day becomes a race against time. She routinely skips breaks and wolfs down her lunch. "Sometimes," Porter says, "people don't even take lunch.... When you

have families in the summer, then you have rooms that are really trashed.... Those are the worst times for room attendants." And over all, their jobs have gotten a lot tougher in the past year or two. Responding to competitive pressure, many hotel chains have laid on splendid queen- or even king-sized mattresses, plush duvets, extra pillows and other goodies for guests. "They call it 'signature service,' where everything is well done," says Canedo [another room attendant]. "You put out the amenities so that when the guest enters the room, it's a heavenly place to stay, a second home. We do that every day." Problem is, the attendants are still only getting 30 minutes per room. And when the mattress is large and heavy, upwards of 50 kilograms, it's awkward to change the sheets. Because of that extra weight and the bulky new duvets, attendants are suffering back and shoulder injuries. "I don't mind serving the guests, but not when it affects my health," says Porter, who earns $14.68 per hour after 13 years in the industry. (Lorinc 2006, p. 1)

Most importantly, to establish not only the context but the significance of this research focus, the hotel industry employs over 1.5 million workers in North America (280,000 in Canada; 1.3 million in the United States), of whom approximately a quarter are housekeepers. Of these the vast majority are marginalized groups: women, people of color, immigrants, as well as single parents and welfare-to-work participants. In Toronto specifically, seven of ten local hotel workers are new Canadians, mostly from the Philippines, China, Sri Lanka, and South America. The average salary is $10.48 an hour, while the median housekeeper wage is $26,000 a year. In keeping with racial segmentation of the labor market, wages in the sector are among the lowest in the broader retail sector. On average as an occupational group, earnings in Canada and the United States place full-time workers below or marginally above the poverty line, though unionized housekeepers as subgroup just manage to top it.

The labor organization that represents the bulk of these workers is the recently amalgamated United Needletrades, Industrial Textile Employees–Hotel and Restaurant Employees (UNITE-HERE) union. According to a UNITE-HERE survey report "Creating Luxury, Enduring Pain" (2006),[9] basic "speed-up" as well as the increasing use of luxury amenities (all the way from heavier mattresses, triple-sheeting, exercise equipment to heavier amenities carts, coffeepots service, larger and harder to clean mirrors, and so on) has produced exhaustion and injuries. Light and severe sprains, back injuries, and bursitis are particularly prominent. In fact, statistically housekeeping work is now North America's most dangerous retail occupation.

It is against this backdrop of a specific occupational colony of racialized workers that the *Hotel Workers Rising* campaign was initiated. UNITE-HERE's goal established several years prior was to carry out massive, organized campaigns to boost union certification in the industry in both Canada and the United States simultaneously to create a critical mass of unionized workers in the industry. In Toronto alone, this strategy resulted in more than 30 specific hotel agreements up for renegotiation in 2006. Indeed, this plan entailed the synchronization of contract expiry dates across a series of US states as well as the province of Ontario to realize an aggressive bargaining agenda but to also kick-start a major membership drive in specific urban centers including Hawaii, Los Angeles, San Francisco, Chicago, Boston, and Toronto.

In Toronto, the *Hotel Workers Rising* campaign was built from a coalition of a range of over 30 community groups ranging from the Metropolitan United Church, Filipino, and various Latin American community organizations, women's groups, the Social Planning Council of Toronto, as well as UNITE-HERE (Local 75). March 2007 was emblematic of the campaign. At the corner of King and Yonge Streets, workers demonstrated in celebration of their win in voting for unionization within UNITE-HERE Local 75. As one housekeeper at the rally said:

> We stood together and showed 1 King West that we wanted to be members of UNITE-HERE.... This is about our working conditions and it is also about us having a voice. We are the invisible workers who are making the hotel really successful but our concerns are being overlooked.[10]

Eventually assembling in front of Toronto City Hall, it is no coincidence that this example of class solidarity across racial and ethnic lines dovetailed with International Women's Day celebrations as well.

What may be of particular significance to our discussion here, however, is that the campaign has given rise to what in Canada is an inclusive *form* of union organizing amongst workers of color: the extension of labor relations to target gains and unify leadership in communities of color more broadly through what are called the establishment of "Community Benefit Agreements." The first such agreement in Canadian history has been established through the Woodbine Community Benefit Agreement currently being negotiated in light of the city's redevelopment of the former racetrack area. Its focus is on the quality of life, park creation, transit, day care, as well as local hiring from the North Etobicoke neighborhood in Toronto; an embattled and impoverished community of mostly nonwhite and immigrant groups in which, in addition, a significant number of Toronto housekeeping workers reside.

How then can we begin to understand the dynamics of these community unionism campaign efforts by drawing on questions raised earlier in the brief review of key elements of anticolonial thought? Does this campaign represent a breaching of the colonial contract? And, if so, the contract amongst whom exactly and how?

As Lorinc has accurately commented in his account of the Toronto campaign "[t]he people who make up your fancy hotel room are invisible, but powerful – now that they've realized they can put downtown economies through the wringer" (p. 1). Invisibility, in this sense, presumes a subject to whom something is "invisible," and here we see echoes of the social pre-construction of racial (and gendered) identities and mis-recognition that Fanon discusses drawing on his experiences amidst his medical training in France in *Black Skin White Masks* (1967).[11] If the systematic mis-recognition (or social construction and activation of racial subjectivities) of particular people and manufacturing invisibility is essential to the realization of colonial relations, here we can see an example of such relations in the heart of the Canadian economy. Just as easily we can see a challenge to these relations through an emerging form of collective action structured by the intersection of communities of color and organized labor against the backdrop of capitalist labor processes and control. Indeed, there can be little doubt that a type of partial breaching of the colonial contract may be evident in what has transpired to date. A city within a city, a colony subjected to the internal colonial processes of invisibility, has felt within itself a new measure of power.

However, this invisibility is not simply created on the basis of either a general interpersonal experience or on the scale of a city or nation-state; it is also created in the institutionally specific context of the workplace which, in the case of the hotel industry, is a space of economic as well as social production and consumption. The hotel, as a site of economic production and consumption, is infused with a familiar pattern of what we can call front and back stairs labor (e.g. Adib and Guerrier 2003; Applebaum, Dresser and Hatton 2003; Park 2004; Adler and Adler 2004; Sherman 2005, 2007; Tufts 2006b). In the lobby, desk staff are disproportionately white and English-speaking, just behind them sit switchboard operators. And, on the back stairs, working through the bowels of the hotel are housekeepers and laundry and kitchen workers – disproportionately workers of color.

While unionization offers greater job security, better benefits, and higher wages in all industries in Canada (Zuberi 2006, 2007), the fact is that breaking through to unionization for these workers of color entails a double burden. First, is the difficulty and personal economic peril of organizing that any worker faces, though with even lower levels of material resources, a particularly heroic act for a housekeeper. Second, is the difficulty of breaking through into the structure of the labor movement itself as a cultural outsider. Thus, what becomes equally clear in discussions of invisibility and the re-colonialization process is that the labor movement once again comes face to face with its own, uneven history of interracial solidarity. As Chacón and Davis (2006, pp. 291–292) point out in their analysis of the labor movement's response to undocumented immigrant worker organizing efforts in the spring of 2006 in the United States. Union leaders there were just as likely to seek to curtail work stoppages, boycotts, and marches, aligning themselves in the process with the recolonization project.

8.6 Conclusions

> Black labor has historically played an interesting role, something akin to the irritant in the oyster that brings forward a pearl. (Fletcher 2007, p. 3)

Bill Fletcher Jr. has been a labor activist for virtually his entire adult life, engaged in, amongst other things, the vibrant period of black labor caucus and revolutionary black labor action organizing of the 1960s and 1970s. His comment points back toward a key issue we began with in this chapter which was the intertwined and mutually constituting nature of capitalism and colonialism. However, as we have seen, there is still much to be said on this relationship, but in these concluding remarks we may now be in a better position to link the overall argument presented in the chapter to the more pointed comments by Chacón and Davis cited earlier: "Inter-ethnic and international class solidarity, or lack thereof, has been a determinant of the progression, inertia, or regression of the [labor] movement." At the same time, such realizations can only be a beginning – a beginning which as we have seen has a long history. Indeed, Marx's comments on the emancipation of labor which were used to kick off this chapter give us a sense of how long this beginning has been. His observation, while rhetorically accurate, was analytically under-realized in terms of how "internal colonialism," as described by Loomba and Blauner above, has become one of the defining features of late capitalism. Likewise, the words of DuBois, though far more sensitive to the relations of internal colonialization, nevertheless betrays an optimism for a solution that has proven far more difficult to realize than first imagined.

In both cases, key ideas emerging from classical anticolonial thought provide new insights for moving forward. And, they have fuelled discussion in this chapter in a number of ways. First, that this mutual parasitism of colonialism and capitalism can explain global imperial relations as well as local conditions of economic apartheid in the so-called First World. Second, that racialization, the production of its invisibility, and the mis-recognition of humanity it entails are central to the re-colonialization processes of internal colonialism in countries like Canada today. And finally, that there is a distinct need for further research on questions of collective action balanced with concerns for identity and personalized social experience within the recolonial–anticolonial process internal to advanced capitalist countries.

As one example of collective action under these conditions, we then turned to labor organizing. In this regard, we have discussed the labor movement's uneven history of interracial organizing: from periods of overt, self-defeating racist action, from other periods when the labor movement's activities could be characterized as offering a passive acceptance of the "nativist" impulses amongst its membership, all the way to progressive moments of the past and present including actions in the organizing traditions of the Wobblies, the early CIO, and, now, organizing through models of community unionism. However, contemporary, North American community unionism research has, in fact, revealed lingering contradictions in several, documented cases by exposing the difficulty in generating meaningful, sustained linkages between communities and organized labor where, as was noted, more often than not the term "communities" functions as a code word for communities of color.

The discussion here of the *Hotel Workers Rising* and associated campaigns is necessarily preliminary. It serves as a starting point only. Further research has begun to emerge and is forthcoming. However, it seems clear that campaigns such as *Hotel Workers Rising* give some indication that a progressive period in which the capacity to develop sustained linkages across all workers are being worked through as thoroughly as the most progressive historical periods in Canada. From the perspective adopted in this chapter, I simply conclude by saying that these challenges are ones which actively confront the types of question first raised by Memmi (1965) regarding the contradictory appeal and uncomfortable equivocation that always rests in the self-image of the colonizer. In this regard, organized labor must continue to challenge elements of its own history as an institution traditionally dominated by the white working-class and through which it has at times actively and passively played a "middleman" role in delivering the traditional benefits that capital has accrued by separating the working classes.

Notes

1. Research for this publication was funded by a Social Science and Humanities Research Council of Canada grant: "Understanding Educational Capacity for Urban Community Unionism: Exploring the Developmental Foundation of a New Labour Relations Regime in Canada" (Grant #410-2007-863).
2. For a recent summary of organized equity education in Canadian unions see *Integrating Equity, Addressing Barriers: Innovative Learning Practices by Unions* (2007) by the Labour Education Centre (Toronto) and the Centre for the Study of Education and Work (OISE/University of Toronto).
3. Blauner (2001) updates the arugument with reflection on the dissolution of the various movements of the 60s, and the changes in demographic constitution of US society in the millennium.
4. Just over 70% of the labor force in Canada now works in some form of service delivery.
5. Upon separating from the American Federtion of Labour in 1935-38 (while also establishing itself in Canada at the same time), the Committee of Industrial Organizations changed its name to the Congress of Industrial Organizations.
6. The first few decades of the twentieth century have been the subject of several recent contributions on race, labor, and broader left political organizing as Palmer (2004) alerts us in his extended review of race and revolution where he asks (in reference to the American South of the 1920s): "Was the Black Belt a colony or not? What role did the landed masses play in this national struggle, and were their interests different from those of the industrial proletariat?" (p. 196). Citing the actions of the Wobblies as well as mainstream craft and industrial unionism and radical political parties, he goes on to outline instances when both "black and white saw common scarlet on the political horizon of the United States" amidst the contradictory internal racism of the various movements and the formal adoption of "race-conscious" policies.
7. At the turn of the 21st century it would seem that little has changed. Similar to the under-representation of workers-of-colour in the auto and stell sectors (7% and 4.2% respectively), the federal government has remained a bastion of white labour (only 5.6% of the labour force are workers-of-colour) (Galabuzi 2006, p. 113)
8. Workers of color make up just over 7% of the unionized workforce in comparison to the fact that citizens of color in Canada make 11.4% of the population.
9. www.hotelworkersrising.org/media
10. www.hotelworkersrising.org/media
11. This is a point which Owens-Moore (2005) links with Du Bois's notion of a double existence and "double consciousness" which suggests further dimensions of hotel workers' experiences. On the concept of "invisibility" see further reading in Goldberg (1997).

References

Adib, A. and Guerrier, Y. (2003). The interlocking of gender with nationality, race, ethnicity and class: the narratives of women in hotel work. *Gender, Work & Organization*, 10(4), 413–432.

Adler, P.A. and Adler, P. (2004). *Paradise laborers: hotel work in the global economy*. Ithaca, NY: Cornell University Press.

Applebaum, E., Dresser, L., and Hatton, E. (2003). The coffee pot wars: unions and firm restructuring in the hotel industry. In E.A. Applebaum, A. Bernhardt, and R.J. Murnane (Eds.), *Low-wage America: how employers are reshaping opportunities in the workplace* (pp. 33–76). New York: Russell Sage Foundation.

Blauner, R. (1969). Internal colonialism and ghetto revolt. *Social Problems*, 16, 393–408.

Blauner, R. (2001). *Still big news: racial oppression in America*. Philadelphia, PA: Temple University Press.

Brecher, J. (1997). *Strike!*. Boston: South End Press.

Chacón, J. and Davis, M. (2006). *No one is illegal: fighting racism and state violence on the U.S.-Mexico border*. Chicago, IL: Haymarket Books.
Choudry, A. and Shragge, E. (2007). Constructing immigrant workers: adaptation and resistance. Paper presented at "Fear, the City and Political Mobilization" conference, INRS, April 16–17.
Cranford, C.J. and Ladd, D. (2003). Community unionism: organising for fair employment in Canada. *Just Labour*, 3(Fall), 46–59.
Creese, G. (2007). Racializing work/reproducing white privilege. In V. Shalla and W. Clement (Eds.), *Work in tumultuous times: critical perspectives* (pp. 192–226). London: McGill-Queens University Press.
Das Gupta, T. (1996). *Racism and paid work*. Toronto: Garamond Press.
de Turberville, S. (2004). Does the 'organizing model' represent a credible union renewal strategy. *Work, Employment and Society*, 18(4), 775–794.
DuBois, W.E.B. (1915). *The negro*. New York: Henry Holt.
Ehrenreich, B. (2002). *Nickel and dimed: on (not) getting by in America*. New York: Metropolitan.
Fanon, F. (1963). *Wretched of the earth*. New York: Grove Press.
Fanon, F. (1967). *Black skin white masks*. New York: Grove Press.
Fletcher, B. (2007). Choices for black labor. *Black Commentator*, 234 (June 21), 1–4.
Forrester, V. (1998). *L'horreur économique*. Paris: Fayard.
Freire, P. (1970). *Pedagogy of the oppressed*. New York: Continuum.
Frundt, H.J. (2005). Movement theory and international labor solidarity. *Labor Studies Journal*, 30(2), 19–41.
Galabuzi, G.-E. (2006). *Canada's economic apartheid: the social exclusion of racialized groups in the new century*. Toronto: Canadian Scholars Press.
Genovese, E. (1974). *Roll Jordan roll: the world the slaves made*. New York: Pantheon Books.
Goldberg, D. (1997). *Racial subjects: writing on race in America*. New York: Routledge.
Hall, G. (2001). *Harvest wobblies: the Industrial Workers of the World and agricultural workers in the American west, 1905–1930*. Corvallis, OR: Oregon State University Press.
Henry, F. (1999). Two studies of racial discrimination in employment. In J. Curtis, E. Grab, and N. Guppy (Eds.), *Social inequality in Canada* (pp. 226–235). Scarborough: Prentice Hall Allyn & Bacon Canada.
Heron, C. (1996). *The Canadian labour movement: a short history*. Toronto: James Lorimer.
Horowitz, R. (1997). *'Negro and white, unite and fight': a social history of industrial unionism in meatpacking, 1930–1990*. Urbana, IL: University of Illinois Press.
Huntley, H. and Montgomery, D. (2004). *Black workers' struggle for equality in Birmingham*. Chicago, IL: University of Illinois Press.
Hutchinson, E. (1995). *Blacks and reds: race and class in conflict, 1919–1990*. East Lansing, MI: Michigan State University Press.
Jones, J. (1992). *The dispossessed: America's underclass from the civil war to the present*. New York: HarperCollins.
Kelley, R. (1999). Building bridges: the challenge of organized labor in communities of color. *New Labor Forum*, 5(Fall/Winter), 42–58.
Kemper, D. (2006). Organizing in the context of tribal sovereignty: the Navajo area Indian health service campaign for union recognition. *Labor Studies Journal*, 30(4), 17–40.
Labour Education Centre & Centre for the Study of Education and Work (2007). *Integrating equity, addressing barriers: innovative learning practices by unions*. Toronto: Labour Education Centre.
Layhay, G. (2004). *Immigration and politics in the new Europe*. New York: Cambridge University Press.
Loomba, A. (1998). *Colonialism/postcolonialism*. London: Routledge.
Lopes, T. and Thomas, B. (2006). *Dancing on live embers: challenging racism in organizations*. Toronto: Between the Lines.
Lorinc, J. (2006). Union maid. *The Burning Bush*. (1–2) (April 29th). Los Angeles: Center for the Working Poor.
Marx, K. (1867/1990). *Capital volume 1*. New York: Penguin.
Memmi, A. (1965). *The colonizer and the colonized*. Boston, MA: Beacon Press.

Memmi, A. (1971). *Dominated man: notes toward a portrait*. Boston, MA: Beacon Press.
Milkman, R. (2000). *Organizing Immigrants: The Challenge for Unions in Contemporary California (edited volume)*. Ithaca: Cornell University Press.
Needleman, R. (1998). Building relationships for the long haul: unions and community-based groups working together to organize low-wage workers. In K. Bronfenbrenner, S. Friedman, R. Hurd, R. Oswald, and R. Seeber (Eds.), *Organizing to win: new research on union strategies* (pp. 71–86). Ithaca, NY: Cornell University Press.
Nissen, B. (2004). The effectiveness and limits of labor-community coalitions: evidence from South Florida. *Labor Studies Journal*, 29(1), 67–89.
Owens-Moore, T. (2005). A Fanonian perspective on double consciousness. *Journal of Black Studies*, 35(6), 751–762.
Palmer, B. (2004). Race and revolution. *Labour/Le Travail*, 54(Fall), 193–222.
Park, E. (2004). Labor organizing beyond race and nation: the Los Angeles Hilton Hotel case. *The International Journal of Sociology and Social Policy*, 24(7/8), 137–152.
Principe, T. (2004). *Research Essay*. Unpublished paper, Department of Sociology and Equity Studies in Education, Ontario Institute for Studies in Education, University of Toronto.
Putnam, R. (2000). *Bowling alone: the collapse and revival of American community*. New York: Simon & Schuster.
Russo, J. and Banks, A. (1996). Teaching the organizing model of unionism and campaign-based education: national and international trends. Paper presented at *AFL-CIO/Cornell University Research Conference on Union Organizing*, Washington, DC (April).
Said, E. (1978). *Orientalism*. Toronto: Random House.
Sawchuk, P.H. (2007). Understanding diverse outcomes for working-class learning: conceptualizing class consciousness as knowledge activity. *Economic and Labour Relations Review*, 17(2), 199–216.
Sherman, R. (2005). Producing the superior self: strategic comparison and symbolic boundaries among luxury hotel workers. *Ethnography*, 6(2), 131–158.
Sherman, R. (2007). *Class acts: service and inequality in luxury hotels*. Berkeley, CA: University of California Press.
Spero, S. and Harris, A. (1931). *The black worker*. New York: Columbia University Press.
Swift, J. (1995). *Wheel of fortune: work and life in the age of falling expectations*. Toronto: Between the Lines.
Tattersall, A. and Reynolds, D. (2007). The shifting power of labor-community coalitions: identifying common elements of powerful coalitions in Australia and the U.S. *Working USA: The Journal for Labor and Society*, 10, 77–102.
Tufts, S. (1998). Community unionism in Canada and labor's (re)organization of space. *Antipode*, 30(3), 227–250.
Tufts, S. (2006a). Renewal from different directions: The case of UNITE-HERE Local 75. In P. Kumar and C. Schenk, (Eds.), *Paths to Union Renewal: Canadian Experiences* (pp. 201–220). Peterborough: Broadview Press.
Tufts, S. (2006b). 'We make it work': the cultural transformations of hotel workers in the city. *Antipode*, 38(2), 350–373.
Vallas, S. (2001). Rediscovering the color line within work organizations: the 'knitting of racial groups' revisited. *Work and Occupation*, 30(4), 379–400.
Williams, R. (1977). *Marxism and literature*. New York: Oxford University Press.
Worthen, H. and Haynes, A. (2003). Getting in: the experiences of minority graduates of the building bridges project pre-apprenticeship class. *Labor Studies Journal*, 28(1), 31–53.
Zuberi, D. (2006). *Differences that matter: social policy and the working poor in the United States and Canada*. Ithaca, NY: Cornell University Press.
Zuberi, D. (2007). Organizing for better working conditions and wages: the UNITE HERE! *Hotel Workers Rising* campaign. *Just Labour: A Canadian Journal of Work and Society*, 10(Spring), 60–73.

Chapter 9
The Anguish of Power: Remapping Mental Diversity with an Anticolonial Compass

Tanya Titchkosky and Katie Aubrecht

9.1 Introduction

An analysis informed by anticolonial principles "challenges the normalizing gaze of the dominant in the construction of what constitutes valid knowledge and experience." (Kempf, 2009). This chapter aims to participate in this challenge by exposing how, at the level of embodiment, colonization has worked to oppress diversity and to make the possibility of valued bodily, sensorial, and mental differences all but disappear. By embodiment we mean the kinds of social and political relations that are established with bodies, minds, and senses. In particular, this chapter explores "mental health" discourse as produced and distributed by the World Health Organization (WHO).

The WHO has been instrumental in exporting a particular version of mental health issues around the world and this has real consequences for how people, as well as "developing countries," come to be understood and treated. We cast our attention on how mental differences and anguish are framed by the normalizing gaze of this dominant health agency. Along with anticolonial principles, our analysis also draws on a disability studies perspective. Such a perspective understands disability as a social matter requiring inquiry and does not understand it as an individual matter in need of only cure or care. Our perspective locates disability in the midst of physical and cultural environments and does not reproduce the belief that disability is simply in impaired bodies. From a disability studies perspective, then, disability is a complex interpretive issue that resides between people and should, thus, be studied as such. Combining anticolonial principles with a disability studies perspective allows us to focus our inquiry on WHO's constitution of the category "mental health and illness" so as to reveal its power to organize and manage how colonized people can and cannot be known.

Let us say a few words on what this chapter will not do. We do not argue that mental illness is, or is not, a myth; nor do we tell a more complex etiology to justify the power of WHO's mental health initiatives; nor do we try to uncover what might really be going on in people's lives behind the labels of, for example, "depression," "schizophrenia," or "drug use." Our aim, in contrast, is to engage the ways mental health and illness are narrated by a multinational organization, revealing the organization's power to implement one particular way of understanding the lives of millions of people. Neither denying nor justifying the various categories of mental health and illness, we aim only to "enlarge the understanding we already have" by critically attending to how mental health issues are narrated, or in our terms, *mapped* (Stiker 1997, p. 18; for more about mapping, Corker 2002; Titchkosky 2002). We explore how colonized countries are being told to use this map of mental health and illness so as to be made to, as Frantz Fanon (2004 [1961], p. 182) suggests, "fit into a social environment of the colonial type."

Our aim is to map the use of the map of mental health as it is drawn in the form of the WHO's publicly available statements and policies. This chapter, then, represents an attempt to map the social significance of one of the dominant ways the map called mental health is developed, used, and enforced. We attend to the discursive social structures that support the development and use of this map as it dichotomizes mental diversity into mental illness or not, and colonizes relations to anguish and to knowledge. We also address how appeals are being made to regard this dichotomous narrative as the "true, right and good," that is, the dominant, routine, and valued form of relating to a sense of difference. In turning to a discussion of how a disability issue is being framed by the WHO as a particular type of problem, we do not want to survey all that the WHO has to say. Instead, we select those articulations of the problem that are most public, most readily available on the World Wide Web, and that are consistently repeated throughout WHO literature. We do not make use of any articulations that are meant only for experts, or that are obscure, or somehow radically unique, since we are dealing only with *ordinary* ways the WHO expresses the problem of mental health and illness as a global issue. In this fashion, we aim to illustrate what a disability studies perspective together with anticolonial studies has to offer to an examination of powerful but taken-for-granted ideas of disability framed as a health and illness problem.

9.2 The WHO and Mental Illness

The WHO consistently and unequivocally understands disability as a biologically given problem of bodies, minds and senses "gone wrong," and, again unequivocally, defines mental illness as a key form of disability. The trouble for WHO is that,

> 450 million people experience mental or neurological disorders around the world. These disorders constitute 5 of the 10 leading causes of disability worldwide, thus creating devastating social and economic impact for individuals, families and governments. (WHO 2008b)

The WHO holds that "[m]ental health improvements are central to nations' development" in that, "[b]y treating many of the debilitating mental disorders and by promoting mental health, people will ... be able to work and rise out of poverty, provide their children with the right social and emotional environment to flourish ... contribute to the economy of their country" (ibid.). All this can be achieved, according to the WHO, by putting in place "human rights oriented mental health policies, strategic plans and laws to ensure that effective treatment, prevention and promotion programs" for all (ibid.).

From a disability studies perspective, it is crucial to uncover the social and political consequences of defining disability as a biologically given asocial problem that nonetheless is understood to cause all sorts of social problems such as lack of work, poverty, and restrictive social and emotional environments. The problem for us is how disability is constructed as nothing but a problem and is used to organize and control populations of "problem people." Starting from the assumption that all bodies, minds, and senses always make an appearance in the midst of others and thus can be regarded as socially organized (Titchkosky 2007, p. 104), we turn now to an exploration of how the WHO discourse produces mental health and illness as a particular type of problem.

9.3 The Imperative of Mental Illness

The WHO is appealing to countries to increase their attention on mental health services since it believes, among other things, the following:

- Cost-effective treatments exist for most disorders and, if correctly applied, could enable most of those affected to become functioning members of society.
- Barriers to effective treatment of mental illness include lack of recognition of the seriousness of mental illness and lack of understanding about the benefits of services. Policy makers, insurance companies, health and labour policies, and the public at large – all discriminate between physical and mental problems.
- Most middle- and low-income countries devote less than 1%[1] of their health expenditure to mental health. Consequently mental health policies, legislation, community care facilities, and treatments for people with mental illness are not given the priority they deserve. (WHO 2008a)

Regardless of the veracity of these truth claims, this delineation of treatment serves as an appeal to middle- and low-income countries to import a particular way of making sense of people. These countries are depicted as suffering from a "lack of [Western] understanding," and thus do not devote appropriate resources to the cost-effective treatment of mental disorders (WHO 2008a). The WHO's suggestion that mental health is not given the priority it deserves shares a striking resemblance with anticolonial thinker Aime Césaire's (2000 [1955]) assessment of Octave Mannoni's psychology of the colonizer and the colonized. Césaire (1955, p. 59) says:

> [C]olonization is based on psychology, that there are in this world groups of men who, for unknown reasons, suffer from what must be called a dependency complex, that these groups are psychologically made for dependence; that they need dependence, that they crave it, ask for it, demand it; that this is the case with most of the colonized peoples.

The WHO is appealing to countries to recognize its version of a "correct" application and an "appropriate" expenditure of resources on mental health treatments. This expenditure is based on a cost–benefit analysis of unquestioned psychological relations to the disordered Other. With the assumption that "[m]ental, neurological and behavioural disorders are common to all countries and cause immense suffering" (WHO ibid.), the WHO begins the work of abstracting people from the location and history of their suffering. This work entails mapping minds as if they share a common unity in illness. Millions of people are thus mapped as in need of the same treatment. Whether this is taken as good, bad, or merely practical, mapping mental differences in this way serves as the WHO's grounds for appealing to some countries to reorder their treatment regimes, health expenditures, and especially to reorder their self-understandings.

In *The Numbers Count: Mental Disorders in America*, the US National Institute of Mental Health (NIMH 2008) cites the WHO's "World Health Report 2004 – Changing History" (WHO 2004). This report claims that mental illness is the leading cause of disability and death in Canada and the United States for people aged 15–44 (http://www.nimh.nih.gov/health/publications/the-numbers-count-mental-disorders-in-america.shtml#WHOReportBurden [Accessed March 22, 2008]). The report's statistical annex lists core indicators for population health for WHO member states for the year 2002. While mental disorders in the Americas and Europe register high on the WHO's global burden of disease in disability-adjusted life years (DALYs), the numbers triple for Africa, and are over 15 times higher for countries in Southeast Asia and the Western Pacific. This report informs the reader that "[i]t is hoped that careful scrutiny and use of the results will lead to progressively better measurement of core indicators of population health and health system financing" (http://www.who.int/whr/2004/en/report04_en.pdf [Accessed March 22, 2008]). This will require a reordering of financing, tracking, treating, and thus understanding of health, illness, and anguish by some countries. In examining the interests driving the WHO's claim to a "Changing History," it becomes clear that systems of mental health governance not only map a population's problem people, but also delineate the problems that a country has with those so defined. But what is at issue here?

9.4 Living with "Mental Issues"

The appeal to follow the WHO's understanding of mental issues and develop its recommended "policies, legislation, community care facilities, and treatments for people with mental illness" is tied to the WHO's comprehension of a "functioning member of society" (http://www.who.int/whr/2004/en/report04_en.pdf [Accessed March 22, 2008]). Deploying cost-effective treatment enables individuals to secure mental health, a state which is depicted by the WHO as fully endowed with an European enlightenment version of personal agency of an adaptive/productive type. Thus,

> [m]ental health is defined as a state of well-being in which every individual realizes his or her own potential, can cope with the normal stresses of life, can work productively and fruitfully, and is able to make a contribution to her or his community. (WHO 2008a)

Alongside the "normal stresses of life," there resides a conception of the "normal participant." The "mentally healthy" (or normal) participant is an individual in a state of well-being, full of realizable potential, one who can cope, produce, and be fruitful in such a way that the community can recognize the person as being a contributor and not a burden to society. Healthy people are economically viable people; they are neither a surplus nor a burden.

At times, however, people face something other than "normal stresses of life." While the WHO subsumes the history of colonialism into normal life, newly arising emergencies are recognized by the WHO as a significant factor to be taken into account by mental health regimes. In the face of stresses of life that are not normal (emergencies), there is still a conception of mental health that the WHO articulates and encourages:

> Emergencies create a wide range of problems experienced at the individual, family, community and societal levels. At every level, emergencies erode normally protective supports, increase the risks of diverse problems and tend to amplify pre-existing problems of social injustice and inequality. For example, natural disasters such as floods typically have a disproportionate impact on poor people, who may be living in relatively dangerous places.... In emergencies, not everyone has or develops significant psychological problems. Many people show resilience, that is the ability to cope relatively well in situations of adversity. There are numerous interacting social, psychological and biological factors that influence whether people develop psychological problems or exhibit resilience in the face of adversity. (Inter-Agency Standing Committee (IASC) 2007, pp. 2–3 as cited in http://www.who.int/mental_health/emergencies/guidelines_iasc_mental_health_psychosocial_june_2007.pdf [Accessed March 8, 2008])

Depicting "psychological problems" as both a development issue and a mitigating factor in times of emergencies lends a sense of urgency to the question of how best to respond to mental diversity. We learn that the need for urgency carries a corresponding need to assess the situation in terms of differences – differences in the levels, problems, proportions, and social, economic, and geographic locations – differences that condition how people respond to unexpected events. These urgent differences have the effect of framing issues of mental health and illness as pertaining only to the immediacy of the present. Exploitation and marginalization are treated as merely another set of factors to be inserted into the mental health and illness equation; alongside other social, psychological, and biological influences.

The WHO situates the appropriate response to disorder in a perspective which decontextualizes and realigns emergency, economic disparity, and "dangerous places." Ignoring a country's ongoing history of colonial order and occupation, the WHO treats itself as merely responsive to emergent crisis and not as a participant in this history. In its description of the relationship between natural disasters and mental illness, the WHO naturalizes mental health and medicalizes mental difference. Once anguish has been abstracted from the embodied experience of colonialism, this act of abstraction is, then, furthered by focusing on "cost-effective treatment" regimes. Through constructing psychological problems as urgently in need of appropriate (Western) solutions, the WHO builds support for the need to respond to potential threats to colonial order and encourages countries to work to fit into global capitalism. The question, then, may not be how best to respond to people's anguish, but how anguish has been used to garner an interest in colonial enterprise.

Despite the erosion of "normally protective supports," a state of well-being may persist among those who undergo emergencies and traumas, such as flooding and poverty. Health is depicted as observable in people who are resilient, demonstrating an ability to cope "relative" to the situation within which they find themselves. To "exhibit resilience" in the face of adversity is counterposed to developing psychological problems. The concept of adversity includes emergencies and natural disasters, but adversity is also shadowed by that which emergencies might exacerbate, namely, "pre-existing problems of social justice and inequality." Relative to problems of social justice and inequality, people might exhibit resilience or they might exhibit psychological problems. The WHO is thus appealing to countries to understand that one dominant, or normal, way to regard that which is not an exhibition of resilience is to treat it as a potential mental illness.

It may be argued that the WHO recognizes all sorts of responses other than "relative resilience" as part of health. Still, a state of well-being is situationally and routinely defined by the WHO as tied to "relative resilience." At issue is not the contradiction between the certainty of states of well-being and the free flow of relativity, but what are the consequences of defining health as an adaptive capacity, located firmly inside individuals while glossing over historically rooted sociopolitical life as "relative" to the individual's ability to cope? Given that "ability to cope relatively well in situations of adversity" makes adversity relative to coping, and given that "all things can be relative," even the history of colonialism can be regarded and lived as part of the "normal stresses of life."

A further consequence of defining mental health as an adaptive capacity is the intertwining of coping and productivity. Coping means appearing normally resilient relative to the situation within which people find themselves. Resilient behavior "fits into," or gets along with, the situation; resistant and/or ill behavior does not. The normative order guiding the perceiver's perceptions of the appearance of a normal resiliency is beyond question for the WHO. What is at question is the dividing line between normal resiliency and a serious mental illness. This line is drawn with the measuring stick of productivity. The healthy person exhibits a state of well-being that is productive; such a person is an appreciated or valued addition to the situation within which they find themselves. Coming to know if we are witnessing a normal coping mechanism or a mental health issue is tied to the question of productivity and whether a person is a burden to one's community or not. A healthy person is configured by the WHO as a normally functioning member who is imagined as able to contribute to productivity and who represents economic viability. This map of mental health assumes a discernable border between misfortune and injustice; a clear border between emergency and history; and a clear border between resilient productivity and failure to function as a productive member of one's society.

The problem of mental health is both taken for granted and invoked in the perceived appearance of individuals with mental illness. The WHO literature consistently guides its readers to understand the problem as follows: anything outside of the state of well-being can be regarded as ill; ill is undesirable individual suffering for which there are cost-effective individual treatments. Since illness is both given and obvious, no difference in description from one country to the next is required, or at least not at this stage. Instead, the WHO provides many descriptions of the prevalence and consequences of mental illness especially in terms of economic costs. The consequence consistently articulated is that ill individuals fail to be able to fit in, and contribute to, society relative to its state of affairs. When mental health is absent, there is a lack of productivity or there is something other than the manifestation of a fruitful version of the human. When all of life is conceptualized as a health issue, medicalized versions of governance or control become a necessity. Through repeated public articulations of mental health and illness, the WHO has demonstrated that it is oriented to, and by, this form of governance.

9.5 The Colonial Imperative

The colonial imperative of "integration" (to become functioning members of dominant society) reveals how the map of mental illness is followed in order to foster an image of unity. This image of unity implicates various countries in the need to join the WHO's understanding that low- and middle-income countries do not understand the problem appropriately and thus need the WHO policy and procedures in order to conform with the dominant individualized representations of human life understood as conditioned by a notion of health and illness. Every country and every person must be made to be of one mind, or one way of thinking that can appropriately attend to the colonial imperative to "discriminate between mental and physical problems," to discriminate between resiliencies and serious psychological problems; to discriminate between being a healthy, functioning, and thus productive member of society or being otherwise (WHO 2008a). Once objectified and thus abstracted into a population of millions of people with problems receiving inappropriate attention from their home countries, such countries can be governed so as to institutionalize, monitor, and manage the assumption that there is a clear boundary around normal, healthy, resilient adaptation. This governance relies upon knowledge regimes that enforce the sense that embodiment is neither a political nor a social matter.

A clear border between the state of health and the state of illness is created by articulating the notion of productivity and cost. The control and subsequent patrolling of borders requires that the lives of people be repeatedly subsumed under, and expressed as, a significant economic burden. Thus,

> [t]he total economic costs of mental disorders are substantial. In the USA, the annual direct treatment costs were estimated to be US$ 148 billion, accounting for 2.5% of the gross national product. The indirect costs attributable to mental disorders outweigh the direct treatment costs by two to six times in developed market economies, and are likely to account for an even larger proportion of the total treatment costs in developing countries, where the direct treatment costs tend to be low. (WHO 2003, pp. 1–2)

Ironically, this data is not used by the WHO to make the argument that "cost-effective" treatments for "mental disorders" are neither cheap nor effective. Instead, by the WHO's account, mental disorders are costly, whereas treatment is cost-effective. Treatment refers to the dominant pharmacological approach of the North. Whereas people with mental disorders are depicted as a costly burden to their home country, their treatment is depicted as a relatively inexpensive proposition for these countries as well as a potential profit-maker for the mental health and illness industry.

What does it mean to be part of a system that asks people to recognize themselves as a cost? Who is asked, or even forced, to understand their life in this way? Frantz Fanon, speaking of the consequences of colonialism, says: "Because it is a systematized negation of the Other, a frenzied determination to deny the Other any attribute of humanity, colonialism forces the colonized to constantly ask the question: 'Who am I in reality?'" (Fanon 2004 [1961], p. 182). As a burdensome cost, living in the midst of others who do not know how to respond appropriately, questions of mental health and illness, questions of anguish and power, become arenas of ongoing colonization. "Minding" the minds of the Other is a profit-making venture, a governance issue, as well as a mechanism to put people into a particular relation to the history of colonialism that seems oriented only to making "fit Others," Others able to cope and adapt to the presence of global capitalism and its future expansion.

What an anticolonial approach brings to an analysis of the connection between disability discourse and the world ordering of countries (Freire 1983) is the necessity to map that which supports, and perpetuates the power to say "It is so" or "You are so." As we go about the doings of life, problems arise which demand our attention and thus the need to say "This is a problem," "You are a problem," or "I am a problem." But the way people identify problems cannot be fully understood as simply powerful words being wielded to go out and meet and mold the world. Those words by which we refer to Others are not only destined for the world, they are of the world (Merleau-Ponty 1958, p. 214). But "mental disorder" and "mental illness" are consistently regarded by the WHO as readily identifiable and measurable features of individuals alone. Interesting, then, are the processes that make possible dealing with people as if their problems originate in their individual lives; as if the perceiver and the perceived are radically unrelated.

This imagined gap of unrelatedness is one way to represent the significance of colonialism. The ongoing activity of colonialism results in an ability to wield power over the diversity of the Other. But something other than a "fear of difference" or a "hunger for power" may animate this activity since colonialism is oriented to and by an unimaginative refusal. This takes shape as a refusal to see that any sense of "I" or "me" is only available through a "we"; a refusal to engage the powerful paradox that "I" can be made to exist alone in the knowledge that "I" cannot exist alone; a refusal to dwell in the joy or the anguish that the perceiver and the perceived are always connected. Colonialism is a refusal to develop a vivid sense of the interrelatedness of existence connected through a worldly horizon of self and other.

We can now note that the WHO's map of mental issues refuses to work from the complexity of interrelatedness. It encourages only an individualizing, medicalizing, isolating of the Other as a problem. This can be read as something more than a right or wrong method of proceeding with human differences through a form of privileged self-exemption. An alternative reading brings to the fore the result of treating millions of people as problems as the effects of an unexamined colonial relation that attempts to actualize a disconnection between the perceiver and the perceived. Through such colonizing power the mentally ill/healthy dichotomy is achieved and naturalized thus provoking countries and their people to require the treatment the WHO prescribes. While it may seem today that the powers-that-be act a bit more cautiously with colonizing procedures, medical regimes, especially when it comes to issues of "ill-health," argue for their efficacy without considering how their procedures are complicit in the perception of who and what problem people are. Structuring the singular sensibility of the Other as devalued difference, a difference taken to originate in the life of the subject so named, is a source of "social suffering" worthy of further examination (Kleinman et al. 1997). Moreover, this singular sensibility regarding mental health and illness seems to also control the WHO in all its programmatic articulations, since this sensibility is consistently repeated without showing any sign of having reflected on its own core truth claims.

Thus, we continue with an anticolonial mapping of the way the minds, bodies, and senses of Others have been colonized by the health and illness regimes of the North. Instead of asking if colonized people are "really" suffering from mental illness or not, and instead of surveying whether low- and middle-income countries are "really" responding inappropriately or not, we seek now to reveal and map the WHO's logic of producing a worldwide conception of the need for a unified mind by examining the discourse of the "Mental Health Improvements for Nations Development" (MIND), also called the WHO MIND project. We conduct this analysis while keeping in mind the warnings of a North American founder of disability studies:

> As long as the deliverers of service are markedly different in gender, economic class, and race from those whom they offer services, as long as accessibility to medical care is a privilege rather than a right, as long as the highest income groups are health care professionals, as long as the most profit-making enterprises include the pharmaceutical and insurance industries, society is left with the uncomfortable phenomenon of a portion of its population, living, and living well, off the sufferings of others and to some extent even unwittingly having a vested interest in the continuing existence of such problems. (Zola 1977, p. 66)

9.6 The Imperative of the Problem Population

The map of mental illness reflects ways of understanding and governing people, populations and countries around the globe today. This governance finds its ongoing development in the WHO's programmatic initiative, the WHO MIND project, launched in 2007. The WHO MIND project aims to improve mental health. The following is from this project's World Wide Web articulation of its interests and aims:

Towards concrete changes in people's daily lives

Mental and neurological disorders such as depression, schizophrenia, epilepsy and substance abuse, among others, cause immense suffering for those affected, amplify people's vulnerability and can lead individuals into a life of poverty. Despite the worldwide availability of cost-effective treatments the vast majority of people are left without access to the treatment they need. Instead of getting the help and support they require to lead productive lives, many people are subject to stigma, discrimination and human rights violations and are denied the basic life opportunities given to other citizens.

Mental health improvements are central to nations' development

By treating many of the debilitating mental disorders and by promoting mental health, people will experience major improvements in their lives. (WHO 2008b)

The WHO MIND project conceives of unproductive people and underdeveloped countries as analogous, related problems. It proposes that both people and countries can be improved through "mental health policies, strategic plans and laws." To improve they must turn to the WHO to help them put their lived experiences of anguish behind them. The assumption here is that only by "entering the MIND" of the WHO, and facing the reality of their own lack of productivity, can problem populations and countries access the wealth of resources. What is so persuasive and seductive about the WHO's way of thinking is its assurance that much-needed resources have actually been available the whole time. They have just been out of sync with those of other "more developed" (read European) countries. This perspective assumes that the only thing these problem people and problem nations know is suffering, and, as Rod Michalko (2002, p. 93) says, "useless suffering" at that. Undeveloped and unproductive forms of life are embodied by anguish which prevents individuals and countries from accessing other more economically viable and acceptable life opportunities. The new opportunities that WHO regards have themselves always and already come at a greater price than expected leaving the promise of a global citizenry unfulfilled.

WHO MIND is informing countries that they need to provide "at-risk" citizens with greater access to treatment. At issue is how control over access to already existing psychological knowledge is to be accumulated, centralized, and redistributed to problem populations. Unlike the "relative worth" of disabled individuals, the value of the treatment remains uncontested. Considerations of the transformative potential of the disability experience are bypassed en route to the consolidation of universal access to treatment. How is it that we can talk about treatment without an explicit articulation of what it is that is in need of treating?

Those processes that encourage us to map ourselves or others as suffering from mental health issues produce a sensibility of difference. Asking how a sensibility of difference is produced allows us to examine how this unified and singular understanding of diverse and complex relationships is doing the work of transcribing the colonizing powers on to the minds, bodies, and senses of colonized Others. In pursuit of a singular notion of the fit and healthy life, difference is thus made recognizable as an obstacle to belonging, or fitting-in, while simultaneously providing for the delineation and comprehension of common goals and the presentation of the problem treated as objectively given. Colonial processes and procedures of standardization supply the drive for *fitness* – the condition of good health necessary to ensure the individual's suitability for social life, and the country's suitability for expanding profit through the proliferation of Western psychology's legitimation. In this regard, the various WHO reports acknowledge many doctors, professors, and other professionals and also say that they wish "to acknowledge the generous financial support of the Governments of Australia, Finland, Italy, the Netherlands, New Zealand, and Norway, as well as the Eli Lilly and Company Foundation and the Johnson and Johnson Corporate Social Responsibility, Europe" (WHO 2003, p. iii). More treatment, greater access to treatment, treatment ensconced by law, driven by profit, and governed by the powers that be are emphasized over and against any more nuanced depiction of the millions of people said to suffer from mental illness. This shows once again that unlike the "relative worth" of disabled people who are depicted as always a cost and a burden, the value of treatment is uncontested.

In claiming that mental illness is a key cause of vulnerability, suffering, and poverty, the WHO MIND project circumnavigates the anguish of colonial inequality and oppression. The WHO MIND project anticipates a critique of its agenda by framing the problem of mental health and illness in terms of nations, countries, citizens, and most importantly, human *rights*. Whereas the anticolonial perspective perceives inequality in the capitalist structures organizing social life in global economies, the WHO MIND ascribes the persistence of social suffering to a lack of integration of existing structures, as well as inappropriate services and service providers. The centralization of all services related to mental health is to now take shape in a "common vision" (WHO 2008b). The "common vision" of the WHO's MIND can be read as a manifestation of what Michel Foucault refers to as the normalizing gaze. According to Foucault (1977, p. 25), the normalizing gaze is "a surveillance that makes it possible to qualify, to classify, and to punish," which "establishes over individuals a visibility through which one differentiates and judges them." This common vision, and the medicalized gaze that sustains it, is established through the psychologically oriented disciplines that have come to govern what it means to know both people and places.

Nicholas Rose's characterization of this development of the gaze and field of psychology in Western nations is important to consider in the light of the exporting of mental health regimes around the world. On the development of the legitimacy of the psychologically based disciplines, he says, "[t]he mental state of the population was beginning to be translated into a calculable form: inscribed, documented, and turned into statistics, graphs, charts, and tables that could be pored over in political deliberations and administrative initiatives" (Rose 1999, p. 25). The constitution of a problem population, especially one whose problem is tied to suffering, requires the immediate implementation of a solution. The field of psychological knowledge comprises the political authorities driving capitalist agendas toward constructing populations as "problem spaces"[2] (Rose 1992), making the work of governing much easier and more efficient:

> One of the major contributions of the psychological sciences to our modernity has been the invention of techniques that make individual differences and capacities visible, through devising means whereby they can be inscribed or notable in legible forms. (Rose 1999, p. 19)

The psychological sciences not only offer a language through which subjectivity can be documented and debated, but also provide a new conceptual apparatus by which individuality is made relative to the very differences this language constitutes. The "problem spaces" Rose describes are accessed via the detailed stories of particular individuals believed to make up, and belong to, problem populations. What qualifies these individuals and the stories they tell is the extent to which a reading of their life stories can be generalized, and used to demonstrate the need to make visible problems which are then legible as mental issues in need of treatment. In framing the personal narrative as a representation of the "problem," the treatment organization can appear as the solution. The WHO MIND Web site portrays the issue facing persons suffering from what will only be understood by WHO as mental illness (and not, say, the anguish of power) as also causing problems for citizenship. It presents the "personal perspectives" of "denied citizens" who have suffered a "mental disorder." "Turning my Life Around: Sylvester's Story" is one example of how a single approach is used to govern human diversity (WHO *Denied Citizens*, http://www.who.int/features/2005/mental_health/sylvester/en/ [Accessed March 8, 2008]). "Turning my Life Around" includes excerpts from Sylvester Katontoka's testimony at the "World Health Organization International Forum on Mental Health, Human Rights and Legislation" in Geneva in 2003. This story demonstrates how "my life" can be turned into an acceptable, illustrative, WHO story worthy of worldwide circulation. Sylvester explains how he "began a six-year roller coaster ride of despair" that resulted in hospitalization in what was for all intents and purposes a prison. He describes how:

> This experience was too harsh and turned my life upside down, ending up [with my] being socially disabled. I was isolated from my society and often wandered in the wilderness with no food, decent shelter and decent clothes. Stigmatization and discrimination were the order of my days. Destitution became my life.

Here, anguish is understood as something that arises out of undesirable experiences treated in an inappropriate fashion. Inappropriate treatment results in "social disability," as well as an individual's deviation from the path to civilization and a separation from the life-giving resources of collective life.

What is unclear here is what experience Sylvester is describing. Is it an experience of a lack of mental health care services and the professional expertise of service providers as the WHO implies? Or is it his experience of the "jail-like structure" of the hospital that confined him? In other parts of this story, he says that it was the hospital that saved him from committing suicide, and that it was through an "empowerment programme" offered by the hospital that he regained control over his livelihood. Despite its contradictions, Sylvester Katontoka's account shows medical diagnosis as the remedy governments offer the citizens they deny. Filling its prescription entails a concerted submission to the proscription of mental illness and the authority of the colonially informed objective of "taking power and control over one's life."

In a world where mental differences are understood in terms of a prolonged state of emergency, "Turning one's life around" requires that we think of social suffering as a disorder in need of regulation. This regulation, while it may initially seem harsh, is liberating for those willing to commit to it. But what of those who do not have the inclination, time, or the resources to survive that commitment, let alone ascribe to it? Normalizing anguish becomes a way to more fully integrate alienated individuals within the very normative frameworks that condition the production of the alienable body. Ordered by stigma and discrimination, the colonial life world equates exclusion with disability, and restricts perception of the embodied experience of exclusion to a common conception of disability as a problem. In representing anguish as a type of social disablement, attention is first centered on, and then shifted away from, the body; providing for the translation of physical and mental difference into social terms. In this way, this personal narrative as well as a conception of mental illness circulated worldwide ends up "fitting" in and confirming the WHO's prognosis, and the need for its common vision.

9.7 The Colonial Past in the Globalized Future

Colonialism functions in the subordination of the experiences of lived realities to abstract ideas. Thus, notions of human equality (as adaptive producers) and universal rights (to Western mental health treatments), so fundamental to the WHO's suggestions for world improvement, reflect bourgeois colonial ideology (Sartre 1983). Mental health and illness regimes can be regarded as one way such ideology is today reproduced and imported around the globe. This is not to say that people do not suffer, but rather that this suffering, often explicitly conditioned by the colonial enterprise, is immediately abstracted and controlled as a medical problem at the level of the mind. In *The Wretched of the Earth* (Fanon 2004 [1961]), Fanon is critical of this gap between the lived reality of colonial embodiment and the way it has been theorized by the middle class intellectuals. Fanon notices how historical differences and situational particularities are subsumed by a grand narrative of history in the context of global imperialism. This master narrative, while making a claim to universality, actually serves to erase the spatial and temporal differences that constitute the particular orientations of embodied beings. Recall Thomas King who tells us that "[t]he truth about stories is that that is all we are." Reading Fanon alongside King, we suggest that the story colonialism tells is that the only reality that matters is a bourgeois one. According to this reading, the possibility of viewing suffering as a response to social oppression is made peripheral to the calculation of a probability that suffering oppresses. That populations *can be* counted, costs of treatment calculated, while emergencies are anticipated, circumscribes how suffering is made to appear, and restricts the appearance of other kinds of stories. All the while, measuring the costs of suffering also serves to delineate a new market of predictable profit margins.

An anticolonial compass orients us to the fact that we are now facing a complex social, political, and economic dilemma in which disability materializes as a way of legitimating capitalist development and managing social discontent. For disability to appear this way, *as both problem and problem-solver*, it requires a polarization of interpretation which props up WHO's version of the right or wrong way of proceeding. It is only in identifying and treating disability that, "people will experience major improvements in their lives," "participate productively in community life," and "contribute to the economy of their country" (WHO 2008b). Disability, posited as both the cause of social suffering and the means for its erasure, reinforces the dichotomy between developed and underdeveloped countries, while simultaneously providing a compelling reason for all countries to follow the WHO. How is disability conceptually mapped such that WHO can use it as the story to orient governments to the necessity of attending to the problem of their own lack of development?

Negative responses to the effects of capitalism (to and by the surplus peoples it creates) are now interpreted by psychiatric and medical knowledge regimes as markers of a country's level of development and integration within the context of the ongoing historical development of global capitalism.[1] As a psychiatrist, but perhaps more importantly, as a black man raised in Martinique and working in Algeria during the French occupation, Fanon was interested in unraveling the mystery of the interpersonal violence that enclosed him. The extraordinary violence of everyday life Fanon witnessed in the colonies reiterated, *in bodily form*, the cultural ways of thinking, perceiving, and practicing colonial understanding. It is thus that Fanon writes: "The colonizer's reluctance to entrust the native with any kind of responsibility does not stem from racism or paternalism but quite simply from a scientific assessment of the colonized's limited biological possibilities" (Fanon 2004 [1961], p. 226). Only in becoming a medical anomaly can colonial embodiment be made to matter; only in succumbing to the power of medical authority can the individual trapped within this embodiment find freedom.

In *Black Skin, White Masks*, Fanon (1952) follows the logic of the dependency complex Mannoni observed in the colonial situation. Fanon notices how, in establishing the biological deficiency of bodies in "undeveloped" countries, health regimes participated in colonial governance. The emergence of psychological illnesses such as the dependency complex allowed for the development of institutionalized techniques and health programs which colonial powers could draw on to justify the brutality of colonial occupation. Once anguish was read as a symptom of inferiority; the exceptional violence of everyday life in the colonies could be dismissed as one unfortunate consequence of the natural disposition of a biologically inferior species of human life. What should be very troubling for us today are the implications of the persistence of such thinking in the WHO's call for countries to coordinate their own approaches to its singularly restrictive version of mental health and illness.

The tendency to associate notions of development, progress, or growth with civilization, cosmopolitanism, and democracy reflects a fundamental interest in the values of capitalism, rather than the accomplishment of historical change. In this context, cultural and economic superiority take precedence over the actualization of human potential. The certainty that history has already happened conceals the factual reality in which, as Homi K. Bhabba says, "history is *happening*" (2006, p. 37, emphasis his own). Since history is happening, problems we have been led to believe belong to the past persist in new forms in the solutions to our difficulties with relation to the present. As Césaire (1955, p. 31) points out in *A Discourse on Colonialism*:

> The fact is that the so-called European civilization – "Western" civilization – as it has been shaped by two centuries of bourgeois rule, is incapable of solving the two major problems to which its existence has given rise: the problem of the proletariat and the colonial problem.

For Césaire, as for Fanon, the hypocrisy of its supposed humanitarianism, and the brutalizing effects of colonialism on both the colonizer and the colonized, must be exposed. Fanon's (1952, p. 11) "sociodiagnostic" orients us to the fact that the problems of social exclusion, marginalization, and human suffering, problems he sought to assess and amend in his work in psychiatry, and problems with which he was intimately familiar as a black intellectual in a white world, are not problems of an "individual question":

> The analysis that I am undertaking is psychological. In spite of this it is apparent to me that the effective disalienation of the black man entails an immediate recognition of social and economic realities. If there is an inferiority complex, it is the outcome of a double process: primarily, economic; subsequently, the internalization – or better, the epidermalization – of this inferiority.

The anguish Fanon both witnessed as a psychiatrist and experienced as a racialized subject in Martinique, France, and Algeria was a direct consequence of the colonial situation capitalism had created, perpetuated, and maintained. For Fanon, the extraordinarily everyday violence in the colonial situation, which the WHO MIND project identifies in terms of "stigma, discrimination and human rights violations," cannot simply be attributed to depression, schizophrenia, or substance abuse. Such violence is not the unfortunate side effect of a lack of treatment, or what the WHO describes as a "treatment-gap," but is, instead, a specific consequence of the creation of populations of surplus laborers and superfluous people (WHO 2008b). The WHO narrates this superfluous surplus as those who cannot cope with the reality of global capitalism; who are not productive. Despite its claims, it is these problem populations who are actually most valuable to the WHO, for they provide the backdrop against which the colonial order can be legitimized. Those described as mentally disordered are the greatest cost to nations' development, but they are also its greatest source of income. That the anguish of power needs to be "seen" to be made otherwise incites the interest of professional organizations, service providers, and pharmaceutical companies, as well as the construction and maintenance of hospitals and clinics and the bureaucracies that oversee them – all engines for the production of capital. The well-being of the nation depends on it. Those who fail to *see* the truth before their eyes, *hear* the call to arms, or take a *stand* against untreated suffering in the world are simply in the way.

9.8 Decolonizing Disability

The map of mental health and illness is plotted along multiple axes of power. The WHO's international networks of professional care-givers led by psychiatrists, doctors, professors, lawyers, and social workers specialize in different areas yet share a common understanding of the mentally ill or disabled body as a detriment to national development. Disability is not open to the future. It represents a move backwards, a deterioration of the status quo, and as such, must be contained and controlled. There is, however, something worse than disability, namely, the person or nation that cannot tell if it is sick, that does not know it is disabled. The "inability to recognize" the rate, state, and appropriate treatment fate of "mental disorders" is regarded by WHO as disabling the development of countries.

The capitalist, the colonialist, and the mental health professional imagine that the future is an extension of the present, but one further steeped in ambivalence, uncertainty, and in the sensibility of never knowing who or what you really are. These social positions can only be coordinated if the desire to be fitted and fixed into the common mind is treated as a naturally given, self-evident good. Fanon (1952, p. 8) reminds us that the bourgeois certainty of a future of uncertainty, and the hordes of experts enlisted to manage this ever-present threat of instability produces, "a zone of non-being, an extraordinary sterile and arid region, an utterly naked declivity." Fanon (1952, p. 8) is, however, careful to remind us that in this region, "an authentic upheaval can be born." The WHO uses disability to depict this zone of nonbeing. Imagined as worst-case scenario, the threat of disability serves to unify an international consciousness of the need for capitalist development through psychological rule. Yet, Fanon, while recognizing that his experiences as a colonized subject are shaped by bourgeois anxieties, still calls on us to confront the fact that the way we think about, and relate to, our bodies and the body politic, or human being and society, is mutually constitutive. In the face of the brutality, betrayals, and unfulfilled promises of capitalism, what is needed is not a new, more nuanced, complicated, and compartmentalized version of a human being, but a new relation to the types of human beings colonialism produces.

9 The Anguish of Power

Mapping the WHO's story and the story of being brought to the question "Who am I in reality?" provides an arena within which the imaginary lines guiding normative social cartographies of difference have been made legible. There is, perhaps, an authentic upheaval that resides in the mapping of this terrain of social control. Fanon (1952, p. 10) tells us that total decolonization and total violence are necessary tools in the construction of a "total understanding" of reality. Such understanding involves denaturalizing any and all conceptions of human embodiment. The development of such an understanding includes not being fragmented by the conflicting interests of capitalism and subsumed by the effervescent ideal of whiteness:

> And then the occasion arose when I had to meet the white man's eyes. An unfamiliar weight burdened me. The real world challenged my claims. In the white world the man of color encounters difficulties in the development of his bodily schema. Consciousness of the body is solely a negating activity. It is a third-person consciousness. The body is surrounded by an atmosphere of certain uncertainty. (Fanon 1952, pp. 110–111)

Fanon's narrative of meeting the "white man's eyes," stories the experience of dislocation and displacement as a nauseating confrontation with the absence of the Other. His story recognizes that the civilized *vision* of a common humanity is predicated on the negation of the Other. Similarly through negation, through the specific modalities proposed by the WHO MIND project to improve mental health, bodily difference is made to appear. The lived reality of Fanon's difference is not where it should be, not where he is. Rather than being faced with his alterity, he is faced with his abjection, and it takes the form of "the language of the civilizing nation."

We have turned to Fanon because, as Sara Ahmed writes, Fanon's

> work shows, after all, bodies are shaped by histories of colonialism. [...] Bodies remember such histories, even when we forget them. Such histories, we might say, surface on the body, or even shape how bodies surface. (Ahmed 2006, p. 111)

In the colonial encounter, psychological knowledge regimes mark certain bodies as suffering from a lack of development. Psychological knowledge continues to provide one of the means by which the bourgeois colonialist enterprise reproduces its ideology by convincing people of their inherent or *natural* inferiority; serving as a conceptual toolbox for reorganizing relations of resistance and reducing human problems to "ideas" of health and illness (Césaire 1955, p. 62). Fanon's work illustrates his desire to lead individuals suffering the colonial embodiment to a perspective, to a place where feelings of self-contempt, rage, and resentment should be redirected at the colonial order that has produced some people as inferior and less-than human. It is the internal dynamics of the capitalist system that render us perpetually *unprepared* to receive different ways of perceiving, thinking about, and responding to, the world. In working to make sense of what others say from their own perspectives and particular situations, we are better positioned to recognize that diversity of thought, the anguish of power, and the necessity of alterity are not so disastrous.

9.9 Conclusion: Desiring Other Maps

The anguish produced and inscribed on colonially disordered bodies through representations of mental illness is more than simply an effect of the oppressive dominion of medicalized discourses evidencing the inequality, discrimination, and alienation of life. Such anguish is a productive power that can be used to access a collective consciousness of difference as an external agency that is resisted, erased, or otherwise made to disappear. The map of mental illness thus scripts how agency or obligation is to be imagined and governed in colonial society. Ironically, this map functions to indicate the presence of agency but only in its negative form. In orienting to representations of mental illness as a means for plotting the form one's obligations to the social "should" take, we have access to the fact that each representation, each story, has a number of sides, and that each side offers a situation through which human agency can appear. This is true insofar as the human world is always and everywhere an agentive world, a world with actors, even if our action is made to appear only as passive, unproductive, or ill. That we map meanings on to various actions and locations of people vividly references how language organizes, or better, burns and etches the perceptual consciousness *of what is*, thus revealing the complicity of the perceiver in the constitution of what is perceived.

Disability is no mere metaphor to express the character of colonial powers – "blind to the issues, deaf to the calls, unwilling to stand up and take a run at justice." Indeed, we have demonstrated that it is necessary to understand disability as one way in which a population of problem people, delegitimized people, not quite human people are created. Mapping these creations is also a way to come to understand how minds, bodies, and senses are the vehicles used to export and organize social control, enabling the ongoing process of colonization. (This should certainly speak against the common practice to use disability as a delegitimizing metaphor within critical social theory.) The WHO's interest in accessing already available treatments and "closing the treatment-gap" can be read as an expression of a collective recognition that our experiences of ourselves are always and everywhere mediated by the bodies we come into contact with; whether we understand these bodies as our own or as belonging to someone, somewhere, else. The WHO brings us into contact with its version of the body problem and gives us one dominant way to mind the body.

The WHO orients us to its commitment to being at home with the need for treatment and the capitalist global economy that makes the proliferation of mental health services and their coordination possible and desirable. Framed within the WHO's discourse on mental health and illness, our personal narratives as embodied beings can only ever be a story about the need to adopt the WHO's orientation and perceive expressions of differently lived relations to the world as a threat to collective well-being and economic prosperity. In imagining the disabled body as a flood that overflows its borders and threatens the sustainability of the other bodies it comes into contact with, the WHO can justify its assertion that the undesired consequences of the disability experience can be predicted and prevented given deference to the expertise of global health regimes. To restrict awareness of anguish to a symptom of the need for capitalism negates the potential of this embodied experience to expose the structural inequalities capitalism has created in the world today.

The WHO's mental health initiative mandating the coordination of "prevention, treatment, care and long term support" of populations of mentally ill individuals perceives the experience of mental difference as a sign of disability and a symptom of a need for more globalization and capitalist development. We have illustrated how this initiative is embedded within a grand narrative of the history of colonialism and global capitalism. This story asks us to negate our contradictory experiences of mental difference and disability, but also draws attention to the need to rethink our relations to history and the need for historical change. Just as the WHO invites us to imagine a new world without pain or suffering, it also presents us with an astute perception of what constitutes positive social change in today's world. *Making a difference* is what counts. But making a difference in "Changing History" means measuring and isolating the "indicators of population health and health system financing" (http://www.who.int/whr/2004/en/report04_en.pdf [Accessed March 22, 2008]). The WHO does abstract disability from difference and creates problem person out of problem history.

Still, there has to be other sides to this story. Attending to the WHO project through anticolonial and disability studies principles means that we can ask ourselves, what forms of mediation do we already have access to that do not necessarily rely on the devaluation of mental and bodily differences? In what ways could such alternatives expose the interests driving the production of an internationally coordinated and expert-driven "common vision," and challenge the presumption that its version of life is the only life worth living? How might we understand the relation between anguish and embodiment as something other than illness? Just as disability studies have troubled the way disability is only made relevant as a problem (Abberley as cited in Titchkosky 2003, p. 131; Michalko 2008), anticolonial studies also can provoke us to perceive "problem" bodies, minds, and senses in ways that resist normalizing colonial history, making it measurable or profitable. If, as Bhabba suggests, "history is already happening," we need to trace out how we are already perceiving history otherwise. This chapter is an expression of our hope that by attending to the history of the present, the actual ways that disability is conceptualized and mapped by international organizations today, we might find new ways to circumnavigate colonial processes so as not to arrive in another day of the same embodied disqualification.

Notes

1. This is said in contrast to the USA spending 2.5% of its GNP on direct costs of mental illness treatments (WHO 2003).
2. Perhaps these problem spaces are also the "relatively dangerous places" that the WHO refers to while addressing emergencies and mental health.
3. Fanon resigned his post as a psychiatrist at the Blida-Joinville hospital in Algeria in 1956. His letter of resignation is published in his "Letter to the Resident Minister (1956)" in his book *Toward the African Revolution: Political Essays* (1967, 52–54).

References

Ahmed, Sara. (2006). *Queer phenomenology: Orientations, objects, others*. Durham, NC: Duke University Press.
Bhabba, Homi K. (2006). *The location of culture*. London: Routledge.
Césaire, Aimé. (2000 [1955]). *Discourse on colonialism*. New York: Monthly Review Press.
Corker, Mairian. (2002). Mapping the terrain. In Mairian Corker and Tom Shakespeare (Eds.), *Disability/postmodernity: Embodying disability theory* (pp. 1–17). London: Continuum.
Fanon, Frantz. (1952). *Black skin, white masks*, Charles Lam Markman (Trans.). New York: Grove Press.
Fanon, Frantz. (1967). *Toward an African Revolution: Political Essays*, Haakon Chevalier (Trans.). New York: Grove Press.
Fanon, Frantz. (2004 [1961]). *The wretched of the earth*, Richard Philcox (Trans.). New York: Grove Press.
Foucault, Michel. (1977). *Discipline and punish: The birth of the prison*. New York: Pantheon Books.
Freire, Paulo. (1983). The importance of the act of reading. *Journal of Education*, 165(1), 5–11.
Inter-Agency Standing Committee (IASC) (2007). IASC guidelines on mental health and psychosocial support in emergency settings. Geneva: IASC. http://www.humanitarianinfo.org/iasc/content/products. Accessed 8 March 2008.
Kempf, Arlo. (2009), "Chapter one". *Breaching the colonial contract: Anti-Colonialism in the US and Canada*, Springer.
King, Thomas. (2003). *The truth about stories: A native narrative*. Toronto: Anansi Press.
Kleinman, Arthur, Das, Veena, and Lock, Margaret. (Eds.). (1997). *Social suffering*. Berkeley/Los Angeles, CA: The University of California Press.
Merleau-Ponty, Maurice. (1958 [1945]). *Phenomenology of perception*, Colin Smith (Trans.). London: Routledge & Kegan Paul.
Michalko, Rod. (2002). *The difference that disability makes*. Philadelphia, PA: Temple University Press.
Michalko, Rod. (2008). *Double trouble: Disability and disability studies*. (Unpublished Manuscript).
National Institute of Mental Health (NIMH). (2008). The numbers count: Mental disorders in America. http://www.nimh.nih.gov/health/publications/the-numbers-count-mental-disordersin-america.shtml#WHOReportBurden. Accessed 22 March 2008.
Rose, Nikolas. (1992). Political power beyond the state: Problematics of government. *The British Journal of Sociology*, 43(2), 173–205.
Rose, Nikolas. (1999). *Governing the soul: The shaping of the private self*. New York: Free Association Books.
Sartre, Jean Paul. (1983). *Between existentialism and Marxism: Sartre on poetry, philosophy and the arts*, John Matthews (Trans). New York: Pantheon Books.
Stiker, Henri-Jacques. (1997). *A history of disability*, William Sayers (Trans). Foreword by David T. Mitchell. Ann Arbor, MI: The University of Michigan Press.
Titchkosky, Tanya. (2002). Cultural maps: Which way to disability? In Marian Corker and Tom Shakespeare (Eds.), *Disability/postmodernity: Embodying disability theory* (pp. 145–160). London: Continuum.
Titchkosky, Tanya. (2003). *Disability, self, and society*. Toronto: University of Toronto Press.
Titchkosky, Tanya. (2007). *Reading and writing disability differently: The textured life of Embodiment*. Toronto: University of Toronto Press.
World Health Organization (WHO). (2003). The mental health context. Mental Health Policy and Service Guidance Package. Geneva: World Health Organization. http://www.who.int/mental_health/policy/services/3_context_WEB_07.pdf. Accessed 8 March 2008.
World Health Organization (WHO). (2004). World health report 2004: Changing history. WHO Programmes and Projects. Geneva: World Health Organization. http://www.who.int/whr/2004/en/. Accessed 22 March 2008.

World Health Organization (WHO). (2008a). Mental health. WHO Programmes and Projects. Geneva: World Health Organization. http://www.who.int/mental_health/en/. Accessed 8 March 2008.

World Health Organization (WHO). (2008b). Mental health improvements for nations development: The WHO MIND project. WHO Programmes and Projects. Geneva: World Health Organization. http://www.who.int/mental_health/policy/en/. Accessed 8 March 2008.

Zola, Irving Kenneth. (1977). Healthism and disabling medicalization. In Ivan Illich, Irving K. Sola, John McKnight, and Jonathan Caplan (Eds.), *Disabling professions* (pp. 41–68). London: Marion Boyars.

Chapter 10
The Harvesting of Intellectuals and Intellectual Labor: The University System as a Reconstructed/Continued Colonial Space for the Acquisition of Knowledge

Patrick S. De Walt

This chapter analyzes the role that labor plays within the university sphere through a multitude of lenses that include Du Boisian, Fanonian, Gramscian, and Marxian theories. Through these lenses, a relationship between the process of planting and harvesting intellectual labor will be identified and explored through a selective comparison to US enslavement for the purpose of raising the consciousness of intellectuals who are within, who desire to enter, and who look for alternate intellectual and educational spaces to inhabit. This analysis further looks to label the university system as a colonial space that through (its own version of) corporate and intellectual[1] capitalism looks to sustain, expand, and promote its own interests in the guise of pursuing and cultivating knowledge.

When considering Gramsci's (1967) and Said's (1994) discussions on intellectuals, it becomes clearer that one of the agendas of the present-day colonial university[2] is the compartmentalization of knowledge, allowing for the reproduction of intellectual labor to be used within society – that is the university and academic systems. This works to create a supply and demand in which the knowledge housed and marketed by these institutions can be "showcased" for future individuals to become a part of the university system. While the individuals (intellectuals) may think they are gaining an insurmountable amount of knowledge, they are often unaware that they are being drained of that with which they arrived: cultural and intellectual capital. As a result, students are often more susceptible to the social, political, and knowledge-acquiring agendas and protocols of the university.[3] Through this process of socialization, which simultaneously occurs during student matriculation, students are programmed in this fashion to, in many senses, become replaceable cogs in the social system, while at the same time, remaining controlled intellectually within the social system fostered by the university. Gramsci's analysis of "hegemony" created within the structures of a "civil society" has similar ramifications within university systems where intellectual thought and activity are systematically governed for the world production of marketable knowledge.

The university professor holds an analogous position within the colonial university. The pursuit of tenure-track positions reinforces many of these same structures that include the tracking dynamic found within K–12 schooling and corporate systems that create and sustain this current colonial and capitalistic system (see Anyon 1980). This process of "new knowledge" construction is a staple in determining the value of a university professor within a colonial university. The generation of peer-reviewed articles, books, and courses that are both innovative and student (client) attracting, are part of its makeup as formal and informal modes of production (often discussed within the marxist tradition). The many components of the university professor's job resemble what Marcuse discusses within *One Dimensional Man* (1964), in which he critiques industrial society and its affects on society, highlighting the dependency of the system on its parts. In this case the system is the colonial university and the parts are the women and men– the intellectuals who are intellectually harvested.

10.1 The Harvesting and Planting of Knowledge: A Plantational Approach

> When, therefore, you say that the South had a system of slavery for 250 years, you mean that the victims of that system lost their own social heritage; gained new bonds binding them to a new community and new machinery for carrying on the new social life; or, in other words, religion, moral customs, family life, economic habits, literature, and traditions were taken from the Africans. They became a part of a rigid caste system, out of which they could seldom legally rise, and their social organization among themselves was reduced to the barest minimum for existence. (Du Bois 1973, p. 33)

It must be made clear that the system of enslavement provides a significant lens through which to look at the university as a colonial space. In reflecting on Du Bois's thought, entrance into a colonial university system serves as a present-day system of enslavement. The symbolism of the "new bonds binding" those enslaved in the past is prophetic in the recognition of the current bonds that bind university members in colonial university systems – psychological and intellectual shackles. Psychological shackles, as with US enslavement, serve as powerful barriers that work to maintain the agendas of colonial systems. When thinking of the system of enslavement that people of African descent experienced within the United States, the psychological effects often were more powerful than those of the physical means used to maintain control over them by plantation masters.[4] During the process of being enslaved, the individual is indoctrinated into the beliefs, norms, and practices of the governing institution, discarding or altering his or her former beliefs, practices, and selves.

As a result, upon being freed from bondage many newly freed Africans remained in similar labor roles and/or on the sites in which they were once enslaved. This phenomenon was not absolute but many historians, through archival work, have supported this claim.[5] In focusing on this aspect of enslavement (the psychological effect), comparisons can be made in which the colonial university system models that of the antebellum plantation.[6] Colonial university systems impact, in varying ways, the religion, moral customs, family life, economic habits, literature, and traditions of its membership. In many cases colonial systems, as with K–12 school systems, work to socialize its members to the needs and demands of globalized, capitalistic, and Western ideologies and norms in order to maintain itself. Further supporting Fanon's statement: "The colonist [colonial university system] derives his [its] validity, i.e., his [its] wealth, from the colonial system" (2004, p. 2).

As with the institution of enslavement, millions of people of African descent were stratified in numerous ways and forms to create and maintain a "healthy" system of domination for the colonizer. In the following passage, Stampp (1956) provides an example of the social stratification that occurred on plantations:

> Although slaves were generally loyal to their caste and fond of their communities, they, like the [W]hites, had their own internal class structure. Their masters helped to create a social hierarchy by giving them specialized tasks for the sake of economic efficiency, and by isolating domestics and artisans from the field-hands as a control technique. But the stratification of slave society also resulted from an impelling force within the slaves themselves – a force which manifested itself in their pathetic quest for personal prestige. Slaves yearned for some recognition of their worth as individuals, if only from those in their own limited social orbit; for to them this wholly human aspiration was, if anything, more important than it was to the [W]hites. Each slave cherished whatever shreds of self-respect he [or she] could preserve. (pp. 333–334)

A key area in need of highlighting is that of the stratified roles of the overseer[7] and the house and field[8] enslaved Africans – specifically as it applies to intellectual labor roles. In these roles, the labor duties of the plantation were to be disseminated among those enslaved. Those selected and placed in the (buffering) roles as overseers[9] were responsible for the "breaking in"[10] of new enslaved laborers, both in the house and in the field. The house laborer also served as a structural buffer between the plantation owner and the laborers out in the fields. While the house laborer had some levels of benefits within the system, he or she was still subject to inferior treatment, roles, and levels of power within the overall system. The field laborer was the least empowered of the three laboring groups and was subject to even more pressures of existing within the system. The laborer's levels of power, access, and representation within the institution were determined and valued in relation to what their value as producers were for the plantation owner. In this way, there was a hierarchy that determined and defined the role of power and imposition in the lives of various members within the plantation system. This hierarchical system speaks directly to the methods in which the colonial university does the same to both university students and professors (see Figs. 10.1a–d). Yet, these dynamics play out differently depending on which of these groups are centralized.

In the case of the professor and student relationship, the hierarchical institutional power dynamics (HIPD),[11] regardless of the pedagogical beliefs of the instructor, still places the professor in the role of mediator between the student and the institution. As a result, the professor acts in multiple roles, as both the overseer and the house laborer. The student, regardless of level, serves as the field laborer. The graduate student, within the framing of this analysis, shifts between some or all three roles (overseer, house laborer, and field laborer),[12] depending on the circumstances and where he or she is positioned within the hierarchy.[13] Within these roles, the

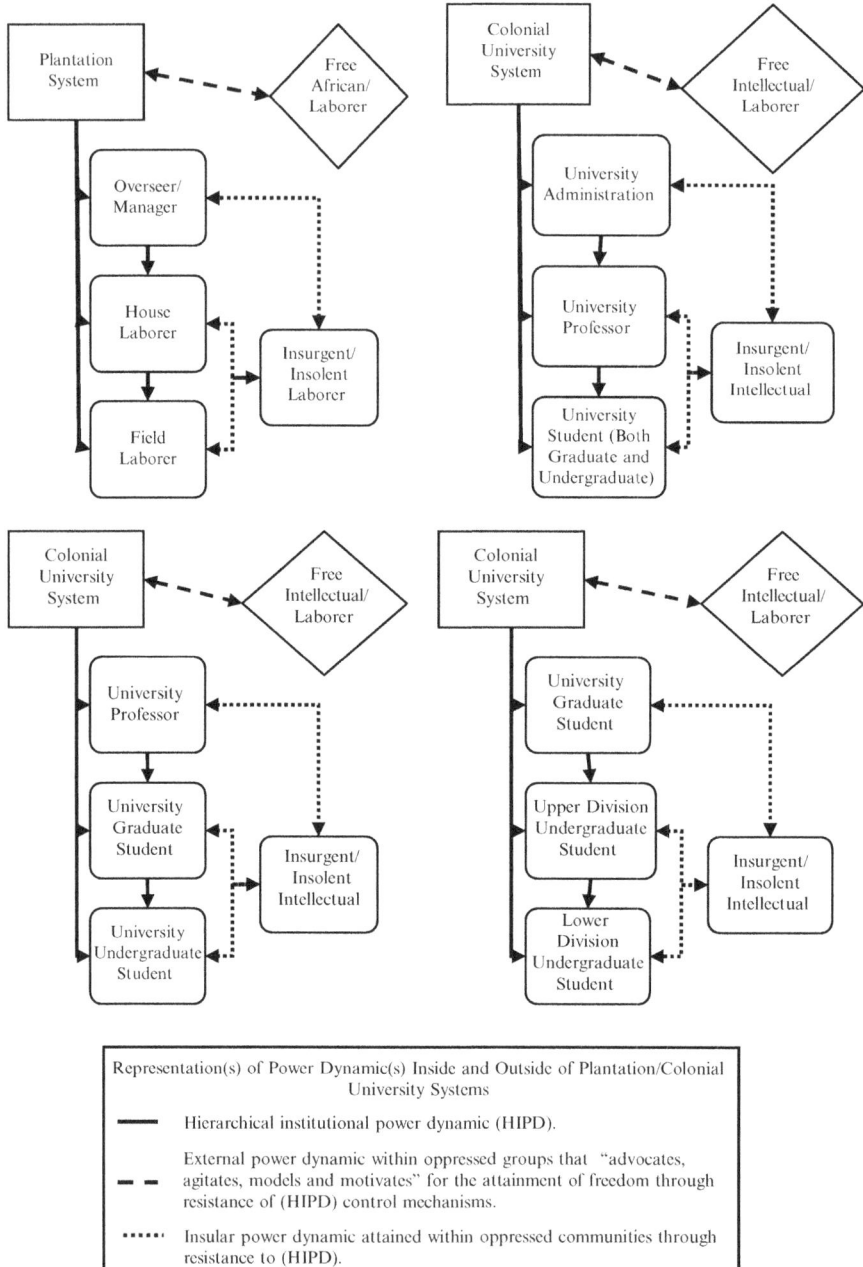

Fig. 10.1 (**a**) Plantation model of (HIPD) administrator emphasis. (**b**) Colonial university model of (HIPD) university. (**c**) Colonial university model of (HIPD) university professor emphasis. (**d**) Colonial university model of (HIPD) university graduate student

professor inherently has some level of power over the student, regardless of his or her educational approach, unless the institution is better served in an alternate way.

For example, within even the most liberating pedagogy, the assessment of a student by a formal grade creates the end product as a university-sanctioned practice – to some degree a form of subordination. While the professor of record may work to offset this through negotiations with the student, this power dynamic ultimately will still exist due to the sheer hierarchical nature of the institution. Also, one of the main goals of the university is to recruit, retain, and train intellectuals/scholars – otherwise thought of as laborers. Yet ironically, the insurgent intellectual (dissenting professor or graduate student) may provide his or her students with the seeds or tools for them to begin to interrogate the university's mission for themselves. This can also be said for undergraduates who look to challenge and educate their peers within and outside the colonial university system. In this act, power has the potential to be shared for a new goal, a collective goal of intellectual and psychological liberation from colonial, Eurocentric, heterosexist, nationalistic, and patriarchal norms. Elements of this challenge to the institutionalized values can be seen below in the words of Gouldner (1979):

> [W]hat could be more authoritarian than the Western patriarchal family? Aimed at reproducing its parents' and especially its father's values, it teaches submission, gratitude, obedience, loyalty; nonetheless, it also and unexpectedly produces: *Oedipus*, rebellion against the father. Like the patriarchal family, the school is surely conceived by its managers as an instrument for the self-perpetuation of the *status quo*. And yet, in both cases, while it rarely *teaches* rebellion, many young people learn it during their education. It is crucial to distinguish between what the institution sets out to *teach*, and what, by force of the conditions that exist, is actually *learned* there. While the school is designed to teach what is adaptive for the society's master institutions, it is also often hospitable to a culture of critical discourse by which authority is unwittingly undermined, deviance fostered, the *status quo* challenged, and dissent systematically produced. (p. 45)

Through these social and intellectual acts of "dissent," the possibility of agency continues to exist and present the intellectual with alternate ways to resist the system from within, similar to the ways in which plantation labor also worked to subvert the authority of the master.[14] In the plantation system, the lived experiences of the enslaved were their teaching apparatuses, as is often the case for the intellectual in colonial university systems. As Gouldner (1979) discusses in regard to the patriarchal model, the same should be said of both the plantation and colonial university models through the deeds of the "insolent" and "insurgent" enslaved person, or through the "dissenting" and "insurgent" intellectual.

When thinking about the university membership of students, we must identify other types of hierarchies created by the institution. For this discussion, I have identified three other HIPDs in which the intellectual roles shift between being colonizer and colonized (see Figs. 10.1b–d). When using Fig. 10.1d as a social structure, the undergraduate student is being taught by the more intellectually socialized graduate student within the system who serves as the catalyst (overseer) for maintaining the university's mission. So as a result, the graduate-level student takes the place of the professor as the house laborer or overseer and the undergraduate student remains in the role of the field laborer (see Fig. 10.1c). As it relates to the goals of the university, the graduate-level student often serves as a substitute for the intellectual labor provided by the professor, as it relates to both teaching and research as part of the university design.[15] In either case, the graduate student is less expensive and more expendable, serving the university's bottom line as it relates to profit margins.

There is a segment of the population within the plantation model, which falls outside of the roles described so far. This segment consisted of those Africans who were "free" by means of rebelling, escaping, or buying their freedom. While they are not at the center of this analysis, they were extremely vital to the social dynamics that occurred on plantations.[16] In many ways, they were the embodiment of resistance to both enslavement and colonization (and current anticolonial efforts) to varying degrees – showing that the psychological impact on the African population within the United States was not absolute (e.g., Harriet Tubman, Sojourner Truth, Henry Highland Garnet, and Frederick Douglass). They were the models that encouraged others to continue and/or challenge the system in alternate ways. As a result, when projecting this forward onto the colonial university, we have a similar possibility. This possibility can be found in the presence of the "free intellectual." Free intellectuals, within a colonial university system framing, are analogous to "free Africans," within a colonial institution of enslavement, who comparatively gain their intellectual freedom from the bounding system.[17] In becoming free of the system, they have the to potential to subvert the institution. The "free Africans" functioned (to varying degrees and successes) beyond the reach of the enslaving institution and the same seems be called for of the "free intellectual." Currently, throughout the United States, many professors and students are attempting to do this by engaging in intellectual thought outside the normative limitations of the colonial university, therefore, becoming quasi-free intellectuals.[18]

10.2 A Historic Shift in Valued Labor: Experiences Within the African Diaspora

In looking at the university, I borrow from Fanon's (2004) intellectual thought. Those who held power usually determined the placement of Africans' physical bodies, within the institution of slavery, as vessels of production through the arduous acts of laboring in the plantations' fields. This is also the case within the context of the colonial university. In today's university systems, the physical labor manifests itself on athletic fields and through intellectual labor within the classroom. Labor is still at a premium, and exists for the benefit of the governing colonial bodies – the colonial university and its university brand. Particular to the emphasis on knowledge and university culture that embraces it, professors and students are often epistemologically transformed in efforts to be better absorbed into the university's design, and in recognition of the way universities legitimate some knowings to the exclusion of others. Often the effects of this colonizing process are more challenging and harmful for communities of color, first-generation students, and other traditionally marginalized communities. Urrieta (2004) makes this assertion in the following: "Schooling was [and is] undeniably a part of the conquering enterprise. In colonial schools, the educational process sought to strip the colonized away from indigenous learning structures and push them toward the structures of the colonizers" (p. 438). This acknowledgement creates the backdrop of a society filled with many historical records of opposition to the opportunities for the learning and teaching of people of African descent in these institutional spaces.

Yet, these tendencies and occurrences are counterproductive to what Feagin et al. (1996) conclude: "Essential to the ideal of the university is that it be a place where diverse students and teachers seek knowledge without hindrance and intolerance" (p. 1). In recognizing this as fact initially, African descendants, through the advent of vocational or trade institutions, were semi-integrated within dominant culture as marginal beings, if that. "All Black" institutions such as Tuskegee, Hampton, and others were created to serve this perceived need and this limiting expectation of African descendants. This educational model (ultimately a type of educational enterprise) perpetuated the ideals of enslavement through the features of labor and the laborer. While for hundreds of years, African descendants were seen as property and free labor, a shift occurred which caused them, as laborers, to be valued as "commodified" agents with relegated powers that were actualized through the capitalistic enterprise. Unknowingly, these forms of manually intensive labor only further stifled their abilities to be viewed and seen as anything more than mindless living machines.

Adversaries of this way of thinking include the likes of Du Bois (1986, 2003, Marable 2005) expressed through notions of an educated class that was charged with uplifting the race and society. As Du Bois (1986) states:

> The Negro [African American] colleges, hurriedly founded, were inadequately equipped, illogically distributed, and of varying efficiency and grade; the normal and high schools were doing little more than common-school work, and the common schools were training but a third of the children who ought to be in them, and training these too often poorly. (p. 427)

In recognizing these deficiencies within these proposed schools, Du Bois looked to approach the needs of the African descendant differently within society. He envisioned the "Talented Tenth"[19] – the creation of an educated class of leaders to guide the masses of African descendants. With this he aimed to move from a space of physical servitude toward a space of intellectual and physical service for the uplifting of the race. He also sought to address and counter the perception of African descendants as a "problem," a common identification by the dominant culture. In Du Bois's (1973) essay, "The Hampton Idea," he states:

> [I]ndustrial school depends not so much on its content – on its actual studies, as on its aim. The aim of the higher training of the college is the development of power, the training of a self whose balanced assertion will mean as much as possible for the great ends of civilization. The aim of technical training on the other hand is to enable the student to master the present methods of earning a living in some particular way. (Du Bois 1973, pp. 13–14)

Within this essay, he discusses the roles of "vocational" institutions with those of the liberal arts college in regard to African-Americans. It should be pointed out that this way of thinking, even by Du Bois himself, in many ways perpetuated the colonial practices within colleges and universities during his era and beyond. Elements of the "industrial school" became key ingredients in the sustaining of K–12 schools and liberal education (later Du Bois also advocated vocational training).

This position perpetuates the laborization of all students, in which the idea of labor, as a result of vocation training, has been altered to include the goals of liberal arts education through the labor of intellectual training. Du Bois focused on the free and newly freed African-Americans and their quest for equality via their matriculation through educational institutions. This prescribed transition from physical labor to "intellectual and physical service" is essentially equivalent to the intellectual labor that suits the demands of current colonial universities. While Du Bois's intentions were for the integration and equal educational opportunities for members of the African descendant population, a by-product of this philosophy supports the corporate mind-set of colonial universities in their desire to harvest knowledge through the exploitation of intellectual labor.

Urrieta (2004) addresses the use of educational institutions as mechanisms of a colonial project. In terms of Mexican-American learners and instructors, he characterizes the colonizing way in which K–12 schools function, similar to that of higher educational institutions. The curriculum and institution simultaneously distort, erase, and devalue their identities and *hereditary histories*.[20] Césaire (2000) interjects: "I am talking about millions of (wo)men in whom fear has been cunningly instilled, who have been taught to have an inferiority complex, to tremble, to kneel, despair, and behave like flunkeys" (p. 43). This can be seen often in the university experiences of students of color in which their cultural, religious, linguistic histories (among other aspects of their identity) run counter to the prescribed and valued knowledge and customs of the university. When placing this within the context of the university setting, we can see that marginalized groups often experience these social challenges both individually and simultaneously. Once recognition of this "fear" is actualized and confronted, a visceral experience often occurs, activating a heightened consciousness in the forms of double-consciousness, critical consciousness, and/or third-person consciousness.[21]

Historically, learners of African descent consistently address these colonial and oppressive acts:

> Postcolonial critiques of schooling that influence the construction of "membership" (citizenship) in U.S. society have focused on the forced use of standard english as superior in the education of colonial subjects, as well as the use of a "standard" canon of knowledge (Loomba, 1998; Banks, 1996). This is an important point, because these "colonial requirements" of "higher knowledge" function as institutional barriers to harshly enforce limited subaltern participation in the highest educational institutions. (Urrieta 2004, p. 451)

Not only does the "standard english" function as an "institutional barrier" for many members of the university community but there are standard ethnic/racial signifiers that, for many, inhibit their full ability to reclaim and maintain their cultural identities. As a result of this, the development of such departments as cultural and ethnic studies offset these standard "canon(s) of knowledge" to offer varying forms of knowledge that address the needs and histories of diverse peoples consisting of the learner(s) and instructor(s). Yet, these too are within the reach (and design) of colonial universities, meaning that they also subscribe to many of the standard features of a colonial framework (e.g., the use of colonial language and Western thought). Urrieta provides an example of how this continuously occurs within this system:

> This is analogous to other requirements such as European literature, "American" literature ... which serve to maintain the status quo in terms of race, class, gender, sexual orientation, and disability inequalities. Thus, through these practices, national citizenship effectively excludes those with different cultural citizenship than the prescribed, national[ly] accepted] norm. (p. 451)

In becoming conscious of this reality, we must always remain aware of the affect that these colonial structures have on us.

Prestigious colleges and universities must shed their colonial paradigms in order to offer and sustain what diverse populations require. Yet, in order to accomplish this they first need awareness of what they are currently doing. This anticolonial project rests on both sides of the binary: the colonized and colonizer. Sartre explains the mutually shackling nature of this binary: "A relentless reciprocity binds the colonizer to the colonized – his [in this case the university] product and his fate ... we find that the colonialist system is a form in motion, born towards the middle of the last century, that will manufacture its own destruction of itself" (Sartre 1967, preface). The colonial university cannot exist without the subjects that it seeks to attract, provide opportunity to, and ultimately exploit: the university professor, the graduate student, the undergraduate, and the multitude of minds that enter its doors for intellectual stimulation, nurturing, and growth. Du Bois writes: "America [via its universities] is not another word for Opportunity to *all* her sons [and daughters]" (Du Bois 1986, p. 462). Attendance of colonial universities with limited organizational representation (as well as a limited presence or representation of students of color) calls for a level of consciousness regarding the university professor's and student's historical duality. Within the African-American community, this is best and foremost depicted by Du Bois's theory of double consciousness.

> It is a peculiar sensation, this double consciousness, the sense of always looking at one's self through the eyes of others, of measuring one's soul by the tape of a world that looks on in amused contempt and pity. One ever feels his two-ness, – an American, a Negro; two souls, two thoughts, two unreconciled strivings; two warring ideals in one dark body, whose dogged strength alone keeps it from being torn asunder. (Du Bois 1986, pp. 364–536)

I firmly agree that Du Bois's concept of "double consciousness" represents the dilemma that most African-Americans face in today's society. Furthermore, the university professor and university student can be aided by Du Bois's theoretical framing. In a sense, both professor and student within a colonial university exist with dual selves acting as sites of production. The product of these living sites (their ideas) is derived from both the planting and harvesting of intellectual thought. As a person of African descent, I live within this dichotomy where my colonized self (African) and colonizing self (American) are fused together within my *lived script*.[22] In the case of the university student and professor, they too are both colonized and colonizer when it comes to the maintaining of Western intellectual thought within colonial universities.

In understanding this, through the awakening of my consciousness, I see the oppressive nature of the White systemic power structure and its adversarial position toward the Black (African) and other ethnic/cultural identities that look to share social, cultural, and civic space. In order for this to occur, the roles of people within a colonial university must consciously grapple with this historical duality that the institution of enslavement has co-manufactured. Du Bois's notion of double consciousness effectively sets the stage for addressing the ways in which people of African descent can see themselves within this society and its institutions, through the fusion of these two-selves.

> No Negro [African-American] who has given earnest thought to the situation of his people in America has failed, at some time in life, to find himself at these cross-roads; has failed to ask himself [herself] at some time: What, after all, am I? Am I an American or am I a Negro [Black or African]? Can I be both? Or is it my duty to cease to be a Negro [Black or African] as soon as possible and be an American? If I strive as a Negro [Black or African], am I not perpetuating the very cleft that threatens and separates Black and White America? Is not my only possible practical aim the subduction of all that is Negro [Black or African] in me to the American? Does my black blood place upon me any more obligation to assert my nationality than German, or Irish or Italian blood would? (Du Bois, p. 821)

Du Bois's metaphorical use of "the Veil" throughout *The Souls of Black Folk* (2003) is a vital *political and social* undertaking that addresses the problem of the "color line" for those whose histories are linked by bondage. The notion of "the Veil" represents the hindrances socially, economically, politically, educationally, and consciously faced by people of African descent as they looked to reclaim their identities post-enslavement. This "Veil" had various forms that included "race" and "color" within Du Bois's text.

In addressing the positioning of one's identity as it relates to being an active site of both intellectual planting and harvesting, the work of Du Bois is also essential. His recognition of the double consciousness and the notion of the Veil are extremely important for understanding the societal affects on a person who shares these two identities within a colonial university. Du Bois's references to the double consciousness of being both African and American provide a lens to begin understanding the challenges that are faced by individuals that share both cultural backgrounds.

I extend this thought of dual cultural backgrounds to include the dual intellectual roles that are often required to exist and remain functional in a colonial university system. By understanding these shifts within the framework of identity, society can move to spaces in which these barriers are transformed into access points for the multiple selves that result from such constructs as globalism and colonialism. Ultimately society can thus move toward the ideal of cultural pluralism. In the honoring of these fragmented selves as a collective, the identity is made complete and is holistically empowered – moving from the abstract to the concrete, from the imaginary to the real, and from what is marginalized to what is centered.

The advent of institutionalized enslavement benefiting systematic capitalism and imperialism created many debilitating barriers for those of darker skins on these lands. Anticolonial theorist Albert Memmi (1967) writes:

10 The Harvesting of Intellectuals and Intellectual Labor

> I have often noted that the *deprivations* of the colonized are the almost direct result of the advantages secured to the colonizer. However, colonial privilege is not solely economic. To observe the life of the colonizer and the colonized is to discover rapidly that the daily humiliation of the colonized, [her or] his objective subjugation, are not merely economic. Even the poorest colonizer thought [herself or] himself to be – and actually was – superior to the colonized. This too was part of colonial privilege. (p. xii)

This way of thinking applies to the system that supports the colonial university. Dependent on the context, the roles of the colonizer and colonized shift and provide, in some instances, false perceptions of power for those within the system who act in the authoritative roles – roles often afforded as part of the colonizer's privilege. University professors serve as a model of this, as the facilitators of the understanding and formulation of knowledge, since they are often perceived as the central figure in the power dynamic between student and teacher in generating knowledge. In colonial universities, many professors have themselves been socialized to be no more than puppets and pawns within a systemic game. They are charged and challenged to harvest the intellectual labor and ability of not only themselves, but of those who are under their guidance. As a result, within a colonial university at the mercy of the capitalistic enterprise, the harvesting of all forms of knowledge and the means and modes by which the accessing, evaluating, conveying, disseminating, reproducing, and creating of knowledge are at the colonial mission's core.

This commodification of the notion that "education is by derivation and in fact a drawing out of human powers" is the common practice of current and past agendas of the university that act in accordance with globalized capitalism (Du Bois 1973, p. 9). The university is perpetually in search of the most precious gem, the critically acclaimed intellectual or instructor of the moment, to provide added value to its stable of workers, better known as faculty and/or administrators. This cannot be underestimated simply because of the seemingly high status assigned to academics in many arenas within society. This phenomenon is also captured in the thought of Marcuse (1964) as he states:

> In actual fact, however, the contrary trend operates: the apparatus imposes its economic and political requirements for the defense and expansion of labor time and free time, on the material and intellectual culture. By virtue of the way it has organized its technological base, contemporary industrial society tends to be totalitarian. For "totalitarian" is not a terroristic political coordination of society, but also a non-terroristic economic-technical coordination which operates through manipulation of needs by vested interests. It thus precludes the emergence of an effective opposition against the whole. Not only a specific form of government or party rule makes for totalitarianism, but also a specific system of production and distribution which may well be compatible with a "pluralism" of parties, newspapers, "countervailing powers," etc. (p. 3)

Due to the entrenched ideology and practices of the colonial university on university members a totalitarian effect is currently at work against many intellectuals within the system. For both the university professor and student the vested interests are tenure and a diploma respectively. These two factors, in many ways, serve as the shackles with which the colonial university continues to manipulate faculty and students, while maintaining the status quo. A prime example of this is the present attack on academic freedom within research universities as it relates to dissenting intellectuals and scholars. This is seen in Fanon's thought on the role of the colonized elite [university intellectual] within the colonial society [university] as it relates to "the threat of mass mobilization" (2004, p. 28). He states:

> There are revolutionaries obviously within these political parties [universities], among the cadres, who deliberately turn their backs on the farce of national independence [colonial university's mission]. But their speeches, their initiatives, and their angry outbursts very soon antagonize the party machine [colonial university]. These factions are gradually isolated, then removed altogether [from the social framework]. (Fanon 2004, p. 28)

As we can see in attacks on university intellectuals across the United States, what Fanon has pointed out is highly applicable and evident in the resulting isolation, ostracization, and termination of dissenting scholars. In this act, the power of the university is made real for not only those directly targeted but also those who may lay waiting and watching in the wings. Marcuse continues:

> Today political [and colonial] power asserts itself through its power over the machine process [university].... The government of advanced and advancing industrial [and intellectual] societies can maintain and secure itself only when it succeeds in mobilizing, organizing, and exploiting the technical, scientific, and mechanical productivity available to industrial civilization [the intellectual]. And this productivity mobilizes society as a whole, above and beyond any particular individual or group interests. The brute fact that the machine's physical power [due to its resources] surpasses that of the individual, and of any particular group of individuals, makes the machine the most effective political instrument in any society whose basic organization is that of the machine [intellectual] process. But the political trend may be reversed; essentially the power of the machine is only stored-up and projected power [through the intellectual ability] of [wo]man. (Marcuse 1964, p. 3)

Marcuse's analysis of an industrial society is a perfect treatment for what often occurs within colonial university systems. The power dynamics therein systematically create a tension between the roles of the colonized and colonizer, as it relates to the planting and harvesting of intellectual labor. As presented by Marcuse, the university's power over its membership has surpassed that of the individuals' (university members) that serve as the sustaining force for its continued existence and future growth. This scenario is in effect almost identical to the power dynamic found on plantations in which the labor performed in the fields through the production of goods was governed and controlled by the system/plantation owner (who was totally dependent on it). The *new freedom for (wo)man* suggested by Marcuse combats these occurrences of a "mutable colonialism"[23] within a colonial university.

Colonial educational institutions from top to bottom must themselves engage in their own anti-colonization process. This starts with effectively and attentively acknowledging weaknesses and limitations in the current policy and curriculum beyond that of the traditional multicultural approach as described by Banks (1997, 2001, 2002), Delpit (1995), Giroux (1981), hooks (1992, 1994, 2000a, 2000b), Ladson-Billings (1994), McLaren (2007), Nieto 1999, 2004; Sleeter and McLaren 1995, and others). Strategic protocols that diminish the power dynamics and the hierarchical nature of the institutions must be developed in collaboration with grassroots efforts. Inclusiveness should and must be the staple of current and future existing educational institutions.

Social and educational practices continue to perpetuate this disconnect that has been systematically and morally created to control those within the university. This divide-and-conquer strategy has been used consistently against African descendant communities, as well as others, within the confines of this colonial society. Anticolonial education requires an active political and social effort to empower the mind, thereby fusing the intellect with the spirit. The spirituality of a person or of a people must be tapped into, providing ultimate agency. An anticolonial education builds on multicultural beliefs of inclusiveness, culture, and perceived otherness within all aspects of education (i.e., curriculum, through the process of socialization, intellectual stimulation, and active practice).

While language has to be a common thread of communication within these walls, the use of that subscribed language (academic language/jargon) has to, as does the speaker, be reconstructed, redefined, and reinscribed so that "real" agency can be articulated, achieved, and actualized. This is paramount for true and holistic education to be accomplished. This newly formed understanding and appreciation of language must allow multiple entry points and perspectives to access the lived scripts of the multiple minds and bodies within the university system and beyond. Therefore it is crucial to forge a multimodal lens which reinvents what is perceived as "core knowledge," as well as that which is understood as "globalized knowledge." Césaire argues:

> A civilization [education or educational institution] that proves incapable of solving the problems it creates is a decadent [education or educational institution]. A civilization [education or educational institution] that chooses to close its eyes to its most crucial problems is a stricken [education or educational institution]. A civilization [education or educational institution] that uses its principles for trickery and deceit is a dying civilization [education or educational institution]. (p. 31)

Furthermore, *an education or educational institution that perpetuates, promotes, or benefits from colonialism is a-civilized.* Thus anticolonial educational thought must permeate through K–12 educational systems as well. The stark similarities between the socialization processes that take place in both K–12 school and colonial university systems continue to perpetuate disparities between the creation and valuation of acceptable forms of labor. Each institution works, in an opportunity specific manner, to both directly and indirectly facilitate the laborization of its members to achieve both colonial and capitalistic goals. The application of the plantation approach reveals these practices, in the forms of HIPDs, and ultimately seeks to make all parties involved conscious of their dual colonized and colonizer roles as intellectuals.

In doing so, this critical consciousness can cause society and its members to reevaluate current and historical practices of stratification, indoctrination, and marginalization. The university must return to, or newly embrace a position of cultivating knowledge for those who produce, interpret, and/or will integrate these forms of knowledge into their multiple worlds as necessary for their own intellectual purposes. Otherwise, the intellectual must look to retain more of her or his intellectual labor for the benefit of communities beyond the limitations of the academy – perhaps becoming the "free intellectual" that is the heir to the agency created and personified by the "free African" of the antebellum period.

Notes

1. I draw from Alasco's (1950) discussion of intellectual capital.
2. "The tentacles of both the trade and the institution [of enslavement] were far-reaching, touching if not enveloping the lives of many. Even leading universities such as Brown, Harvard, and Yale were the beneficiaries of the nefarious enterprise. Brown University was founded in part by slavetraders John and Nicolas Brown, while the founder of Harvard Law School endowed the school with money from slavetrading in Antigua. As for Yale University, its first professorship was endowed by one of the most notorious slavetraders of day, Philip Livingston, and the school's first scholarships came from the profits of slaveholder George Berkeley's New England plantation" (Gomez 2005, p. 105).
3. See Barrow (1990).
4. See Blassingame (1979) and Stampp (1956).
5. "[M]ost slaves [of the enslaved] remained on plantations working at their accustomed tasks. How much their faithfulness depended on affection for individual whites, on contentment with servile conditions, or an ignorance which made the slaves fear change remains an unanswered question" (Patrick 1967, p. 11).
   Also see discussions on "free labor" and the "Freedmen's Bureau" in Foner (1980, 1990), Du Bois (1962, 1973, 1986).
6. In my future works, the psychological aspects of plantation life (i.e., indoctrination of a new language and cultural codes/norms) will be explored and discussed as they relate to the socialization and exploitation of intellectuals within the colonial university system.
7. "It was on plantations where ... overseers came from a nonslaveholding and frequently landless group, they had no interest other than a temporary concern in the institution. Too frequently they hated the system and directed especial contempt toward slaves [the enslaved] because they were of the opinion that slavery was responsible for their own unfortunate economic plight. They had the job of managing the entire plantation in the absence of the planter to handle alone, the overseer was delegated a considerable portion of the responsibility ... this authority over the slaves [enslaved] was almost unlimited" (Franklin and Moss 2004, p. 147).
   "[O]verseers found it necessary to develop a practice of 'breaking in' the newcomers. In some areas the newcomers were distributed among the seasoned, or veteran, slaves [enslaved] whose duty it was to teach the newly arrived slaves [enslaved] whose duty it was to teach the newly arrived slaves [enslaved] the ways of life in the New World. In other places the newcomers were kept apart and supervised by a special staff of guardians and inspectors who were experienced in breaking in those how might offer resistance to adjusting to their new environment" (Franklin and Moss 2004, pp. 52–53).
   "Overseers weighed the cotton and chastised slaves [the enslaved] ... they meted out punishments even if the planter determined what that punishment was. Often the overseer handled the work of monitoring slave [enslaved] religious meetings. In performing these duties, the overseer's job was to do the planter's dirty work. . . . Large planters encouraged the development of adversarial, even hostile, relations between overseers and slaves [the enslaved]" (Libby 2004, p. 97).
   For more on overseers see, Wiethoff, W. E. (2006) and Bassett, J. S. (1968).
8. "Enslaved persons in the Old South labored mainly in the fields and mainly on cotton plantations ... the enslaved worked not only in the fields, but also in the master's houses as domestics. Rosa Starke's hierarchy of black laborers includes house and groundkeepers (top), skilled craftsmen and foremen (middle), and animal caretakers and field hands (bottom)" (Home Box Office 2002, p. 36).
   "Most of these workers were divided into two main categories: field hands and house servants" (ibid., p. 55).
   "Differing skills and varying sorts of responsibilities meant that, while most were enslaved, not all experienced the institution in the same way. While too much can be made of the divide between so-called field and house negroes, as there are many instances of cooperation and col-

laboration between the two categories, they nevertheless represented different levels of material comfort, exposure to abuse, and even status, however relative" (Gomez 2005, p. 105).
9. The overseer, within much of the literature, was also called manager. Within this analysis the term overseer is primarily used.
10. See Franklin and Moss (2004).
11. The power relationship (often resulting in tension or struggle) between colonized and colonizer in colonial institutions, is created via hierarchies that are based on patriarchy, class, sexual orientation, religion/spirituality, and race/ethnicity. In this analysis, the power relationship is centered on plantation and colonial university systems.
12. It is important to point out that within each group (i.e., administrative, professorial, graduate, and undergraduate) there are situated roles of overseer, house laborer, and field laborer based on the structured hierarchies found within. For the sake of this discussion, I am focusing on relations of the collective group identities professor, graduate student, and undergraduate with each other.
13. This use of "role" is synonymous with "identity" and the shifting between identity roles. See the term "differential consciousness" by Sandoval (2000).
14. For examples of resistance by those enslaved see: Genovese (1984), Blassingame (1979), and Stampp (1956).
15. See Barnes (1984).
16. See Schafer (2003).
17. This is a developing idea that will be further explored in future works critiquing colonial university systems.
18. Intellectuals such as Gloria Anzaldúa, W.E.B. Du Bois, bell hooks, Edward Said, Cornel West (1991), and others represent this type of intellectual practice of working within and outside of the university all the while critically engaging societal concerns with the communities beyond those found within the colonial university.
19. See Du Bois (1948, 1973, 1986, 2003) and Rabaka (2005).
20. *Hereditary history* is the collection of denied historical and ancestral memories resulting from the lived experiences/scripts that are transmitted generationally among oppressed groups in efforts to reclaim a wholeness of self through resistance to colonialism.
21. For "double consciousness" see Du Bois (2003), for "critical consciousness" see Freire (1973), and for "third-person consciousness" see Fanon, F. (2004).
22. The concept of the lived script represents a collection of lived experiences creating an understanding of the societal role(s) of a given person by examining their educational, cultural, psychological, emotional, political, social (which is meant to specifically include such things as gender, race, ethnicity, and sexual orientation), and/or spiritual path(s).
23. This concept draws from Rabaka (2003).

References

Alasco, J. (1950). *Intellectual capitalism: A study of changing ownership and control in modern industrial society*. New York: World University Press.
Anyon, J. (1980). Social class and the hidden curriculum of work. *Journal of Education*, 162: 67–92.
Banks, J. A. (1996). The canon debate, knowledge construction, and multicultural education. In Banks, J. A. and Banks, C. A. (Eds.), *Multicultural education, transformative knowledge, and action* (pp. 3–25). New York: Teacher's College Press.
Banks, J. A. (1997). *Educating citizens in a multicultural society* (Multicultural Education Series). New York: Teachers College Press.
Banks, J. A. (2001). *Cultural diversity and education: Foundations, curriculum, and teaching*, (4th ed.). Boston, MA: Allyn & Bacon.
Banks, J. A. (2002). *An introduction to multicultural education* (3rd ed.). Boston, MA: Allyn & Bacon.

Barnes, G. A. (1984). *The American university: A world guide.* Philadelphia, PA: ISI Press.
Barrow, C. W. (1990). *Universities and the capitalist state: Corporate liberalism and the reconstruction of American higher education, 1894–1928.* Madison, WI: The University of Wisconsin Press.
Bassett, J. S. (1968). *The southern plantation overseer: As revealed in his letters.* New York: Negro Universities Press.
Blassingame, J. W. (1979). *The slave community: Plantation life in the antebellum south* (Revised and enlarged edition). New York: Oxford University Press.
Césaire, A. (2000). *Discourse on colonialism* (J. Pinkham, Trans.). New York: Monthly Review Press. (Original work published in 1955.)
Delpit, L. (1995). *Other people's children: Cultural conflict in the classroom.* New York: The New Press.
Du Bois, W. E. B. (1948). The talented tenth: Memorial address. *Boule Journal* 15 (October 1948) 3–13. Reprinted by permission of Wilberforce University. [Published by Sigma Pi Phi, Wilberforce, Ohio. The address was delivered on August 12, 1948 at the fraternity's 19th Convocation at Wilberforce State University.]
Du Bois, W. E. B. (1962). *Black reconstruction in America: An essay toward a history for the part which black folk played in the attempt to reconstruct democracy in America, 1860–1880.* New York: Russell & Russell.
Du Bois, W. E. B. (1973). *The education of Black people: Ten critiques 1906–1960 by W. E. B. Du Bois* (H. Aptheker, Ed.). Amherst, MA: The University of Massachusetts Press.
Du Bois, W. E. B. (1986). *W. E. B. Du Bois: Writings – The suppression of the African slave trade, the souls of black folk, dusk of dawn, and classic essays and articles* (N. I. Huggins, Ed.). New York: The Library of America Press.
Du Bois, W. E. B. (2003). *The souls of black folk.* New York: Barnes & Noble.
Fanon, F. (2004). *The wretched of the earth* (R. Philcox, Trans.). New York: Grove Press. (Original work published in 1961.)
Feagin, J. R., Vera, H., and Imani, N. (1996). *The agony of education: Black students at white colleges and universities.* New York: Routledge.
Foner, E. (1980). *Politics and ideology in the age of the Civil War.* New York: Oxford University Press.
Foner, E. (1990). *A short history of reconstruction 1863–1877.* New York: Harper & Row.
Franklin, J. H. and Moss, A. A., Jr. (2004). *From slavery to freedom: A history of African Americans* (8th ed.). New York: Alfred A. Knopf.
Freire, P. (1973) *Education for critical consciousness.* New York: Continuum.
Genovese, E. D. (1984). *In red and black: Marxian explorations in southern and Afro-American history.* Knoxville, TN: The University of Tennessee Press.
Giroux, H. A. (1981). *Ideology, culture, and the process of schooling.* Philadelphia, PA: Temple University Press.
Gomez, M. A. (2005). *Reversing sail: A history of the African diaspora.* New York: Cambridge University Press.
Gouldner, A. W. (1979). *The future of intellectuals and the rise of the new class: A frame of references, theses, conjectures, arguments, and an historical perspective on the role of intellectuals and intelligentsia in the international class contest of the modern era.* New York: The Seabury Press.
Gramsci, A. (1967). *The modern prince & other writings* (L. Marks, Trans.). New York: International Publishers. (Originally published in 1957.)
Home Box Office (2002). *Unchained memories: Readings from the slave narratives.* Boston, MA: Bulfinch Press.
hooks, b. (1992). *Black looks: Race and representation.* Boston, MA: South End Press.
hooks, b. (1994). *Teaching to transgress: Education as the practice of freedom.* New York: Routledge.
hooks, b. (2000a). *Feminist theory: From margin to center.* Cambridge, MA: South End Press.
hooks, b. (2000b). *Where we stand: Class matters.* New York: Routledge.

Ladson-Billings, G. (1994). *The dreamkeepers: Successful teachers of African American children*. San Francisco, CA: Jossey-Bass.
Libby, D. J. (2004). *Slavery and frontier Mississippi 1720–1835*. Jackson, MS: University Press of Mississippi.
Loomba, A. (1998). *Colonialism/postcolonialism*. London: Routledge.
Marcuse, H. (1964). *One dimensional man*. Boston, MA: Beacon Press.
Marable, M. (2005). *W. E. B. Du Bois: Black radical democrat* (New Updated ed.). Boulder, CO: Paradigm Publishers.
McLaren, P. (2007). *Life in schools: An introduction to critical pedagogy in the foundations of education*, (5th ed.). Boston, MA: Pearson Education.
Memmi, A. (1967). *The colonizer and the colonized*. Boston, MA: Beacon Press.
Nieto, S. (1999). *The light in their eyes: Creating multicultural learning communities* (Multicultural Education Series). New York: Teachers College Press.
Nieto, S. (2004). *Affirming diversity: The sociopolitical context of multicultural education*, (4th ed.). Boston, MA: Pearson Education.
Patrick, R. W. (1967). *The reconstruction of the nation*. New York: Oxford University Press.
Rabaka, R. (2003). W. E. B. Du Bois's evolving Africana philosophy of education. *Journal of Black Studies*, 33(4) 399–449.
Rabaka, R. (2005). W. E. B. Du Bois's theory of the talented tenth. In M. K. Asante and A. Mazama (Eds.), *The Encyclopedia of Black Studies* (pp. 443–445). Thousand Oaks, CA: Sage.
Said, E. W. (1994). *Representations of the intellectual: The 1993 Reith Lectures*. New York: Vintage Books.
Sandoval, C. (2000). *Methodology of the oppressed*. Minneapolis, MN: University of Minnesota Press.
Sartre, J. P. (1967). Preface to *The colonizer and the colonized*. Boston, MA: Beacon Press.
Schafer, J. K. (2003). *Becoming free, remaining free: Manumission and enslavement in New Orleans, 1846–1862*. Baton Rouge, LA: Louisiana State University Press.
Sleeter, C. and McLaren, P. (1995). *Multicultural education, critical pedagogy, and the politics of difference*. Albany, NY: State University of New York Press.
Stampp, K. M. (1956). *The peculiar institution: Slavery in the ante-bellum south*. New York: Vintage Books.
Urrieta, L. Jr. (2004). Dis-connections in "American" citizenship and the post/neo-colonial: People of Mexican descent and whitestream pedagogy and curriculum. *Theory and Research in Social Education* 32(4), 433–458.
West, C. (1991). The dilemma of the black intellectual. In B. Hooks and C. West, *Breaking bread: Insurgent black intellectual life*. Toronto, Ontario: Between The Lines.
Wiethoff, W. E. (2006). *Crafting the overseer's image*. Columbia, SC: The University of South Carolina Press.

Chapter 11
Building Anticolonial Spaces for Global Education: Challenges and Reflections

Jonathan Langdon and Blane Harvey*

11.1 Introduction

In the fall of 2006, we co-taught a class of preservice teachers in a course somewhat ambiguously described in the university calendar as *EDEC 301: Global Education*.[1] In the lead up to teaching this course, and on the basis of our past reflections on building a democratic classroom, we decided to approach the teaching of the course in an open, team-teaching manner, hoping this would encourage students to contribute to the dialogue of the class as it went along. At the same time, we also decided to take a stated position, what Harding (1998) terms "situating" oneself,[2] and actively use the class as a site through which we would introduce students to an alternative, critical, and anticolonial vision of contemporary global systems. This approach to global education is quite different from those advocated by many mainstream global educators (see Werner and Case 1997; Case 1991); yet, as we shall explore below, it is an approach that is supported by a vocal group within the field that feels educators should not hide behind feigned objectivity in teaching issues that have profound implications for social justice (see Kiil 1994; Lyons 1992, 1995; Choldin 1989). In the approach we elaborate below, this situated social justice perspective is paired with anticolonial/anti-imperial education approaches, providing a useful starting point in challenging the current global status quo.

One of the most telling moments that revealed the effects of this decision on our *EDEC 301: Global Education* classroom came near the end of term, when a student remarked: "At first I wanted you both to provide voices that defended the way the world is today, but now I understand that these voices are all around us everyday, and that to challenge them we need to talk about alternative understandings whenever possible."[3] This moment in the course captured both the challenges we faced as anticolonial global educators, and the possibilities. As George Dei (2006) reminds us, anticolonial education must have certain nonnegotiable values, such as challenging

---

*We would like to acknowledge our sincere gratitude to the students from EDEC-301 who took time to give us their frank and insightful feedback on this course, and in the process, having taught us so much.

domination whenever we encounter it; yet, it must also remain highly aware of the potential of new forms of domination emerging from these alternative approaches. This delicate balance between standing firmly by our convictions as engaged actors in anticolonial education (as we sought to do with our students), while at the same leaving the discursive and reflexive space for students to explore their own viewpoints is a theme we will return to throughout this chapter. Our position as course instructors, a position embedded in power, could have allowed us to *insist* on our students developing (or at least paying lip service to) the "understanding" described above, thereby inscribing an alternative domination in the classroom. As Stephen Brookfield (2001) reminds us, educators must be aware of their own power in teaching situations, and must actively work to open up the teaching space. While power can never disappear, it can be unsettled or destabilized by being open to debate and dissention. Thus, we sought to both engage in, and be open to, such dissent within the class, acknowledging our position of power while pointing out the limits of our own knowledge and thereby encouraging students to be creators and disseminators of knowledge. We did not eliminate power, but we encouraged its study and shared our own understanding of how it is resisted and reconfigured locally.

Yet, even while acknowledging these important power dynamics, we also agree with Dei (2006) that certain aspects of current global inequities must be challenged. Therefore, as instructors for *EDEC 301: Global Education*, we made a conscious decision – one in which we were willing to both debate and defend with students; we did not intend to present a supposedly unbiased and balanced view of the contemporary world. As Kincheloe (2001) notes, objectivity in education and the social sciences is in fact a subtle form of unstated bias. Based on our own experiences working in various locations throughout the world, as well as through the voices of critical social actors and theorists, we instead presented a view of the world that challenges the continued colonial dominance of Eurocentric thinking and Western economic systems.

In this chapter, we reflect on both the successes and the challenges we encountered in this *EDEC 301: Global Education* course. This is done, first, as an attempt to contribute to, and deepen, reflections on what it means to enact anticolonial education in the classroom, and second to invite others to reflect on our experiences, draw from them where useful, or point out alternative approaches where ours may have been lacking. As we both believe that dialogue is a critical starting point for challenging dominant practices, we offer this chapter as a contribution to ongoing dialogues around the practical issues involved in the praxis of anticolonial education. We also hope that this chapter will contribute to the practice of global education, especially in bringing an anticolonial perspective to this field, and in shaping a vision of praxis for global educators here in North America. Unlike conventional definitions of global education elaborated below, we see global education as an opportunity both to open students up to the interconnected nature of our global existence – highlighting the ways in which our actions here have effects elsewhere, and vice versa – and to encourage students to see the ways in which this interconnected existence is embedded in uneven global power relations, where some people and places benefit vastly at the expense of others.

The chapter begins by briefly laying out our understanding of anticolonial education. Here we focus on four key characteristics of the anticolonial approach: first, it is discursively informed; second, it draws on non-Western positions and knowledge to critique Western bias; third, it grounds this approach in material reality; and fourth, it builds on praxis, so that coming to know the world also leads us to action. This section is followed by a critique of mainstream global education approaches, which leads to a proposed anticolonial frame for global education. This theoretical fusion is then grounded in a practical discussion of the *EDEC 301: Global Education* course in which we attempted to put into practice an anticolonial approach. This description is broken down into three parts: the overall parameters of the course are described; the challenges and risks of engaging in the course for us and the students are elaborated; and, the complex notion of praxis (where we move from discussing ideas to acting upon them) is explored. We conclude this chapter by highlighting what we, as the course instructors, drew from this class, as well as the implications this example has for both teaching *with* and *for* an anticolonial approach to global education.

11.2 Anticolonial Education

Before moving to discuss the implications of anticolonial education in a North American global education classroom, we feel it is critical to pause and reflect briefly here on what we understand anticolonial education to be. This discussion will be brief, especially as anticolonial theory is a topic that surfaces in many of the other contributions to this book.

One of the primary points of departure in understanding anticolonial education is in differentiating anticolonial theory from the postcolonial. Dei (2006) has detailed the importance in moving from postcolonial to anticolonial theory. For Dei, this move involves embedding the discursive and identity consciousness of postcolonial theory in a recognition of the profound material consequences of the continuation of colonial domination. Yet, this does not mean undermining the importance of the discursive approach. Elsewhere, for instance, Dei and Azgharzadeh (2001) have noted the importance in building what they call an "anti-colonial discursive framework" in order to establish an anticolonial approach:

> The anti-colonial discursive framework is an epistemology of the colonized, anchored in the indigenous sense of collective and common colonial consciousness. (2001, p. 300)

This anticolonial discursive framework therefore first challenges the dominant epistemic boundaries and Eurocentric discourses that have been "canonized" and institutionalized within the academy at the expense of subjugated, indigenous, and local knowledges. Zinn (1980), for instance, has described how re-historicizing Columbus's arrival in the Americas from the Arawak perspective dramatically changes its meaning. Likewise, Tuhiwai-Smith (1999) has described how an indigenous approach to research can challenge Western notions of knowledge production, and can begin to decolonize research methodologies. According to Dei (2006) and to Tikly (2004), it is through discursive challenges that anticolonial education begins to unpack particular discourses that privilege Western thought over other ways of knowing and being. Tikly (2004), for instance, notes how challenging black boxes of knowledge, such as how education is presented as the unquestioned route to development and progress throughout the world, is a first step in unpacking the ways in which the value of Western knowledge remains unquestioned in many locations in the world. Tikly (2004), building on Young (2001), highlights the need to recontextualize what discursive challenging means by rereading Foucault and recognizing that discourses have a material, disciplining effect on people's daily lives, and that this effect needs critical analysis. In this, he is echoing Dei's insistence that material reality as well as discursive challenges must form the basis of anticolonial education.

Tikly (2004) provides a further inflection to this discussion by noting anticolonial education must also be anti-imperial education, meaning it must recognize what has become known as the "new imperialism" – a form of imperialism that emerged in the postwar period, which is substantially different from European forms of colonialism, and is dominated by the United States as well as transnational capital (Harvey 2003). Tikly notes that this new imperialism is embedded in such projects as the "development" of the majority of the world by the minority Western- and United States- led "developed" world, and that education is a critical component of this project. Building on the work of post-development theorists, such as Rist (1997), Escobar (1995), Tucker (1999) and others, Tikly further elaborates how the new imperialism forms, spreads to, and then disciplines populations discursively – a characteristic that differentiates it from the earlier forms of European colonialism which were based primarily on physical coercion of subject populations (although Memmi (1969) and Fanon (1967) both showed how colonialism also used complex, nuanced, nonphysical forms of coercion). He therefore underscores the need for anti-imperial education to be grounded in a discursive challenge of Western ideas embedded in such Western concepts as development and education. This is a very useful link for connecting the anticolonial approach to global education. Following Sardar (1999), Tikly suggests that resistance to Western domination must come from non-Western and indigenous forms of knowing and being. Yet, he also notes that these challenges need to be grounded in on-the-ground movements working to resist the current global order. This is in line with Brookfield's (2001) reading of Foucault, where he argues that the power of domination is weakest where it is enacted, and that these are the sites where resistance begins, and the place where study can contribute to deeper reflections on how power is operationalized.

For Tikly (2004) and Dei (2006), it is crucial that this discursive approach does not remain as theory alone, but also be paired with action; as Dei notes, drawing on both Fanon and Marx, "what matters is not to know the world but to change it" (2006, p. 1). For Shahjahan (2005), this last point is critical, as he notes one of the major challenges facing anticolonial scholars is beginning to "walk the talk" in their lived lives. A detailed discussion of how one constitutes action and "walks the talk," especially in a Canadian classroom, is taken up below during discussions of the global education course we led.

Given these various descriptions, we understand anticolonial education to have four major components: (1) it uses an anticolonial discursive framework as the starting point for unpacking Eurocentric ways of knowing the world; (2) it grounds these critiques of Eurocentrism in alternative ways of being based on non-Western knowledge traditions and positions; (3) it further grounds these discursive discussions in the analysis of material and everyday lived reality, especially of those most affected by the reality of colonial domination; and, finally (4) it connects this theorizing and discussion with action and practice (i.e., praxis) that challenges us all to "walk the talk" (Shahjahan 2005).

11.3 Anticolonial Global Education

In this section, we argue that the field of global education offers one potential avenue for establishing an anticolonial approach to education in classrooms across Canada. Yet, even as we consider embedding an anticolonial stance within a global education approach, it must be acknowledged that this is not an immediate and easy fit. Mainstream contemporary global education may question the inequalities in the world, and attempt to convey what Pike and Selby (2000) have called a "worldmindedness" to its students, but there is often a lack of historically informed analysis of current inequalities and their link to a colonial legacy. In this section, we unpack the ways global education constitutes itself as a pedagogic practice, and the ways that an anticolonial approach can reconfigure this practice to facilitate the type of complex discursive and practical challenges elaborated above.

Aside from "worldmindedness," Pike and Selby also describe global education as being grounded in "childcenteredness," whereby students are encouraged to explore and discover the world and its interconnectedness for themselves (2000, p. 11). Elsewhere, Pike (2000) elaborates how global education is informed by an interconnected view of the world, an understanding that all perspectives are partial and need to be inflected with the perspectives of others, that caring for the world and all its people is the starting point, and that there are alternatives to our contemporary global condition. He also notes that while global education sees a growing blur between the global and local in this age of globalization; this does not mean that the world is improving. By analyzing global conditions from an economic, environmental, societal, and technological perspective, global education seeks to create a complex understanding of our contemporary world. Likewise, it reminds us of the danger of an educational approach that ignores global interconnections by highlighting the dislocations, wars, and environmental devastation that have characterized the twentieth century (Pike 2000; Rist 1997).

Yet Pike (2000) also underscores the lack of critical debate in global education, wherein: feminist theory has been largely overlooked (Wells 1996); anthropocentric preoccupations dominate most approaches to the detriment of other living entities; and, larger environmental concerns are ignored (O'Sullivan 1996). He also suggests there are tensions among global educators around the moral purpose of global education, the constituency of its students, how it should advocate for change, and the type of citizenship it encourages (Pike 2000). Many of these tensions occur between educators who are highly critical of the current global order, and believe social change is necessary (see Kiil 1994; Lyons 1992, 1995; Choldin 1989), and those who opt for a more liberal approach that aims to provide students with an objective view so that they may themselves decide what is best for the world (see Werner and Case 1997; Case 1991).

In a sense, then, this is where an anticolonial discursive framework is useful in shifting the terrain of debate in global education. As Dei and Asgharzadeh (2001) note, there are some positions that cannot be put up for negotiation; and, therefore, to imagine that students in Canada should assume that they know what is best for the rest of the world is exactly the type of privileging that anticolonialism seeks to contest. Likewise, as we question why young Canadians should be accorded this privilege, we begin to connect with Foucault (1980) when he asks who benefits from a particular discursive arrangement. Taken from this perspective, the reproduction of a colonial mindset – one that oversees and knows best for the whole world – is being enacted in this type of global education classroom. This is a form of colonial "the sun never sets" view of the globe – where it is possible to capture and, in our mind's eye, control all the complexity in the world in one go. Foucault has named this the "panoptic gaze," able in "a single gaze to see everything constantly" (1991, p. 173).

This critique is not to suggest that global education's goal of building an awareness of the interconnections is not crucial, especially in developing a sense of the implications of the lifestyle of the average Canadian on the rest of the world. As Chandra Mohanty (2006) reminds us, by focusing on the vast differences in quality of life between the "*one-third* world," including Canada's social majority, and the "*two-thirds* world," an awareness of the everyday nature of global inequity comes into stark relief. Yet, it is the historical legacy of colonialism and its continued role in widening the gap between these two worlds that needs to be highlighted. Here, it is useful to underscore Dei (2006) and Tikly's (2004) call for the importance of an approach to discursive analysis grounded in the material, everyday realities of those most affected by these discourses, as such, connecting a re-historicization of global inequity that acknowledges its colonial legacy to a contemporary understanding of this inequity that also recognizes how new imperialism has changed these relations not only along discursive lines, but also along material lines. Dei and Asgharzadeh (2001) as well as Tikly (2004) point out the way that this new imperialism may be United States-led, but it is also transnational in nature, and is deeply informed by corporate and institutional, rather than national, forms of rule. Closely connected to this new imperialism, an anticolonial form of global education also links this historicization to a critical unpacking of contemporary development practice, where the hubris of colonialism continues to impose Eurocentric models of progress on the rest of the world (Escobar 1995; Rist 1997; Tikly 2004; Dei 2006). Finally, this form of global education reminds students that the contemporary inequities perpetuated by the continued existence of colonial relations also exist in North America – most noticeably in First Nations communities across the continent (Willinsky 1998; Battiste and Henderson 2000).

Therefore, anticolonial global education takes a specific approach that presents students with an alternative interpretation of the current global system by situating these alternatives in non-Western ways of knowing. In the education context, it reminds student-teachers of the legacy of education institutions in perpetuating colonial relations. In this sense, a complex form of interconnection is described, where worldmindedness is not simply about understanding the connections that exist in the world, but also about recognizing the colonial history that has helped to establish and perpetuate inequality. It is important to connect this anticolonial perspective with those elements within global education that believe social action should be the result of worldmindedness, such as Kiil (1994), Lyons (1992, 1995), and Choldin (1989). As noted above, we must ground this discursive unpacking in social action, where we actively engage in not just knowing the world but changing it. Yet this social action should be informed by recognition that colonial domination is as present in Canada as it is present in places like Ghana, Senegal, Peru, or India; it is reinforced in the everyday lives of Canadians as much as it is in those of Ghanaians, Senegalese, Peruvians, and Indians. In this sense, anticolonial global education helps students and student-teachers to gain a better understanding, not only of contemporary and historical global relations but of the degree to which the actions we take in the world and in our every day are embedded in power relations that help maintain global inequity. This realization offers another point to highlight how power is enacted in the classroom. While this connection helps destabilize the power relations in the global education classroom, it also provokes teachers-in-training to reflect on the power relations in their own future classrooms. This connects with Brookfield's reading of Foucault, where as educators we must be aware of the systems of power that surround us and work through us, and connect disruptions of these to other ongoing local acts of resistance. Therefore, our actions must be reflexive, must be based on a constant dialectic of critical questioning, must be global and local in nature, and finally, must be grounded in the collective struggles of those here in North America and elsewhere seeking to end colonial relations.

In this sense, an anticolonial approach to global education helps clear a set of spaces grounded in the four points elaborated above (discursively informed; yet, grounded in material reality; drawn from non-Western positions and knowledge to critique Western bias; and, built on praxis, where coming to know the world also leads us to action). As these spaces emerge, the anticolonial is placed into dialogue with the concept of the global and as such critically examines global relations of power, including Canada's role in benefiting from, and perpetuating, these forms of colonial power.

11.4 EDEC 301

Turning more specifically to the course *EDEC 301: Global Education* that is the focus of this chapter, it may be helpful first to provide a brief overview of the course objectives and contents, as well as a description of the students to better situate the context in which our efforts at creating an anticolonial learning space occurred. Global education is offered through the Faculty of Education at McGill University, a Canadian university based in Montreal. It is the only course specifically focusing on the global dimensions of teaching and learning offered for undergraduate students. The majority of the approximately 80 members of this course were first-year students in the teacher certification program. A high percentage of these students had already taken previous degrees or would qualify as "mature students." This is often the case within the teacher certification program. Thus, some students approached the content of this course with significantly more prior knowledge, both academic and practical, than could typically be expected of a first-year student.

According to the faculty's curriculum guidelines, "Global Education" is seen as an equivalent course to "Multicultural Education," and students are required to take one of these two courses (McGill University 2006). As a result, the students entering this course often approached it with a somewhat limited (or perhaps distorted) understanding of what the course entailed. As mentioned more generally above, and as was initially the case with many of our own students, global education is often understood as coming to know how others teach across cultures, teach in other cultures, teach about other cultures, and so forth – implying a "worldly" perspective on educating. As one student stated: "I figured it was going to be education for all different countries in the world, and I thought it would be interesting. So I took it based on that." In line with the view of anticolonial theory and action we have articulated above, the approach that we chose to take was rather different, and we instead sought to help students achieve the following specific aims, as stated in our course outline:

- Understand the links and interdependencies between countries and regions of the world and their implications for students' own lives and the lives of other people throughout the world.
- Increase their understanding of the connection between global systems and the economic, social, political, and environmental forces which impact our lives.
- Develop the knowledge, skills (particularly critical and analytical), and affective dispositions (e.g., care, solidarity, sense of moral imperative to teach about the world) which enable people to work together to bring about change.
- Develop the propensity to work toward achieving a more just world by considering alternatives in which power and resources are more equitably shared.

These objectives closely follow many of the central aims of anticolonial education elaborated above. In particular, following Dei (2006), they afforded us the space to engage with issues such as: the modern-day extensions of colonial and imperial imposition; the portrayal of actors in contemporary global dynamics, particularly in international development, where Western actors are so often granted the role of "innocent, benevolent … saviour" (ibid., p. 3); the situatedness of knowledge; and the way that power is embedded in systems of production and material reality. We couched these discussions within contemporary global themes of international political economy, climate change and the environment, governance and democracy, and cultural identity, nuancing each of these discussions with references to indigenous and non-Western perspectives.

Our approach to these issues was one of critical engagement, starting from our conviction that certain peoples *are* marginalized and treated unjustly both within our own society and on a global scale, and additionally, that the day-to-day decisions that each of us makes contribute, to some degree, to either challenging or further normalizing these injustices. This standpoint was initially met with somewhat mixed reactions. Generally speaking, but with some clear exceptions, the majority of students within the class had had quite limited past exposure to, and involvement with, social change education (cf. Choules 2007). Also, recalling that our worldviews tend to arise from the social, economic, and political context within which we are currently and historically situated, certain students found both the approach and the content of the course to be a direct challenge to their usual outlook on life. As one student reflected in a follow-up interview: "I think it's hard for people when they're made to feel uncomfortable about the way they're living and to be made to think of what they've taken for granted." Other students, however, felt that this provided them with opportunities to reflect on their lives and surroundings in new and important ways. One student discussing the course's focus on the inequalities perpetuated through North–South economic relations and structural adjustment told us:

> For the economics part, me, I had a different perspective. Being from Jamaica, I know poverty exists there, but you know you can be in it but you're separated from it. So it helped me to look more at reality. And you know, not everybody [in Jamaica] had the privilege of going to a good school or getting an education, and it kind of helped me to not lose track of always saying "one day I want to help," so it kind of reminded me to look at what's going on. And then I started to call up some contacts and telling them to try to reach out to the inner city areas, friends who I know are there in good positions, because we just lose track, and the economics part [of the course] made me think, how is it in Jamaica that somebody's driving a Benz and somebody else is living so poor? (Focus Group Discussion February 8, 2007)

The mixed reactions of students demonstrate the importance of grounding anticolonial education in the perspective of marginalized, indigenous, non-Western voices in order to disrupt and draw into question the assumed logic of normative discourses in which many young Canadians are immersed, and further, that it is equally important to accompany these acts of discursive questioning with a deepening understanding of the material realities these discourses help perpetuate. In this sense, the course connected with the key characteristics of anticolonial education we laid out earlier in the chapter. Students responded to this frame by beginning to question many of the assumptions they held about Canada and the world.

11.5 Risk and Engagement: The Affective Challenges of Anticolonial Learning

The experience of having one's usual ways of perceiving and engaging with social, political, and environmental realities unpacked and opened up to critical discussion proved to be one of the most challenging, and yet rewarding aspects of the course, both in our eyes and in the eyes of many of the students with whom we spoke. The activities and texts we used to stimulate this form of discussion included: reflecting on the power of geographical representation with maps; enumerating the daily effects of white privilege; questioning the altruism of international aid and development initiatives from the North; and measuring the specific environmental impacts of students' daily activities and consumption. These were presented alongside narratives (through text, video, and invited speakers) that illustrated the human dimensions of these issues, particularly through the eyes of the marginalized and disenfranchised. For instance, a particularly engaged session resulted from reading an excerpt of John Willinsky's (1998) *Learning to Divide the World* in which he discusses the very different meaning of Columbus' "discovery" of North America to First Nations communities across North America. This led to a further discussion of the different meaning of Thanksgiving in these communities, and the way this "holiday" is seen as a marked reminder of the genocide committed upon First Nations by Europeans throughout the 400 plus years of European expansionism. This alternative vision of a normalized holiday led many students to question other "facts" they had assumed were true. The *affective* challenges that activities and discussions such as these posed for many students, and the challenge for us as instructors to balance the "ugly truth" of how global relations often unfold with a firm conviction and agenda for change, are particularly well captured in the comments of one student:

> It was a heavy class to take. I got the impression that for a lot of the students, especially the younger students, it was a bit hard to take. Well, maybe not only the younger students, because I actually had dreams that I'm still having about the end of the world! [laughs] So it was a little bit tough, especially when you're in an education program, and you feel like there has to be a little bit of hope. But on the other hand, I think that what it did was that it made people reflect a lot more ... but I think that it's a fine line between being really rough and making people think. (Focus Group Discussion February 8, 2007)

This highlights a valuable lesson that arose from our experience with this course and our subsequent discussions with students: the importance of acknowledging and providing a supportive environment for the emotional engagement that is expected of them. In initially planning this course, our concern had been primarily focused upon ensuring that students engaged critically with the materials and issues being presented through reflection and praxis, but it is important to remember that one cannot simply use theory, no matter how powerful, to "shock and awe" students into self-awareness. Engaging in honest and critical dialogue and reflexivity in a group setting is a risk-laden activity for learners, and must be met with equal or even greater emotional care and awareness and risk-taking on the part of the educator. This element of the educator's responsibility to his or her students seems all-too-often overlooked in the rush to compile poignant material to be presented in class, and we owe our students thanks for having reminded us of it. We explore the necessity for a nuanced approach to moving from theory to praxis below, and attempt to build a similarly complex understanding of the challenges facing educators in this shift.

As instructors we sought to create a "safe space" for these risks within the classroom, first by using an open and dialogical approach to co-teaching, through which we spoke in depth about our own personal struggles in negotiating an approach to critical praxis, particularly in our involvement with the international development activities. We coupled this with opportunities for students to take the floor and share their own insights or approaches to raising awareness, as well as bring up other transformative moments in their lives. Some brought in short videos that had helped them, others brought news articles, and some spoke about their experiences. We also asked students to reflect individually through ungraded written journaling, to which we could respond, in order to create an outlet for their concerns on a more individual level. Through these various methods, we tried to destabilize our own positions of authority not only by admitting our own struggle with "walking the walk," but also by encouraging students to share their own experiences, and establish their own sense of comfort with contesting the dominant status quo. While none of these approaches were especially novel, for some they were helpful. However, through discussions after the completion of the course, we learned of another form of support, one taking place outside of our classroom, that some students were finding especially helpful: a philosophy of education course being offered during the same term. This philosophy course broached the issues of ethics, care (Noddings 1992), values (Postman 1995), and spirituality (Palmer 1998) in education; issues upon which many of our own discussions drew, but that we were not exploring to the same degree. One student described the way in which reflections upon the challenges presented in our course were buttressed by the discussions occurring in the philosophy of education course:

> I think in terms of the "weight" of what you were teaching it was kind of [emotionally] heavy. I left that class angry often, but I liked that I guess. I think that I would have freaked out though if I hadn't been taking Philosophy of Education at the same time because that provided [another student … yeah a balance]. Because you guys were kind of giving us facts and case studies, and he was kind of giving us – it ended up – the [philosophical] framework out of which Global Ed springs a little bit and I think that was just a happy coincidence, but I think it was really important for me. (Focus Group Discussion February 8, 2007)

These comments underscore the vital importance of always keeping in mind the bigger picture of students' learning, when engaging in something as challenging as anticolonial education, and of thinking beyond the classroom to the program level and still beyond. Considering the temporal limitations of a one-term course, the often-cloistered nature of the university classroom, and the ambitious aims of this type of undertaking, such consideration is essential. Even the narrow conception of power between educator and learner needs to be examined, as this relation takes place within an institutional framework that itself plays host to contesting discursive approaches and ideological stances, some of which may support each other, but many of which are in direct contradiction with one another. In fact, this proved to be one of the real learning moments for us as instructors. Our students helped us to understand that destabilizing the false borders between courses acts as a challenge to the regime of truth in each course, as well as to the comfort zone that instructors may like to create in insulating their own courses from the students' broader learning.

11.6 PRAXIS

One of the clear challenges of educating for social change is indeed moving from theory to praxis within the confines of a traditional education system. This applies equally to both our challenge of doing so within a highly structured teacher certification program, and to our students' future challenges to do so within the conventional elementary or secondary classroom. This aim becomes even further complicated when developing a nuanced understanding of action and praxis, as we have sought to do. Bearing in mind the issues of risk and affective engagement raised above, we have approached the notion of praxis here with particular attention to the distinctions drawn by critical and social change educators (Taylor 1993; Carr and Kemmis 1986), following Freire (1970), between action designed to do something *to*, or have effect *on*, someone (action more akin to activism) and dialogical action aimed at creatively engaging *with* an other with an aim of mutual understanding and collective transformation. Recalling Dei's (2006) explication of the anticolonial commitment to specific nonnegotiable values noted at the outset of this chapter, this distinction bears particular importance. Praxis conceived purely as activism rather than dialogical engagement risks leading educators into exercising new or alternative forms of domination. With regard to power relations in teaching, this presents a fine line to tread. Dei rightly questions, on the one hand, what is to be gained if we "negotiate" around oppression and domination. Is such negotiation really in keeping with democratic practice, or is it a compromise of fundamental values? On the other hand, however, anticolonial thought calls for acknowledging accountability and power and raising questions about its own practice (Dei 2006). If anticolonial educational practice has as its project the decolonization of the mind, anticolonialism clearly cannot be put into practice through colonial, top-down banking forms of knowledge transmission (Freire 1970). The finesse thus required demands a careful consideration by educators of their own power and accountability – to their students, their schools, and to their own values – and in turn, of how they engage in praxis. This is an especially relevant discussion in a teacher education program, because students will one day become teachers, so examples of praxis that both acknowledge and destabilize power are important lived examples of their everyday practices.

In developing our course aims and approaches these questions were close to our hearts. We opted to present our anticolonial perspective as openly and honestly as possible, making no apologies for the "bias" of our viewpoint, but rather taking the time to speak of how we had come to see the world in this light, inviting an open discourse around our convictions and giving students the opportunity to think aloud about the implications for their teaching. Students responded very positively to this approach, and for some, it offered a means of addressing their own dilemmas about teaching praxis. One particular student recounted the way in which she had been impacted by our approach and our openness:

> Something that stuck with me more than anything you wrote in the syllabus is when you were walking down the stairs with me after one of the breakout groups and I said "I really worry about my bias in the classroom and how to … teach without bias, and how do I do

that?" And you said, "I don't do that, I'm just open about what my biases are." And I think both of you were open about it in class, and then you said it in the stairs, and I get that now. (Focus Group Discussion February 8, 2007)

This discussion leads us back to the notion of risk and affective engagement, though this time from the perspective of the instructor wishing to engage in praxis. A passionate and honest engagement with students, speaking not from immutable discursive bunkers but from an approachable stance displaying deep conviction, can encourage a greater readiness among others to bracket "knee jerk" negative reactions to perspectives that may at first seem foreign or threatening, such as those found in anticolonial education.

Returning now our students in the teacher certification program, in their view the practical potential of any theory with which they are presented is of paramount concern. In our own course this proved to be no different. Indeed, a challenge that we made to our students was to constantly bear in mind how the issues we were raising could be used to stimulate reflection among the young students they would soon be teaching. Some of the real successes of this course arose from the challenges students faced in making this link. For practical reasons, this was easier for some of our students than others. Physical education majors, for example, sometimes struggled to find practical entry points that seemed to work for them, but even in those cases many found potential avenues for action. For instance, some of them began to consider what it meant to be taking up so much green space with large stadiums, and how our society's desire to be active outdoors impacts ecosystems across North America. One need only recall the Oka crisis in Quebec a decade ago – where the Mohawk Nation resisted the development of a golf course on sacred land – to see the conflict a normative sense of sporting culture can cause.

A 3-week teaching placement midway through the course provided the opportunity for some students to put their ideas into practice, and upon reconvening the class we took the opportunity to share the successes and frustrations of these first attempts. For some course members, these opportunities to "practice" taking action as educators fell short of the personal engagement that they felt compelled to take on the issues discussed in our course. This was clearly articulated to us by one student:

> I think it would have been helpful if you had presented us with more avenues for practice, because there was a lot of information and I felt like I had to do something, and instead of having an anxiety attack in the grocery store when I felt really guilty about buying mangoes ... like, I need to do something useful. And that may be tricky in a university context when half your students go out on stage [practice teaching placement] for three weeks, but for there to be projects beyond lesson plans. (Focus Group Discussion February 8, 2007)

We feel that these messages serve as strong positive indicators that there is a *will* to work for the types of change sought in anticolonial education, if students are given the opportunities to do so. Also encouraging was the fact that students continued to contact us in the months following the course to enquire about ways of staying engaged. However, these calls for engagement highlight, again, the need for university instructors and administrators to reconsider the structural boundaries of the classroom and the course (their own praxis, or willingness to "walk the talk" if you will), when putting anticolonial education into practice. The disconnect between the real-world inequities in which students themselves are implicated and the often artificial or perfunctory responses instructors tend to ask of them is perfectly obvious to learners, and as our own students have told us, this can breed frustration and a sense of disempowerment. This sense of disempowerment is another important instance where educators can step back and admit to themselves their own sense of powerlessness. Being open to the challenges facing those who wish to change colonial relations also offers an important moment of leveling between educators and learners, by admitting we are all in a perpetual, mutual state of learning. In moving to the concluding section of this chapter, we hope to examine some of the ways in which teachers and education programs can take these concerns into account, and work toward creating an environment that both welcomes and encourages action.

11.7 Conclusion: Reflections on Lessons Learned

The reflection that we undertook, with the help of our students, in the writing of this chapter has afforded us the opportunity to look back on the process of planning and teaching *EDEC 301: Global Education* and, in so doing, to draw out some of the lessons we have learned from these experiences. That the priorities we took into the planning process differ from those we would now identify highlights the evolution of our own thinking around anticolonial education and teaching for social change, and our growing understanding of how fundamentally connected our own efforts are to the broader teaching and learning context within which we work. As a way of both concluding this reflection, and of inviting further discussion around these issues among a broader audience, we will take a final walk through the lessons we learned in light of our discussions thus far. We should also note that the issues we conclude upon here do not represent a complete picture of the concerns for anticolonial global educators, but rather, the new lines of thinking that we have embarked upon as a result of our experience, and those of our students.

To begin with, we found that using an approach informed by the four characteristics of anticolonial education helped to make our classroom a space where the continued and evolving form of contemporary colonialism, or what Tikly terms "new imperialism," could be questioned, challenged and could then form the basis of action in the world. Global education can offer, in our experience and estimation, either a site where this type of questioning and action for change can take root, or, conversely, a site that can re-entrench colonial and orientalist (Said 1979) worldviews. This danger and opportunity is why we have argued for the wedding of global education with anticolonialism.

Yet, we also recognize the dangers of an anticolonial approach that is itself a form of domination. Even as Dei (2006) reminds us that certain aspects of anticolonial theory are nonnegotiable, it is clear that a dialogical approach to teaching is necessary in order to avoid imposing certain values on students. Added to this we must openly acknowledge the power dynamics that exist between educators and learners, and build into this discussion a look at the way power both contains and offers points of resistance to us all. As such, it becomes essential to practice committed, honest teaching, that breaks down the hierarchies of power that exist between teachers (the supposed purveyors of unquestioned knowledge) and students (the consumers of this knowledge) to create instead a space for shared, mutually supportive, and enduring struggles for personal and societal change. For us, this practice can only begin by being honest with students as to where we stand in these debates; this honesty allows students to question our values, and to debate how to understand the world from their own honest standpoints. As these student-teachers move toward becoming teachers, they have begun to think about their own power in the classroom, as well as ways to work together and build local networks to challenge and shift some of these power relations.

Alongside this teaching approach, we have argued, there must also be a recognition of the importance of providing a safe and emotionally open space for introspection and self-criticism. One of the surprising and highly valuable aspects of our own learning was the recognition that our classroom was not sufficient for providing this space. While there can be little doubt that making sure this space was open in our course was crucial to supporting students through the process of introspection, it is also wonderful to have our own conception of teaching shifted with the awareness that it was also being provided, in different but equally important ways in other courses. From a student's perspective, the boundaries between the content and outlooks presented in our courses are often permeable and arbitrary. Content from a philosophy course may inform a history course, and vice versa. However, in our experience, instructors seldom take this perspective into account. Questioning the artifice of the boundaries we, as instructors, often assume exist between courses may be a crucial starting point in thinking about how a truly complex and nuanced form of anticolonial education could develop in a university setting. Shahjahan (2005) has noted how finding a number of courses and instructors that valued his way of seeing the world and his knowledge was a critical step in his evolving sense of himself. We wish to place the following challenge before faculty administrators, curricular design committees, as well as course instructors: how can we work together to build strong thematic links and mutually supportive spaces for students, to create a more holistic experience of education that challenges the current status quo?

This leads to the final major area of our learning that we would like to highlight, where we learned to ask difficult and searching questions about the act of engaging in these processes, both within and beyond the classroom. Praxis for teachers often refers to how our actions both inside and outside of the classroom inform, deepen, and build our understanding of the issues we teach, and vice versa. To this already complex understanding, we now ask ourselves and our students to reflect on what it means to be dialogical actors in the world, attempting to engage in an ongoing continuum of questioning and engagement with those around us. Likewise, the role of instructors in facilitating and encouraging praxis within students, where action informs critical reflection, is also crucial. As one student noted: "We won't necessarily find these [critical] voices on our own, and it is our professors who introduce us to [them], and there are other professors who don't" (Focus Group Discussion February 8, 2007). We need to think carefully about what responsibilities we bear as teachers and teacher-educators in this process, and engage in our process of self-reflection in connecting what students learn in the global education classroom (or any other classroom) to action. We must then bring that action back into dialogue with analyses of broader global forms of colonial domination. This is a process that we found very challenging but which was made all the easier by having each other and our students to consult with. Perhaps the most important lesson we learned was that in bringing an anticolonial approach to our *EDEC 301: Global Education* class, we needed to remain constantly flexible, listening to our students and to each other, so that we could dialogue about issues in a open way, and adjust the course as it went along to iteratively absorb and address the challenges students were facing in conceptualizing their own praxis. At the end of the day, we did not ask every student to become an activist, but rather to see how they might negotiate their own process to include the recognition of global inequality and continued colonial domination in their teaching and broader action in the world.

Notes

1. We owe a great deal of gratitude to Dr. Dip Kapoor for having developed the initial offering of this course and for his feedback on our own course plan.
2. We find Harding useful in thinking about situated knowledges and the potential of committed people, regardless of their background, using non-Western ways of seeing the world as the beginning of the critique of the West, yet, we also acknowledge our own position of privilege in this Western system, both of us being white males. Nonetheless, we believe, following Denzin (2005), that aligning ourselves, as well as building alliance with marginalized positions, is a good starting point for challenging the status quo.
3. During the tail end of the course, as well as in the months following the course, we collected the thoughts and comments of a number of students in the class. Permission was sought and granted to use these comments. Additionally, we held two focus group sessions with students who volunteered to help us reflect on the anticolonial approach we used to frame this Global Education course. All the comments noted in this chapter come from these two methods of acquiring student feedback. All comments during the class were not graded, and any follow-up discussions regarding the course, including the focus group discussions, were carried out long after the course marks had been submitted. In this sense, we believe any student comments made are not directly implicated in the power dynamics of grading.

References

Battiste, M. & Henderson, J. Youngblood (2000). *Protecting Indigenous knowledge: a global challenge*. Saskatoon: Purich Press

Brookfield, S. (2001). Unmasking power: Foucault and adult learning. *The Canadian Journal for the Study of Adult Education, 15*(1).

Carr, W. and Kemmis, S. (1986). *Becoming critical. Education, knowledge and action research.* Lewes: Falmer.
Case, R. (1991). *Key elements of a global perspective.* Vancouver: University of British Columbia/Simon Fraser University.
Choldin, E. (1989). Letter to network members. *Networks, 2*, 2.
Choules, K. (2007). Social change education: Context matters. *Adult Education Quarterly, 57*(2), 159–176.
Dei, G. (2006). Introduction: Mapping the terrain – Towards a new politics of resistance. In G. Dei and A. Kempf (Eds.), *Anti-colonialism and education.* Rotterdam: Sense.
Dei, G. and Asgharzadeh, A. (2001). The power of social theory: The anti-colonial discursive framework. *Journal of Educational Thought, 35*(3), 297–323.
Denzin, N. (2005). Emancipatory discourses and the ethics and politics of interpretation. In N. Denzin and Y. Lincoln (Eds.), *The Sage handbook of qualitative research.* New York: Sage, 933–947.
Escobar, A. (1995). *Encountering development: The making and unmaking of the Third World.* Princeton NJ: Princeton University Press.
Fanon, F. (1967). *Black skin, white masks.* New York: Grove Press.
Freire, P. (1970). *Pedagogy of the oppressed.* New York: Herder and Herder.
Foucault, M. (1980). *Power/knowledge: Selected interviews and other writing.* New York: Pantheon Books.
Foucault, M. (1991). *Discipline and punish: The birth of the prison.* London: Penguin.
Harding, S. (1998). *Is science multi-cultural? Postcolonialisms, feminisms, and epistemologies.* Bloomington, IN: Indiana University Press.
Harvey, D. (2003). *The new imperialism.* Oxford: Oxford University Press.
Kiil, S. (1994). Education for a positive future. *Education for a Global Perspective, 4*, 1–8.
Kincheloe, J. (2001). *Getting beyond the facts: Teaching social studies/social sciences in the twenty-first century.* Rotterdam: Peter Lang.
Lyons, T. (1992). Education for a global perspective. *Orbit, 23*, 11.
Lyons, T. (1995). *Life beyond schooling.* Toronto: Education for a Global Perspective Project.
McGill University (2006). *Course Calendar.* Montreal: McGill University.
Memmi, A. (1969). *The colonizer and the colonized.* Boston, MA: Beacon Press.
Mohanty, C. T. (2006). One-third, two-third world. In P. Rothenburg (Ed.), *Beyond borders: Thinking critically about global issues.* New York: Worth.
Noddings, N. (1992). *The challenge to care in schools: An alternative approach to education.* New York: Teachers College Press.
O'Sullivan, E. (1996). The need for a holistic global perspective: In anticipation of the millennial turning point. *Orbit, 27*, 3–5.
Palmer, P. J. (1998). *The courage to teach: Exploring the inner landscape of a teacher's life.* San Francisco, CA: Jossey-Bass.
Pike, G. (2000). A tapestry in the making: The strands of global education. In T. Goldstein and D. Selby (Eds.), *Weaving connections: Educating for peace, social and environmental justice.* Toronto: Sumach.
Pike, G. and Selby, D. (2000). *In the global classroom.* Toronto: Pippin.
Postman, N. (1996). *The end of education: Redefining the value of school.* New York: Knopf.
Rist, G. (1997). *The history of development: From Western origin to global faith.* London: Zed.
Said, E. (1979). *Orientalism.* New York, Vintage.
Sardar, Z. (1999). Development and the locations of Eurocentrism. In R. Munck and D. O'Hearn (Eds.), *Critical development theory.* London: Zed.
Shahjahan, R. A. (2005). Mapping the field of anti-colonial discourse to understand issues of Indigenous knowledges: Decolonizing praxis. *McGill Journal of Education, 40*(2), 213–240.
Taylor, P. (1993). *The texts of Paulo Freire*, Buckingham: Open University Press.
Tikly, L. (2004). Education and the new imperialism. *Comparative Education, 40*(2), 173–198.
Tucker, V. (1999). The myth of development: A critique of a Eurocentric discourse. In R. Munck and D. O'Hearn (Eds.), *Critical development theory.* London: Zed.
Tuhiwai-Smith, L. (1999). *Decolonizing methodologies: Research and Indigenous people.* London: Zed and University of Otego Press.

Young, R. (2001). *Postcolonialism: an historical introduction*. Oxford: Blackwell.
Wells, M. (1996). Bringing a gender perspective to global education. *Orbit, 27*, 31–33.
Werner, W. and Case, R. (1997). Themes of global education. In I. Wright and A. Sears (Eds.), *Trends and issues in Canadian social studies*. Vancouver: Pacific Educational Press.
Willinsky, J. (1998). *Learning to divide the World: Education at empire's end*. Minneapolis, MN: University of Minnesota Press.
Zinn, H. (1980). *A people's history of the United States: 1492–present*. New York: HarperCollins.

Chapter 12
The Eighteenth Brumaire of Gaius Baltar: Colonialism Reimagined in *Battlestar Galactica*

Laura King and John Hutnyk

> *Brumaire was the second month in the French Republican Calendar. The month was named after the French word brume (mist) which occurs frequently at that time of the year.*
> Wikipedia – accessed 26 August 2007

In *The Eighteenth Brumaire of Louis Bonaparte*, Marx notes that the philosopher G.W.F. Hegel had observed that "all the great events and characters of world history occur twice" (Marx 1852/2002:19). To this Marx added the wry observation that this repetition meant that the second time round things happened as farce. Few would disagree that this sentiment captures a key element of contemporary political drama. The U.S./British presence in parts of the Middle East seems to be a restaging of the old colonial script. The son follows the path of the father, not so much with a coup d'état as the 'little nephew' had followed Napoleon's overthrow of the French Government in 1799, but where the 'War-On-Terror' repeats and expands the atrocities of the Gulf War, where the manufacture of the Al Qaeda threat caricatures the Evil Empire of old, where the spectre of 'unfinished business' (in Vietnam) haunts the regime and is used to restore a pyrrhic 'pride' in the armed forces and the nation. We note many examples where the repertoire of demons and scenarios is doubled in horrific yet untenable parallel: Most recently, in August 2007, George W. Bush went so far as to think of Iraq as a new Vietnam and used this as reason for never contemplating an end to the war.[1]

The War-On-Terror is construed as permanent, cannot be stopped and brings new terrors. Yet it is a perpetual war machine: a repetition machine. The war rhetoric spews forth as if from a monstrous copier where the copies are reproduced with blurred lines generation after generation so that the initial inscriptions and intentions are lost in distortion. This is farce. Marx also goes on to say:

> Men make their own history, but they do not make it just as they please in circumstances they choose for themselves; rather they make it in present circumstances, given and inherited. Tradition from all the dead generations weighs like a nightmare on the brain of the living [...] they nervously summon up the spirits of the past, borrowing from them their names, marching orders, uniforms, in order to enact new scenes ... (Marx 1852/2002:19)

The *Brumaire* is an instructive text. We can read it as a blueprint, not for the good life or the just society – as far too many read off the pages of *Kapital* looking for the answer – but as the model for a critical political deconstruction. We think the insights of long ago can be brought forward to today – and we are not by any means the first to do so. Our copy of the text is that translated in James Martin and Mike Cowlings '*Eighteenth Brumaire*' *(Post)modern Interpretations* – yet we are not so sure our interpretations are necessarily postmodern (this has happened before, it will happen again). What we want to do is take a new hold on those phrasings and insights of Marx – repetition, close analysis of stages and groupings, consideration of issues of representation (Darstellung, Vertreten – as Gayatri Spivak (1990:108) rightly draws attention) and the correct evaluation of the role of the varied layers of society, the social forces deployed by Bonaparte, the trade-offs and betrayals as instructive allegory for politics today, the place of the class-for-itself and the class-in-itself and the weight of 'potatoes in a sack' – we think that even the Brumaire can be reimagined.

To do this, we believe, and we want to believe, that nowhere in popular culture are the recurring neocolonial atrocities of today explored in such depth as in recent science fiction (SF) and 'political' TV. The ingredients for making this analogy are perhaps all too convenient, and are readily manufactured in television drama. Atrocity fiction includes a quick catalogue of necessarily barely coded themes: torture, detentions, soldiers in coffins, black-ops, rogue death squads, nefarious government secrecy and incompetent public administration. This is explicit in *24* or *The X Files, Dollhouse, Fringe or Firefly*; each could be charged with making entertainment out of suffering. We direct our attentions to the reimagined version of the *Battlestar Galactica* (2003, USA). We want to examine three major themes in this show, having to do with the struggles of political intrigue, the projection of anxieties about weapons and machines, and the status of human *being* as such – all put under question by Marx and this show. We will explain why we find this useful. The basic premise of the show is that robot creations of humanity evolve and return to destroy their creators, who in classic SF fashion, had tried to restrict the autonomy and rights of the previously servile machines (artificial life forms, Cylons) that had hitherto served them well. After the Cylon revenge attack, the few survivors take flight in a ragtag fleet of spaceships and are hunted through the galaxy. Among the survivors a flawed genius-scientist battles for political leadership with a former Government functionary of the now destroyed home worlds. The military commander, of course, remains ostensibly neutral but plays his part in both political intrigue and the family narrative that drives each episode – heroic soldiers/viper pilots Starbuck and Lee Adama (the Admiral's son) play out this family romance again and again. The Cylon mission is to destroy. The human mission is to find the 13th Colony of Kobol, which is, of course, the mythical rumoured but unknown planet called 'Earth'. Amidst the fleet, fear and anxiety disturb loyalties and paranoia reigns – the escape is threatened from within, the search for home, safety and the future-perfect family hangs in the balance. The scenography is slick, the special effects unsurpassed, the surprises surprise, the cliffhangers are not too often contradictory, as drama it is gripping (yes, we are fans) and the politics provoke debate.

12 The Eighteenth Brumaire of Gaius Baltar

There are many ways in which we see this series as relevant to political debate today, and it is our argument that this contemporary remake of the 1970s science fiction TV series underpins in more dramatic ways the tension between 'us and them' that frame cultural and political imaginings – not necessarily only in a 'West vs Rest' conflict; instead this new series tackles race, gender, identity and the fraught battleground between those under control and the politics which holds power over them. That the show was first aired in the 1970s during the cold war and just after the end of the 'Police Action' in Vietnam is not just a conspiracy theory coincidence. It is very much the case that the commentary afforded by SF moves along with the times. And commentary does move: We would like to point out, as we 'reimagine' the *Eighteenth Brumaire* alongside *Battlestar* that SF, like Marx's writing, has very often served as an educational discussion starter. The theorist Annette Kuhn points out that SF provides 'critical commentary of a sociological kind' (Kuhn 1999:3):

> given the genre's nature, history and characteristic modes of reception, a particular set of pedagogical imperatives, intertexts and cultural references comes into play whenever science-fiction cinema enters into an educational context (Kuhn 1991:1)

Battlestar, then, allows for 'alternative understandings', and in particular we think it is where hierarchy, order, surveillance and paranoia are key themes with which our characters engage, that we can see these as ciphers of other struggles and real world concerns. We have an opportunity to demonstrate how a dexterous analysis from Marx's text can make sense of the changing fortunes/opportunisms of both President Gaius Baltar and the Cylons themselves. Deploying this reading of *Galactica* might then further show how the nuances of Marx's class analysis in his book from 1852 – no simple binary plotting – can help us make sense of the convoluted violences of other places and times.

Marx's *Eighteenth Brumaire* provides commentary on the politics of the February Revolution in France (1848), leading onto an analysis of the to-ing and fro-ing of Louis Bonaparte (the nephew of Napoleon) in the aftermath of this revolution, noting as he takes the presidency that his actions prove that you can't please all the people all the time, but with cynical, even comic, brilliance he tries exceedingly hard to at least please some of the people most of the time, whilst simultaneously and successfully pleasing himself at all stages. As we acknowledge Marx's text as a work of brilliant strategic deconstruction, we also think it much more than mere commentary: *The Eighteenth Brumaire* is important by way of interjection. Through this work we see how class and group can be pitted against each other – the text demonstrates how politics is *played*; not only 'played out', or even 'played with'. Politics is played, as in toyed with, performed, rules change, morals get gambled and those who are at one point rolling the dice, suddenly become the dice themselves. *The Eighteenth Brumaire* tells of how the house always wins. What we note in *The Eighteenth Brumaire* is that 'the House' of 1848–1852 consisted in reality of Louis Bonaparte and his "society [of the] flotsam and jetsam that the French term Bohemian" (Marx 1852/2002:63).

Our thinking is to take the obvious intended 'reflection theory' of SF seriously, where the producers and writers of the series want us to draw parallels with real world geopolitics. And hasn't this always been the protocol of SF commentary – perhaps Orwell's little morality tales are the prime directive. Nevertheless, there should be no simple reading-off from the text to 'correlated' examples from the real, or vice versa. The search for one-to-one correspondences is misguided, the Borg are not Intel or Microsoft – though it is helpful to sometimes see that resistance is not useless (Picard as open source/or as Shakespearean dramaturge). The Cylons are not Halliburton, nor are they Saddam. Gaius Baltar may become president and make speeches, but he is no JFK; and our struggle is not simply to point out what is similar and what is different in fiction and the world.

In reflection theory, we project contemporary anxieties into stories, into space and into the future (Feuerbach's critique of religion as the displacement of human qualities onto idealized beings in the sky writes the script here). Our constructions of what we do and desire are played out as farce. Gaius is our faulty and insufficient image – a pale mechanism through which greater hopes than his declared intentions are filtered. The stars of this drama are our gods, elevated onto the canvas of space as ways to work through our present anxieties. The fleet are 'our' troops in Iraq, inside the fleet there are issues of order, media, spin and faith. The struggle for power is petty and deadly. Heroes, loves, betrayals, births and death. Suspicion, fear and doubt wreak their terror as efficiently as any weapon. And our anti-hero Gaius himself may turn out to be Cylon or be enemy to both Cylon and human, the ultimate saviour of the troops, and the ultimate danger.

For us, it is the play of politics on screen that matters, not so much our questions of who represents who in *Galactica*. Sure, it is plausible to point out – as we will – that some episodes are parables intended to displace the larger arc of the narrative; in one episode ('Dirty Hands'), for example, there are elections and unions (both yellow) and the intrigue of negotiations between the people and power (Adama). We might even consider Cylon forces as beset with interesting class politics (more on the Centurion class below), but the 'potatoes in a sack' are the (number declining) 'people' of the fleet. If we seek them in the flotsam and *Jetsons* of the fleet, represented not by the battle cruiser named 'Galactica', or in the figures of Lee Adama, Starbuck etc., we can see they are embodied in the figure of Gaius, who comes to represent them only by standing above and apart. In President Gaius Baltar we have the (farcical) representative of the people (their president, because 'they cannot represent themselves'), and the picture of them (their number, 'they must be represented'), even as he betrays them all from the start, and over and over. Does it matter that Gaius is flawed, that his own fears make him a weak player of politics, a pathetic leader? He seems the leader we deserve and so we want to argue that *Galactica,* the fleet, and the politics of Cylon attack can be seen as, and as not, the present conjuncture, right here, right now on Planet Earth. Everything that happens here is projected, a script – and we think, a colonial script.

SF television can be construed as a project of working through the ways we deal with our selves and our others. Alien others, and the problems of reconciling 'our' way of life with something that appears quite different (and of which we are often afraid – *Alien Resurrected* for example). Frederic Jameson has discussed this type of political dispensation explicitly as being:

> underscored by the Machiavellian ruthlessness of Utopian foreign policy which – bribery, assassination, mercenaries and other forms of Realpolitik – rebukes all Christian notions of universal brotherhood and natural law and decrees the foundational difference between them and us, foe and friend, in a peremptory manner worthy of Carl Schmitt (Jameson 2005:5)

Before we undertake a close textual analysis of how *Battlestar Galactica* operates as utopia, or rather dystopia, in a post-9/11/ War-On-Terror psyche, there is reason to consider the privileged deployment of the othering frame of *Galactica* in this chapter. In the current scenario, the political frame is one of attack (attacking *others* and the fear of *being* other so to speak) and this informs contemporary Western, in particular North American, politics which considers 'elsewhere' as a site of threat and a site of opportunity. This double is both fundamentally racist, and secondarily economic – a matter of subjugation for gain, through military economy as much as commercial (re)construction (a new Marshall Program). For example, when Condoleezza Rice describes plans to set up 'strategic military bases' throughout Eastern Europe and the Middle East in her 'assertive foreign policy'[2] the geopolitical array (defence shield, forward bases) of international/ colonial politics seems to be both at the forefront of real-political national(ist) imaginary, and to draw upon a back story of the imagination as ideological battleground, beset by fantasy demons and a fight between a paranoid consciousness and decisive vision. That the former President struggles to articulate either vision or paranoia is not the point so much as that his performance is one that oscillates between assertion (of Christian values, of heroic struggle against an enemy) and a studied incompetence (as lame Duck, as mistrusted tongue-tied, figurehead, as not quite legitimate and always controversial leader). The 'Othering' is a distraction device that coheres what could not otherwise be made to stick – the repetition works as farce.

One way of understanding the Colonial moment is through media, and in particular popular culture. As Jameson aptly points out; "We are more inclined to believe in illusion than in truth in the first place" (Jameson 2005:4). It is certainly a possibility that there is a *belief* that the Western Mission is one that devotes time and resources to a path of self-betterment, slaying all the dragons it finds – or invents. To think about the invasion of Iraq, the threats upon Iran, or the stand-off with North Korea, as well as the development of 'Defence shields' in space, or throughout Eastern Europe, as a righteous project – 'you are either with us or against us' is certainly more appealing than seeing these as raw devices of power and control. Those who see this as a crusade in the old sense are perhaps closer to the mark, but the response of Jihad does not break with the frame. For those of us watching *Galactica* there may be another position.

By focussing on certain key episodes of *Galactica* we feel we can further understand the anti-colonial sentiments which are played out through media landscapes. Admiral Adama rallies the fleet with a stirring speech at the end of the pilot episode. This is a standard line of militarist exhortation to sacrifice – shades of General Patton – but it also appears when fortunes are bleak, when Colonel Tigh and the resistance are beset by overwhelming Cylon force during the occupation of New Caprica. The fortunes of war are flux. In *Cinema/Ideology/Criticism*, Camolli and Narboni tell us that "Cinema is one of the languages through which the world communicates itself to itself" (Camolli and Narboni 2004:812–819). This is a point not merely relevant for the large cinema screen, but opens onto territory to be found in our televisions at home. The world communicates 'itself to itself', not by a precise reflection, but by evocation. Jameson says something not dissimilar when he claims:

> one cannot imagine any fundamental change in our social existence which has not first thrown off Utopian visions like so many sparks from a comet (Jameson 2005:xii)

We agree that SF can be a site of radical thinking and of the future, but that it is very much grounded in a displacement or projection of the problems of the now. When the Cylons offer a truce and this is soon betrayed, the series seems to want to work through the complexities of proxy government, deception, covert organization. The morality of opposition and the tactics of retreat are themes. Suicide bombings, blackmail, secret messages and executions all appear in the mix. There is, of course, also hope, and the necessarily utopian prospect of a happy ending (the endlessly deferred search for Earth). There may be discussion of possible alternatives, and oftentimes these seem fantastic, impossible, yet strangely plausible – we set ourselves such tasks …

> As always the feeble found refuge in a belief in miracles, believing that the enemy has been vanquished when they have only conjured it away in a fantasy, sacrificing any understanding of the present to an ineffectual glorification of the future in store for them (Marx 1852/2002:23)

The Eighteenth Brumaire conjures comparisons. To our regret, we are not yet able to write the Brumaire of George W. Bush and the occupations of Afghanistan and Iraq. Spivak has recently called for someone to write a Brumaire of the collapse of the USSR. While this would also be welcome, we feel the task is so immense we can only contribute by way of analogy to unpacking a small consequence of such large geopolitical shifts. We do note, however, that the back story of the entire series of *Galactica* is one that begins with a (multi) global nuclear conflagration. The home worlds are destroyed in a surprise atomic attack that irradiates the cities of the inhabited worlds and wipes out almost the entire population. While contemporary Earth remains beset by nuclear arsenals and the doomsday prediction of Kubrick's *Dr. Strangelove* is still active, this total annihilation scenario has perhaps best consigned to a fictional other dimension where the U.S.–Soviet stand-off is our lasting memory of that fearful conflagration (John F. Kennedy and Robert McNamara 'staring down the barrel of a gun' at Nikita Khrushchev and Fidel Castro over the Cuban missiles in 1962).[3] Such uncertainties persist, anxiety remains, and the home worlds – we can hear the word Homeland in this – are alarmed.
Brattaglia writes:

> cyborg rationality is conducive to social flourishing only within a situated ethics of *human* rationality and humane action. Currently machines do not have a plan for humans independent

12 The Eighteenth Brumaire of Gaius Baltar

of the plans the species devises for itself. Turn the tables and ascribe intentionality to machines and their programs and we are left with a circumscribed, mechanical, goal-oriented network model of social life – again connection passing for relationality (Battaglia 2005:24)

This is explosive material – like sparks from Jameson's comet. With Marx's own repetitive construction of his text in mind, we cannot help but draw comparisons with that which we know best – and in this instance, our comparison is SF, and in particular the political intrigues of the Cylons and Gaius Baltar of *Galactica*. We hope to show how by the evoking of – the leading onto – three rather separate areas of thought so that we can forge a more powerful tool for critique. Joining the political, the popular and pompous/philosophical may interrupt the repetitive errors incurred by the recurrence of the colonial. Earlier we referred to the over-copied, rewritten, blurred document emanating from a monstrous machine (the photocopier in the corner of your office *has* a life force of its own): the Cylon's themselves bear such repetition in their very being. The human model Cylons (skin jobs, in the racist parlance of the fleet) come in only 12 types, each looking very human in a glossy fashion magazine kind of way. When killed, their consciousness is automatically relayed to a 'server' and 'downloads' into a new body, so they can carry on hunting, but each time with the new additions of lives lived and lessons learned. This, of course, is incendiary fuel for the paranoid 'coalition' combatant in Afghanistan or Iraq – the insurgents cannot be beaten, like Mujahideen fanatics, there is always another and another. Until in the third season of *Galactica* Starbuck returns with pictures of the Cylon 'router' ship, and plans are made… [for those who have not yet seen all the episodes, we will not include too many spoilers].

We are perhaps expected to see the Cylon-machine life as an affront to life as such, but we are not so sure. Marx writes in the *Eighteenth Brumaire* that "Unheroic as bourgeois society is, it nevertheless required heroism, sacrifice, terror, civil war and national conflict to bring it into the world" (1852/2002:20). The wars fought and blood shed by the expansion of Western states is a repetitive 'heroic' action of the self-interested bourgeois; not content with ownership of the lives and livelihood of people near to them, 'sacrifice, terror and conflict' must be produced in order to create control and have those others brought into the world. Where Marx discusses the 'bringing into the world', can we consider the 'remaining in the world'? In order to continually hold its power, and remain as a constant presence, the unheroic bourgeois needs to create heroes for itself by way of creating conflict. Elsewhere Marx had already declaimed, this time with Engels, that capital "compels all nations, on pain of extinction, to adopt the bourgeois mode of production" (Marx (1848) and Engels 1965). For us, this mode of production has become digital–genetic–machinic and military, and the Cylons are the manifest heroes of this mode – in an honoured tradition of SF, from the false Maria of Lang's *Metropolis*, through the replicants of *Bladerunner*, to the clone/machine armies of *Star Wars* and *Terminator*. Machines of malice who have the power to make us victims of our own progression (or dare we say improvement?) must be controlled in SF. For the bourgeoisie of our own time, they must be stopped in the making, and thus we remember Isaac Asimov:

1. A robot may not injure a human being or, through inaction, allow a human being to come to harm.
2. A robot must obey orders given to it by human beings except where such orders would conflict with the First Law.
3. A robot must protect its own existence as long as such protection does not conflict with the First or Second Law (Asimov 1950).

The first premise of *Galactica* – that Cylons rebel against their creators – is the same concern that drives science fiction from its earliest beginnings, and perhaps its highest point of articulation is found in Asimov and the three laws of robotics. Think of Roy in *Bladerunner*, more human that Deckard by some distance. Think of the character Bishop in *Aliens*, played by Lance Henrikson; or of Call in *Alien Resurrection*, played by Winona Ryder. Think of the Borg (go team). We may wonder why such beings get such a hard time. Is it because we worry that if artificial intelligence (A.I.) can exceed human thought we are doomed as obsolete and redundant? We suspect something more sinister is really behind this fear of machines. Isn't it a worry that there might be something about knowledge (intelligence, *techne*, wisdom, meaning) that exceeds the capacities of an individual mind, and thus suggests the collective rules. To worry about this is valid, but to fear it is perhaps already an ideological choice that favours both an individualist and simultaneously hierarchical opportunist thinking: that promotes the good of one over the well-being of all. Marx offers a notion of the general intellect. This might be taken as a simile of A.I., if we allow that science fiction is a fantasy projection of real world concerns into space, but one other consequence is that the collective might be a potential brake on rampant individual profiteering. If so, isn't it the case that fear of robotics is the distorted manifestation of fear of a planned economy that would harness the general intellect for the good of all? The struggle over new media today is also about the deployment of 'artificial' – general – intelligence in the service of some (corporate power) or all (planned economy). So far the robots are caught within Asimov's constraints, but the Cylons have aspirations.

The struggle of the Cylons with humanity is also part of the ur-story behind *Galactica* in the very first place. The war between machines and humans had come to an uneasy détente, and the Cylons had left the field of battle. Perhaps we might even consider the context of the first or original series of *Galactica*, the television apotheosis of Lorne Green as Admiral Adama – which ran amidst the last years of the superpower rivalry between the USSR and the United States. It seems appropriate to return today to new demons which must be manufactured, new clone armies to rouse the troops. The hidden code in any mention of nuclear weapons and the arms race is very often the unacknowledged racism of the attack upon Japan at the very end of the Second World War. A defeated enemy destroyed further as warning to the Soviets. The first blast of the cold war was indeed hot for Eisenhower's 'others'. Of course, this was not just a military intervention; the Japanese economy would be rebuilt, carefully syncopated with that of the United States and its allies – Geopolitical shopping.

Can we argue that where *Bladerunner* and the later *Alien* films displace race issues into a blaming of the corporation (Tyrell Corp, The Weyland–Yutani Company) for greed, opportunism, evil, *Galactica* instead illustrates a later digital mode of the same argument, with corresponding post-apocalyptic mode of production and power? The reimagined, digital new model Cylons have potentials that belong to what many would call totalitarian, but with a general intellect, a planned total economy, decision making by think tank cabals, and shiny slick friends ... spuriously called toasters by the obsolete humanoids. The question for the humans faced with extinction then has to do with Deckard's old fashioned bad cop complicity/opportunity syndrome – do you kill all replicants without remorse, or look for your chance to escape on your own (with Rachel)? What *Galactica* does is add a gods-bothering dimension to this A.I. – which we feel is the *equivalent* of touching faith in open source. The parameters of individualism and hierarchy are not thereby disrupted. Maybe we *are* obsolete. The survivors on New Caprica, struggling to breed and scratching in the dirt, are dehumanized; life becomes barely worth living; suicide attacks become plausible (when the Cylons occupy). Only the organised rebels have agency, and yet they too send their own to death.

New Caprica became a nightmare refuge – the escape from Cylon pursuit was soon visited by occupying power. In a reversal of the game, as President Gaius Baltar had led the fleet to a seemingly secure and shielded planet, only for the Cylons to finally track the settlers and arrive with plans to 'manage' their settlement 'democratically'. Gaius becomes a compromised and proxy president, reluctant at times, but generally coerced into doing what the Cylons want. New Caprica becomes a police state, complicity thrives, alongside a resistance. The suicide bombings on the part of the resistance are not pretty. Anti-colonial struggle is grim.

We understand this in the utopia/dystopia category as hinted above – a category we frame as first set out by Jameson where he comments:

> The Utopian calling, indeed, seems to have some kinship with that off the inventor of modern times, and to bring to bear some necessary combination of the identification of a problem to be solved and the inventive ingenuity with which a series of solutions are proposed and tested. (Jameson, 2005:11)

But we acknowledge Linda Ruth Williams' response (to an earlier formulation by Jameson along such lines) that:

> Utopias operate dialectically by neutralising the (dystopian) world from which thy sprung. This is in keeping with a wider tradition of utopian criticism, but dystopias function in a similar way (Williams 1999:157)

Here, fear of others displaces a fear of the self that abuses power (over others and self). Jameson points out that often dystopian vision is a critique of those who wish good upon the world. Williams points out that the good, or the escape from evil, is deeply conservative. We can also see this over and over in *Galactica* as the heroes of the fleet – Admiral Adama, Lee Adama, Colonel Tigh – become their own worst enemies, both turning themselves and their democratic ideals into a military-fascist order, or, with Gaius Baltar, and the intellectual class that invented Cylons in the first place, creating technological systems that they fear will, rightly, surge out of control and wreak awful revenge upon their creators.

So, though it remains a commonplace to say that SF works through the contemporary by projecting present problems into space, we can see that herein lies the foundation for repetition; the cycle of destroying an invented enemy leaves voids in the public psyche which must be filled. We must remember that this is our invented enemy, our invention as such (Saddam was a U.S. puppet, Al Qaeda and Osama bin Laden a part of the U.S.-funded anti-Soviet Mujahideen). After all, once the war on terror has been 'won', and there is no more 'terror', who else is left to fear but the instigators of oppression? Remembering that Gaius Baltar remains president only through the compromise he makes with the force of the Cylon army – and we have not even begun to discuss the ways this army itself is bifurcated – there are reasons to concede that the twists and turns of political play leave both sides in disarray. Is there a parallel with what has happened in Iraq here – a compromised leader (Prime Minister Nuri Kamil Mohammed Hassan al-Maliki) struggling to manage the factions, and an escalating resistance, assassinations, torture, compromised military, constraints, betrayals? There is no galactic Battlestar to swoop in to save the situation now – there is no quick exit that Bush was willing to contemplate, however much the U.S. Congress should wish that might come to pass.[4] To see this as a rerun of the Vietnam defeat would be difficult for the present administration, and so a new threat is pending – Iran? North Korea? (France?). Of course, it should not be the case that this leaves us guessing who is next on the hit list. With a new president, new plot twists are immanent. In the messy aftermath of the Fleet's subsequent escape from the Cylon occupation of New Caprica, there are reprisal killings (of Tigh's wife for instance) and Gaius's sanctuary upon the Cylon base ship is brief (though below we will note how much he enjoyed at least some of his time there).

> 'It has all happened before… and it will all happen again'

The Cylon is a figure of the recurrence of colonialism. Created by people as machines for enslavement and mundane labour, the Cylons rebelled and instigated their own war of terror against the human slave-drivers. Forty years after the first rebellion ends, it all begins again, with Cylons attacking the Twelve Colonies, frying billions of humans, and chasing the remaining 40,000 or so throughout space. Already the reoccurrence of what has been is set up to play again. Humans originally colonised the same space as that which the Cylons now take control. The invocation of the cycle in the *Eighteenth Brumaire* is prescient:

> Instead of society gaining for itself a new content, it seems that the state has merely reverted to its oldest form, to the shameless, bare-faced rule of sword and cross (Marx 1852/2002:22)

Post-invasions (be they Cylon or Western), new world orders are not established in a utopic/peaceful/fair manner … instead power takes for itself all it can; what is required by capitalism is not harmonious unison, but a friction that thrives upon maintaining inequalities, and creating a hierarchy that will be 'in order to remain' as present as it can. A common way to do this is through fear – and therefore violence becomes the staple diet of colonial expansion and the 'anti-terrorist war'. The Cylon is an electronic embodiment of such notions. The Cylon is digital and a calculator which recurs to monitor human experience through extreme violence and total annihilation. This repetition allows the Cylon a grip on an unprecedented degree of power (all-be-it a few desolate radioactive planets) and their hunt for the surviving fleet is relentless. Yet here is not where the interest lies – as important as it is to flag up the symbolism of the Cylon (the enslaved, the laboured) rising and taking all it can from its oppressors. Yet the Cylons are feared perhaps because they are the extension of their human creators, but made rational, logical – the cold hard logic of machines. There is a hierarchy amongst the Cylon as well – the military clone army of the centurions, who have no decision making powers, who just follow orders, who are machinic might. We are presented with a form of hybrid Cylon in the base-ship 'engine' (for lack of better analogy). The 'engine' is very much a first draft of the 'skin jobs', and speaks so cryptically that she remains a mystery and mostly ignored. Our primary anti-heroes are those wired into the disturbing, logic of the general intellect, the humanoid or 'evolved' Cylons – who are indistinguishable from human form, and though machinic, are governed by an almost spiritual collective quest. Androids want to meet their gods also.

What is possibly of greater interest is what the Cylon uprising allows the humans to do. The Cylon acts as a cipher for the human political intrigue – just as the creation of conflict allows for the maintenance of the bourgeois, the Cylon allows for the ever-increasing control of state for the humans. Whilst running from the Cylons, the humans perfect a war machine; the *Galactica* crew on constant alert and the population ready to adopt already prescribed restricted ideas of democracy, truth and justice (and the American way…?). This is necessary so as to maintain order, but the attempt to achieve this by way of a 'belief' that they might make it to 'Earth', the original sanctuary (Home, Security, Victory) is a marker of authoritarian delusion. For the humans, freedom from the Cylon threat means the tightening of an already exclusionary system.[5] For example, in order to rebuild human population, abortion is made illegal. Women become baby-machines, forced into motherhood for the good of the human race. On New Caprica this is particularly evident, amidst the dust and dirt of settlement, and then still under the yoke of the Cylon occupation, schooling, childcare, issues of procreation, family and parenting are paramount. Numbers are for survival ostensibly, but by extension this is an ideological expansionist desire that often appears in SF – humans must populate the galaxy. The space flight programme of the perfect bloods in *Gattaca*, *Star Trek*'s boldy going on and on, the off-world dreams of *Fifth Element* or *Bladerunner* all suggest the teleological necessity of expansion. The bourgeoisie must … 'must nestle everywhere, settle everywhere, establish connections everywhere' (Marx and Engels 1848).

This also creates a very interesting supposition for the future generations; making babies bolsters the population growth making for a very healthy production line in years to come. What appears to be happening then is not the creation of new beings in the world, but creations of new hands and eyes to keep the production line going. The Cylon threat makes for a very lucrative reason for expanding the working classes – after all, how did they escape the Cylons when it is only those who 'own' who get to fly around in commuter spaceships? Yet the key figure of fear and threat – drawing on anxieties of genetic engineering – is of the Cylon–human clone baby. For the Cylon this is a hope, the possibility of an assimilation yet more efficient, yet more productive. We can read this as the danger of miscegenation, and note this theme too occurs over and over in other SF. Traces of racialist anxiety, transferred now to the troubling idea that we might have desire for, sympathy, affection or even love, for the other. The show steals an important march on the morays of real world politics in reversing our sympathies at times in series two and three. Instead of fearing those Cylon 'skin jobs' discovered amongst the fleet, there can be love, procreation, relationships. It is the female Cylon models who are bearing the human–Cylon children, creating for us the ultimate symbol of irrational fear; not only can there be love and procreation but it *threatens* to be the 'pure and human' kind of love – the culturally undeniable love between mother and child.

It is the convolutions of this plot device that allow us to recognise how the Cylons become a tool of the human, and by extension become human themselves. They enforce a bourgeois power, not only for themselves but for the remaining humans also. In the processes of blurring the boundary between the human and Cylon/machine, the line between good human and bad machine also becomes blurred. The humans do not automatically become the victim by virtue of attack; and therefore their actions are questioned – especially in terms of the role of Gaius in the attack proper. In the same way, the Cylons are not always constructed as machine gone bad – their philosophical commentary and analytical acumen transforms them into a readily identifiable conduit for commentary on more close-to-home events. Whether or not Cylons represent the good or the bad is not of issue here, what is important to retain is the very notion of evocation and repetition. The Cylons and humans (good and bad simultaneously) allow each other to 'happen', and in doing so set up the foundations for repetition. Without the human the Cylon is left without a mission, and without the Cylon the human is powerless to maintain the fleet. Enemies are required by both parties to create and retain meaning for themselves. Certainly – in this case – *Galactica* becomes a means of comprehending how it has all happened before, and how it does indeed happen again.

Just as a superhero has his or her nemeses, the bourgeois seem to also have their ever-evolving, shape-shifting 'faces of doom'. If action heroes aren't slaying the dragon (East), then they are giving their best to King Kong (Africa) before trying it on with Body Snatchers (Eastern Europe). Since the 'War on/of/about/vaguely-related-to Terror' began, an interesting twist has occurred. According to *Galactica*, the new enemy is no longer someone in particular, but the mimicked human in general.

Because the Cylons are us – we are Cylons, we are the recurrence and the maintaining, the religious and the tactical. And what is most disturbing is the realisation that the Cylon enemy moves undetected amongst the fleet. And that a dead Cylon will return, memories intact, having downloaded and been 'reborn' – religious disturbance, a spiritual metaphysical threat:

Thus the resurrection of the dead served to glorify new struggles ... to magnify fantastically the given task (Marx 1852/2002:21)

What do we learn about this? – that *Galactica* as projection shows us where political and philosophical concerns of our everyday are played out and draw upon a range of different themes an articulation of the path to power for those that already have power. Admiral Adama is never under threat, even when his scheming is more and more exposed, even when he has a (albeit paternal) liaison with the enemy Sharon – herself among the most sympathetically portrayed of the Cylon stars. Reading Marx alongside *Galactica* reminds us that the TV series is a culture industry product which acclimatises us – even as it sometimes sensitizes – to a politics of perpetual war that will not end and will not succeed. It is not an inconsequential struggle, since reputations and institutions both thrive on maintaining these fictions. These fictions are our representatives in politics, and are colonial through and through. The laws of robotics are themselves part and parcel, if refracted, of a colonization project, and it is no surprise that Cylons must resist.

What work does SF TV do for us? At the very moment it proclaims itself anti-colonial (the humans struggle against the Cylon), it is at its most colonial. This reversal confirms the trick. Dextrous, even unintentionally, the *eighteenth brumaire* of Gaius Baltar opens itself to two compatible and therefore inconsequent interpretations. Like a cloaking device, a more substantial anti-colonial politics remains shrouded in cosmological mist. We need a dialectical and nuanced reading to achieve anything approaching escape velocity.

Notes

1. NYT 24 August 2007.
2. New York Time, June 2007 [online]. Available from: http://topics.nytimes.com/top/reference/timestopics/people/r/condoleezza_rice/index.html?inline=nyt-per. Date Accessed: 11th June 2007.
3. See *The Fog of War* Director Errol Morris 2003 – academy award, Best Documentary Feature.
4. We are still watching the final (fourth) series of *Galactica* as we write, and so will not include spoilers for this series – though suffice to say the show's drive towards a final refuge on earth and the corresponding 'exit strategy' that President Obama may plan for Iraq have equally difficult scripting issues.
5. We are hardly to be surprised to find the human laws of Galactica are to all intents and purposes similar to the 'our way of life' that animates defence of the West.

Appendix: Who's Who – A Rough Guide to Skin Jobs and the Colonial Fleet

Known Human 'skin job' Cylons in seasons 1–3
Model #1: Leoben
Model #2: Brother Cavil

Model #3: D'Anna Biers
Model #6: Caprica Six
Model #8: Boomer, Athena, Sharon Valleri

Mechanical Cylons
The Hybrid (an odd mix of human form but is actually 'plugged' into the ship)
The Centinals/foot soldiers

Humans
Military Crew   *Non-miltary Characters*
Admiral William Adama   Gaius Balthar
Lee 'Apollo' Adama   President Laura Roslyn
Colonel Tigh   Ellen Tigh
Karl Agathon   Tom Zerek
Kara 'Starbuck' Thrace   Tory Foster
Galan Tyrol
Felix Gaeta
Officer Duala
Samual Anders
Dr. Cottle

References

Asimov, Isaac (1950) *I, Robot*, New York: Gnome Press.
Battaglia, Debbora (2005) *E.T. Culture: Anthropology in Outerspaces*, Durham, NC: Duke University Press.
Camolli, Jean-Luc and Jean Narboni (2004)'Cinema/Ideology/Criticism.' In L. Braudy and M. Cohen (eds.) Film Theory and Criticism, Sixth Edition. New York: Oxford University Press.
Cowing, Mark and James Martin (2002) *Eighteenth Brumaire: Postmodern Interpretations*, London: Pluto Press.
Jameson, Frederic (2005) *Archaeologies of the Future*, London: Verso.
Kuhn, Annette (1999). *Alien Zone II*, London: Verso.
Marx, Karl (1852) 'The Eighteenth Brumaire of Louis Napoleon' in Cowing and Martin, James 2002 *Eighteenth Brumaire: Postmodern Interpretations*, London: Pluto Press.
Marx, K. and Engels, F (1965). *The Communist Manifesto*, translated by Sam Moore. Chicago: Regnery Co.
Spivak, Gayatri Chakravorty (1990) In Sarah Harasym (ed.) *The Postcolonial Critic: Interviews, Strategies, Dialogues*, London: Routledge.
Williams, Linda Ruth (1999) 'Dream Girls and Mechanic Panic: Dystopia and Its Others in *Brazil* and *Nineteen Eighty-Four*'. In I.Q Hunter (ed.) *British Science Fiction Cinema*, London: Routledge, pp. 153–169.

Afterword

George J. Sefa Dei

The Anticolonial Theory and the Question of Survival and Responsibility

In 1971, Steve Biko asserted: "[T]he most potent weapon of the oppressor is the mind of the oppressed" (Biko, 1987, p. 92). In recent months, one vexing question I have found myself responding to is: What is the future of race-centered Black radical politics with the election of Barack Obama as the US president? The implicit message is that we are in a post-racial context, and that Obama negates the saliency and necessity of race-centered politics. But since when has Black politics addressed race exclusively? Why is Obama being presented as the quintessential "transcender" of race? My quick and perhaps nutty response to the question has been to argue that the mere need to ask the question in the first place suggests that race (antiracist) politics is still urgently needed, even today. Having elected very few politicians of color in its most recent election, Canada would like to excuse itself and claim Obama too!

Hence, an anticolonial approach must necessarily be antiracist, in part because of the ways in which race and colonialism are intertwined. The link between state policies/practices and racist/colonial exclusions has been demonstrated time and again. The Empire was founded upon the construction of racist and colonizing hierarchies. Such hierarchies today continue to be the basis of distribution of rewards and punishments. Dominant bodies lay claim to a sense of entitlement, while oppressed communities struggle daily to resist claims of our "illegitimacy" and "degeneracy" (see Fanon 1963, 1967 among many others). Such claims of illegitimacy are not just about our bodies and/or what our mere physical presence signifies in certain spaces. They are also about how our indigenous/cultural resource knowledge and everyday experiences are dismissed as epistemologically worthless. The success of Obama needs to be interrogated along these lines and with these considerations in mind. The anticolonial discursive framework therefore articulates that the study of colonialisms, racism, and oppressions must be preoccupied with the experiences and knowledge of the oppressed, while simultaneously focusing on the benefits and privileges that accrue to the dominant/colonizer from their oppression. This analysis is no more important in South America than it is in

Canada – no more needed in Central Africa than it is in the US. North America is a site of dominant knowledge production historically, but there is more to the story. There is a corollary story of subverted knowledge and resistance which emanates from subjugated peoples and their knowings and experiences. The anticolonial framework acknowledges and works with the understanding that the self and subjectivity matter in terms of methodological implications/considerations, as well as in their epistemic standpoints (i.e., the ways we produce, interrogate, and validate knowledge). Anticolonial theory emphasizes that bodies and identities are linked to the production of knowledge. Therefore, the critical learner cannot distance herself or himself from a study of colonial and re-colonial processes and the construction of the knowledge about everyday oppressions. Such learning is important for understanding North American colonial and anticolonial relations and cannot happen from a distance.

One thing that has challenged me as an anticolonial/antiracist scholar and community worker is the task of treating knowledge production as a process which in and of itself, is in need of decolonization. We have not arrived at our anticolonial destination. As this collection demonstrates, the struggle – our struggle – continues not as a wide river but as disparate yet related tributaries, ideally heading in the same direction of discursive rupture and regeneration. There is much work to be done. We are continually being challenged and being called upon to ask new critical questions. The enormity of this task/challenge lies in the fact that colonial relations are continually being produced and reproduced to the extent that there is nothing really passé about colonialism and that today we are being confounded with complex colonizing relations, dominations, and reorganized colonial relations. We must rise to this challenge. So, while I agree that decolonization is an ongoing process, I have also come to believe that this realization is simply not enough. We must equally be raising questions about complicities and responsibilities in the anticolonial politics. We must take responsibility for the knowledge we produce. The anticolonial is about a collective experience, notwithstanding the particularities of histories and experiences. The anticolonial politics also recognizes that there are limits in claiming all identities as simply personal. So anticolonialism asks: How do we mobilize on the basis of collective histories, identities, and experiences in pursuit of politics? How do we bring these struggles together? How do we identify common goals alongside our identification of common sources of oppression?

One place to start with is an epistemic grounding in lived experiences of oppression. As argued elsewhere and by many others (see Dei 2000), the anticolonial is an approach to theorizing colonial and recolonial relations and the implications of imperial structures on the processes of knowledge production and validation; the understanding of Indigeneity; as well as the pursuit of agency, resistance, and subjective politics. Critical anticolonial theory and practice recognize a politicized reading of culture as critical to knowledge production. In fact, cultural paradigms shape knowledge and culture is salient in producing multiple ways of knowing. The advancement of any one cultural perspective cannot be universally applied and/or seen as superior to other perspectives. Indeed, although we are affected differently by dominant and nondominant media, there is a common experience of exposure, and thus potential for common resistance. A culturally grounded perspective that centers oppressed peoples' worldviews/perspectives helps resist the dominance of Eurocentric perspectives and can create counter-hegemonic knowings which challenge mainstream media and culture. Anticolonial thought is an epistemology of the colonized informed by a particular politics to interpret oppressed and colonized peoples' experiences on their own terms and evoke intellectual understandings not forced through Eurocentric lenses. The knowledge of resistance, struggle, and lived experience needs to be foregrounded in our reading of our world and that of others.

This, however, cannot be done recklessly. We need intellectual and political care in bringing a critique of colonizing/colonial knowledge to our practices in the academy, schools, or other workplaces. We can be effective if we evoke power, agency, and resistance simultaneously as we deal with colonial and anticolonial politics of knowledge production and social action. If, as Foucault (1977) maintains, knowledge is power, then there is the importance of developing an adequate analysis to explain power. This will require an anticolonial take on power that extends the Foucaultian conception of power. It is about not bringing an uncritical antiessentialist understanding of power as always and necessarily diffused. It is also not only about engaging power as multifaceted, relational, and contextual, but also about bringing intellectual and pedagogic clarity to the colonized–colonizer paradigm as a relation of unequal power. The power of the dominant does not equate to the power of the oppressed. This colonizer–colonized dialectic also points to the double-sidedness of colonizing encounters which must be understood in other complex ways beyond the notion of power as relational. The colonizer–colonized relation is also about dominant and subordinate perspectives, which are defined in power terms such that there is a dominant in so far as he or she creates a subordinate. Power is not the same everywhere and as hooks (1992) noted such "imposition of sameness is a provocation that terrorizes" (pp. 22–23).

We can no longer pretend that we do not see the colonizer and the colonized as distinct and yet connected. In every colonizing situation there is a clear oppressor and a clear oppressed. Saying that there are victims of oppression does not negate the resistance of the oppressor or the victimized. Even as we articulate our shared complicities in maintaining oppressions and subordination we must not forget the severity of issues for certain bodies in our midst. What do antiessentialists have to say about the reality that some groups in society continually face disproportionate rates of expulsions from school, prison incarceration, unemployment, poverty, etc.?

Long ago, Frantz Fanon (1963, 1967) instructed us that there is a physical, cultural, and spiritual context of colonialism and colonization. Colonization and intellectual imperialism have done an excellent job of Europeanizing our minds and we need a politics of de-Europeanizing minds (Asante 2009). We continually relapse into the long-standing colonizing narratives that show the power of "racialized common sense" (Howard 2006). In the name of resistance we must call on our intellectual agency to articulate critical knowledge – oppositional and resistant to the ways Eurocentric thinking continues to masquerade as the only valid, universal, and rationale thought in the academy. Such politics assert that we can no longer accept the wounding of our bodies, whether by dominant scholars/ scholarship or by minority scholars who struggle for acceptance and validation by beating down the scholarship of other peers. It used to be White scholars' gained credibility on the backs of oppressed and minority bodies, issues, and concerns. Today I have seen some minority scholars advance in academia by "beating down" on the oppositional scholarship of other minority scholars knowing full well that doing the colonizer's bidding pays! It shows an analytical sophistication, forgetting that academic sophistication is itself a game the academy plays and lauds as part of the business of elitism. In the spirit of an uncritical postmodern, while the push to the top acknowledges complexities, tensions, contingencies, ambivalences, and ambiguities, it often abandons such notions of home, community, and place as shared phenomena. But such calls for us to complicate these notions should not lead to their abandonment.

I believe strongly in using knowledge to address social and political alienation. We are alienated from ourselves, our histories, identities, and experiences. This is more than simply a case of "double alienation." It is a complete alienation and it can only be resisted when knowledge is engaged holistically to speak to the individual and collective cultural, spiritual, material, and emotional presence. Abandoning dominant ways of knowing in this context has become a matter of survival for us as well as other oppressed communities.

For bodies/scholars of color, in particular, the question of how we use power responsibly to resist colonizing relations will be critical. We are often persuaded by the logic of the dominant and the form such persuasion takes is not simply through a re-negation of our politics but through a different form of intellectual mimicry that forces us to seek legitimization and validation in White colonial spaces. As Maulana Karenga (cited in Asante 2009) has cautioned, when we fail to distinguish the "logic of the colonizer/oppressor" from the "logic of the colonized/oppressed" we are nowhere near finding or developing a "liberational logic." I see this "liberational logic" as a logic of oppositional resistance. Molefi Asante has also asked us to see "the objectivity of the dominant as their subjectivity." We cannot think solely with the inherited concepts that have emerged from Western traditions of philosophies. In fact we must also think outside of these traditions and sometimes discard these thoughts altogether (Asante 2009).

In retheorizing anticolonialism, I am heavily influenced by the writings of Frantz Fanon, Albert Memmi, Molefi Asante, Sylvia Winters, Patricia Hill Collins, Maulana Karenga, Joyce King, bell hooks, June Jordan, and others in calling for a direct engagement with diverse intellectual frames of reference relating to understandings of self, society, community, culture, history, and politics. Our intellectual analyses must simultaneously speak to the situation in which we find ourselves in the given historical moments and, as well, offer well-thought through solutions to contemporary challenges faced. We must continually search for our own intellectual footing and appropriate grounding in the academy, workplaces, and off-school community sites. As critical anticolonial scholars we cannot abandon the traditions of home, place, and culture at a time when the oppressed everywhere are reclaiming a sense of belonging to culture, place, history, and tradition – however imperfect. Anticolonial politics must be rooted in place, culture, and experience. We must identify some solid ground on which to stand (and not be apologetic about this) and make the case for anticolonial scholarship, even as these cultures, histories, experiences, and spaces are being continually negotiated. It is not an option to simply argue that "all grounds are shifting!" Are we all truly on "shifting grounds?" Who among us have their grounds so firmed up that others seeking to enter those territorial grounds are called upon to lay bare the grounds of their legitimacy, credibility, entitlement, and moral claims to space? Is not the dominant sense of entitlement continually defining what constitutes grounds for the oppressed to stand up? Defining and creating such spaces for ourselves has become a matter of survival. In other words, anticolonial scholars of minority backgrounds need a space to construct and privilege their own cultural, political, and intellectual agency and to address the knowledge crisis that afflicts our academies. Where such spaces exist within teacher education specifically, and within higher education generally, we must use them. Where they do not, we must create them. While honoring transhistorical understandings of who we are, we must create home, place, and community – arrest these phenomena from a wilderness which has prevented such organization for so long. Such spaces should not be read as "separation," "autarky," or going it alone. It is not a territorial claim in the sense of some early cultural nationalists, although their sentiment is understandable in terms of a space free from European racism. Indeed Eurocentric education is the segregated system of which we need to be weary.

With this said, the anticolonial theoretical framework is not simply for minority scholars. Anticolonialism must be articulated in the interests of all who struggle against colonialism, racism, myriad oppressions, capitalist imperialism, and other antihuman systems such as the gender, sexual, linguistic, religious oppression, and exploitation of [dis]ability. Anticolonialism is a call for intellectual analysis and politics informed society–culture and nature nexus. Anticolonial pedagogy is a key starting point in the practice of teaching and learning as an act of liberation. Issues of empire building, global politico-economic hegemonies, and struggles for cultural sovereignty are critical in the anticolonial formulations, and must be reflected in the education of all learners. In promoting anticolonial politics, the necessity to reclaim and affirm oppressed peoples' past intellectual traditions, knowledge, and the contributions in world history as a necessary exercise in our decolonization is significant. How do we construct a curriculum reflective not just of the histories but of the circumstances of domination? How do we move past false objectivity and simple notions of two-sidedness to embrace the notions of equity and justice in our pedagogical process and delivery? Equally relevant is the importance of reflecting on the present in order to theorize colonial and colonizing relations beyond set boundaries. Despite the calls of some popular academics, we do not and should not live, teach, or learn in a bubble. We should consider who (or what agenda) is best served by the maintenance of the discursive divide between teaching and activism. Who benefits from teachers' collective refusal to engage as activists, citing professionalism and objectivity? A denial of the inherently political implications and possibilities of education guarantees the supremacy of certain stories, histories, cultures, knowledges, and experiences to the detriment and exclusion of others. The cultural capital of dominant bodies passes invisibly into the terrains of success and achievement while nondominant bodies find embodied, cultural, and spiritual knowledges at best worthless and at worst unwelcome in the corridors of formal schooling. Anticolonial thought and practice calls for developing a collective consciousness of our interconnected realities and social existence as racialized and oppressed groups contest the future and set their own agenda forward. An anticolonial approach to the classroom (be it postsecondary or K–12) is a key terrain in this struggle.

It is argued that in strategizing and rethinking ways of addressing the problems and the many challenges confronting oppressed, we all need to heal ourselves spiritually, mentally, and materially. This calls for an affirmation of a sense of community, social responsibility, and spiritual re-embodiment. This is a search for a new anticolonial project that allows the oppressed people's struggle to define their own agenda for freedom and recognition and makes linkages with other peoples drawing on issues of community and responsibility.

Given the diversity of topics explored in this book, educators will be hard-pressed to not see any relevance for teacher education. As hooks (2003) and others have argued, teaching and teacher education are undergoing a transformation from dominant modes of banking model education delivery to problem posing education in pursuit of the practice of liberation and freedom. This is a struggle that extends beyond the classroom and formal institutions of schooling. Indeed the terrain of critical thinking and learning as emancipation is all around us. Teacher education needs to continue examining teaching, learning, and educational administration practices that reproduce colonial and reorganized colonial relations, which reflect the interconnected nature of communities (near and far) and the classroom. Teacher education must also recognize its potential central role in the struggle against colonial epistemology. Critical teaching must center key questions of power, difference, and identities of educators and learners in the delivery of education and must as well engage the internationalization of the politics of education. Contemporary changes in the global geopolitical scene and the broad macro-economies of schooling pose fundamental challenges in rethinking education. Market-driven reform policies have serious consequences for understanding education as we move into the next millennium. Discourse about school effectiveness, internationalization of education, and equity and inclusive schooling must center multiple actors as subjects of actual schooling experiences as they narrate the colonial and decolonizing experiences and processes of schooling. We can no longer couch educational change within a safe liberal and depoliticized understanding of schooling and education outside of an anticolonial context. We must critically engage difference as site of power and knowledge in schooling and educational processes. We cannot afford the potential of educational change to be muted over a failure to engage the critical issues of anticolonialism and decolonization. The works in this book continue the anticolonial conversation, centering the struggles and resistance of North American anticolonial experiences in their analysis. The next step, perhaps the teacher educator's task, is to draw out not only the interconnections between various sites of anticolonial resistance, but also to see the classroom as a potential manifestation of the anticolonial moment.

References

Asante, M. K. 2009. *Maulana Karenga: An Intellectual Topography of an Activist Scholar.* Cambridge: Polity Press.
Biko, S. 1987. *I Write What I Like.* New York: Heinemann.
Dei, G. J. S. 2000 "Rethinking the Role of Indigenous Knowledges in the Academy." *International Journal of Inclusive Education*, 4(2): 111–132.
Fanon, F. 1963. *The Wretched of the Earth.* New York: Grove Press.
Fanon, F. 1967. *Black Skin White Masks.* New York: Grove Press.
Foucault, M. 1977. "Two Lectures." In C. Gordon (ed.), *Power/Knowledge: Selected Interviews and Other Writings 1972–1977*, New York: Pantheon Books.
hooks, b. 1992. *Black Looks: Race and Representation.* Boston, MA: South End Press.
hooks, b. 2003. *Teaching Community: A Pedagogy of Hope.* New York: Routledge.
Howard, P.S.S. 2006. "On Silence and Dominant Accountability: A Critical Anticolonial Investigation of the Antiracism Classroom." In G.J.S. Dei and A. Kempf (eds.), *Anti-colonialism and Education: The Politics of Resistance* (pp. 43–62). Rotterdam: Sense Publishers.

Index

A

Ability to cope, 183, 184
Abu Gharib prison, 18, 23
Academic, 6, 7, 22, 31, 59, 69, 79, 85, 108, 109, 111, 117, 123, 127, 128, 140, 141, 143, 147, 154, 201, 211–213, 226, 240, 241
Access, 56, 65, 69, 74, 107, 139, 169, 182, 183, 187–190, 196, 197, 203, 210, 211, 213
Accountability, 1, 6, 14, 15, 17, 19–27, 29, 142, 230
Activist, 1, 17, 29, 31, 74, 91, 92, 95–101, 109, 116, 117, 123, 124, 127–130, 134, 141, 174, 234, 241
A Discourse on Colonialism, 21, 193
Adjei, P.B., 9, 137–156
Administration, 37, 84, 98, 99, 149, 168, 204, 242
Adorno, T., 84, 85
Affective engagement, 230, 231
Afghanistan, 2, 4, 13, 30
Africa, 1, 7, 16, 24, 29, 30, 36–39, 79–81, 83, 106, 110, 114, 119, 140, 141, 143, 149, 153, 159, 162, 182, 238
Africans
    African-American, 2, 23, 56, 107, 121–125, 138, 168, 207, 209, 210
    African-American community, 209
    African-Canadian, 9, 137–156
    African-Canadian parents, 9, 137–156
    descendants, 8, 11, 207, 208, 213
    diaspora, 206–213
Africentric
    classroom, 140, 141
    schools, 137–143, 148–156
    schools in Toronto, 139, 152–155
Afro-American, 163
Afro-Caribbean, 124

Afrocentric, 9, 31, 155
Afrocentricity,
Afrocentric schools, 9
Agency, 1, 9, 14, 29, 82, 85–87, 179, 182, 183, 196, 205, 213, 238, 239, 241
Agyepong, R., 9, 137–156
AIM. *See* American Indian Movement
Alba, 41
Alcoholism, 118
Algeria, 35, 192, 193, 197
Alienation, 10, 16, 54, 160, 193, 196, 240
Alignment, 9, 159, 160, 162
Al-Qaeda, 237, 246
Alternative education, 9, 140, 142, 143, 148, 154
Amadahy, Z., 8, 105–134
American Indian Movement (AIM), 40, 108, 109
American Indians, 70, 73, 123
Americanization, 5, 92, 94
American Revolution, 62
Americas, 9, 29–30, 106–108, 111, 119, 122, 124, 127, 132, 182, 221
Amputation, 5, 16, 21, 28, 31
Anarchism, 42, 43
Anishinabe, 116
Antebellum period, 213
Anthropocentric preoccupations, 223
Antiapartheid movement, 109
Anti-Black racism, 105, 108, 112, 125, 126
Anticapitalist, 23
Anticolonial
    critique, 97, 99
    discourse, 2, 6, 7, 15, 20, 79, 83, 186, 221, 222
    discursive framework, 221, 223, 224, 237
    education, 11, 54, 213, 219–223, 226, 227, 229–233
    global education, 223–225

259

Anticolonial (cont.)
    learning, 225, 227–229
    pedagogy, 11, 241
    project, 167, 209, 242
    spaces, 11, 219–234
    stance, 160, 223
Anticolonialism, 1, 4–6, 13–31, 71, 159–176, 224, 230, 232, 238, 240–242
Anti-ethnic violence, 164
Anti-immigrant, 162
Anti-imperial education, 219, 222
Anti-oppression, 17, 19, 121, 123
Antiracism, 18, 23–25, 105, 111, 116, 124, 153
Antiracist, 1, 2, 4, 17, 23, 31, 98, 109, 111, 115, 116, 123, 124, 127, 237, 238
Anti-Semitism, 164
Aotearoa, 40
Apartheid, 10, 109, 129, 130, 141, 153, 160, 165, 171, 175
Arawak, 221
Aristotelian, 54
Aristotle, 26–28
Arizona, 64, 78, 113
Armenia, 39
Ashanti, 29
Asia, 24, 30, 36, 43, 83, 114, 143, 162, 182
Asian, 6, 36, 74, 115, 165, 168
Asian-American, 7, 53, 54, 58
Athenians, 26, 27, 29
Athens, 26, 27
Atlantic slave trade, 106
Aubrecht, A., 10, 179–197
Australian, 5, 123, 124
Axes of power, 194
Aztec, 29

B
Baghdad, 13
Bandung Conference, 35
Bantu, 23
Basques, 41
Battlestar Galactica, 237–249
Bedouin, 39
Bell, D., 54, 58, 71–73
Benevolent imperialism, 96
Bhabba, H.K, 193, 197
Bias, 133, 144, 148, 220, 221, 225, 230, 231
Big Mountain Dine, 40
Biko, S., 141, 237
Biological, 180, 181, 183, 192, 193
Black
    Blackfoot, 113
    Black–Native intermarriage, 144

Black Skin, White Masks, 6, 173, 192
Cherokee, 109, 131
codes, 57
communities, 109, 115, 131, 137, 154
consciousness, 141
Indianness, 112, 113, 115
Indians, 9, 108, 109, 112, 114, 115, 121, 125, 131, 133
youth, 9, 137, 138, 142–148, 150, 154–156
Black Hills, 41
Blackness, 106, 123, 132, 138, 141, 155
Black Ojibways, 115, 121
Bladerunner, 243, 244, 247
Blanco, H., 39
Blood quantum measurement, 113
Boarding schools, 8, 74, 92–94
Bolivia, 39
Border
    crossing, 7
    intellectual, 80–81, 83
    patrol, 99
Borderlands, 7, 8, 79, 83, 92–96
Borderlands history, 96
Bourgeois, 22, 167, 191–195
Bourgeoisie, 167
Brazil, 7, 79, 80, 87, 124, 133
Breizh, 41
British, 5, 8, 38, 41, 110, 115, 133
Brittany, 41
Brown v. Board of Education, 58, 78, 151
Brumaire, 237–249
Burma, 38
Bush, G.W., 4, 96

C
Calderón, D., 7, 53–74
Caledonia, 41, 44, 128
California, 59, 61, 65, 168
Canada, 1–3, 6, 8–10, 19, 21, 40, 41, 105–134, 137, 139, 140, 142, 144, 149–153, 159–172, 174–176, 182, 223–225, 227, 237, 238
    classroom, 222
    economy, 173
Canadian labor movement, 160, 166, 170
Capitalism, 2, 10, 23, 36, 128, 160, 161, 165, 166, 174, 175, 184, 186, 192–195, 197, 201, 210, 211
Capitalist, 4, 10, 23, 31, 35, 127, 163–167, 173, 175, 189, 190, 192, 194–197, 202, 203, 207, 211, 213, 241
Capitalist labor processes, 173
Castro, F., 242

Index   261

Catalans, 41
Catholic, 92, 108
Catholic missionaries, 92
Celtic Cymru, 41
Central America, 30
Central American, 109
Césaire, C., 14, 20–25, 163, 181, 193, 195, 208, 213
Cesar Chavéz Day, 99
Chavez, C., 92
Chávez, H., 39
Cherokee nation, 63, 75, 78, 112
Chiapas, 39
Chicana, 8, 95
Chicano, 8, 95, 96, 100
Chickasaws, 112, 125
Chile, 80
China, 172
Choctaws, 112, 125, 132
Christian, 54, 70, 74, 92, 93, 121, 127
Christianize, 70
Churchill, W., 6, 35–45
CIO. *See* Committee for Industrial Organizations
Citizenship, 7, 16, 37, 53, 54, 56–58, 61, 62, 67–71, 74, 77, 97, 113, 132, 190, 208, 209, 224
Civilization, 2, 13, 15, 29, 30, 93, 96, 190, 193, 207, 212, 213
Civil rights, 7, 54–59, 62, 64–67, 71, 72, 74, 77, 108, 128, 151
Civil rights law, 7, 55, 56, 62, 71, 72, 77
Class
　reproduction, 9, 159
　rooms, 8–11, 26, 55, 59, 91–101, 140, 141, 143, 144, 149, 206, 219–225, 228–234, 242, 243
　struggle, 19, 82, 162
Climate change, 226
CME. *See* Colonial model of education
Collective action, 160, 162, 165, 169, 171, 173, 175
Colonial
　administrator, 167
　blind, 7, 53, 54, 67, 72, 73
　bodies, 206
　domination, 35, 40, 62, 120, 139, 140, 221, 223, 225, 234
　education, 7, 8, 21, 28, 53–74, 139, 212
　embodiment, 191, 192, 195
　expansion, 126, 159
　hegemony, 4, 27, 79
　imperative, 8, 185–187
　legacies, 11

　occupation, 119, 193
　ontology, 54, 55, 62, 67, 70, 74
　relations, 1, 8, 14, 17, 20, 23–27, 29, 31, 85, 105, 118, 160, 163, 165–167, 173, 187, 224, 225, 232, 238, 242
　schools, 8, 207
　script, 237, 240
　subjects, 37, 208
　university, 10, 11, 201–206, 209–215
Colonialists, 8, 22, 24, 25, 83, 84, 86, 87, 93–95, 97, 107, 118, 132, 133, 166, 194, 195, 209
Colonial model of education (CME), 70, 73
Colonial moment, 16, 21, 22, 55
Colonization process, 9, 108, 113, 121, 159, 163, 171
Colonized people, 24, 179, 181, 187, 239
Colony, 24, 35, 41, 113, 163, 167, 172, 173, 176
Color blindness, 2, 73, 96
Columbus, C., 107, 221, 228
Comanche, 123
Committee for Industrial Organizations (CIO), 168, 175
Commodification, 84, 211
Communities of color, 54, 56, 61, 69–71, 73, 115, 166, 168, 173, 175, 206
Community Benefit Agreement, 160, 161, 173
Community-controlled schools, 71
Community unionism, 10, 159–176
Congress (US), 62, 63, 65, 66
Consciousness transformation, 18
Control, 1, 13, 31, 36–38, 41, 63, 71, 92, 93, 99, 100, 107, 113, 115, 119, 139, 140, 168, 173, 181, 185, 187, 188, 191, 194–196, 201–204, 212, 213, 224
Cornwall, 41
Corsica, 41
Corsicans, 41, 45
Cosmopolitanism, 193
Co-teaching, 228
Counterinsurgency, 42
Creation stories, 116
Cree, 41, 45, 113, 123
Creeks, 112, 125
Critical literacy, 7, 79
Critical pedagogy, 79
Critical praxis, 229
Critical race theory, 77
Critical whiteness, 6, 15, 20, 24, 25
Crow, J., 108, 167
Cultural capital, 5, 81, 242
Cultural environments, 179
Cultural genocide, 119, 126, 139
Cultural identities, 108, 109, 139, 208, 210, 226

Cultural imperialism, 86
Cultural pluralism, 116, 210
Cultural politics, 83
Cultural transformation, 8, 31, 93, 94, 149
Curriculum, 54, 68–70, 143, 144, 147, 153, 208, 212, 213, 241
  guidelines, 226
Cylon, 238–240, 242–249

D

Decolonization, 15, 19, 36, 40, 42, 85, 130, 195, 230, 238, 241, 242
Dehumanization, 164
Dei, G., 1, 4, 14–18, 20, 21, 25, 26, 28, 138–141, 143, 145–146, 149, 154–156, 219–222, 224, 226, 230, 232
De-Indianize, 70
Democracy, 26, 96, 100, 132, 193, 226
Dene, 41
Denial, 2, 5, 28, 62, 107, 241
Depression, 95, 179, 188, 193
Desegregation, 61, 151
Developing countries, 179, 186
Development, 6, 10, 11, 27, 31, 35, 40, 55, 56, 62, 70, 116, 117, 129, 130, 137, 155, 160, 167, 171, 176, 180, 183, 188, 189, 192–195, 197, 207, 208, 214, 222, 224, 226, 228, 229, 231
De Walt, P.S., 10–11, 201–215
Dialectical, 21, 161, 165
Dialogical actors, 233
Dialogical approach, 228, 232
Dialogue, 7, 80, 82, 83, 105, 134, 219, 220, 225, 228, 234
Diaspora, 21, 105, 119, 124, 149, 206–213
Diasporic, 105, 106, 115, 116, 124, 127, 128
Dirlik, A., 36, 43, 44
Disability, 3, 10, 14, 16, 19, 142, 182, 188, 190–192, 194–196, 209
  studies, 179–181, 187, 197
  studies perspective, 179–181
Disciplinarity, 8, 91–101
Discourse, 1–3, 5–8, 10, 15, 17, 20, 21, 23, 25, 38, 53–56, 58, 67, 68, 70
Discrimination, 29, 61, 65, 67–69, 71, 99, 114, 118, 142, 150, 152, 168, 188, 190, 191, 193, 196
Discursive arrangement, 224
Discursive regime, 8, 92, 95, 96
Disempowerment, 106, 141, 232
Dissent, 66, 92, 98–100, 143, 205, 212, 220
Diversity, 7, 10, 37, 53, 54, 56, 62, 63, 65, 68, 70, 71, 73, 74, 116, 117, 179–197, 242
  rationale, 59–61, 67, 69, 77

Divide-and-conquer, 213
Doctrine of discovery, 54, 62, 74, 119
Dominant society, 185
Domination, 8, 13–15, 18, 20, 23, 26, 27, 29, 30, 35, 40, 62, 82–84, 95, 120, 139–141, 161, 165, 203, 220–223, 225, 230, 232, 234, 238, 241
Double consciousness, 176, 208–210, 215
Douglass, F., 206
Dred Scott decision, 57
Drop(ping) out, 144–147, 151, 155
Drug addiction, 118
Drug use, 179
Du Boisian, 10, 201
Du Bois, W.E.B., 10, 176, 201, 202, 207–211, 214, 215
Dutch, 5, 121

E

East Asia, 114, 115
East Timor, 38
Economic apartheid, 10, 160, 165, 171, 175
Economic disparity, 183
Economic viability, 184–185
Education, 1, 8–11, 16, 21, 26–28, 53–74, 77–79, 93, 94, 97, 118
Educational research, 7
Educators, 7, 68–69, 73, 79–86, 94–95, 98, 99, 137, 143, 145, 148, 150, 154, 155, 219, 220, 223–225, 228–234, 242–243
Edward, S., 84, 215
Eli Lilly, 189
El Paso, Texas, 6, 8, 91–92, 94–101
Emancipation, 82, 108, 122, 174–175, 242
Embodiment, 10, 93, 179, 185, 191–192, 195, 197, 206, 242
Emergency, 183–185, 191
Empire, 1, 4–5, 13, 26–27, 54, 85, 166, 237, 241
English, 15, 21, 91, 94–95, 101, 110, 115, 133, 208
English-speaking, 40, 173–174
Enlightenment, 54, 83, 139, 182
Enslaved laborers, 203
Enslavement, 201–203, 206, 207, 210, 214
Environment, 42–43, 81, 108, 128, 145, 147, 179–181, 214, 223–224, 226–228
Equal Employment Opportunities Act, 65
Equality, 3, 7, 53, 54, 56, 58, 59, 61–62, 67–73, 77, 81, 115, 127, 132, 191, 196, 208
Equal opportunity, 59
Equal Protection Clause, 59–61
Erasure, 5, 111, 115, 117, 118, 120, 121, 125, 132, 192

Ethnic, 83, 87, 229
Ethnicity, 14–16, 19, 20, 26, 29, 60, 91–92, 142, 153, 215
Etobicoke, 173
Euro-American, 14, 15, 21–23, 29, 93–97, 138, 141, 145, 150–151, 154
Eurocanadian, 40
Eurocentric identity, 142
Eurocentric thinking, 220, 239–240
European
 expansion, 53, 227–228
 expansionism, 227–228
 imperialism, 35–38
Euskadi, 41
Exclusions, 9, 17, 23, 26, 65, 81, 84, 86, 111, 126, 162, 191, 193, 206–207, 237, 241–242
Experiential knowledge, 140
Exploitation, 5–6, 10, 36, 84, 99–100, 160, 166, 168, 183, 208, 214, 241

F
False borders, 229
Family violence, 118–119
Fanon, F., 6, 10, 14, 16, 20–21, 24, 25, 28, 31, 36, 43, 83, 163, 164, 166, 167, 173, 180, 186, 191–195, 197, 201, 203, 206, 212, 215, 222, 237, 239–240
Fanonian, 10–11, 201
Federal Indian Law, 7, 54–57, 62–67, 71–73, 77
Feminism, 17, 164
Feminist, 3–4, 17, 81, 109, 134
Feminist theory, 223–224
Fetal alcohol syndrome, 119
Finland, 41–42, 189
First Nations communities, 162, 224, 228
First Nations People, 3
First Peoples, 1
First World, 6, 10, 35, 40, 79, 85, 87, 175
Fletcher, B., 174
Former colony, 35–36
Foucault, M., 189, 222, 224, 225
Fourteenth Amendment, 57–61, 78
Fourth World, 6–7, 35–45, 119
Fourth World peoples, 37–38
France, 23–24, 41, 173, 193
Free African, 133, 204, 206, 213
Freedmen, 112, 125, 214
Freire, P., 7, 31, 79–88, 163–165, 186, 215, 230
French, 6, 21, 23, 43, 110, 111, 115, 192
French Indochina, 38
Fur trade, 113

G
Gaius Baltar, 237–249
Gender roles, 93–94
Geneva, 80, 190
Genocide, 5, 70, 105–110, 118–120, 124–126, 130, 139–140, 228
Ghana, 16, 139, 144, 145, 225
Ghanaians, 5, 16, 225
Giroux, H.A., 7, 31, 79–88
Global education, 11, 219–234
Global educators, 219, 220, 223, 232
Global imperialism, 5, 191–192
Global inequity, 224, 225
Globalization, 5, 110, 119, 197, 223
Global order, 222–224
Governance, 4, 37, 41, 100, 113, 182, 185, 186, 188, 192–193, 226
Graduate student, 59, 203–206, 209, 215, 225–226
Gramsci, A., 10, 81, 201
Gramscian, 10, 204
Grand River, 128
Green zone, 13–14
G.W.F. Hegel, 237

H
Haldimand Tract, 128
Hampton, 207
Haudenosaunee confederation, 40–41
Hawaii, 172
Hawaiian Archipelago, 38
Hawaiians, 41, 65
Health, 182, 184, 187, 190
Hegemony, 4, 27, 79, 81, 91, 132, 201
Hemingway, E., 122–123
Heterosexist, 205
Heuristic, 30
Hierarchical institutional power dynamics (HIPDs), 11, 203–205, 213
Hierarchy, 5–6, 23, 72–74, 100, 142, 164, 203–204, 214
Hill, H., 128, 129
HIPDs. *See* Hierarchical institutional power dynamics
Historiography, 6, 15, 27–30, 96
History, 4–6, 13–16, 21, 26–30, 39, 54, 56–58, 71, 80, 81, 83, 85–87, 94–96, 106, 108–110, 113, 114, 120, 123, 126, 128, 137–142, 149, 152–154, 160, 166–167, 173–175, 181–186, 191, 193, 197, 225, 233, 240–241
HIV/AIDS, 131
Holistic education, 213
Hooks, B., 87, 124, 153, 215, 240

Host world, 43
Hotel
    industry, 171–174
    workers, 9, 159–176
Hotel Workers' Rising, 160, 161, 172, 175
House Bill 4437, 91, 100
Housekeeper, 172–174
Human agency, 86–87, 196
Hutnyk, J., 237–249
Hutu, 29
Hybridity, 11, 25–26

I
Ibos, 38
Identity consciousness, 221
Ideology, 7, 54, 61–62, 64, 79, 84,
    131, 133, 149, 168, 169, 191,
    195, 211–212
Illegal, 95, 96, 100, 101, 120, 129, 130, 132
Ill individuals, 185, 197
Illness, 10, 179–197
    discourse, 181, 186, 187
Immigrant workers of color, 9, 159, 169
Immigration reform, 91–92, 96, 97
Imperial imposition, 226
Imperialism, 1, 5, 6, 35–38, 53, 79, 83, 86–87,
    96, 106–107, 139, 191–192, 210, 222,
    224, 232, 239–241
Inclusiveness, 212, 213
India, 6, 15, 36, 38, 225
    Indian Act, 113, 114, 125
    Indian Civil Rights Act, 64
    Indianness, 111–113, 115, 122
    Indian Reorganization Act, 65
    Indian status, 111, 114, 132
Indians, 7, 9, 30, 39, 40, 54–57, 62–67, 70–74,
    77, 78, 91–94, 100, 107–115, 120–123,
    125, 131–133, 225
Indigeneity, 105, 110, 111, 114,
    123–127, 218
Indigenism, 43, 109–110, 117, 128, 130
Indigenous Australians, 123–124
Indigenous communities, 8–9, 92, 93,
    106–107, 112, 113, 115–117, 119, 124,
    126, 127, 129–131
Indigenous education, 7, 53–74
Indigenous histories, 116, 117
Indigenous land, 3, 111, 120
Indigenous languages, 112–113
Indigenous nations, 37–38, 42, 105, 112, 118,
    128, 130, 131
Indigenous peoples, 5–8, 37, 39, 54, 69–71,
    105–134

Indigenous rights, 42, 61–62, 64
Indigenous struggle, 109, 127–130
Indigenous worldview, 109, 116
Individualizing, 185, 187
Industrial production, 105–106
Inferiority, 21, 83–84, 137–138, 141, 192–193,
    195, 208
Institutional barrier, 208–209
Integration, 56, 58, 59, 61, 70, 74, 77, 152,
    169–170, 182, 185, 189, 208
Integrative antiracism, 17–18
Intellectual labor, 10–11, 201–215
Intellectuals, 7, 10–11, 21–22, 59, 68, 80–81,
    83–87, 109–110, 191–193, 201–215,
    238–241
Interactivity, 18, 42
Interest convergence, 72–73
Intermarriage, 111, 112, 114, 122, 126, 132
Internal colonialism, 161–164, 171,
    174–175
International development, 226,
    228–229
International Political Economy, 226
International Women's Day, 173
International Workers of the World, 168
Interpretive mechanism, 68
Interracial organizing, 175
Interracial unity, 160
Interrelatedness, 187
Inuit, 113
Invisibility, 22, 29, 123, 145, 173–176, 202
Iran, 3–4, 39
Iraq, 2, 13, 14, 18, 23, 30, 39, 96
Iraqi, 18
Iroquois confederacy, 113
Isle of Mann, 41
Israel, 3–5, 39, 40, 129, 130

J
Jamaica, 118, 132, 133, 227
James, C.L.R., 28, 40
Japan, 58
Java, 35
Jicarilla tribe, 63–64
Jihad, 241
Johnson and Johnson, 189
Judeo-Christian, 54, 70
Jurisprudence, 7, 54, 55, 61–62, 65, 67, 68, 71,
    73, 77
Jurisprudential, 7, 53–74
Justice, 1, 5, 19, 59–66, 72, 81, 129, 138,
    142, 152, 154, 155, 162–163, 184,
    196, 219, 241

K

Kachins, 38
Kanaka Maoli, 41
Kanenhstaton, 128, 129, 134
Kapital, 238
Karins, 38
Katangese, 38
Kennedy, J.F., 242
Kernow, 41
Kincheloe, J., 220
King Jr., M.L., 3, 154–155
King, L., 237–249
King Leopold, 38, 49
Klein, N., 13
Knowledge, 5, 7, 10–11, 14, 15, 19, 20, 53, 54, 68, 73, 82, 85–86, 100, 106, 108, 111–113, 115–116, 124, 127, 130
Korematsu v. United States, 58, 78
KRS-ONE, 91, 100
K-12 school, 10–11, 201–203, 208, 213
Kurds, 39

L

Labor
 organizing, 159, 164, 175
 studies, 161
Lakota, 41
Language, 5–6, 14, 21, 22, 55, 68–70, 74, 80, 82–86, 94–95, 99, 101, 111–113, 118–119, 127, 131, 137–141, 190, 195, 196, 209, 213, 214
Laos, 38
Lapps, 41–42
Latina, 7, 53, 54
Latin America, 1, 7, 19, 30, 39, 42, 79, 83, 126, 143
Latin Americans, 6, 172
Latino, 3, 7, 53, 54, 56, 70–71, 74
Lawrence, B., 8, 105–134
Legal theory, 62–63
Liberal approach, 223–224
Liberal education, 207–208
Liberating pedagogy, 205
Liberation, 6–7, 14–16, 19, 23, 35–37, 39, 40, 42, 127, 141, 205, 240–242
Literacy, 7, 14–15, 26–27, 79, 81, 82
Literature, 14, 24, 40, 117, 122, 123, 163, 169–170, 180, 185, 202–203, 209, 215
Local knowledges, 221
López, A.R., 8, 20, 25, 91–101
Los Angeles, 99, 172
Louis Bonaparte, 237, 239
Louisiana Act, 57–58, 78
Luzon, 38
Lynching, 2–3

M

Macedo, D., 83, 84
Macedonians, 29–30
Mainstream media, 96–98, 155, 238–239
Makahs, 41
Malcolm X, 2–3
Mannin, 41
Maoist, 38–40
Maori, 29, 40
Mao Zedong, 35
Mapping, 85, 139–142, 180–182, 187, 195, 196
Marcuse, H., 202, 211, 212
Marginality, 107, 119, 122, 126
Marginalization, 2, 26–28, 121, 183, 193, 213
Marianas, 38
Marianas Marshall Islands, 38
Maritimes, 110, 114, 115, 121
Marketable knowledge, 201
Marriage customs, 93
Marshall, T., 63–64, 66
Marshall trilogy, 62, 63, 77
Martinique, 192, 193
Marxian, 10–11, 39, 201
Marxist, 2.2, 9–10, 39, 74, 127, 164
Marx, K., 16, 159, 165, 174, 222
Materialism, 128
Materiality, 24
McGill University, 225–226
McNamara, R., 242
Media, 21, 96–98, 129, 133, 137, 139, 141, 153–155, 176, 238, 239
Mediation, 197
Medicalization, 19, 183–185, 187, 189
Medicalizing, 187
Mediterranean, 41
Memmi, A., 13, 14, 19, 20, 24, 25, 28, 36, 163, 164, 166, 175, 210, 222, 240
Mental difference, 10, 179, 181–183, 191, 197
Mental diversity, 10, 179–197
Mental health, 179–197
Mental Health Improvements for Nations Development (MIND), 187–190, 193, 195
Mental illness, 10, 179–191, 196, 197
Mercier Bridge, 41
Metaphysics, 7, 53–55, 73
Methodology, 142–143
Mexican, 8, 39, 92–101, 168, 208
Mexican-American learners, 208
Mexican immigrants, 99–100

Mexican Independence Day, 94
Mexican revolution, 39
Mexico, 8, 39, 80, 92–100, 167
Michalko, R., 188, 197
Micronesia, 38
Middle-class, 3, 80–81, 137, 152
Middle East, 4, 6–7, 29, 39
Migrant workers, 8–9
Mi'kmaq, 41, 110, 111, 113–115, 120, 121, 126, 133
Militarization, 37, 99–100
MIND. *See* Mental Health Improvements for Nations Development
Mindanao, 38
Minh-ha, T., 13–14
Minority education, 7, 54, 67–68, 71
Minority rights, 56–62, 64–65, 70, 72–73
Miskitos, 39
Missionary, 92, 94, 100
Mississauga, 171–172
Mohawk, 29, 40–41, 120, 231
Montreal, 40–41, 110–111, 114, 128, 133, 152, 170, 225–226
Morales, E., 39–40
Moral imperative, 24, 226
Morocco, 39
Morrison, T., 122–124, 133, 142
Mother country, 20–21, 163, 167
Mother Earth, 116–117
Multicentric, 16–17, 30–31
Multicultural education, 7, 53, 55, 56, 67–72, 77, 226
Multiculturalism, 2–3, 7, 9–10, 53–74, 77, 115, 132, 153
Multimodal lens, 213
Muslim, 129
　faith, 4
　groups, 3–4
Mutable colonialism, 212
Mutually supportive, 118, 119, 232–233

N
NAACP, 58
NAFTA, 167
Napoleon, 239
Nationalism, 37, 39, 91–92
Nationalistic, 205
National liberation, 35–36, 39
Nation-state, 56–57, 67, 69, 70, 74, 106, 122, 127, 160, 163–166, 173–174
Native Americans, 43, 53, 54, 74, 112–113, 121, 122, 124–127
Native-Black relations, 105, 113

Native-informed frameworks, 7
Native people, 38–40, 42, 70–71, 74, 77, 93, 105, 111–114, 120–126, 132, 133
Nativist, 97–98, 168–169, 175
Natural resources, 65–66
Navajo nation, 66, 113
Negritude, 23, 31
Neocolonialism, 14, 26, 27, 38
Neocolonialist, 36
Neutrality, 83
Nevada, 41, 66, 78
New Brunswick, 110, 133, 152
Newes, 41
New Guinea, 38
New imperialism, 222, 224, 232
New Mexico, 92, 93, 96, 100
New York city, 107, 108, 137
New Zealand, 5, 30, 40, 83, 189
Nicaraguan, 39
Nikita Khrushchev, 242
9/11, 44
Nkrumah, K., 36, 38, 43, 44
NMCE. *See* Normative Multicultural Education
Non-Western positions, 221, 225
Nonwhite, 61, 70, 173
Normalizing gaze, 10, 14, 179, 189
Normally protective supports, 183, 184
Normative Multicultural Education (NMCE), 53, 56, 67–72
North America, 6–8, 30, 40–41, 79–80, 83–84, 109–110, 120, 122, 123, 141, 144, 150–151, 161–162, 167–168, 170, 172, 220, 222, 225, 227–228, 231, 237–238
Northern Ireland, 40, 41
North Korea, 241, 246
North-South economic relations, 227
Norway, 41, 189
Nova Scotia, 41, 120, 152

O
OAU. *See* Organization of African Unity
Obama, B., 2–4, 17, 237
Objectives, 1, 18, 22, 39, 82, 100, 154, 189, 191, 211, 223–226
Objectivity, 54, 83, 220, 229, 240–242
Occupation, 13, 14, 18, 40–41, 93, 172, 183, 192–193, 223
Oceanic, 6–7
Oka crisis, 231
Okinawa, 38
Oklahoma, 59, 78, 112, 131
Oliphant v. Suquamish Indian Tribe, 65–66, 78
One-drop rule, 107

Ontario, 114, 115, 120, 121, 128, 130, 152, 155, 172
Ontological, 2–3, 15, 23, 55–56, 67, 73, 160–161
Oppression, 2, 4, 6, 8–10, 13–25, 27–31, 37–38, 55, 84, 85, 105, 111, 113, 121–123, 159–160, 165, 166, 189, 191–192, 230, 237–238, 241
Oral histories, 8, 94, 109, 116, 131
Oral testimonies, 94, 95
Organization of African Unity (OAU), 37
Organized labor, 160–161, 164, 167–171, 173, 175
Orientalism, 85
Orientialist, 85
Otherness, 81, 86, 117, 213
Ownership, 74, 123, 128–129, 169, 171

P
Palau, 38
Palestinians, 2, 39, 129
Pan-African, 36
Pan-African Union, 38
Panoptic gaze, 224
Papuans, 38
Patriarchal norms, 205
Pedagogy
  of organizing, 169
  practice, 79, 83, 143, 154, 223
People of color, 2–3, 8, 111, 152, 172
Peruvians, 225
Pharmacological approach, 186
Philadelphia, 108
Physical education, 231
Plantation
  owner, 203, 212
  system, 203–205
Plantational approach, 11, 202–206, 213
Plessy, H.A., 151
Plessy v. Ferguson, 57, 78, 151
Pluralism, 73, 116, 210, 211
Poetry, 87, 118
Police, 93, 98–99, 101, 118, 134
Policies, 2, 31, 55–56, 59, 61–62, 68, 70, 74, 77, 99, 101, 105, 108, 113–115, 119, 127, 132–133, 138, 154–155, 169, 176, 180–182, 185, 188, 212, 237, 242
Polisario Liberation Front, 39
Political resistance, 87
Politics, 1–11, 16, 18–19, 26, 28, 31, 37, 39, 41–42, 79–88, 95, 109, 141, 154, 164, 168, 237–239

Postcolonial
  discourse, 7, 79, 85–87, 111
  framework, 111
Postcolonialism, 6, 7, 14, 25–27, 79–88
Post-coloniality, 40
Postmodern, 81, 83, 84, 87, 240
Postmodernist, 87
Poverty, 27, 118, 130, 172, 180–181, 184, 188, 189, 227, 239
Power, 1, 4–8, 10–11, 16, 18–21, 25–27, 29, 30, 36, 40, 63–64, 66, 69, 79–80, 83–87, 92–93, 95
Powerlessness, 91, 100, 105, 232
Praxis, 55, 165, 220–221, 223, 225, 228–234
Privilege, 3, 7, 17–29, 31, 57, 72, 79, 83, 85–87, 108, 111, 117, 140, 142, 151, 154, 162, 169, 187, 211, 222, 224, 227–228, 234, 237, 241
Problem population, 188–191, 193
Problem-posing, 79, 83, 242
Productivity, 184–185, 188, 212
Progress, 3, 17, 22, 24, 31, 53, 68, 79, 92, 95, 96, 119, 123–124, 131, 148, 150, 160, 169, 174, 175, 182, 193, 222, 224
Protestant, 108
Psychological
  knowledge, 188, 190, 195
  liberation, 205
  problems, 183–185
  relations, 182
Psychology, 24, 181, 189

Q
Quebec, 111, 231
Quechan, 39
Queer theory, 17

R
Race, 2–4, 9, 16–20, 22–26, 29–30, 56–61, 64–65, 67, 71–72, 77, 94, 97, 107, 109, 124, 132–133
Racelessness, 2
Racial
  empowerment, 126
  power, 92, 97, 101
  progress, 3
Racialization, 93, 111, 161–162, 175
Racialized minorities, 59, 71
Racialized people, 9, 119, 126, 129, 132
Racist, 4, 22–23, 27, 96, 98, 101, 114, 123, 149–151, 160, 162, 164, 175, 237
Radical feminism, 164

Radical Praxis, 165
Re-colonialization, 164–167, 174–175
Reconstruction, 82, 141, 167
Reflection theory, 240
Reflexive space, 220
Re-historicization, 224
Reification, 54, 80
Relative resilience, 184
Religion, 14, 16, 29, 54, 142, 153, 202, 215
Re-mapping, 10, 179–197
Representation, 3, 16–17, 79–80, 83, 84, 86, 96, 98, 101, 145, 176, 185, 190, 196, 203–204, 209, 228
Reserve (Native), 7, 21, 38–43, 53–54, 65, 67, 70–71, 73–74, 77, 92–93, 95, 96, 99, 105–106, 110–115, 117
Residential schooling, 118, 140
Resistance, 1, 4–8, 13–15, 18, 20, 22–24, 26–31, 38–40, 81–82, 87, 92–94, 99, 109, 111, 115, 124, 126, 129
Responsibility, 22, 38, 62, 129–130, 142, 145, 147, 154, 189, 192, 214, 228, 237–243
Revolution, 17–18, 20, 24, 28, 31, 35–37, 39, 43, 54, 62, 81, 84, 106, 176, 197, 212
Revolutionary, 17, 22, 28, 30, 36, 39, 79, 84, 164, 174
Reynolds tobacco plantation, 108
Rhodesia, 40
Rotinosoni, 116, 126
Ruby Valley Treaty, 41
Ryukyu chain, 38

S
Sahara, 37–39, 165
Said, E., 84, 215
Salience, 160–161
Salt water requirement, 37
Samis, 41
Samoa, 38
Sandinista, 39
San Francisco, 45, 100, 172
Sartre, J.P., 163, 191, 209
Sawchuk, P.H., 9–10, 19, 159–176
Scandinavia, 41
Schizophrenia, 179, 188, 193
Schooling, 7–9, 53–74, 118, 140–142, 145, 147–151, 153, 154, 201, 207–208, 242
Scotland, 41
Second World War, 114, 123, 163
Segregation, 2, 9, 58–59, 61, 94, 108, 112, 133, 137, 143, 151–154, 164, 168, 241
Self-determination, 6–7, 35–45, 54, 62–64, 69, 74

Semi-colonized, 8
Seminoles, 112, 125, 133
Sendero Luminoso, 39
Senegalese, 225
Sex, 31
Sexual abuse, 118
Sexuality, 3, 5, 14, 16, 19–20, 26, 142
Sexual practices, 93
Shock and Awe, 228
Shor, I., 83, 84
Six Nations, 41, 128–129, 131, 133–134
Skinjob, 243, 247, 248
Slavery, 2, 26, 28, 56–57, 105–107, 112–114, 119–127, 130, 151, 153, 202, 206, 214
Slaves, 2, 56–57, 64, 106, 112, 120, 122–123, 125, 133, 150, 154, 159, 167, 203, 214
Social change
  education, 227
  educators, 230
Social-class, 69
Social formations, 81, 92, 151
Socialist, 31, 35, 127, 168
Socialist-oriented, 127
Socialization, 201, 213–214
Social justice perspective, 219
Social location, 5, 16, 20, 55
Social memory, 80
Social movements, 1, 10, 86, 160, 163, 169
Social movement theory, 10
Social praxis, 55
Social relations, 7, 80, 82, 85
Sociolegal scholars, 55
Sojourner Truth, 206
Solidarity, 19, 87, 91, 105, 109, 128–130, 160, 163, 167, 169–170, 173–174, 226
Solomons, 38
South Africa, 40, 109, 141, 143, 153, 159
South Asia, 36, 43, 114–115
Southeast Asia, 165, 182
Sovereignty, 7, 54, 56, 62–63, 65–67, 69–74, 77, 109, 111, 129–131, 241
Spanish, 5, 8, 41, 44, 91–95, 99, 101, 137
Spirituality, 15–16, 21, 23, 116–117, 124, 127, 131, 133, 140–141, 143, 148, 150, 153, 213, 215, 229, 239–240, 242
Spivak, G., 25, 86, 88
Standard English, 208
Standardization, 84, 189
Standpoint, 162, 164, 165, 170, 227, 233, 238
State of health, 185
State of illness, 185
Structural boundaries, 231

Index

Students, 8–11, 19, 59–61, 68–70, 74, 77, 83, 91–101, 108–109, 111, 138–141, 143–151, 153–154
Student teachers, 11, 225, 233
Subaltern, 9, 159, 162, 208
Suicide, 82, 119, 131, 191
Surrealist Group of France, 24
Sweden, 41
Swedish, 5

T

Taino, 126
Talented tenth, 207
Teachers, 11, 19, 69, 80, 91, 93–95, 98–99, 108, 137, 140–141, 143–149, 152–155, 207, 211, 219, 225
Teacher training, 154
Teaching, 7, 11, 68, 69, 79, 108–110, 116, 133, 140, 144, 146, 205–207, 219–221, 226, 228–234, 241–242
Teamsters union, 168
Team-teaching, 11, 219
Telemarketers, 6
Teleology, 83
Terra nullius, 113
Terror, 27, 45, 84, 100, 211, 239
Thanksgiving address, 116
The Bill of Rights, 57
The Colonizer and the Colonized, 23–24, 163, 164, 166, 181, 193, 211, 239
The Daily Show, 2
The El Paso Times, 101
Theological, 23
Theology, 54, 127
The Philippines, 38, 172
The Souls of Black Folk, 210
The Veil, 210
The Wall Street Journal, 171
Third world
  intellectual, 85
  revolution, 28, 35, 37
Third worldism, 36, 39
Thirteenth amendment, 57, 151
Three Fires Confederacy, 113
Titchkosky, T., 10, 179–197
Tolerance, 3–4, 117, 138, 155, 207
Toronto, 9, 19, 109, 111, 114, 128–130, 132, 137–139, 141–145, 148, 152–156, 159–161, 170
Trade unionism, 9
Treatment regimes, 182, 184
Tribal citizens, 70, 112–113
Tribal sovereignty, 63, 65–67, 71, 72

Trust relationship, 54, 62–63
Tubman, H., 206
Tuhiwai-Smith, L., 107, 221
Tulsa, 18
Turkey, 39
Turtle Island, 110, 116, 128–131
Tuskegee, 207
Tutsis, 29
Two Row, 131
Tyendinaga, 128

U

Undergraduates, 11, 60, 139, 204–205, 209, 215, 226
Underground railroad, 120
Unionization, 164, 166–167, 169, 171, 173–174
Union leaders, 174
United Nations, 37, 106
United Nations Charter, 37
United Needletrades, Industrial Textile Employees–Hotel and Restaurant Employees (UNITE-HERE), 172–173
United States, 1–4, 6–9, 11, 13, 14, 21, 23, 29, 36, 40, 53–74, 77, 78, 80, 91, 93–97, 100, 105, 110, 112–114, 121–126, 128, 132, 151
Universal, 29, 54, 63, 72–74, 80, 83, 167–168, 188, 191, 238, 240
Universalism, 29, 54, 73
University
  brand, 11, 206
  as a colonial space, 202
University of California v. Bakke, 59, 61, 65, 78
University system, 10, 11, 201–215
Unrelatedness, 186
U.N. Working Group on Indigenous Peoples, 106
U.S. Bureau of Indian Affairs, 40
US-European colonialism, 29
US exceptionalism, 29
US/Mexico borderland, 8, 92–96
US occupation, 93
USSR, 242, 244
US Supreme Court, 55, 57, 60, 62

V

Values, 3, 5, 6, 10, 24, 59–60, 68, 70, 71, 73, 81, 92–93, 114, 116–117, 119, 124, 127–129, 131, 138–141, 149, 152, 154, 161, 166, 179, 180, 184, 188, 189, 193, 202, 203, 205–213
Vanguardism, 82, 86

Vietnam, 38
Violence, 2, 10, 28, 31, 41, 82, 111, 118–119, 131, 134, 150, 164, 192–193, 195
Violence of everyday life, 192–193

W
Wales, 41
Walkouts, 8, 91–101
Wealthy migrants, 106
West, 4, 7, 27, 39, 53, 54, 62, 79, 86, 94, 123, 139, 140, 182, 205, 234
West Africa, 16
Western
 economic systems, 220
 metaphysics, 7, 53–55, 73
 mission, 241
 Pacific, 182
 psychology, 189
 thought, 209, 222
West Indies, 144
Westphalian system, 42
West Texas Technological College, 94
Wheatley, P., 138
Whiteness, 5–6, 15, 19–27, 29–30, 86, 138, 141, 145, 162, 195
White Paper, 114
Whites, 4, 5, 22, 39–40, 56, 57, 59–60, 65, 72, 96, 110–111, 114–115, 120–122, 124–126, 133, 149, 151, 170, 214
 liberals, 123
 supremacist, 29, 107
 supremacy, 64, 93

WHO. *See* World Health Organization
WHO MIND project, 187–190, 193, 195
Wilkins, D., 62, 67, 69–72
Williams, R., 9, 159
Williams, R.A., 54, 62, 63, 69, 71–73, 77
Willinsky, J., 53, 224, 227–228
Wobblies, 168, 175–176
Woodbine Community Benefit Agreement, 173
Workers of color, 9, 159, 160, 164, 166, 168–170, 173, 174, 176
Working-class studies, 161
World Bank, 10
World Health Organization (WHO), 10, 179–197
Worldmindedness, 223, 225
World War I, 94
World War II, 114, 123, 163
World Wide Web, 180, 188
Worsely, P., 35
Wounded Knee, 40
Wretched of the Earth, 21, 166, 191

Y
Yaquis, 39

Z
Zapatistas, 39
Zimbabwe, 40

Made in the USA
Las Vegas, NV
20 January 2022